Insights into Teachers'
Thinking and Practice

Insights into Teachers' Thinking and Practice

Edited by
Christopher Day
Maureen Pope and Pam Denicolo

 The Falmer Press

(A member of the Taylor & Francis Group)
London • New York • Philadelphia

UK   The Falmer Press, Rankine Road, Basingstoke, Hampshire, RG24 0PR

USA   The Falmer Press, Taylor & Francis Inc., 1900 Frost Road, Suite 101, Bristol, PA 19007

First published 1990

British Library Cataloguing in Publication Data
Day, Christopher, *1943–*
   Insights into teachers' thinking and practice.
   1. Teachers, Role – Case studies
   I. Title   II. Pope, Maureen   III. Denicolo, Pam
   371.1

   ISBN 1-85000-660-1
   ISBN 1-85000-661-X   pbk

Library of Congress Cataloging-in-Publication Data

Insights into teachers' thinking and practice/edited by
   Christopher W. Day, Maureen Pope, and Pam Denicolo.
   Selected papers of the 4th ISATT Conference held in 1988.
   Includes bibliographical references.
   ISBN 1-85000-660-1 – ISBN 1-85000-661-X (pbk.)
   1. Teaching-Congresses.   2. Teachers-Attitudes-Congresses.
3. Thought and thinking-Congresses. I. Day, Christopher, ACP. II. Pope, Maureen L. III. Denicolo, Pam. IV. ISATT Conference (4th: 1988)
LB1025.2.I6444 1990   90-32218
371.1'02-dc20   CIP

Jacket design by Caroline Archer

Typeset in 10/12 California by
Chapterhouse, The Cloisters, Formby L37 3PX

Contents

Introduction

It is now six years since the formation of the International Study Association on Teacher Thinking (ISATT). If attendance at the fourth ISATT conference (September 1988) of delegates from eighteen different countries is one measure of activity then one can say that it is a progressive field of research. This book represents but a small selection of papers initially presented at the 1988 conference.

Clark (1986) demonstrated in his paper on the development of conceptions that have influenced research on teacher thinking that such research has a longer history that ISATT. Nevertheless the decade 1975–85 showed a period of rapid growth and the beginning of a new focus within the research field.

What then is the current focus within research on teacher thinking? For many researchers it is the *teacher's subjective school related knowledge*. The following quote by Halkes and Olson (1984) from the first ISATT volume captures the views of many researchers on teacher thinking with respect to this focus.

> Looking from a teacher thinking perspective at teaching and learning one is not so much striving for the disclosure of 'the' effective teacher, but for the explanation and understanding of teaching processes as they are. After all it's the teacher's subjective school related knowledge which determines for the most part what happens in the classroom; whether the teacher can articulate his/her knowledge or not. Instead of reducing the complexities of the teaching learning situations into a few manageable research variables, one tries to find out how teachers cope with these complexities (p. 1).

The thrust of much educational research in Britain and elsewhere is towards national criteria for selection and performance appraisal and creation of performance indicators for serving teachers. Much of the blame for 'quality deficits' is often placed on personal qualities of teachers, their lack of technical expertise or incompetence as a subject specialist. These do little to raise the morale of teachers and the emphasis seems misplaced. As far back as 1963 Getzels and Jackson noted that despite many decades of work on teacher personality 'very little is known for certain about the nature and measurement of teacher personality or about the relation between teacher personality and teacher effectiveness' (p.547). Likewise, as Lowyck (1984) suggests, correlational research aimed at isolating specific teaching behaviours in effective teaching has had limited success. He claims that this was due not only to problems of methodology but to the concept of teaching behaviour in use.

> Teaching cannot in its wholeness be conceived as the sum of a limited number of isolated effective teaching behaviours often called 'skills'. Teaching behaviour has to be understood in relation to the intentions of the teacher and to the situational complexity (p.9).

The chapters in this book essentially represent the efforts of the authors to present students' and teachers' lives and experiences in authentic ways. As expected, theoretical and empirical research is represented, and approaches range from the so-called scientific traditions of cognitive psychology to inductive approaches associated with phenomenographic naturalistic inquiry. The vast majority are small scale qualitative studies which rely upon combinations of interview, questionnaire, naturalistic observation, descriptive, biographical and autobiographical data presented as analytic description (case studies and vignettes).

All the authors affirm implicitly the continuing need for research to demonstrate a holistic view of teacher as person rather than teacher as segmented object, to bridge the descriptive-prescriptive divide. All are concerned with the nature, formation and use of teachers' knowledge — the construction, reconstruction and reorganization of experience which adds to its meaning.

The current focus is therefore trying to understand and interpret the ways in which teachers make sense of and adjust to and create the educational environment within their schools and classrooms — not an easy endeavour and certainly one that has necessitated a shift in educational research thinking and practice.

Whilst sharing a focus and an ideological commitment to viewing teachers as active agents in the development of educative events, the field of teacher thinking research is diverse in terms of theoretical and methodological approaches. This is not surprising given the complexity of the phenomena to be studied and the diverse backgrounds of the researchers themselves. The community of teacher thinking scholars embraces a wide range including psychologists, sociologists, curriculum specialists, anthropologists, philosophers, linguists and 'subject' specialists for example, mathematicians, physicists.

Within teacher thinking research there has been a recognition of the complexity of the phenomena to be studied and the need for more qualitative data gathering processes.

Shifts in methodological perspective within teacher thinking research reflect those within social science generally. For example, Nagy (1984) referred to a 'methodological crisis amongst those who are engaged in the task of deciphering the true meaning of *cognitive structure*' (p.iii). This crisis was in part due to continued debate regarding the appropriateness of quantitative and qualitative research strategies and the diversity of assumptions regarding the nature of 'cognitive structure'.

Recent emphasis has been on research being of value to practitioners and the participants within the research. In order to enhance this within teacher thinking research a change of relationship between teachers and researchers is developing and the goal of teacher thinking research has become that of 'portraying and understanding good teaching in all of its irreducible complexity and difficulty. Quality portraiture may be of more practical and inspirational value than reductionistic analysis and technical prescriptiveness'. (Clark, 1986: p.4).

As in other fields of social enquiry methodological debates regarding appropriateness of particular paradigms exist within educational research, see for example Popkewitz (1984) *Paradigm and Ideology in Educational Research.* If one considers Habermas's categories of positivist, interpretative, and critical research as applied to teacher thinking research all three forms can be identified within the field. The current scene is predominantly interpretative although one can detect more of the critical form in recent years.

Elbaz's work in the first part of this volume adopts a critical stance. She challenges any tendency towards complacency amongst teacher thinking researchers by raising important issues such as non linearity of tacit knowledge, inarticulateness of ordinary folk, the difficulties of reporting on teachers' narratives, the distortion in telling someone else's stories. She advocates the development of new ways of disseminating such narratives if teacher thinking researchers truly aim at giving teachers 'voice' and wish to avoid the risk of 'taking teachers' stories out of their hands'. Buchman's chapter raises a philosophical question regarding the relationship between thinking and action by considering the role of contemplation in teaching and its practical aspects. Elbaz and Buchman's chapters open Part I which focuses on general methodological and theoretical debates within teacher thinking research.

Within pre and in-service professional development teachers are being encouraged to rethink the 'metaphors they live by' (Lakoff and Johnson, 1980). The reflective practitioner (Schön, 1983) needs to critically reflect on the meaning of his/her thoughts and actions as a route to the enhancement of professional practice. Teachers may find consideration of their current constructs threatening, especially if they deduce that change is needed. Threatening and revolutionary this may be but some teacher educators see this as empowering the teachers to make education a positive experience for learner *and* teacher. Haandal and Lauvas (1987) advocate the promotion of reflective teacher education and that within teaching practice 'supervision' the teachers' 'practical theory' should be discussed given its role in practical classroom decision-making.

Kremer Hayon's chapter challenges the notion of reflection and its relationship to the development of professional knowledge. In particular she expresses the need for greater conceptual clarity regarding 'reflection' and poses a potential conceptual framework for considering the processes involved. Olson adds an important dimension to the arena of discourse within teacher thinking — that of the moral. Using case studies of teachers' responses to the implement-

ation of new technology within the curriculum Olson traces the moral impera-
tives within teacher thinking, an issue developed in Massey's chapter in Part II.
No direct connection with morality is implied in Brown and Kompf's chapter on
'Lies teachers tell'! These authors focus on the methodological dilemmas
inherent in obtaining commentary from teachers and the importance of tools
which allow for expression of teachers' views in their own words. Their starting
point embraces personal construct psychology but within the chapter they
comment on the need to go beyond the repertory grid as a technique for
gathering data about teachers' intentions.

The final chapter in Part I provides an overview of recent research in
teacher thinking. Lowyck traces the development of theory and method in this
field and raises questions as to the legitimate aims of such research. Should researchers seek to describe teaching situations and teachers' views regarding their
craft or should prescription as to good practice prevail? Lowyck advocates the
need to form bridges between descriptive accounts and the implications of such
results for practice. In order to effect such bridges within teacher thinking
research new relationships with the teaching community need to develop. In
seeking an integrative way of looking at the way teaching 'is' and 'ought to be'
Lowyck suggests that teacher thinking reseachers should attempt to integrate
some of the findings of the process-product paradigm in order to avoid
parallelism between various approaches in research on teaching. Lowyck also
notes that if the descriptive research outcomes are to function as inspiration for
practitioners there is a need to consider potential alienation due to 'the transcoding inside scientific models' of the concepts deduced from the real life of
teachers. This echoes some of the concerns expressed by Elbaz in her chapter.

An attempt is made in Part II to illustrate some of the preceding points by
including papers which describe current empirical work in the field. In terms of
methodology, these papers demonstrate a range of divergence from or
adherence to the traditional scientific research design. Indeed, for some the
essence of the paper is a report on issues related to methods in use, for instance
Denicolo and Pope are concerned with the epistemology of an approach and its
ramifications, while others are concerned more with alerting readers to issues
worthy of investigation because of their peculiar salience to particular groups of
teachers, for example Massey, in addressing the roots of teachers' perspectives,
notes an ideological theme which emerged during the process of research.

Thus the reader will find that for some authors their fieldwork provides
only the background to a discussion of issues emerging from it while for others
the issue relates more strongly to the methods themselves as vehicles for the
improvement of practice by promoting reflection on it. It is noteworthy that all
the studies presented focus on the real life practice of teachers, mainly in the
form of case studies, and each author has made an attempt to convey the participants' perspectives as authentically as possible. Gudmundsdottir and
Naeslund in particular provide us with some graphic insights into aspects of
their participants' worlds.

The section starts with a paper by Denicolo and Pope, the intent of which is not to present a formal report of a research project, thus avoiding the potential alienation as described by Lowyck, but which does seek to illustrate an approach grounded in a particular philosophy of teacher education. Although some research results are presented, they are included only as exemplars to support an evaluation of an innovative research instrument. The main proposition discussed is that the subsuming approach, using similar complementary devices, is a fruitful tool for raising the awareness of both researchers and teachers alike, whatever their respective experience levels.

The professional experience of the teacher-participants in the research addressed in the subsequent papers moves along a continuum from that of student teachers and novice teachers to that of experienced teachers, reaffirming that development of professional practice is a continuous process.

Thus, the study in the second paper is set in a teacher-training context. Although a more traditional overall design is used by Huber and Roth, the case study presented incorporates the perspectives of student teachers and their teachers on a very relevant issue in teacher development, that is, orientation to aspects of uncertainty versus certainty of situations. It is proposed that this orientation is one of the determinants of teaching style which in turn interacts with the orientation in this dimension of the learners. This paper adds to the growing literature about the conflicts between teaching and learning styles and has particular relevance in educational settings in which independent, student-centred learning is promoted and non-traditional teaching methods advocated in counterpoint to the prior experience of either teachers or learners.

The arena of initial teacher education also forms the context of the case studies described in Massey's paper in which the reflections of novice teachers on their practice are considered in conjunction with their presuppositions and their ideal or technological realities. An emergent issue to which our attention is directed is the moral base of teaching, an issue which has been sadly neglected in the past while the literature and research has been preoccupied with more overt indicators of professional skills development. Redressing the balance somewhat, this paper, like others in this section, addresses the concerns and dilemmas which occupy the practitioners and which, indeed, ultimately influence practice.

By contrasting case studies of novice and experienced teachers, Gudmundsdottir's illustrative research illuminates differences in practice between the two groups in the realm of ability to communicate their subject knowledge. The central thesis is that the creation of meaning in a discipline area involves, within the curriculum, the making of a story by linking the ideas inherent in the continuing syllabus. From this paper we receive insights into the development of teachers-as-storytellers, addressing a skill related to their content knowledge but having a significant contribution to make to the development of pedagogical skill.

Continuing the shift of focus towards the practice of more experienced teachers, another author, Naeslund, redirects our attention to teaching style, this time with respect to the illusive concept of effectiveness. By using vignettes of teachers with very different styles, he demonstrates the variety of definition of effectiveness in terms of success in the teaching role while also delineating the consequences that different perspectives of this role have for individual teachers. In doing so, an argument is developed against too tight a prescription of role nature and performance by teacher educators or politicians. We are reminded that good professional practice is neither simply definable in terms of descriptions of orientation and style of role enactment, nor is it necessarily something which can be attained by the elapse of time or confrontation by certain kinds of experience.

The theme of experienced professionals also needing opportunities to consider their practice is taken up in the next paper in which Ben Peretz *et al* provide us with a synopsis of their evaluation of some of the innovatory ways in which teachers in Israel are encouraged to do this. Of particular interest in this study is the range of motives that teachers have prior to engaging in these forms of professional development and the consequent relationship of intentions, choice of study programme and reflections on the value of that selected programme. This paper will serve not only to alert planners of in-service staff development programmes to considerations which deserve attention prior to implementation but may also encourage teachers to reflect on the limitations which they themselves impose on their possibilities for development.

The final paper in this section also considers a developmental tool for in-service work with teachers but in this case Hanke reports on an investigation of a method related to critical incident analysis which encourages teachers to consider, in conjunction with their own reflections, the perspectives of the other actors in the incident, that is, their pupils. 'Structured dialogues' concerning the interpretation of both parties and the consequent decisions taken enable teachers to become more alert to alternative perspectives and hence modes of reaction. It is of relevance to note that the research led in turn to the development of materials which may be used selectively for individual diagnosis and training, the selection being made by the teachers themselves. Thus, in this small way, they too can be self-directed learners, emancipated from externally generated criteria, an issue which is taken up in the next section.

In Part III, which reports research into recent developments in thinking and practice, in her paper entitled 'Relations Between Thinking and Acting in Teachers in Innovative Work' Ingrid Carlgren describes Swedish teachers' perceptions of the implementation of externally generated innovation through the implementation of school-based curriculum development. The research provides useful empirical data which demonstrates the ways in which teachers modify externally generated innovation to their own individually perceived needs. Although in doing so the original intentions of the innovation may become 'contaminated' or 'distorted', the benefits of transfer of ownership are that new practices may be adopted, developed, and tested to greater or lesser degrees. Carlgren posits three relationships between means and ends which may result from innovation: a taken-for-granted relationship in which innovations are adopted; a theoretical relationship in which innovations are developed by teachers; and an empirical relationship in which innovations are tested by teachers. She uses this analysis as a means of exploring the significancies of different relationships between teachers' thinking and acting. In a sense the research is an investigation of the limitations on the development of teachers' thinking and acting of external innovation which fails to provide as an integral part of the design the appropriate means of support for the process of implementation. Thus, innovation which only extends current thinking and practice is likely to produce only 'surface' change. Neither innovation itself, nor its application to school-based curriculum development work will necessarily contribute to the development of teachers as reflective practitioners.

In contrast, Lynne Hannay and Wayne Seller's work in Canada on 'The Influence of Teachers' Thinking on Curriculum Development Decisions' reports on researcher facilitated processes of deliberation and change. Their report focuses on the work processes of a school-based curriculum development committee over one school year. One of the researchers was involved in a participant-as-observer role, facilitating and encouraging the curriculum deliberations of the committee, whilst the second acted in a non-participant observer role. They suggest that curriculum deliberation, defined as an exploration of what is in order to examine what should be, results in individuals taking decisions and sharing them with others. Their research examines the thinking and action processes which contribute to these results and in particular how they are influenced by previously held practical knowledge, personal and professional beliefs, rules of practice, image, and the environment in which teachers work. The research demonstrates how teachers' images of themselves as (in this case geography) teachers, teaching itself, students, rules of practice and the curriculum development process itself affected significantly their deliberations and shows how these images were modified as a direct result of participation in curriculum development discussions which took place over time with the facilitation of an external agent. In this sense, the paper, like Day's, reports a research and development project which provides opportunities for teachers to engage in systematic reflection on personal practical knowledge. The motivation for the meetings was the need to respond to externally proposed innovation from the Ministry of Education. The initial response of token change and minimum participation gradually changed as its members began to feel ownership of and responsibility for their own decisions within the framework of Ministry imposed guidelines — further empirical evidence which, whilst supporting the findings of Carlgren's research that school-based curriculum development in response to external innovation may be at surface level only, implicitly takes this into account through the provision of external intervention strategies, critical support for what might be described as 'emancipatory' curriculum discussion amongst equals which re-empowered them as curriculum decision takers. Hannay and Seller identified three phases in the development of curriculum decision making — 'cut and paste', 'cognitive dissonance' and 'assimilation' and found that factors which facilitated the curriculum development process included the particular nature of the deliberative process itself, facilitative leadership of these processes by one of the researchers, and a supportive group climate in which public reflection was accepted and encouraged.

These factors are further examined by Christopher Day in 'The Development of Teachers' Personal Practical Knowledge through School-Based Curriculum Development Projects'. This paper reports and evaluates the impact on teachers' thinking and practice of active involvement over time in five school initiated school-based curriculum development projects which were managed, like that described in Hannay and Seller's paper by 'communities of equals', groups of like-minded people, on a voluntary basis. However, in the work described by Day, the teachers were participants in the action of curriculum development as well as its formulation, and the researcher took an observer-as-non-participant role. The work, like that described by Carlgren, was intended to lead to change. Unlike the Swedish experience, however, it was initiated by management inside rather than outside of the school. Nevertheless, problems of commitment and ownership were identified in those projects which were intended to implement rather than critically consider policy issues determined by management. Essentially, the paper provides empirical evidence which supports the views of teachers as potential reflective practitioners (Schön, 1983) active meaning makers, connoisseurs and researchers, expressed over the years by Stenhouse (1975) in England, Eisner (1983) and Schön (1983) in America, Smyth (1987) in Australia, and Connelly and Clandinin (1985) in Canada among others.

Potential for the development of personal practical knowledge does, it seems, in order to be realized, need certain conditions, identified in the paper as being positive school climate, tangible, planned opportunities for self reflection, defined as a dialectical process of reflection both in and on the action, peer support and collaboration, ownership and control of learning, and the support by the institution for locking into institutional practice the learning achieved. However, reflecting in and on the action is not simply a matter of providing optimum conditions. It must be recognized that each teacher's motivation and learning commitment will vary in intensity because of personal and professional developmental and socialization factors — and that each will be at a different stage of development.

As in Letiche's paper, Day's study reveals that the development of personal practical knowledge must take into account all of these factors. Research on teacher thinking must continue to seek to identify developmental stages in teachers' professional growth and conceptualize these in terms of both psychological, sociological and environmental factors.

In, 'Teachers Never Stop Thinking About Teaching: Sharing Classroom Constructs with Expert Volunteers', Michael Kompf and Donald Dworet test the hypothesis that constructs about teaching remain constant in inactive teachers by placing them for three months as 'expert volunteers' alongside practising teachers in elementary school classrooms. Volunteers and hosts were matched according to experience, qualifications and preferences. Although initially both groups expressed concerns, the learning results perceived by both exceeded expectations. All the participants perceived this to be due to the construct match between teachers and expert volunteers, and the authors argue for a 'permanent corps' of volunteers within interested boards of education as a means of adding to classroom teaching quality. Like Day, Kompf and Dworet recognize the need for occasional but significant intellectual and effective challenge and support for teachers in classrooms, and their research emphasizes that in achieving this there is much to be gained by paying careful attention to matching of teachers' personal professional constructs.

Hugo Letiche's paper on 'Polytechnic Careers: Development in Instructor Thinking' reports on the results of research aimed at discovering if effective instructors use certain patterns of meaning making in their work with students in order to move towards the development of a theory of personal development. He presents a critique of Torbert's (1987) six stages of development — impulsive, opportunistic, diplomatic, technician, achiever, and strategist, within three ('I/me', 'self/other', 'beliefs/reality') levels of the teacher's belief systems as his initial analytic framework. Through data on career history (collected through interviewing), he analyzes teachers' belief systems, their tacit assumptions about interaction, authority and expression and uses these empirical data to present his own seven stages of personal development. He then analyzes, within what he describes as 'situational conflict psychology' the forces that lead to lecturer change.

Using case studies as apt illustrations, he concludes that for the polytechnic lecturer to develop more insight into her career she must have 'sufficient personal, collegial, institutional and social commitment', and that if career development is to occur, 'the process of reflective critical self-definition has to be strengthened and the movement into dialogical inclusive insight has to be facilitated'. Although writing in a different context from Hannay and Seller, Letiche identifies the significant effect that existing practical knowledge and the environment have upon teachers' development, and the need for facilitative intervention which provides support for reflection and environments in which (*vide* Day) self and other confrontation may occur.

Finally, in 'Social Aspects of Teacher Creativity', Peter Woods investigates the possibilities for creative teaching in a context which has been described as giving 'little encouragement for teachers to view themselves as originators of knowledge'. He identifies four basic criteria associated with his use of the term 'creativity' in relation to teachers whom he regards as connoisseurs rather than technicians — innovation, ownership, control and relevance. He reports research in primary schools in England in which teachers are in control of innovations which belong to them, and in which they are culturally attuned to pupils and able to adapt to unexpected classroom responses to their planned programmes. He presents observed examples of creative teaching, 'round a structural base', 'breakthroughs' and 'creative projects'; and he argues that time, resources, supportive school ethos and appropriate pupil culture are necessary for inspiration and incubation of ideas which will not only be produced but also take root. There is a sense in which Wood's views on the need for establishing conditions which will optimize opportunities for teacher creativity links directly with the research and development projects presented in this section. Certainly deliberative reflection, the development of teachers' personal practical knowledge described by Day, Hannay and Seller, and Letiche require conditions to be negotiated in which teachers do have time to reflect in a supportive environment and challenge their own and colleagues' existing thinking and practices.

Although this book is presented in three sections which move from mainly methodological and theoretical discussions through case studies of professional practice towards teacher thinking within the context of innovations several major themes recur throughout, namely, teachers' belief systems and thought processes, their personal and professional knowledge in action and the relationships between espoused theories, theories-in-use, ideals and actual behaviour.

Much of the research considers the role and significance of contemplation in teaching, through investigations of reflection 'in' and reflection 'on' action, for example influences on teacher decision-making processes, teacher practitioner perspectives, the use by teachers of objective-based and practice-based language, teachers' innovative strategies, life-cycle research, logs and diaries, school-based work, curriculum development, uncertainty-certainty orientations of teachers; guiding metaphors, aspects of student-teacher thinking and relationships between them.

All recognize implicitly the dynamic between theory and action, and together they demonstrate a rich and complex tapestry of research which represents a real evolution of a perspective on teacher thinking and action.

Christopher Day
Maureen Pope
Pam Denicolo

References

CLARK, C. M. (1986) 'Ten years of conceptual development in research on teacher thinking', in BENN-PERETZ, M., BROMME, R. and HALKES, R. (Eds.) *Advances of Research on Teacher Thinking*, Lisse, Netherlands, Swets and Zeitlinger.

CONNELLY, M. F. and CLANDININ, D. J. (1985) *On narrative method, personal philosophy and narrative unities in the study of teaching*, paper presented at annual meeting of NARST, Indiana.

EISNER, E. W. (1983) The Art and Craft of Teaching, *Educational Leadership, January 1983.*

GETZELS, J. W. and JACKSON, P. (1963) 'The teacher's personality and characteristics' in GAGE, N. L. (Ed.) *Handbook of Research on Teaching*, Chicago, Rand McNally.

HAANDAL, G. and LAUVAS, L. (1987) *Promoting Reflective Teaching: Supervision in Action*, Milton Keynes, Open University Press.

HALKES, R. and OLSON, J. K. (Eds.) (1984) *Teacher Thinking: A New Perspective on Persisting Problems in Education*, Lisse, Netherlands, Swets and Zeitlinger.

LAKOFF, G. and JOHNSON, M. (1980) *Metaphors We Live By*, London, Duckworth and Co.

LOWYCK, J. (1984) 'Teacher Thinking and Teacher Routines a Bifurcation?' in HALKES, R. and OLSON, J. (Eds.) *Teacher Thinking*, Lisse, Swets and Zeitlinger.

NAGY, P. (Ed.) (1984) *The Representation of Cognitive Structures*, Toronto, Dept of Measurement, Evaluation and Computer Applications, The Ontario Institute for Studies in Education (OISE).

POPKEWITZ, T. (1984) *Paradigm and Ideology in Educational Research*, Lewes, Falmer Press.

SCHÖN, D. A. (1983) *The Reflective Practitioner: How Professions Think in Action*, New York, Basic Books.

SMYTH, J. (1987) *A Rationale for Teachers Critical Pedagogy: A Handbook*, Geelong, Deakin University Press.

STENHOUSE, L. A. (1975) *An Introduction to Curriculum Research and Development*, Heinemann Educational, London.

Part I
Reflections on Teachers' Thinking and Action

Chapter 1

Knowledge and Discourse: The Evolution of Research on Teacher Thinking

Freema Elbaz

This chapter will examine the evolving discourse of teacher thinking research with a view to discerning the directions in which it has been developing. Three themes will be treated: voice, the opposition of the ordinary and the extraordinary, and story. 'Voice' is a term used increasingly by researchers concerned with teacher empowerment; the term expresses an implicit critique of the prevailing tendency in earlier studies of teaching to reduce the complexity of teachers' work, and to privilege theoretical formulations over the concerns of teachers themselves. The second theme picks up on a tension between the concern to give an account of good teaching, the 'extraordinary' work of the master or expert teacher, and to find what is special in the 'ordinary', the work of every teacher in all its familiarity. Finally, 'story' is another important focus: as researchers try to present teachers' work and experience in authentic ways, they make use of accounts, portrayals, narratives, biographies, portraits, conversations; the term 'story' seems to me to be particularly appropriate to our methodological and epistemological search.

The chapter deals with the language of teacher thinking research, and does so in terms of the perspective elaborated by post-structuralist theoreticians such as Foucault (1970, 1979) and Reiss (1982). On this view one looks at the ongoing praxis of a given community or cultural group through the various forms of discourse which make up the social text of that group; the particular signifying practices of a given group are both constituted by and constitutive of the discursive field within which members of the group live and function. Another way of putting it is that 'language provides the conceptual categories which organize thought into predetermined patterns and set the boundaries on discourse' (Bowers, 1987). Further, the ability to determine these conceptual categories constitutes power, and groups who have the possibility of ensuring that significant aspects of their own reality are reflected in prevailing conceptual categories thereby exercise power over other groups whose situation and experience does not have this legitimacy as expressed in names, concepts and definitions of their reality. This perspective was drawn upon by Bowers in an important study of the conceptual underpinnings of liberal educational thought, a philosophical work which has implications for our own concerns since Bowers sees the teacher as potentially exercising 'a significant form of control over the language process (over how initial conceptual maps are constituted and thus will influence subsequent thought and political behavior)', and thus considers that teachers 'have a responsibility for contributing to the conceptual foundations of communicative competence' (p.154). Thus the perspective I invoke here has a bearing not only on our understanding of what we have been up to as researchers but also on our educational purposes generally. The chapter will be looking at some of the categories in terms of which research in our field has been organized, and will ask where these categories come from and what part of reality — whose reality — they reflect. The chapter does not, however, constitute a review of the research; rather, the three themes were chosen because they seemed to be both interesting and important, and to make it possible to look at a fair selection of examples from the research (though some areas within the research on teacher thinking have not been attended to).

The analysis of discursive practices calls for different kinds of questions from those we are accustomed to asking. First of all we need to ask quite directly about the mode of discourse in the field: around what concepts and distinctions is the field organized, what terms are used and what assumptions, commitments and values underlie this choice of terms? Second, what places are available in the discourse for possible subjects, and who can assume these various subject functions (Foucault, 1979)? Third, what can we say about the way that this discourse is produced and about how it exists in the world: in what situations do we as researchers work with teachers, in what forms do we publish our work and where does it circulate, what is the impact of the particular institutional practices which attend it, and what consequences are there to its presence, whether in book, article, conference presentation or report form?

Each of the three themes would allow us to raise a variety of questions, but they nevertheless seem to map on, in a rough way, to the three sets of questions. Under the theme of 'voice' I will be looking at the way that the language of research on teacher thinking allows us to examine and present the concern of teachers in their own terms. The second theme, 'ordinary versus extraordinary', brings into focus the teacher as subject. The third theme, 'story', relates to the various forms in which we carry out and present our work.

Voice

Town maps registered the street as Mains Avenue, but the only colored doctor in the city had lived and died on that street, and when he moved there in 1896 his patients took to calling the street, which none of them lived in or near, Doctor Street. Later, when other Negroes moved there... envelopes from Louisiana, Virginia, Alabama, and Georgia began to arrive addressed to people at house numbers on Doctor Street. The post office workers returned these envelopes or passed them on to the Dead Letter Office. Then in 1918, when colored men were being drafted, a few gave their address at the recruitment office as Doctor Street. In that way, the name acquired a quasi-official status. But not for long. Some of the city legislators . . . had notices posted in the stores, barber shops, and restaurants in that part of the city saying that the avenue running northerly and southerly from Shore Road fronting the lake to the junction of routes 6 and 2 leading to Pennsylvania, and also running parallel to and between Rutherford Avenue and Broadway, had always been and would always be known as Mains Avenue and not Doctor Street.

It was a genuinely clarifying public notice because it gave Southside residents a way to keep their memories alive and please the city legislators as well. They called it Not Doctor Street, and were inclined to call the charity hospital at its northern end No Mercy Hospital since it was 1931 . . . before the first colored expectant mother was allowed to give birth inside its wards and not on its steps. (Morrison, 1977, 3–4)

The notion of 'voice' has been central to the development of teacher thinking research. The term itself does not appear all that often; Butt and Raymond (1987), for example, speak of facilitating 'the expression of the teacher's perspective and voice' Others are interested in 'The teacher's perspective' (Janesick, 1982; Tabachnick and Zeichner, 1986), the teacher's point of view or 'frame of reference' (Clark and Peterson, 1986); Feiman-Nemser and Floden (1986) identify this area of research in terms of a concern with getting 'inside teachers' heads'. The concern with voice is also implicit in the work of all those who are committed to the empowerment of teachers (Smyth, 1987). As in other areas where the notion of 'voice' is used (feminist research, Gilligan's 1982 redrawing of the terms of moral development), the term is always used against the background of a previous silence, and it is a political usage as well as an epistemological one. Teacher thinking researchers have all been concerned to redress an imbalance which had in the past given us knowledge of teaching from the outside only; many have also been committed to return to teachers the right to speak for and about teaching.

In the passage quoted above, Morrison brings into focus several aspects that are central to our concern with the teacher's voice: the first is the power to name, to define one's own reality and to determine, at least in part, the way the rest of the world must relate to that reality; the second is the power to care for and sustain oneself and others, to maintain the dignity and integrity of those named. Having 'voice' implies that one has a language in which to give expression to one's authentic concerns, that one is able to recognize those concerns, and further that there is an audience of significant others who will listen. The passage also underlines a sense in which voice is already there, already critical, regardless of whether the outside world allows it expression; this should be borne in mind lest we lose sight of the fact that our role as researchers is primarily to remove the obstacles to the expression of teachers' concerns.

In the effort to allow for the expression of the teacher's voice and point of view, researchers have experimented with methodological innovations such as joint writing (Butt *et al.*, 1988), interviews followed by mutual construction of a narrative (Connelly and Clandinin 1986, 1987), collaborative analysis of teachers' journals (Tripp, 1987) as well as more familiar methods such as those of personal construct theory (Pope and Scott 1984). While these directions are both interesting and fruitful, it is important to realize that 'who writes', whether it is biography or autobiography, joint authorship or negotiated accounts, is only one aspect of the issue. The more basic question is, what kind of discourse is being used, and to what extent does it make possible the authentic expression of teachers' experiences and concerns. The issue of 'voice' should not be reduced to the question of who speaks, nor should we be satisfied with a superficial impression that the concerns of teachers are being expressed. If it has been difficult for teachers to voice their own concerns, this is primarily because the discourse of teaching, and of educational research generally, does not allow for the formulation of these concerns. Lampert (1985) provides an example of this when she suggests that teachers do not deal with problems to be solved but rather confront dilemmas, and that any teaching situation simultaneously presents a number of conflicting issues with which the teacher must find a way to live. This formulation underlines the fact that the teaching situation is not in any sense linear, and it is difficult in educational talk, influenced as it is by liberal, western assumptions that problems have solutions and progress is an un-questionable good, to talk about functioning in a complex setting where problems do not have single solutions towards which one moves in a linear fashion.

Thus to a considerable degree the language we have had available to talk about teaching has been both inadequate and systematically biased against the faithful expression of the teacher's voice. In recognition of this inadequacy, re-searchers have shifted their concern from accounting for the mere complexity of teaching to a concern for the authenticity of our accounts of teachers' knowledge, in short with a concern for voice. This has generated efforts to present the teacher's knowledge in its own terms, as it is embedded in the teachers' and the school's culture. Much of the search for terms by means of which to conceptualize teachers' knowledge is a series of compromises in which the researcher proposes terms that do some justice to teachers' knowledge while still being acceptable in the academic context with its requirement of explicit context-free rational discourse. In a sense much of the research on teacher thinking has been a series of developments towards an adequate conception of voice and an ongoing attempt to give voice to teachers.

Looking back over the research as it has evolved, what can we now say about the teacher's voice, and about the way that the language of teacher thinking research gives expression to the teacher's voice?

One starting point for almost all teacher thinking research has been the concern for the tacit aspect of teachers' knowledge and for the paradox implied by this quality: while knowledge must be made explicit if the teacher's voice is to be heard, we thus risk turning teachers' knowledge into researchers' knowledge, colonizing it and thus silencing the voice of the teacher. Some of this risk is voiced by researchers. Brown and McIntyre (1986) write, 'Although we started from the assumption that there is such a thing as teachers' professional craft knowledge, we knew that for the most part this knowledge is not articulated. Was it sensible, therefore, to plan to undertake an investigation of what pupils and teachers construed as good teaching?' And Yinger (1987) asks, 'What would become of efforts to codify this knowledge, to write it down? Would the form of written language distort and destroy its character, stripping it of its meaning and vitality?' (p. 309). Despite the risks, many researchers have made the effort to uncover the tacit dimension, and have attended to a number of aspects of the tacitness of teachers' knowledge: it is nonlinear, it has a holistic, integrated quality, it is at least partly patterned or organized, and it is imbued with personal meaning.

Non-linearity

Since tacit knowledge is not always coherent and consistent, the teacher's voice ought to be able to speak in several registers at once; teachers' knowledge is not logically sequenced and many concerns are being entertained at any given moment. Psychological models of problem-solving or decision-making seem to make it particularly difficult to account, except in negative terms, for this non-linearity of teacher thinking. For example, it is claimed that 'the ability of teachers . . . to process all of the information in their environment is limited . . . people tend to process information sequentially (i.e. step by step) rather than simultaneously . . . Teachers appeared to lack information-processing strategies to make complete, specific diagnoses' (Shavelson and Stern 1981). Yet when research begins from an examination of the teaching situation itself rather than from a theoretical position, this non-linear quality of teacher thought comes to the fore quickly. For example, Lowyck (1986) suggests that the distinction between preactive, interactive and post-active teaching does not fit the way teachers view their work. As suggested above, the notion of 'dilemma' (Lampert, 1985) is a useful term to reflect the dialectical quality of teachers' knowledge.

Integration

Polanyi tells us that tacit knowing is 'an act of indwelling'; for example, in using a stick to feel one's way in the dark, 'we attend subsidiarily to the feeling of holding the probe in the hand . . . The sensation of the probe pressing on fingers and palm, and of the muscles guiding the probe, is lost, and instead we feel the point of the probe as it touches an object' (Polanyi and Prosch, 1975, p. 36). In some such way, it may be that a teacher concerned with, say, the emotional climate of the classroom, becomes unaware of the specific actions taken to enhance the climate yet feels what is happening in the classroom and thus reads the emotional barometer most carefully from moment to moment. This integrated quality of tacit knowing may of course mask errors in the teacher's reading of situations. Olson (1986) gives the example of a group of teachers who seemed to be systematically unaware that their loose, pupil-directed strategy for teaching computer literacy was not working as well as they thought, but suggests that there is no paradox in this: the teachers' concern with the 'expressive' domain took priority, and their sense of pupil enthusiasm and their own enhanced image were integrated to give a tacit view of a successful program.

Patterning of Complexity

The concern with the complexity of teachers' knowledge leads to the search for a 'language of practice' which will allow us to understand how teachers cope with the complexity of their work (Yinger, 1987). This concern for and appreciation of complexity could be seen as simply a matter of identifying all the variables, but it seems more fruitful to look at it in terms of how the whole performance is organized: some of it is 'scripted', i.e. ordered in terms of patterns (Yinger, 1987), routines (Leinhardt *et al.*, 1987), or cycles (Connelly and Clandinin 1985).

Personal Meaning

One of the guiding questions of much research has had to do with the sense-making processes by which teachers invest their work with personal meaning. What is interesting is how teachers come by particular conflicts or dilemmas rather than others, and how they come to elaborate the particular scripts and routines they do use, what meaning these structures have for them. While teachers probably have explicit knowledge of some or even most of their routines, they are less likely to have explicit knowledge of all the meanings attached to the routines or of their sources. Giving expression to the personal quality of teachers' knowledge has not been a simple matter; as Eisner (1988) points out, 'the research language that has dominated educational inquiry has been one that has attempted to bifurcate the knower and the known' (p. 18), such that teachers' concerns come to be spoken of in a detached and dispassionate way: coping with the lively business of the classroom becomes 'classroom management', caring for the welfare and development of each child becomes 'individualization of instruction', and virtually every aspect of teaching has been similarly subjected to some form of labelling that empties the teaching act of any personal significance.

The means deployed to handle the tacit quality of teachers' knowledge, in all of its aspects, have varied considerably; some have already been alluded to. 'Dilemma' addresses the non-linear, dialectical character of tacit knowledge; further, a use of dilemmas in the sense of Berlak and Berlak (1981) also touches on the patterned nature of teachers' knowledge since it helps to show underlying consistencies in pedagogic choices (Tabachnick and Zeichner, 1986). A concept such as 'image' (Elbaz, 1983; Clandinin, 1985) speaks particularly to the integrated nature of teachers' knowledge in its simultaneously emotional, evaluative and cognitive nature, and also conveys the personal meanings which permeate this knowledge. One teacher's sense of her 'classroom as home', another teacher's view of her subject matter sometimes as a barrier 'to hide behind', other times as 'a window on what students are thinking', both provide us with immediate contact with the teacher's experience precisely as she sees fit to express it. Other terms which seem to give us a direct insight into teachers' experience are 'rhythm, cycle, habit and ritual' (Clandinin and Connelly 1985) insofar as these terms allow the researcher to provide an almost physical sense of what the teacher feels, thinks, believes, wants. Other terms, while helpful to us in organizing our own understanding of the tacit, seem to be a step away from the teacher's immediate experience: Yinger's (1987) 'pattern language' is as yet a hypothetical construct which, by analogy with a pattern language in architecture, might allow us to explain how teachers order complexity; the notion of 'routines', and of the teacher as choreographer who selects and rehearses the steps with pupils (Leinhardt *et al.*, 1987) accounts for the order in some classrooms but does not bring us close to the moment at which the teacher creates one particular routine rather than another.

Beyond the specific terms used to generate a discourse on teacher thinking, we also need to look at the discursive strategies by which researchers give a hearing to teachers' immediate concerns. These will be discussed more fully later in this chapter. Here, I want simply to mention an example which brings out the tacitness of teacher knowledge. Connelly and Clandinin's (1986) presentation of 'narrative fragments' in the teaching of a science teacher named Bruce shows how the teacher's understanding of science teaching is tied to, and made comprehensible only with reference to, his tacit sense of what pupils need, what they are learning and will learn later in this and other subjects.

Teachers' concerns are not only complex, multi-faceted and non-linear; they are also heavily dependent on context, as Clark (1986) reminds us. Thus the teacher's voice must speak from an embeddedness within the culture of the particular school, school system, and society the teacher lives and works in. The difficulties this entails are brought into focus by drawing on a distinction made by Hall (1977) between high and low context thinking. Looking at culture with the tools of an anthropologist, Hall suggests that every culture has to work out a balance, within the communication process, between the explicit linguistic code, context, and meaning; a high-context form of communication is one in which 'most of the information is either in the physical context or internalized in the person, while very little is in the coded, explicit, transmitted part of the message', whereas a low-context form of communication is one where inform-ation is conveyed primarily via the explicit language code. We can see that teachers' knowledge is primarily high-context, whereas researchers' knowledge is low context. Further, researchers participate in a 'culture of critical discourse' (Gouldner, 1979), a decontextualized discourse in which everything is explicit, and there is no appeal to authority except the authority of reason.

The narrative of Bruce cited above illustrates well what is meant by 'high context': in order to construct a narrative that makes sense, the researchers have to provide an understanding of the pupils' working class background and language, the limited expectations both they and their families share, of the school science program in the given grade level as well as later on, and particu-larly about the teacher's own position as an inner-city school teacher, given his own background and experience. Without this detail, we cannot understand how a teacher whose classroom strategies appear to be quite traditional (he has students copy notes from the board, for example) has in fact managed to create an environment where the students' own dialect is respected, and where they are enabled gradually to realize that they must acquire the middle-class language in order to succeed. Furthermore, not only do we need to have this context filled in in order to 'hear' the teacher clearly; we need to become aware of context *as context*, that is, not in the form of abstract explanations of Bruce's background and the like, but in terms of the matters that are important to him: his account of a student named Ken who succeeded, his complaint about lack of time to cover all the material, his amusing way of treating science terms and, eventually, his sense of the time frame within which he thinks about his students, such that distortions in scientific language today make sense in terms of keeping them interested and tuned in until the time when they will be ready to take responsibility for their own language.

Following Hall and Bowers, another feature of the teachers' voice insofar as it speaks in a 'high-context' mode, is the fact that the traditions of the school and the culture are a source of authority for what the teacher does and says. I believe that the place of tradition in teacher thinking is a matter we have tended to treat poorly. When a teacher tells us of a particular innovation 'that won't work in my school', we are likely, as educators interested in progress and improvement, to hear this as the voice of teacher conservatism. However, it is just as likely to be the expression of the teacher's tacit understanding of school tradition and culture. Buchmann (1986) argues that in our concern for the personal aspects of teacher thinking we have set aside the importance of role and community:

> In teaching these communities include the profession, the public, and the disciplines of knowledge . . . while it is important to communicate the fact that disciplinary knowledge is not absolute, teachers have to recognize and respect the constraints imposed by the structure of

different disciplines . . . they are not free to choose methods, content, or classroom organization for psychological, social or personal reasons alone. (p. 57)

I believe our difficulty in finding a place for tradition in our own conceptualizations of teacher thinking has to do with the conceptual maps we have ourselves acquired from liberal theories of education according to which progress and change based on dispassionate criticism of the outmoded ways of the past are unquestioned goods, and the traditional is seen as equivalent to the conservative and the archaic. Indeed, when we talk about that which has been handed on to teachers by culture this is usually seen in a negative light; for example, Britzman (1986) talks about 'cultural myths' in teaching such as the myth that 'everything depends on the teacher'. While I acknowledge that these particular bits of tradition do seem to have a negative impact on the work of teachers, I do not believe we have looked hard enough to find positive traditions informing the work of teachers. For example, might there not be a tradition, in elementary schools, of 'the teacher as maker' which underlies the image identified by Clandinin (1985) for one of the teachers she worked with; such a tradition might be a way to understand many forms of teacher activity from crafts and classroom decoration to involvement in school-based development.

The teacher's voice is always a moral voice, always concerned with the good of pupils, as Noddings (1987) so eloquently argues. Sockett (1987) adds an important point regarding the place of the moral: it is not confined to expressions of goals or ideals but pervades every aspect of teaching; 'the language of the means of teaching is as much a moral language as the language of educational ends.' This is well illustrated by Brown and McIntyre's (1986) examination of professional craft knowledge: one might have expected craft knowledge to be largely technical, but in fact much of what teachers talk about has to do with their ways of caring for pupils. Of a list of twelve areas of concern which they identified in teachers' accounts of themselves and of what they do well in teaching, more than half are directly related to teachers' caring for the good of pupils:

Their approaches to taking account of differences among their pupils; . . . attempts to build up confidence and trust . . . concerns for the characteristics of individual pupils; their strategies for . . . making sure that recalcitrant pupils do not become alienated from the work . . . ; efforts to ensure that everyone is involved in the work and all achievements are recognized; . . . how they endeavour to ensure that pupils' creative efforts will not be hindered by technical expertise that is lacking; the ways in which they create a relaxed and enjoyable but, nevertheless, disciplined atmosphere. (pp. 40–1)

Although it is tacit, not elaborated and tied to tradition, it does not follow that the teacher's voice is an uncritical one; rather, being a moral voice, the teacher's voice may be implicitly critical like the voices in the quote which began this section. For example, Sarah, the teacher with whom I worked (Elbaz, 1983) expressed her criticism of the school system, and the particular school in which she worked, through an imagery of conflict that pervaded our discussions. In work with a group of teachers she perceived problems that 'erupted' all at once; the prospect of working with a new group of teachers was 'a whole new potentially dangerous situation', and the work of the group seemed 'like horses, all running on the same track at the same speed', with each teacher concerned to protect her own 'territory'. In the school as a whole Sarah perceived 'occupational hazards' such as the lack of time to reflect, and felt she was 'challenged by people who are suspicious of what I'm doing'; in her work in a reading centre she was 'on trial for the future' and expected to have to 'fight for staffing'. Further, she felt that teachers as a group were vulnerable; following an unpopular strike they had been attacked in the press and 'as a profession we felt completely emasculated'. The cumulative effect of such imagery, in the context of one teacher's particular story, is no less powerful than that of a careful theoretical critique of schooling.

The final point I want to make about the teacher's voice is one on which the field is not in agreement. For many researchers on teacher thinking, there is a direct relationship between thought and action seen as two separate domains; we study teacher thinking, listen to the teacher's voice, in order to learn more about teacher action since the teacher's thought is assumed to direct her teaching (Clark and Peterson, 1986). For others, however, the distinction between thought and action is not valid since a dialectical relationship between thought and action is assumed (Clandinin and Connelly 1987); for example, Tabachnick and Zeichner (1986) studied teacher perspectives under the assumption that 'teacher behavior and thought are inseparable and part of the same event.'

I will expand on this matter further in a later section.

In 1986, Clark gave an account of progress in the study of teacher thinking in terms of increased conceptual sophistication in several areas — the view of teachers and of students, of curriculum and of context, and of research. His analysis also bears on the notion of voice. The field has indeed evolved in terms of giving a more adequate and fair expression to the teacher's voice: (1) the increased attention given to teachers' concerns as they themselves present them indicates that we have been paying attention to the expression of teachers' tacit knowledge, in its complexity, in its embeddedness in context and, to a lesser degree, in a way that shows respect for those traditions that teachers consider meaningful and important. (2) The development of a more complex view of students indicates that we have been paying attention to the moral dimension of teaching in which both teachers and pupils are seen as agents. (3) Attention to curriculum, and to the specifics of particular subject matters, allows us to hear the teacher as talking about something of substantive importance. (4) The increased attention to context in itself has given us a greater ability to allow expression to the teacher's voice, and perhaps will also make us more sensitive in the future to the importance of tradition. (5) Methodological advances, and in particular the increasing role of teachers as partners in research indicates clearly that, however we may conceive and understand teacher thought, we are willing to hear the teacher's version of it, and to admit their critical input as well.

We have been attending to the expression of the teacher's concerns and voice as a discursive phenomenon; the other side of this matter is the nature of the role which teachers play as subjects of the discourse on teacher thinking. To this we turn in the next section.

The Ordinary and the Extraordinary

The second issue to which we will now attend concerns the kind of place which the discourse of teacher thinking research allows for possible subjects, and who can assume these subject functions.

Jackson described the teacher who played a role in earlier research on teaching in a way that underlines our problem. 'Not only is the classroom a relatively stable physical environment, it also provides a fairly constant social context. Behind the same old desks sit the same old students, in front of the familiar blackboard stands the familiar teacher' (quoted in Goodson, 1980). Goodson points out that this way of viewing the teacher represents a subject who is, on the one hand, depersonalized, that is, essentially interchangeable with other subjects, and on the other hand static, seen as existing outside of time or unchanging. That the tendency to view teaching in this way is prevalent does not, I think, require argument: all of us recognize the portrait, and all of us are bothered by it. We are bothered, I believe, for two kinds of reasons: first because we can all bring to mind images of lively, interesting teachers in dynamic classrooms where students are actively engaged in learning, so we know that, at least some of the time, the picture of institutionalized boredom is inaccurate. The second reason is that we would prefer to be associated with a more dynamic image; our 'conceptual map' is one which puts a positive value on progress and change, and whatever does not change is seen as stagnant, as stultified, rather than as simply enduring or stable.

Thus much of our research is motivated in two ways: by a desire to recover and make evident what is alive and interesting about teaching, and by a desire to improve schooling, to find ways of making good teaching more prevalent. These desires are reflected in the discourse of teacher thinking by the provision of several different kinds of positions in which the teacher can be a subject. One such position is that of the 'exemplar': the 'veteran' teacher or the 'expert peda-gogue' as studied by Leinhardt and Smith (1985), Berliner (1986), and Shulman (1987); her counterpart is the 'novice'. In other areas of the discourse on teacher thinking, the prevailing subject position is filled by a teacher whom I will call the 'ordinary teacher'.

The Exemplar

In the discourse of expert/novice research, the position of the expert teacher is indeed, in part, that of a subject in the sense that the researcher gives a portrayal of the teacher's work from the teacher's point of view. It is usually a portrait in the language of research, emphasizing explicit rather than tacit knowledge: 'tacit knowledge among teachers is of limited value if the teachers are held responsible for explaining what they do and why,' argues Shulman (1987); Berliner (1986) on the other hand, accepts Buchmann's (1983) point that 'we have no reason to assume that premises that need to be guessed at, terms without clear definition, oblique references, and beliefs that are debatable must be associated with wrong headed ideas or indefensible lines of action.' Further, the subject is present in the discourse primarily as someone on whom other teachers may model their teaching. Thus if we understand how the expert teacher conducts a rapid and efficient homework review, or how she diagnoses a student's problems in a way that zeroes in on strengths and needs, we can use this knowledge to guide and teach the beginner; the expert's performance 'provides us . . . with a temporary pedagogical theory, a temporary scaffolding from which novices may learn to be more expert.' (Berliner, 1986, p. 6) It also follows from such a position that we will be interested in the teacher as subject only insofar as what she does, or thinks, can be replicated: we would have no reason to be interested in the idiosyncratic or spontaneous aspects of her knowledge. Thus much of what is personal and context-bound, like what is tacit and difficult to formulate, ceases to concern us and in large measure the teacher's voice as characterized in the previous section is muted. The modelling process itself is undoubtedly important, and unexceptionable as such. It begins to be problematic when we find it suggested that the performance of expert teachers be used to serve 'as sufficient guides to the design of better education' (Shulman, 1987), to allow us to 'codify, formalize, and systematize the knowledge of expert teachers' (Berliner, 1986), or to elaborate and illustrate a 'conception of pedagogical reasoning and action' that is normative insofar as it both defines 'a complete act of pedagogy' and lays out a series of processes in which every teacher should be able to engage (Shulman, 1987, p. 1). Shulman's particular conception of pedagogical reasoning and action is not the object of my criticism here (it is criticized by Sockett (1987), on the grounds that it splits reason and action and that it is formulated in a technical language which masks the moral character of teaching), nor is the truth that beginning teachers can learn, in a variety of interesting ways, from those more experienced. Rather, the point is that the researcher has used these teachers, defined as experts by their success within a given school system, to generate a theoretical and normative conception of pedagogy to which other teachers may eventually be expected to conform; the expert teacher occupies a subject position in this discourse, but in this role she risks becoming an instrument of bureaucracy in controlling the work of other teachers. (Shulman is aware of the potential danger in using empirically derived criteria of teaching effectiveness to judge teaching, but fails to see that the same risks are attached to his goal of developing 'codified representations of the practical pedagogical wisdom of able teachers'.)

The Novice

What of the position in this particular discourse of the novice teacher, whose main function is to become like the model? In effect her position is hardly that of a subject at all. To Shulman (1987), for example, the novice teacher is of interest insofar as she allows us to observe how pedagogical knowledge develops; but the emphasis is on the knowledge base, a given if not absolutely fixed body of under-standings, and how it comes into being (pp. 14–19). The novice herself has no contribution to make to the knowledge base, and in this respect she is treated as an object of research. Berliner (1986), for example, tells us that 'because these kinds of studies give us information about the routines, scripts, and schema used by experts, we are helped in identifying the buggy routine or script, or the ill-formed schemata, that might be characteristic of less expert or novice teachers.' (p. 6). The thought that the 'buggy routine' of the novice might teach us something new about what is possible within the constraints and pressures of schooling, that we might learn from the struggle of the beginning teacher to realize something different, that the novice's view of her cooperating teacher's classroom might enlighten the latter, all these possibilities are foreign to a discourse which places educators in a clear hierarchy with the scholar above the expert teacher, who is in turn above the novice.

The Subject as Expert

The hierarchization of expertise in teaching is itself another feature of our western discourse which values expertise, in any domain, where expertise is defined as the 'ability to put skills and knowledge to work in the service of achieving certain ends.' (MacIntyre, 1984, p. 75) In effect, educational research in the past has allowed a subject role only to those persons who are considered experts; only experts are considered to have the understanding and ability to determine ends and to carry them out. This is reflected in Shulman's (1987) statement, 'We believe that scholars and expert teachers are able to define, describe, and reproduce good teaching.' (p. 12) This conception of expertise, however, is highly problematic since it involves us in a circular form of reasoning whereby experts are those who are able to define good teaching, and good teaching is the teaching of those whom the experts identify. Teachers are expected to engage in reasoning about purposes, but since no substantive criteria are offered for doing so, the good teacher is, by default, the one who is effective in achieving the ends defined by the system.

It is difficult for us to break out of this circle because 'effectiveness' is a built-in feature of the conceptual maps with which we view the world; our acceptance of a notion like efficiency influences not only the way we speak but also the way we observe everyday phenomena. Thus we probably have some shared images of poor teaching — the lesson that drones on and on, the chaos of poor discipline — and we do find poor teaching boring, but it is important to understand to what extent this is a matter of perspective. The lesson that does not seem to be going anywhere, the apparently aimless behaviour of disorderly students, are indeed uninteresting if we do not know what the teacher is trying to accomplish, if we do not know why the students are misbehaving. However, if we can stop separating means and ends, and listen to the teacher's own view, the dull or disastrous lesson often becomes interesting.

The point then, is that what we consider interesting or dull, the teacher we recognize as an 'expert teacher' or a novice, are so only by virtue of the bringing to bear of a complex set of schemata which organize our understanding of the phenomena of teaching. And unless we first bring these schemata to awareness, discuss them and come to agreement about our criteria for employing them, it is virtually meaningless to talk about expertise in teaching. Thus, to confine our view to a few teachers whom somebody has given a seal of approval is to restrict our data and impoverish our understanding of teaching.

The Ordinary Teacher as Subject

In this respect, I think we can learn something from feminist researchers who have struggled with the question of how to 'uncover and understand the social experience and perceptions of that vast population of women whose "silence" reflects our own dependence on the written word and our own inability to cope with such an enormous and complicated "data base" ' (Geiger, 1986). The ordinary teacher is the silent subject who has not always been given a position as subject in our discourse. But although, as suggested above, we have been handicapped by our language in giving expression to the teacher's voice, it is sometimes much simpler than we realize to do so. Something of this simplicity is conveyed by the film-maker Chantal Akerman (1977), speaking of her film *Jeanne Dielman*, a film about an 'ordinary' woman:

> I let her (the character) live her life in the middle of the frame. I didn't go in too close, but I was not *very* far away. I let her be in her space ... the camera was not voyeuristic in the commercial way because you always knew where I was ... It was the only way to shoot that film — to avoid cutting the woman into a hundred pieces, to avoid cutting the action in a hundred places, to look carefully and to be respectful. The framing was meant to respect the space, her, and her gestures within it.

This simplicity of approach is a quality for which we should strive in our work, I suggest, because it may make it easier to see the work of teaching, and the teacher as subject, in their own terms. I want to suggest, then, that we turn our attention away from artificially drawn distinctions between the expert and the novice, the ordinary teacher and the master, and look rather at the ordinary stories of ordinary teachers. I am not arguing that we cease to look for the extraordinary or abandon the pursuit of excellence in teaching, only that we give up our predefined notions of what it might be. In looking at ordinary classrooms, sooner or later something extraordinary happens; something moves us to feel appreciation, respect, anger. These reactions are personal but they are grounded in our understanding of teaching as a practice within a social setting, of the values we believe it should foster, of the traditions we want to see preserved. And these can be formulated and subjected to dialogue, among ourselves and with teachers. In this process we uncover and give legitimacy to the extraordinary that is within the ordinary.

One account of teaching which illuminates this dialectic of the ordinary and the extraordinary in a powerful way is Aoki's (1983) 'Experiencing Ethnicity as a Japanese Canadian Teacher: Reflections on a Personal Curriculum'. In this account Aoki takes up the position of an ordinary subject in a number of contexts. As a Japanese-born Canadian he experiences the feelings that must have been shared by many, of being both insider and outsider; his encounters with subtle and overt forms of discrimination were no different from those of others. And the process of becoming a teacher, as he underwent it, is a 'typical' process followed by many other students. But Aoki's perspective as a Japanese Canadian, as a Nisei who experienced the evacuation, gives him a purchase on these experiences which transforms his vision into an extraordinary one: he is able to see vividly, and then to show us, 'that to become a teacher one undergoes a ritual which allows one entry into a culturally-shaped and culturally legitimated world' (p. 324). The difficulties of entering that world were confronted again and again by Aoki as he struggled to realize his own aspirations and hopes. As the first Japanese Canadian allowed to live in Calgary, as a teacher in the closed world of a Hutterite school, as the first teacher of oriental origin to be hired in Lehbridge in 1951, Aoki did ordinary work which became extraordinary by virtue of the social and historical context combined with Aoki's persistence in demanding that he be allowed to be 'ordinary'. These experiences nevertheless created for Aoki a series of 'alternative possibilities in making sense of my world', insofar as he can discern and distinguish between, on the one hand, the western 'paradigm of orderliness reflecting interest in efficiency and effectiveness — values embedded in our very technological world', and on the other hand the oriental 'paradigm of reciprocity of differences, a dialectic world of positives and negatives' (p. 332). Aoki's story shows us how context and perspective transform the ordinary into the extraordinary. Further, the particular form which the extraordinary takes here, Aoki's ability to bring to awareness the social, cultural and historical patterns which shape, and are shaped by his personal experienced history, is important, for in finding the extraordinary in teachers' work we in effect show how teachers bring their knowledge to bear in creating meanings that may transcend given social, cultural and historical patterns.

The device which allows us to comprehend the extraordinary in Aoki's work and life is the simple form of a story told. This choice of form is not surprising, for it is when seen in the frame of a story that our experiences are rendered interesting. Through story, every teacher's work can be seen for the special work that it is. The next section will deal with 'story' as a way of realizing our work.

Story

The set of questions which the notion of 'story' allows us to address involves the modes of existence of the discourse of teacher thinking research. To repeat, how do we carry out our work, in what theoretical and material forms do we present our 'findings', how does our research exist in the world and what difference does it make?

More and more often, researchers seem to be telling stories about teaching. Lampert (1985) tells us, 'Conflicts in the way teachers view themselves and their work will only emerge as they present themselves in the stories they tell about their work to different people and in different settings'; she goes on to illustrate her point with stories from her own teaching and that of a colleague. Clandinin and Connelly (1987) suggest that 'A narrative approach to thought and biography . . . might yield stories linking . . . thought and biography, not as cause and effect, but as one among several possible explanatory narratives'; their work similarly provides examples of such narratives. Butt *et al*'s (1988) retelling of parts of the biographies of Lloyd and of Glenda reflect their belief that 'authentic teachers' knowledge is grounded in the autobiographical story.' Grumet (1987), who uses narrative in work with teachers, tells us that personal knowledge 'is constituted by the stories about experience we usually keep to ourselves, and practical knowledge, by the stories that are never, or rarely related, but provide, nevertheless the structure for the improvizations that we call coping, problem-solving, action' (p. 322). Other researchers perhaps do not label what they present as stories, but stories they are nonetheless: Shulman's (1987) portraits of Nancy and Colleen, Tabachnick and Zeichner's (1986) account of two beginning teachers' experiences during their induction year, and those of Leinhardt *et al*. (1987) of how several teachers structure classroom routines, as well as Day's (1987) retelling of the process of staff development in a primary school. Add to these the current of work on teachers' life histories (Goodson, 1980; Woods, 1987). These are only a few examples of stories to be found in recent research on teacher thinking. The purposes of the telling may be very different from one instance to another, but the first point to note is the sheer presence of story within the body of our work: it makes our research dramatically different from that in many other areas, and the presence of these stories generates a dynamic of its own which will, I believe, bring about even further changes.

Links to Theory and Method

We are not alone in discovering the interest of 'story'. Reid (1988), for example, pays attention to the concept of story in its implications for educational reform:

> As we read accounts of successful reform, such as those provided by Burton Clark, what we encounter is a story of people who saw the shaping of institutions as something brought about by this 'exercise of the virtues' and who prevailed over institutional tendencies to emphasize theory over story, structure over people, and skill over virtue.

The notions of 'story' and 'virtue' which Reid culls from accounts of reform are drawn from MacIntyre's (1984) complex analysis of moral philosophy and the 'modern condition'. MacIntyre suggests that 'man is in his actions and practice, as well as in his fictions, essentially a story-telling animal', and he grounds this claim in a prior argument about the nature of human action, showing that action is 'something for which someone is accountable' and that to give an account is to place an action within both the context of the person's individual history and that of the setting in which it is played out, in short, to write a 'narrative history', which 'turns out to be the basic and essential genre for the characterization of human actions.' (pp. 208–9) Story also has an important cultural aspect; MacIntyre tells us that any account of virtue in a human life is an account in three stages, each of which is bounded by cultural structures and presuppositions. First, we require an account of a practice which provides the context or background for the exercise of the virtues, where a practice is 'any coherent and complex form of socially established cooperative human activity through which goods . . . are realized'; second, we need the individual story, 'the narrative order of a single human life' which likewise follows one or more of a selection of culturally-ordered possibilities; and third, we must call upon a view of tradition as that which both makes it possible for particular practices to be transmitted and transformed and also gives meaning to the individual story, for 'the story of my life is always embedded in the story of those communities from which I derive my identity.' (p. 221) These three features, the practice, the individual story in its particular narrative ordering, and the tradition, all have a bearing on our work and we will come back to them.

A conception of 'story' is also finding a place in psychology. Bruner has recently (1987) written on stories people tell in giving accounts of their lives, and one of his points is that life is lived to a 'story line'; we shape the story and the life together, reshape life as we retell it, and then live it in accordance with the already formed story-in-progress until the next retelling changes its shape yet again. And of course the story shape is never pure invention but is always drawn at least in part from stories made available to us by the culture.

What I have been suggesting so far is that 'story' is beginning to acquire a sort of pedigree in the form of a complex theoretical backdrop for our discussion, one which allows us to see connections between the practice of teaching and the virtues and knowledge proper to it, the institutions of education and their traditions, and the stories of individual teachers through which we see their knowledge enacted. Nevertheless it might still be argued that story is primarily a cosmetic device to make research appear oriented to teachers. In order to gain legitimacy for the notion of 'story' we have to mount one of two kinds of argument. We could indeed argue for the practical value of story in rendering out research more accessible to and usable by teachers; for the moment, however, it is not evident that the use of stories has made our research more appealing to a general audience of teachers, and so I will pursue this argument only indirectly. Rather, I intend to pursue the epistemological argument to the effect that 'story' is that which most adequately constitutes and presents teachers' knowledge.

In our research we find 'story' being used in a number of different ways. In many instances it is primarily a methodological device, an effective way of presenting data that is rich and voluminous and would otherwise be difficult to convey. For others it is methodology itself: the work consists of getting the narrative (for example, for life history) and using it to make a point about the work of teachers. But a few researchers see some form of story as the very purpose of their work: I am referring in particular to the work of Connelly and Clandinin (1986, 1987) on 'narrative' and that of Butt and Raymond (1987) on biography, as well as to my own work (Elbaz 1983, 1988). For this work, the story is not which 'links' teacher thought and action, for thought and action are not seen as separate domains to begin with. Rather, the story is the very stuff of teaching, the landscape within which we live as teachers and researchers, and within which the work of teachers can be seen as making sense. This constitutes an important conceptual shift in the way that teacher thinking can be conceived and studied, and it is also (in my opinion) the direction in which the field should be heading.

Story as Form for the Teacher's Voice

To return for a moment to the argument of the previous section, it is only when we take 'story' in the sense I have been elaborating that we can acknowledge and give a hearing to the teacher's voice. We can relate 'story', and for the moment I am thinking in particular of oral storytelling and not of the formal, written short story, to the conception of the teacher's voice which was developed in the first part of this chapter on almost every dimension: first of all the told story can be elliptical and rambling, and relies on much tacit knowledge to be understood; second, storytelling takes place in a context which gives meaning to what is said; third, it calls on traditions of telling which make possible certain kinds of story, with accepted structures for beginning and end, and so on; fourth, it very often involves a moral or a lesson to be learned; fifth, it is often a way of voicing severe criticism in a form that is socially acceptable or at least not dangerous to the teller; and sixth, the telling of a story reflects the inseparability of thought and action because it is simultaneously the making public of someone's thinking and also a performance in the real world: the story affects those who listen and possibly also the teller through the dialogue that may take place between story-teller and audience, sometimes even changing the story. For all these reasons, then, 'story' seems to be particularly fitting to make public the teacher's voice.

The claim I would like to make, however, is not merely a claim about the aesthetic or emotional sense of 'fit' of the notion of 'story' with our intuitive understanding of the teacher's voice, but an epistemological claim to the effect that 'story' is something implicit in teachers' knowledge, that teachers' knowledge in its own terms is ordered by and as 'story' can best be understood in this way. We already have a body of 'good stories' in the literature of teacher thinking, and these have a force and authenticity that has convinced some readers. There is some research which goes a little way toward making my point; for example, Eraut and his colleagues (Becher *et al.* 1981; Eraut 1982) 'found that teachers never discussed children's work in isolation but always in context. What came before and after, how long it took, how much help they had, whether the child was highly involved or affected by some unusual circum-stance . . .' and so on. Eraut likens this to a film-clip; extended a bit (which it might well have been if the teachers had not been talking to researchers), such a clip readily becomes a story. Two further examples: Ray, a junior high school teacher with whom Butt *et al.* (1988) worked, talks about his image of the class-room as haven; his account of this image as it relates to his own difficult child-hood passes first through a story of one of his students who suffered abuse at the hands of an alcoholic father. And Bruce, when questioned about his use of non-academic dialect in the classroom, also 'responds indirectly by telling the story of one of his students' (Connelly and Clandinin, 1986). It could be objected, of course, that these stories were told for the benefit of researchers already oriented to elicit this form of reply, but I think we have to acknowledge that all of us retain stories of teaching, memorable or hair-raising moments which encapsul-ate something important about our work that we have not found it necessary to elaborate in a formal way.

A Story About a Story

I have one such story which presses a little further the claim that teachers' knowledge is intrinsically ordered in terms of story, and if this seems to be 'merely anecdotal', I can only point out that if one accepts the notion that teachers' knowledge is organized this way we can only hope to convince others by telling stories. So . . . a few years ago I was asked to give a short in-service presentation on evaluation to a group of elementary school teachers. I decided to present a general theoretical framework for talking about evaluation, and then discuss the British Open University's model for classroom evaluation by teachers; the model involves six steps beginning with the question, 'What are the pupils doing?' Illustrating the use of the model was problematic because I did not have local material that could be used with Israeli teachers.

While I was mulling this over I happened to talk to a teacher, Ruth, who had done some interesting work in art education. A social worker by training, Ruth worked in a community youth centre which had been asked by a neighbourhood school to work with its fourth and fifth grade teachers on art activities to be integrated with school subjects. Ruth had played a major role in developing and presenting units on topics such as 'Jerusalem' and 'environmental art'. Her account was particularly interesting because it reflected a number of concerns being treated simultaneously. The first concern had come from the school, which was interested in the use of diverse media to reinforce learning. The second concern, shared by the classroom teachers and Ruth, was to use art works as sources of knowledge; for example, works depicting Jerusalem were used to teach about the way of life in the city a century ago: the pupils learned about distribution of services from the portrait of the water merchant, and so on. Third, art work was seen by Ruth as a context in which to acquire skills: learning to complete a picture, learning to criticize one's work; in this concern Ruth drew on her background as a social worker with children in difficulty. Ruth gave me a number of slides showing the children at work on the environmental art project, and I decided to use these in my presentation.

On the morning of the workshop I found myself facing a group of about twenty elementary school teachers; from the lively conversation that went on before the session began I gathered that many of the participants knew one another either from school or from other workshops. I gave the first half of the presentation — general background, the six-stage evaluation scheme, and an account of Ruth's work in planning the unit on environmental art. One point I emphasized was that unlike other topics which had been chosen to dovetail with the existing curriculum, this topic was contributed by Ruth and her colleagues because it interested them, and because they saw in it an opportunity to get the children totally involved in an art activity. The unit began with a series of short lectures on environmental art illustrated by slides and photographs. The following lesson was a full morning's activity: the children were brought to an empty room at the centre, and shown a pile of fabric, string, wire, paper and other junk which they could use any way they liked. The instruction was to construct an environment in the room using the materials provided. Up to this point in the workshop, the teachers listened politely to the account, asking questions which suggested that they were interested but were skeptical of the practical value of all this. We then took a coffee break and the session resumed in a different room where a slide projector had been set up and drapes were drawn. I mention this point because after the break the seating arrangement was different and this is significant to my story.

The lights were turned off, and the first slide was shown. The teachers looked at the first slide, which showed two pupils apparently examining an arrangement of coloured string and paper, and I repeated the first question of the scheme, 'What are the pupils doing?' A variety of responses were forthcoming, and I went on to the second question, 'What could they be learning?' At this point a voice to my left was raised above the others, and the teacher who belonged to the voice said, 'Just a minute, I can't see the point of these questions. You've told us very little about this class, and we don't even know what the objectives of the lesson are!' When I heard this comment I took a deep breath; I had spent time during the first hour discussing some of the limitations of planning by objectives, but I knew that most teachers had been indoctrinated to view evaluation as the final stage of a sequence that began with the formulation of an objective, and thus the question was expected. Still, I needed to gather my energies to make another stab at it. I had just begun a reply when several other members of the group burst in on the discussion. In the semi-darkness and altered seating they had noticed what I could not, that this teacher had not been present during the first half of the morning, and they let her know in no un-certain terms that her intervention was unacceptable. They explained to her that we were trying to get away from the concept of objectives and look at these slides as data that might allow us to learn new things about what was happening in the class. The teachers then turned back to me, pleased with their own insight, and said, 'look, you've succeeded, all of us would have been inclined to have this response to the slides before we heard the first half of your present-ation.'

The session continued, we looked at the remainder of the slides and discussed the implications and usefulness of the six questions for the evaluation of their own teaching. I do not mean to suggest that the session was a great success: the teachers did get the point, but remained skeptical about their ability to evaluate their own work for a variety of good reasons (time, energy, pressure to conform). The point that I do want to make with the story is that the teachers had been able to hear a message about the limitations of thinking in terms of objectives and an alternative way of analyzing a classroom situation because it had been presented in the context of a story of a teacher's work, and they had been given for analysis a facet of the story, in the faces of these children intent upon their work.

The Discourse of Biography and Narrative

If we are to use the concept of 'story' in carrying forward our work, however, we need some conceptual guidelines. Serious work has been done by Connelly and Clandinin around the terms 'narrative', 'narrative unity' and 'personal practical knowledge' (1986, 1987), by Butt and Raymond using 'biography' (1987), and by Butt *et al.* using 'autobiography', and 'autobiographic praxis' (1988). I want now to address some points of agreement and difference between these two approaches, and between the two and my own understanding of 'story'.

First, there is a common theme in the two sets of studies which relates to how both 'biography' and 'narrative', are viewed. Connelly and Clandinin speak of 'narrative unity', following MacIntyre (1984) as

> a continuum within a person's experience which renders life experi-
> ences meaningful through the unity they achieve for the

> person . . . unity is the union in a particular person in a particular time and place of all that he has been and undergone in the past and in the past of the tradition which helped to shape him. (Clandinin and Connelly, 1985, p. 32)

Butt *et al.* (1988), on the other hand, refer to 'the "whole" story', to 'the full depth and breadth of autobiography' as opposed to the bringing forward of biographic fragments relevant to a particular practice. For Connelly and Clandinin unity is found in the present as a person brings past experience to bear to make present action meaningful. For Butt *et al.* unity or wholeness is found in the long sweep of biography from the past into the present. The formulations differ but both express a similar concern with giving an account of the person that is full and complete, tracing everything that the person has undergone, all that is 'in' his self. Butt *et al.* take this even further in speaking of 'what a teacher knows inside her head . . . unfettered and unshaped by others' questions, ideas and interpretations . . . the teacher's own unadulterated voice.'

Both the above accounts reflect quite clearly some of the ideological presuppositions behind the traditional conception of autobiography:

> that autobiography is a narrative similar to other narratives: it develops linearly from a to n, following a temporal sequence the logic of which is retrospective, (and that it deals with) what belongs to the author alone (or is 'owned' by him), his 'individual life' . . . which is self-consistent throughout its history . . . this statement assumes the existence of a given and knowable empirical reality, and further assures us that the author . . . is in a position of 'authority' with respect to a particular segment of that reality — his own life . . . However, nowhere are we told that such a definition obtains only within a social structure which promotes subjects with 'proper existence', existing as free-floating totalities . . . the completion of autobiography — or biography, or any other narrative — is a myth posited within the discursive reality (Elbaz, 1988).

Thus the treatment of both narrative and biography seem to belie the author's convictions, expressed elsewhere in both sets of writing, that knowledge is constructed, dynamic and changing; their formulations do not always take account of the fact that the teacher's knowledge grows out of a complex, dialectic relationship with the discursive social matrix that shapes it. As such, we could not possibly hope to present the 'whole story'; and 'all' that I have undergone in the past is unavailable: what we can perhaps obtain is that which, according to my present perspective, appears to be relevant, whereas in the future parts of my past that now seem unimportant may become central to my understanding of my history. In short, both Connelly and Clandinin and Butt and Raymond fall back on conceptions of unity and wholeness which are posited within the discursive space of modern thought, conceptions which serve to mask the fragmented nature of modern social life in which facts and values, ends and means, thoughts and actions are split apart and the individual's life is similarly divided up into spheres and roles (private and public, work and play). It is one thing to share the *quest* for unity (as MacIntyre sees it), but it is quite another to see unity because one has posited it before one looks.

With respect to their views of the thought/action relationship, both sets of studies also encounter some difficulties in carrying out the dialectical approaches which they espouse. For Connelly and Clandinin (1985), the intention to treat thought and action dialectically is evident: 'A teaching act is an act of understanding . . . an act of "personal participation" [through which] teachers come to know, and to act upon, teaching and learning situations' (p. 2). Yet in addressing the question of what counts as evidence for the personal in their work (Clandinin and Connelly 1987), they state that 'practice precedes teacher assertions and is ultimately considered more telling in the accounts of teacher knowledge offered'; they nevertheless go on to conclude that 'given this dual evidential base . . . these studies effectively define personal knowledge in terms of both "thought" and action.' One can only conclude that there are inherent difficulties in conceptualizing teaching practice as inseparable from teacher thought: although the dialectical relationship is asserted, it is examined in terms of a 'problematic' (in McKeon's 1952 sense) conception of the theory/practice relationship some of the terms of which are 'problem', 'method', 'outcome' and 'evidence.' Yet in a dialectic view neither teacher assertion nor practice can constitute 'evidence' of knowledge because, to the extent that the teacher and researcher are mutually involved in a process of reconstructing meaning, both are involved within practice and assertion; in the state of being involved, we apprehend coherence, but as soon as we focus directly on the clues to that coherence (whether practice or teacher assertion), 'we change their phenomenal character, and we find that they do not, in their new guise, logically imply . . . the reality that we do find them to imply through an indwelling *tacit* inference' (Polanyi and Prosch, 1975, p. 61).

Butt *et al.* (1988) are clear as to the dialectical nature both of their work and of the multiple relationships between 'thought and action of the teacher (as distinct from theory and practice), the interaction of person and context, teacher's knowledge held and expressed, and the past and the present' (p. 28). In their concern with preserving the 'whole' of the teacher's knowledge and not being limited to that which finds expression in current practice, they argue for the autobiographical method which begins from the historical sweep of a teacher's experience, whereas action in the practical domain 'must also eventually be examined in its own right' (p. 34), thus making a case for a correct starting point for research. A consistently dialectical approach to the theory/practice and the thought/action relationships, however, should make it unimportant where we start. Or rather, the appropriateness of a particular starting point for research on teacher thinking can be, and must be, justified in the context of the study itself. Both Butt and Raymond's biographical work with teachers who are available for reflection because they are already pursuing academic studies, and Connelly and Clandinin's work in the context of a school-oriented project where they play a participative role in the classroom seem to fully justify their particular starting points and emphases. Both have, as Connelly and Clandinin suggest, something special to offer; it should not be necessary to attempt to generalize as to 'the correct method' of studying teachers' knowledge dialectically.

Story as Discourse for Teacher Thinking Research

Insofar as both 'narrative' and 'autobiography' are terms which derive from particular traditions of literature, both tend to carry with them into our discourse some of the positivist assumptions from which we are striving to distance ourselves. I believe that the notion of 'story' might help us to avoid some of the pitfalls of these terms. First, the notion of 'story' is one which keeps the teller of the story clearly in focus: if the story achieves a unity or wholeness, it is because the teller has done so, not because unity has been found to inhere in the stuff itself. Unity is something we seek to accomplish in our lives, and if the teacher achieves this in her working life it is because she has been able to arrange matters in a consistent story line. The accomplishment of story thus always involves both the creation of a coherent meaning and the successful resolution of whatever conflict threatens meaning. 'Story' thus also keeps audience firmly in mind, for what counts as a meaningful story, or a good story depends on the listener who plays an active role in making sense of the story; it is the complicity of the listener which allows the story to repel the threat of meaninglessness. In this respect 'story' is analogous to 'text' (Barthes, 1979) insofar as it implies the collaboration of author and reader, whereas 'narrative' tends to call on a conception of 'work' as a defined object with particular, formal qualities, an object which signifies something else in a relatively straightforward way and is there to be consumed. All this reminds us that teachers cannot function in a totally idiosyncratic fashion: what they do, and how they account for it, have to make sense both in the context of the practice of teaching (with its particular, if contested, base of knowledge) and in the context of the society and its traditions of what it means to teach, learn and become educated. As against narrative (at least the traditional conception thereof), story is not linear and does not have to follow a prescribed shape or form. It can, like Aoki's story, mix genres, giving us historical document, analysis and poetic language in one occasion of telling. As against traditional conceptions of autobiography and biography, story does not assume the authoritative and omniscient narrator who tells the whole truth and nothing but the truth; the teller's perspective is assumed to be a partial one, but honestly assumed, and thus open to criticism.

Another feature of 'story' as opposed to both narrative and autobiography is that as a tale told on an occasion it can change easily, and is unlikely to become frozen into a fixed form. One of the problems with the relationship that holds between teachers and researchers in our academic context has to do with the solidification of our accounts of teachers into published form. In my own case, after the account of Sarah (Elbaz, 1983) was complete I gave it to her to read;

one of her comments was that it read like a novel about someone else. I believe from other discussions we had that Sarah did feel the study told her story, and that participating in it had furthered her own thinking on many issues. But (as Grumet reminds us, 1987) there is inescapably something about the publication in a finished, formal way, of any piece of writing, which involves its alienation from those who produced it. I am not suggesting we stop publishing our accounts of teachers' knowledge, but rather that we experiment with forms that involve less risk of taking teachers' stories out of their hands. Joint publication is one means, appropriate to some situations, but should not be the only one. Grumet suggests that we produce multiple accounts, in part because 'if they undermine the authority of the teller, they also free her from being captured by the reflection provided in a single narrative.' A similar purpose is achieved with 'narrative fragments' (Connelly and Clandinin, 1986), episodes taken from longer conversations with teachers and used to draw the outlines of narrative unities rather than giving us the full narrative account for every teacher.

Finally, the notion of 'story' evokes an image of a community of listeners which is particularly needed at this point in our work. The image of such a community is suggested by Butt and Raymond's account of their collaborative work on autobiography with groups of graduate students, but its presence may not be dependent on one particular form of work. In Connelly and Clandinin's work, for example, each teacher is portrayed as belonging individually to various traditions and communities; nevertheless the fact that teacher and researcher participate in a shared discourse constitutes a small step toward the creation of a new sense of community. In our own work as researchers we have been able, despite significant theoretical and methodological differences, to create for ourselves this sense of community; we should find ways of opening this up to include teachers, and the notion of 'story', I think, gives us increased possibilities of doing so.

References

AKERMAN, C. (1977) 'On *Jeanne Dielman*', *Camera Obscura* 2, pp. 118–19.

AOKI, T. (1983) 'Experiencing ethnicity as a Japanese Canadian teacher: Reflections on a personal curriculum', *Curriculum Inquiry* 13, 3, pp. 321–35.

BARTHES, R. (1979) 'From Work to Text,' in HARARI, J. V. (Ed.) *Textual Strategies: Perspectives in Post-Structuralist Criticism* Ithaca, Cornell.

BECHER, A., ERAUT, M. and KNIGHT, J. (1981) *Policies for Educational Accountability*, London, Heinemann.

BERLAK, A. and BERLAK, H. (1981) *Dilemmas of Schooling: Teaching and Social Change*, London, Methuen.

BERLINER, D. (1986) 'In pursuit of the expert pedagogue', *Educational Researcher*, 15, 7, pp. 5–13.

BOWERS, C. A. (1987) *Elements of a Post-Liberal Theory of Education*, New York and London, Teachers' College Press.

BRITZMAN, D. P. (1986) 'Cultural myths in the making of a teacher: Biography and social structure in teacher education', *Harvard Educational Review*, 56, 4, pp. 442–56.

BROWN, S. and MCINTYRE, D. (1986) 'How do teachers think about their craft?' in BEN-PERETZ, M., BROMME, R. and HALKES, R. (Eds), *Advances of Research on Teacher Thinking*, Lisse, Swets and Zeitlinger.

BRUNER, J. (1987) 'Life as narrative,' *Social Research*, 54, 1, pp. 11–32.

BUCHMANN, M. (1983) 'Argument and conversation as discourse models of knowledge use', Occasional Paper No. 68. East Lansing, Michigan State University, Institute for Research on Teaching.

BUCHMANN, M. (1986) 'Role over person: Legitimacy and authenticity in teaching', in BEN-PERETZ, M., BROMME, R. and HALKES, R. (Eds), *Advances of Research on Teacher Thinking*, Lisse, Swets and Zeitlinger.

BUTT, R. and RAYMOND, D. (1987) 'Arguments for using qualitative approaches in understanding teacher thinking: The case for biography', *Journal of Curriculum Theorizing*, 7, 1, pp. 62–93.

BUTT, R., RAYMOND, D., and YAMAGISHI, L. (1988) 'Autobiographic praxis: Studying the formation of teachers' knowledge', *Journal of Curriculum Theorizing*, 7, 4.

CLANDININ, D. J. (1985) *Classroom Practice: Teacher Images in Action*, Lewes, Falmer Press.

CLANDININ, D. J. and CONNELLY, F. M. (1985) 'Teachers' personal practical knowledge: Calendars, cycles, habits and rhythms and the aesthetics of the classroom', a paper presented at the University of Calgary — OISE Conference on Teachers' Personal Practical Knowledge, Toronto.

CLANDININ, D. J. and CONNELLY, F. M. (1987) 'What is "personal" in studies of the personality?' *Journal of Curriculum Studies*, 19, 6.

CLARKE, C. M. (1986) 'Ten years of conceptual development in research on teacher thinking', in BEN-PERETZ, M., BROMME, R. and HALKES, R. (Eds), *Advances of Research on Teacher Thinking*, Lisse, Swets and Zeitlinger.

CLARK, C. M. and PETERSON, P. L. (1986) 'Teachers' thought processes,' in WITTROCK, M. (Ed.) *Handbook of Research on Teaching*, Third edition, New York, Macmillan, pp. 255–95.

CONNELLY, F. M. and CLANDININ, D. J. (1985) 'Personal practical knowledge and the modes of knowing: Relevance for teaching and learning', in EISNER, E. (Ed.) *Learning and Teaching the Ways of Knowing*, NSSE Yearbook, Chicago, University of Chicago Press.

CONNELLY, F. M. and CLANDININ, D. J. (1986) 'On narrative method, personal philosophy and narrative unities in the study of teaching', *Journal of Research in Science Teaching*, 23, 3, pp. 15–32.

CONNELLY, F. M. and CLANDININ, D. J. (1987) 'On narrative method, biography and narrative unities in the study of teaching', *Journal of Educational Thought*, 21, 3, pp. 130–9.

DAY, C. (1987) 'Sharing practice through consultancy: individual and whole school staff development in a primary school', *Curriculum Perspectives*, 7, 1, pp. 7–15.

EISNER, E. (1988) 'The primacy of experience and the politics of method', *Educational Researcher*, 17, 5, pp. 15–20.

ELBAZ, F. (1983) *Teacher Thinking: A Study of Practical Knowledge*, London, Croom Helm.

ELBAZ, R. (1988) *The Changing Nature of the Self: A Critical Study of the Autobiographic Discourse*, Beckenham, Croom Helm.

ERAUT, M. (1982) 'What is learned in in-service education and how? A knowledge use perspective', *British Journal of In-Service Education*, 9, 1, pp. 6–14.

FEIMAN-NEMSER, S. and FLODEN, R. (1986) 'The cultures of teaching', in WITTROCK, M. (Ed.) *Handbook of Research on Teaching*, Third edition, 505–26, New York: Macmillan.

FOUCAULT, M. (1970) *The Order of Things: An Archaeology of the Human Sciences*, New York, Random House.

FOUCAULT, M. (1979) 'What is an author?' in HARARI, H. V. (Ed.) *Textual Strategies: Perspectives in Post-structuralist Criticism*, Ithaca, Cornell.

GEIGER, S. (1986) 'Women's life histories: Method and content', *Signs*, 11, 2, pp. 334–51.

GILLIGAN, C. (1982) *In a Different Voice*, Cambridge, Harvard University Press.

GOODSON, I. (1980) 'Life histories and the study of schooling', *Interchange*, 11, 4, pp. 62–77.

GOULDNER, A. (1979) *The Future of Intellectuals and the Rise of a New Class*, New York, Seabury Press.

GRUMET, M. (1987) 'The politics of personal knowledge', *Curriculum Inquiry*, 17, 3, pp. 319–29.

HALL, E. (1977) *Beyond Culture*, Garden City, NY, Anchor Books.

JACKSON, P. (1968) *Life in Classrooms*, New York, Holt, Rinehart and Winston.

JANESICK, V. (1982) 'Of snakes and circles: Making sense of classroom group processes through a case study', *Curriculum Inquiry*, 12, 2, pp. 161–89.

LAMPERT, M. (1985) 'How do teachers manage to teach?' *Harvard Educational Review*, 55, 2, pp. 178–94.

LEINHARDT, G., WEIDMAN, C. and HAMMOND, K. M. (1987) 'Introduction and integration of classroom routines by expert teachers', *Curriculum Inquiry*, 17, 2, pp. 135–76.

LOWYCK, J. (1986) 'Post-interactive reflections of teachers: A critical appraisal', in BEN-PERETZ, M., BROMME, R. and HALKES, R. (Eds) *Advances of Research on Teacher Thinking*, Lisse, Swets and Zeitlinger.

MACINTYRE, A. (1984) *After Virtue*, Notre Dame, Ind., University of Notre Dame Press.

MORRISON, T. (1977) *Song of Solomon*, New York, Knopf.

NODDINGS, N. (1987) 'Fidelity in teaching, teacher education, and research for teaching', *Harvard Educational Review*, 56, 4, pp. 496–510.

OLSON, J. (1986) 'Information technology and teacher routines: Learning from the microcomputer', in BEN-PERETZ, M., BROMME, R. and HALKES, R. (Eds), *Advances of Research on Teacher Thinking*, Lisse, Swets and Zeitlinger.

POLANYI, M. and PROSCH, H. (1975) *Meaning*, Chicago, University of Chicago Press.

POPE, M. and SCOTT, E. (1984) 'Teachers' epistemology and practice', in HALKES, R. and OLSON, J. (Eds), *Teacher Thinking: A New Perspective on Persisting Problems in Education* Lisse, Swets and Zeitlinger.

REID, W. A. (1988) 'Institutions and practices: Professional education reports and the language of reform', *Educational Researcher*, 17.

REISS, T. J. (1982) *The Discourse of Modernism*, Ithaca, Cornell University Press.

SHAVELSON, R. and STERN, P. (1981) 'Research on teachers' pedagogical thoughts, judgments, decisions and behavior', *Review of Educational Research*, 51, pp. 455–98.

SHULMAN, L. (1987) 'Knowledge and teaching: Foundations of the new reform', *Harvard Educational Review*, 57, 1, pp. 1–22.

SMYTH, J. (1987) 'Transforming teaching through intellectualizing the work of teachers', in SMYTH, J. (Ed.) *Educating Teachers: Changing the Nature of Pedagogical Knowledge*, Lewes, Falmer Press.

SOCKETT, H. (1987) 'Has Shulman got the strategy right?' *Harvard Educational Review*, 57, 2, pp. 208–19.

TABACHNICK, B. R. and ZEICHNER, K. M. (1986) 'Teacher beliefs and classroom behaviors: some teacher responses to inconsistency', in BEN-PERETZ, M., BROMME, R. and HALKES, R. (Eds) *Advances of Research on Teacher Thinking*, Lisse, Swets and Zeitlinger.

TRIPP, D. H. (1987) 'Teachers, journals and collaborative research', in SMYTH, J. (Ed.)

Educating Teachers: Changing the Nature of Pedagogical Knowledge, Lewes, Falmer Press.

WOODS, P. (1987) 'Life histories in teacher knowledge', in SMYTH, J. (Ed.) *Educating Teachers: Changing the Nature of Pedagogical Knowledge*, Lewes, Falmer Press.

YINGER, R. (1987) 'Learning the language of practice', *Curriculum Inquiry*, 17, 3, pp. 293–318.

Chapter 2

How Practical is Contemplation in Teaching?*

Margaret Buchmann

What sophisticated *ways of looking at people learning* can we initiate intending teachers into? (Wilson, 1975)

In much of research on teacher thinking, teachers' decisions and processes of arriving at them, have been central concerns. Thinking, however, must be construed more broadly than decision-making; it includes a variety of processes, such as imagining, remembering, interpreting, judging, caring and feeling. This philosophical chapter extends previous analyses of teacher thinking by focusing on 'contemplation', and investigating the uses of this 'quiet, absorbed kind of looking' in teaching. In doing so, it clarifies the meaning of contemplation as attentive perception and wonder and discusses an interpretation of the practical that goes beyond defining practice simply as what a teacher does. Instead, the chapter invokes an ethical understanding of human practices that requires attention to intangible ideas of excellence and the exercise of acquired virtues.

To speak of contemplation and practicality in one breath is to be guilty of a contradiction in terms, or so it would seem. Practicality is commonly associated with usefulness and contemplation suspends the qualities of wanting and willing in favor of a quiet, absorbed kind of looking. What could be the uses of this kind of looking in teaching? To address this question, we have to arrive at some understanding of 'practical' and 'contemplation' and a great part of the task of this chapter will be to establish just that.

Research has made much of teacher thinking as decision-making; yet the process of arriving at choices is by no means all there is to thinking. The selective emphasis on teacher decisions reflects a historical trend characteristic of modernity with its emphasis on free choice and an implicit preference for a certain form of rationality in which the calculation of outcomes takes pride of place. In ordinary language, however, thinking is seen as, among other things, an internal kind of gazing: as vision rather than decision. Researchers need to

---

*A precursor of this chapter is my (1988) 'Argument and contemplation in teaching'.

stop and think, to look at the diverse contexts in which people talk about thinking.

When Do We Talk About Thinking?

We comment on a painting by an old Dutch master by saying, 'The girl sits at a table, pen in hand, dreamily looking into the distance; her servant, ready to carry her letter, is smiling conspiratorially: I think the girl is wrapped in thoughts of her lover.' Confronted with a puzzling situation, we turn it over in our mind, not satisfied until we have made sense of it — at least for the time being, for the meaning we attribute to experience is subject to change. Thinking, we also remember the past and we are moved by it, all the while giving it meaning. 'Do you recall when mother told us how she lost her chance to go to high school when her own mother died? — I think she meant to encourage us to go farther and learn more than she was able to do.' We ask someone, 'What is your thinking on that?' and are ready to accept answers that, depending on the context, can derive from logical or conceptual analysis, common sense, or personal judgment based on values and experience.

Are There Experts in Thinking?

Like singing, dancing, and teaching, thinking is part of our human inheritance. We think because we are human, and if someone tells us to think we ordinarily know what to do.

> By birthright we are all not only thinkers but also singers and dancers, poets and painters, teachers and storytellers. This means that the professional singer or painter, poet or teacher, dancer or storyteller, is a professional in a different way from the solicitor or doctor, physician or statistician. (Bambrough, 1980, p.60; see also Popper, 1980)

This is not to say that character, choice, and chance cannot lead people to do more or less singing, dancing, teaching or thinking; and these human activities can be done with more or less engagement or aplomb. If one makes one's living by thinking, dancing, and so on, one becomes a professional without ever being an expert in the sense of someone being proficient, say, at the law of torts or at radiology.

The *Oxford English Dictionary* defines 'to think' as the most general verb expressing mental activity and documents its usage in seventeen senses with numerous subdivisions. To a greater or lesser extent conscious of what they are doing, people engage in the activities of thinking as they go about their lives. To think means 'to form or have in mind as an idea'; 'to consider, meditate on, ponder'; 'to have, or make, a train of ideas pass through the mind'. Forming ideas of people, things, and events, thinking is imagining, conceiving, thus, intellectual construction. Thinking may require effort, as when one applies the mind to something, giving it one's steady mental attention. It may lead to solving a problem by a process of thought, or eventuate in a purpose, the finding out or devising of a plan. Consideration merges with memory in the senses of 'to think' as 'to call to mind, bear in mind, recollect or remember'.

Judgment comes to the fore when thinking involves having or forming an opinion, good or bad, valuing or esteeming something or someone, highly or otherwise. And poets have associated thinking with the claims of the heart; as Wordsworth wrote, "'tis still the hour of thinking, feeling, living'; recall also John Donne's phrase: 'A naked thinking heart.' Holding someone in regard is not just looking at a person but liking what one sees, and imagines. These contexts and examples of usage make clear that thinking is more than an instrument for knowing and doing.

Thinking is related to freedom, for trains of thought can take any point of departure and lead anywhere. People think of many more things than they will, or can, ever do. The thinking process plays havoc with the restrictive conditions of ordinary experience, such as the continuity of time, one's location in time and space, as well as the requirements of necessity related to the social and material aspects of human nature. Being hidden from others, thoughts do not commit one as action does. Hannah Arendt (1978) explains the freedom and insubstantiality peculiar to thinking as follows:

> Thinking is 'out of order' not merely because it stops all the other activities so necessary for the business of living and staying alive, but because it inverts all ordinary relationships: what is near and appears directly to our senses is now far away and what is distant is actually present. While thinking I am not where I actually am; I am surrounded not by sense-objects but by images that are invisible to everybody else. It is as though I had withdrawn into some never-never land, the land of invisibles, of which I would know nothing had I not this faculty of re-membering and imagining. Thinking annihilates temporal as well as spatial distances. I can anticipate the future, think of it as though it were already present, and I can remember the past as though it had not disappeared. (p.85)

Is Thoughtfulness the Opposite of Absentmindedness?

What can we learn about thinking when we consider the absence of thought? First of all, 'thoughtlessness' is not a merely descriptive term: second, it has much less to do with decisions, and hardheadedness, than with consideration and mindfulness. When we say that another person has been thoughtless, we do not mean to imply that she was wavering before acting, or lacking in whatever it takes to arrive at a decision. Neither do we necessarily mean to convey that she suffers from an inability to reason properly.

The attribution of thoughtlessness is, at minimum, a statement about behavior. But people judge one's failure to acknowledge 'the claim on our thinking attention that all events and facts make by virtue of their existence' (Arendt, 1978, p.4), in moral terms. We describe someone as 'thoughtless' who is not taking thought and is wanting in consideration for others, being heedless or imprudent. In her analysis of the Eichmann trials in Jerusalem, Arendt (1978) builds on the assumptions embedded in ordinary language by asking:

> Could the activity of thinking as such, the habit of examining whatever happens to come to pass or to attract attention, regardless of results and specific content, could this activity be among the conditions that make men abstain from evil-doing or even actually 'condition' them against it? (p.5)

Considering how people regard the absence of thought greatly qualifies the freedom we have attributed to thinking. Sometimes people assume that there is a duty to think. There are things that *call for* our attention not just because they are 'thought-provoking' or intriguing but because we ought to pay attention to them, putting aside the claims of the insistent self, its interests and inclinations. Accordingly, being thoughtful or mindful is associated with goodness — kindness and care — and, where it does concern action and decision, with the more sober virtue of prudence.

Being prudent means having the ability to determine the most suitable course of action or conduct (the manner of conducting oneself or one's life), usually with reference to the moral quality of action (good or bad). Hence, in thinking about thinking, we have come full circle to a major area of research on teacher thinking: teachers' capacity to determine suitable courses of action and the dispositions and processes that presumably underlie that capacity.[1] In doing so, we have also traversed other domains, including goodness and evil, and touched on a variety of processes, such as imagining and remembering, interpreting and giving meaning, judging and willing, caring and feeling.

In broadening and diversifying the picture of thinking and hence, of teacher thinking, we have also mentioned the concept of 'attention' related to the binding claims that people, facts, ideas or events have on our consideration, whether thought eventuates in action, dissolves into further thought, or simply peters out. Now it is necessary to pull in the conceptual reins and establish distinctions and priorities. For instance, philosophers distinguish judgment from both theoretical reasoning and imagination and try to sort out how one's feelings influence belief. Are some mental activities more important than others, so that one can establish some precedence in the order of logic or importance? Willing, acting, and, of course, judging, depend on a person's preliminary reflections, on thought's attention to relevant objects of thought: facts, ideas, persons, circumstances and events. In this sense, 'mere' thinking has priority over judging, acting, and willing.

Schopenhauer (1844) went farther in arguing that, under the shadow of the will, it is impossible to see things as they are. A man (and, we might add, a woman) rises to being a knowing subject in and through contemplation which establishes conditions for seeing things, events, and people as they are. He describes these conditions as follows:

> If, raised by the power of the mind, a man relinquishes the common way of looking at things, gives up tracing... their relations to each other, the final goal of which is always a relation to his own will; if he thus ceases to consider the where, the when, the why, and the whither of things, and looks simply and solely at the *what*; if, further, he does not allow abstract thought, the concepts of the reason, to take possession of his consciousness, but instead of all this, gives the whole power of his mind to perception, sinks himself entirely in this, and lets his whole consciousness be filled with quiet contemplation. (p.231)

This brings us to the topic at hand: the process of contemplation and its practicality in the work of teaching. Lost in thought, we may achieve detachment, but we are also lost to the world and its supposed chains of causation. To dispel the appearance of paradox in examining the practicality of contemplation in teaching, we must work with a concept of the practical that goes beyond defining practice simply as what a teacher does — or even thinks about action — as a particular individual swayed by circumstance and desire. We must reconsider what we mean by saying that something is 'practical'.

Is Practice Practical?

A practised carpenter has experience and skill, knows what to do for the purposes of her craft, and is supposed to get more proficient in the doing. Though practice means the habitual carrying on of something, customary or constant action, it also implies an idea of perfection to which individuals will advance to varying degrees, while few or none will ever reach it.

Perfection in practice is something elusive and exalted, denoting a quality, endowment, or accomplishment of the highest order, usually in a good sense. When we speak of carpentry or medicine as a practice, we have therefore much more in mind than people's traits, acquired capacities, or the patterns and outcomes of individual action. We postulate a configuration of excellences — literally surpassing qualities — for that domain of work; these excellences do not only refer to outcomes of action, but to dispositions, skills, and ways of doing and knowing things that are distinctive to carpentry or medical practice as a form of human striving. And, although medicine is people work and carpentry wood work, there are certain ethical universals governing the conduct of doctors, carpenters, and many other practitioners.

Virtues and Practice

Due to special knowledge and skill, and an associated power over others, participants in a practice have to be people that their clients can trust: trust to do their best, to be concerned about how their actions affect others, to be honest and fair, and to wholeheartedly acknowledge the particular claims which their work has on its practitioners. Such claims result in closing certain options to the acting, thinking person as soon as she takes up a practice in earnest. Carpenters cannot choose to make a rickety cabinet with drawers that are permanently stuck while maintaining that they practice carpentry. Such behavior would provoke the indignant question, 'How *can* you call yourself a carpenter (doctor, teacher, and so on)?' — indicating that such titles are more than names, that they presuppose a demand for people to acknowledge and abide by certain standards to the best of their capacity, which they are, moreover, supposed to improve.

Doctors caring more for their own well-being than for that of their patients may hold down a job but do not practise medicine in the sense of practise that we are talking about. This explains the presence of doctors in battlefields and in hospital wards for the victims of infectious diseases, though the amount of risk to be undergone knowingly may be a matter of debate among practitioners. Even work in the ivory tower calls for courage; professors have to stand up for what is best in their field in dealing with student work, are bound to challenge claims to knowledge they consider ill-founded, even if these are put forth by friends or colleagues of high social authority, and are required to publicize the fact that they have made an error in their work. In general:

> If someone says that he cares for some individual, community, or cause but is unwilling to risk harm or danger on his, her or its own behalf, he puts in question the genuineness of his care anf concern. Courage, the capacity to risk harm or damage to oneself, has its role in human life because of this connection with care and concern. (MacIntyre, 1984, p.192)

In the emphasis on a certain *quality* of engagement and interaction, admirable in its own right, care and concern differ vastly from calculations of utility in terms of outcomes.

While on the surface, 'practicality' stands in opposition to ideals and speculation, people cannot participate in a practice — take part and share, in association with others, in some form of human endeavour — when they are mean-spirited and dishonest, as well as ignorant of or careless about the internal goods and ends a practice does not only embody but extend. Here it is important to realize that the impetus for change does not only flow from the facts of history but from the very idea of perfection with its connotations of incompleteness. In reality, human excellence is always a matter of degree, comparative only, as well as somewhat fluid. These considerations underlie MacIntyre's (1984) somewhat formal and dense definition of practice as:

any coherent and complex form of socially established cooperative human activity through which goods internal to that form of activity are realized in the course of trying to achieve those standards of excellence which are appropriate to, and partially definitive of, that form of activity, with the result that human powers to achieve excellence, and human conceptions of the ends and goods involved, are systematically extended. (p.187)

Ideas of Perfection Are Practical

Assuming an idea of, in the words of Shakespeare, 'right perfection wrongfully disgraced', practice turns out to be impractical, starry-eyed rather than down-to-earth. It requires commitment to intangible ideas of excellence (general human virtues and the ideal goods particular to a practice), the exercise of acquired virtues that may not be externally rewarded or even punished, and the living, personal acknowledgment of claims upon oneself. Such claims may not be enforced, or enforceable, by anything except one's sense of what participation in that practice means. It also follows that — while performance depends on skills and habits, formal and informal knowledge, before it can grow into proficiency and artfulness — practice cannot be defined by compiling lists of skills and other endowments of a technical kind in disjunction with an understanding of a commitment to ends: the points internal to a given form of human striving. That these endeavors may change across time and place merely strengthens the case for people's living awareness and examination of ends.

Many things are 'practical', in the literal sense of pertaining or relating to practice, that violate the taken-for-granted opposition of the practical and the theoretical, speculative, or ideal: things incapable of being put to any immediate or obvious account and thus appearing practically useless. These include ideas of excellence and standards of performance relating to the specific goods defining the point, or points, of a practice; dispositions for caring and being concerned about these ideas as one participates in a practice, standing in relation to both other practitioners and people affected by one's work; as well as general human virtues such as courage, justice and honesty, without which it would be difficult to imagine how one could act on ideas of excellence and work, alone and in concert with others, towards the internal goods that constitute a practice.

Becoming a Participant in a Practice

All these things are acquired as we live, study, and work. A newborn child has no more of a notion of honesty than he has of mathematics or teaching excellence. Inducting aspirants to a practice entails helping them form ideas of perfection relating to conceptions of their work and its specific internal goods, fostering dispositions to care and be concerned about those goods and the people affected by one's work, and upholding — as well as feeling the import of — general human virtues such as truthfulness and courage.

John Wilson (1975) makes a certain intellectual and moral seriousness *about teaching* central in considering the preparation of teachers who likewise have to show — and dispense — care and concern for their subjects. 'One could not', Wilson argues, 'properly be described as "doing science" or "learning history" if one simply did not care about the results of experiments or what contemporary historical documents say' (p.111). He stresses that such seriousness is a precondition of further learning, about teaching as well as subjects, thus relating the disposition for caring and being concerned to the development of proficiency, or the comparative excellence which stimulates further effort. It is thus that we make a variety of human goods available to people while extending and refining the virtues of practice.

Hence, helping people form ideas of perfection in a field of human endeavor is a practical job. Although it retains a vital imprecision, an idea of (right) perfection provides a growing sense of order and direction; it

> moves, and possibly changes, us (as artist, worker, agent) because it inspires love in the part of us that is most worthy. One cannot feel unmixed love for a mediocre moral standard any more than one can for the work of a mediocre artist. The idea of perfection is also a natural producer of order. In its *light* we come to see that A, which superficially resembles B, is really better than B. And this can occur, indeed must occur, without our having the sovereign idea in any sense 'taped'. In fact it is in its nature that we cannot get it taped. (Murdoch, 1986, p.62)

Perfection being out of reach and not precisely definable, the idea exercises an authority from 'beyond'. Thinking, therefore, that does not refer to particular actions — their determination, execution, consequences — is practical nevertheless. Indeed, one might say that we are rising instead of descending to the practical where we consider internal goods and excellences. I will investigate these claims by drawing on the scholastic discussion of the active and the contemplative life in teaching.

Teacher Thinking as Star-Gazing

St Thomas Acquinas (1966a) considers the active and the contemplative life in *Summa Theologiae*. Contemplation is an internal activity of looking that requires an agent but no outward effect or recipient; contemplating things, we aim to see them as they are. The contemplative life has the freedom we have associated with thinking, for it is sufficient to itself. In the active life, people work to affect things or other people and are often ruffled by their recalcitrance and the force of circumstance. The contemplative life also involves a kind of application and moral discipline in cognition or meditation. But contemplation is the point where mental activity comes to rest; its essential qualities are those of restfulness and joy, as we attend to some desirable or lovable good — especially any truth whatever — and dwell on it. This requires clarity of vision and serenity in the concentration on looking. In the words of St Thomas, contemplation refers 'to a simple gaze upon a truth' (p.23).

Requirements and Rewards of Contemplation

As an interior act of seeing, contemplation opens the eyes of the mind while engaging the emotions, the will, and the moral virtues, insofar as the latter dispose one towards peace and purity of heart, and help one direct one's attention to worthy objects. Relieved from the quality of wanting in any immediate or distracting sense, the contemplative life does not comprise the accidental rewards of (external) labour; instead, its rewards are intrinsic, lying in ultimate truths and a perfection of the human mind and its happiness, in the sense of a deep and lasting satisfaction that is not revolving around the self. The ends and delights of contemplation stem from the activity itself and from the value of its admirable objects.

Since we are rational animals we see in truth something we love, and desire to be enlightened. This statement appears to move contemplation close to examination or investigation. But, while admiration and joy (though not repose) are compatible with inquiry in any domain, its simplicity and self-sufficiency mark off contemplation from research, logical analysis, or reflection on action which try to penetrate where contemplation aims to receive. In manner and kind, the ascesis of contemplation is likewise different from the 'self-denial' of science and logic, which both encompass assertion or the laying and vindicating of claims. Contemplation requires its very own kind of detachment. Consider the example of a falling leaf:

> A farmer on seeing the leaf fall might mark the arc it describes in its descent, deduce from this the direction of the wind, the imminence of rain, and hurry off to do whatever farmers do when rain is imminent. A botanist may observe the leaf, think that it is falling rather earlier in the year than usual, pick it up and examine its capillaries, look for signs of disease or other causes for the weakening of the tissues and so on. A sensitive soul, on seeing the leaf fall, may be induced to reflect on the transience of worldly glory . . . and generally indulge in sad musings. A poet . . . may be led to think of a metre or rhythm he could use in his next poem, or of a striking metaphor. (Haezrani, 1956, p.35)

What these different people have in common is that each of them only perceives the falling leaf from his or her own system of relevances, looking, at the same time, beyond the leaf and its falling to other phenomena of intention or causation in applied science and natural science, spiritual life and art. Yet contemplation is 'non-volitional, non-emotional, non-analytical . . . an act of unselfish almost impersonal concentration, an incorporeal "gazing" ' (p.36). It requires a disciplined overcoming of self, and selfless respect for reality (see Murdoch, 1986, chapter 2).

The Priority of Contemplation

Though the active and contemplative life can be distinguished, both are forms of human life, and in an actual existence now one, now the other form will predominate. And it is possible for action to lead to contemplation and for contemplation to lead to action: both forms of life are complementary. In accordance with most medieval authors, however, Aquinas (1966a) points out that the 'return to the active life is guided by the contemplative' (p.83); 'divorced from the contemplative life, the active life would be cut off from its source of value' (see p.117).

These are strong, even counter-intuitive, claims implying that action is appropriately guided by vision, or more precisely, by seeing things — objects, concepts, events, relations, people — as they are, and that some kind of 'incorporeal gazing', rather than utility or conformity to desire, is the spring from which the comparative worth and excellence of our actions and experiences originates. In fact, if I have argued earlier that contemplation begins and ends in itself, these claims seem to imply that thought *and* practice begin and end in contemplation.

If we recall the definition of practice by internal goods and excellences — which need to be 'seen' in a way that makes them binding to a person — these claims begin to make more sense. On reflection, we can also see that 'our ability to act well "when the time comes" depends partly, perhaps largely, upon the quality of our habitual objects of attention' (Murdoch, 1986, p.56). In other words, it is not only the activity of contemplation but the quality of the objects (their nature, kind, or character and their peculiar excellences) to which it is attached that accounts for its priority, since those objects direct effort and further attention informed by an idea of perfection. And action, to quote Murdoch again, 'tends to confirm, for better or worse, the background of attachment from which it issues' (*ibid.*, p.71).

Nor is there a *prima facie* difficulty in applying these claims to teaching, where action and decision need to flow from, and return to, the pursuit of understanding subject matter (objects, concepts, events, relations) and people (primarily students), just as they are, and where thinking and acting without reference to the ultimate good of learning would be without rudder. It is this ultimate good, Heidegger (1968) believes, which makes teaching even more difficult than learning:

> And why is teaching more difficult than learning? Not because the teacher must have a larger store of information, and have it always ready. Teaching is more difficult than learning because what teaching

calls for is this: to let learn . . . The teacher is ahead of his apprentices in this alone, that he has still far more to learn than they — he has to learn to let them learn. The teacher must be capable of being more teachable than the apprentices. The teacher is far less assured of his ground than those who are of theirs. If the relation between the teacher and the taught is genuine, therefore, there is never a place in it for the authority of the know-it-all or the authoritative sway of the official. It is still an exalted matter, then, to become a teacher. (p. 15)

Two Objects of Contemplation Intrinsic to Teaching

These considerations should have rendered St Thomas's question, namely, whether teaching belongs to the active or to the contemplative life, at least intelligible. In working out his answer, Aquinas refers to Aristotle, and points out, first, that the ability to teach is an indication of learning. And, since wisdom and truth in the widest sense belong to the contemplative life, teaching belongs to the contemplative life. He extends this point by stating that, 'it seems an office of the contemplative life to impart to another by teaching, truth that has been contemplated' (p. 61). Office here has the meaning of 'good office', a kindness or attention in the service of others; thus he explains in the volume of *Summa Theologiae* following on the one I have quoted from so far, 'just as it is better to illumine than merely to shine, so it is better to give to others the things contemplated than simply to contemplate' (1966b, p. 205).

The subject matter of teaching, or its *first* object, is accordingly, the unending consideration and love of truth in all of its forms, with the teacher taking delight in that selfless consideration and love. Compared to the external acts of teaching, even reflection-on-action, this object and associated mental activities have logical, though not necessarily temporal, priority. In teaching, the contemplative precedes the active life because of its nature, and the nature of teaching, which requires attachments to objects of thought. Without knowing how to look at an aesthetic object and without knowing one for what it is, what can one say about a child's drawing, except that it is 'nice' or 'true to nature'?

One needs to be able to discern the concept of number and enjoy thinking about that concept — thus complicating one's understanding and experiencing its limits — to help others think about what a number may be. Here it is crucial to share, with the learners, in the authentic engagement in looking: concentrating on the object of thought in its own right without assuming that our usual answers in current language have done full justice to what there is. Hawkins (1974) tells a story about a young and very learned physicist that bears on this point.

My wife was asking him to explain something to her about coupled pendulums. He said, 'Well, now, you can see that there's a conversion of . . . Well, there's really a conservation of angle here.' She looked up at him. 'Well, you see, in the transfer of energy from one pendulum to the other there is . . . ' and so on and so on. And she said, 'No, I don't mean that, I want you to notice this and tell me what's happening.' Finally, he looked at the pendulums and he saw what she was asking. He looked at it, and he looked at her, and he grinned and said, 'Well, I know the right words but I don't understand it either.' This confession, wrung from a potential teacher, I've always valued very much. It proves that we're all in it together. (Hawkins, 1974, p. 62)

The *second* object of teaching and, as I will argue, of the teacher's contemplative attention, are students. That one's attention is urged on toward other people as learners follows from the relation that there is, in human life, between what one most delights in and the wish to be sharing it with other people, particularly one's friends. As Aristotle (1985) writes in the *Nicomachean Ethics*:

> Whatever existence means for each class of men, whatever it is for whose sake they value life, in *that* they wish to occupy themselves with their friends and some drink together, others dice together, others join in athletic exercises and hunting, or in the study of philosophy. (p. 1852)

To the extent that the concept of teaching involves as its second object other people — aiming to enlighten and perfect them — teaching belongs to the active life and requires its exertions in the spirit of fellowship and kindness. Aquinas concludes that teaching *sometimes* belongs to the active life and *sometimes* to the contemplative life. Yet, to reiterate, in moving from contemplation to action in teaching we do not subtract the contemplative but add the active dimension. Put differently, teaching is not a life of action tempered by occasional fits of abstraction, but, in the words of St Thomas, the active life in teaching 'proceeds from the fullness of contemplation' (1966b, p.205).

Moreover, the second object of teaching is also, and properly, an object of contemplation, not just of action. This is suggested by Aristotle's words which connect the impulse to share what we value — or the giving of good things — with our valuing of other people. I will adapt an example from Iris Murdoch (1986) to suggest what process the contemplation of other people is, and how that way of looking fits into teaching.

Raising One's Sights to Children

Suppose a secondary school teacher, Miss Jacobs, feels herself affected by a sense of hostility toward a student. From the first day of school, John strikes her as uncouth in behavior and raw in intellect, over familiar, and excitable — always tiresomely adolescent. Miss Jacobs herself is a quiet person, a bit severe and spinsterish but intelligent and well-intentioned. She knows that she is not at her best with rambunctious boys of that age; in fact, she cannot say that she likes adolescents. A term passes. But Miss Jacobs does not perfect her picture of John as an impossible boy, firming it up in outline and elaborating it in detail.

Miss Jacobs has come to see John as endearingly awkward; his raw intellect has become, in her eyes, an untutored intelligence that is a challenge; John seems to her now not over familiar and excitable but trusting and emotional to the point of being vulnerable. Protective, almost tender, feelings supplant her earlier hostility. What has happened? John has not changed; he is still a rather pestilential adolescent. Nor has Miss Jacobs been busy in any external sense, or devising plans of action to change him. On the surface, Miss Jacobs has substituted one set of (moral) words for another, with positive instead of negative meaning. But deep down, she has been thinking, deliberately, until she could raise her sights to John.

There are cases in which such a process might result in delusions. Yet let us further suppose that our case is correctly described by saying that Miss Jacobs has *looked* at John (and beyond the stereotype), that she has focused her attention on *him* (and away from her sensitivities and limitations), achieving an inward stance and progress of intrinsic worth and attraction. Part of this progress stems from a transcendence of habitual and conventional modes of classification; the greater part, however, stems from seeing John not just with accuracy but with kindness.

Iris Murdoch summarizes this attitude and process in the concept of 'attention', a form of contemplation central to the thought of Simone Weil. This process of thinking opens one's mind to seeing another person as an individual, worthy of regard — in the sense of observant attention and kindly feeling. Though it requires being simple, attentive perception is not easy; it is the contemplation of other people, and the delight taken in that consideration, the love and admiration of their truth, which is their individuality, separate and distinct from oneself, one's purposes and needs. In this way of looking, to quote Simone Weil (1977), the 'soul empties itself of all its own contents in order to receive into itself the being it is looking at, just as he is, in all his truth (p.51).

Perhaps when teachers tell us that they decided to go into teaching because they love children, some mean loving to look at children attentively: holding them in regard — noticing, caring, valuing — thus seeing them not only accurately but justly and lovingly. Surely, this form of contemplation is required by teaching as well, though we may shrug off its ordinary manifestations in teacher talk.

The progression associated with the concepts of truth, love, and justice implies that the attentive perception we have associated with both objects of contemplation in teaching is fallible and open-ended, infinitely perfectible and inherently appealing. It is a source of self-sustaining joy not readily exhausted. Contemplation also connects goodness with knowledge, as 'a refined and honest perception of what is really the case, a patient and just discernment of what confronts one, which is the result not simply of opening one's eyes but of a certainly perfectly familiar kind of moral discipline' (Murdoch, 1985, p. 38). Teaching calls, I submit, for contemplation, which has both practicality and priority in teacher thinking.

Note

1   Some researchers have, however, tended to shrink from explicitly making the moral judgment implied in a concept such as prudence or sagacity, preferring, instead, to assume that any action is reasonable from the point of view of the actor; the attendant confusion of what is capable of being understood, or of rational explanation, with what is capable of being justified — a right belief or action — is a troubling matter. (See Buchmann, 1986.)

References

AQUINAS, ST THOMAS (2)

AQUINAS, T. (1966a) 'Action and contemplation', in AUMANN, J. (Ed.) *Suma Theologiae*, vol. 46, New York, Blackfriars.

AQUINAS, T. (1966b) 'The pastoral and religious lives, in AUMANN, J. (Ed.) *Suma Theologiae*, vol. 47, New York, Blackfriars.

ARENDT, H. (1978) *The Life of the Mind*, New York and London, Harcourt Brace Jovanovich.

ARISTOTLE (1985) 'Nichomachean Ethics', in BARNES, J. (Ed.) *The Complete Works of Aristotle*, vol. 2, Princeton, NJ:, Princeton University Press.

BAMBROUGH, R. (1980) 'Question time', in SHANKER, S. G. (Ed.) *Philosophy in Britain Today*, London and Sydney, Croom Helm pp. 58–71.

BUCHMANN, M. (1985) 'Role over person: Morality and authenticity in teaching', *Teachers College Record*, 87, pp. 529–44.

BUCHMANN, M. (1988) 'Argument and contemplation in teaching', *Oxford Review of Education*, 14, pp. 201–14.

HAEZRANI, P. (1956) *The Contemplative Activity: A Study in Aesthetics*, New York, Abeland-Schuman.

HAWKINS (1974) 'I, thou and it', in *The Informed Vision: Essays on Learning and Human Nature*, New York, Agathon.

HEIDEGGER, M. (1968) *What is Called Thinking?* New York, Harper and Row.

MACINTYRE, A. (1989) *After Virtue*, Notre Dame, Ind., University of Notre Dame Press.

MURDOCH, I. (1986) *The Sovereignty of Good*, London and New York, ARK.

POPPER, K. (1980) 'How I see philosophy', in SHANKER, S. G. (Ed.) *Philosophy in Britain Today*, London and Sydney, Croom Helm pp. 198–205.

SCHOPENHAUER, A. (1844/undated translation) *The World as Will and Idea*, (R. B. HALDANE and J. KEMP, Trans.), London, Kegan Paul, French, Trubner.

WEIL, S. (1977) 'Reflections on the right use of school studies with a view to the love of God', in *Waiting for God*, New York, Putnam.

WILSON, J. (1975) *Educational Theory and the Preparation of Teachers*, Windsor, Berks, NFER.

Chapter 3

Reflection and Professional Knowledge: A Conceptual Framework

Lya Kremer Hayon

The recent interest in reflective teaching has resulted in a number of studies in which reflective teaching is proposed as an important aim to be achieved through teacher education programs. Programs for the development of reflective teaching have been proposed, however, attempts at clarifying the meaning of reflective teaching have been scarce. This study proposes an eclectic frame of reference of reflective teaching based upon an analysis of reflection, of professional knowledge and on the juxtaposition of these two concepts. This juxtaposition generates a mapping sentence that consists of several facets and elements and thus provides the proposed eclectic frame of reference. Theoretically, this mapping sentence may serve as a source for the derivation of research hypotheses, practically it is apt to guide practitioners in teacher education.

Perspective

The topic of reflection in teaching has recently attracted the interest of educational researchers and has consequently captured a significant part of the educational literature. The number of studies devoted to this subject is growing constantly. 'Why does the recent educational scene entertain *reflection* to such an extent?', one may wonder, 'What have teachers been doing all these years, have they not reflected?' A negative answer to the latter question will do injustice to many teachers and distort the image of educational realities, as history reveals a number of 'reflective' great teachers, too large to mention here. The rise of reflection in teaching, as a topic of research and one that deserves to be encouraged in teacher professional development programs, may be understood on the background of the interest in teacher thinking. Considering the developmental phenomenon of differentiation of knowledge, reflection may be conceived of as one particular aspect of thinking. This interest is also embedded in the process of professionalization of teaching and in the societal demand for accountability. Nevertheless, the present study suggests that the literature on reflective teaching has limited itself to a great extent to a declared ideology concerning the desirability of reflection in teaching and consequently to the need to include it as a central aim in teacher education programs. Programs and models for developing reflective teaching have been described in a number of studies (Berlak and Berlak, 1981; Peters, 1985; Zeichner and Liston, 1987). However, it appears that no systematic attempts to clarify and elaborate upon the concept itself have been made, and no specific research questions have been posed. The meanings of reflection that have been forwarded are too general and ambiguous to guide research studies and educational practices. The variety of conceptions and descriptions offered in today's literature may enrich the field of enquiry *but* may also lead to vagueness and misunderstandings, if no clarification of the concept is forwarded (Clandinin and Connelly, 1986). Clark's suggestion (1986) that after ten years of research on teacher thinking, it is time to 'chart a new course for research on teacher thinking' (p. 15), and Shulman's call for a disciplined enquiry regarding the concept of pedagogical knowledge (1987), may well be extended to the need to clarify and investigate the concept of reflective teaching. Furthermore, following the line of thought that underlies Yinger's call for the discovery of the 'language of practice' (1985), we advocate the importance of the discovery of a language, or rather of languages of teacher reflection.

In view of the differing educational perceptions and attitudes, no one definition or any single way of describing reflective teaching is to be expected or desired. However, a conceptual framework of reference which will point out the various elements of reflective teaching and their potential interactions may prove to be helpful in broadening the perspective of this concept for theoretical as well as for practical purposes. Such a frame of reference is apt to guide researchers in the derivation of hypotheses and practitioners in better understanding teachers' reflection and in designing programs for its development.

A frame of reference calls for the clarification of the concepts that it hosts, which in the present case are: *reflection and professional knowledge*. One must keep in mind that reflection is a process, a form of thinking, and as such it has to have a content of reference, as no process is independent of the content in which it occurs. It is only natural to expect that the content of teachers' reflection will be professional and based on *pedagogical knowledge*. One may hope, for instance, that the reflection of a graduate of a university teacher education program will differ from the one of a university graduate who has not undergone such a program, should the latter have a chance to teach. How will, or how should it differ? What will be the characteristics of a professional teacher's reflection? Can reflective teaching be developed? Do teacher educators have a frame of reference to guide them in trying to encourage reflective teaching in their students? In attempting to answer these and similar questions researchers as well as practitioners may well profit from a conceptual frame of reference.

In the next paragraphs the concepts of *Reflection and Professional Knowledge* will be elaborated upon and juxtaposed upon each other to form a basis of a conceptual frame of reference.

The Concept of Reflection

Reflection has been described in the educational literature in many different ways. A brief review of the relatively current literature on reflection, of its processes and styles follows: Lowyck (1986) points to the difficulty in arriving at an agreement regarding the definition of the concept, because of lack of conceptualization and empirical research.

It was Dewey at the onset of this century who mentioned the term *reflection* in making the distinction between routine and reflective teaching, the latter being characterized by active and persistent careful consideration of ends and means, and by relating them to social, educational and political contexts (Dewey, 1933). He suggested three prerequisites for reflective teaching: open-mindedness, responsibility, and wholeheartedness. Fully accepting that these are necessary conditions, one may at the same time doubt whether they are sufficient. The concept as it is perceived today encompasses a wider range of connotations and meanings and the question of what the prerequisites of reflective teaching are, still presents a challenge to educational researchers.

How is reflection perceived in more recent studies?

McKay and Marland (1978) refer to reflection as a category of interactive thoughts, and as a process of teachers' thoughts on past occurrences in the classroom. According to these authors, reflection concerns only teaching behaviors that have not been actualized. This perception presents serious limitations to the concept. In referring to evaluation as a 'phase of teaching whereby teachers assess their plans and accomplishments and so revise them for the future', Shavelson and Stern (1981, p.471) actually describe one aspect of reflection, although they do not use the term itself. Clark and Peterson (1986) relate to reflection in general terms, as post-active thoughts, and Lowyck (1986, p.173) uses the term 'post-interactive reflection' to describe the information processing activities of the teacher 'after a lesson or a broader unit of time'. He perceives post-interactive reflection as a present activity with reference to past experiences. Grant and Zeichner (1984) claim that 'reflective teaching occurs when you question and clarify why you have chosen your classroom materials, procedures and content'. They define reflection as an ongoing process that involves re-examination of what was done, and as thinking analytically about goals and actions in order to achieve better results. They add that 'the reflective teacher is dedicated and committed to teaching all students'. The latter quotation entails a value orientation, which does not clarify the process itself: a teacher may be reflective but this does not necessarily indicate which value orientates his/her reflection, or what is the subject of his/her dedication. The attachment of values to reflection may well guide program development, but it also may contaminate the description of the process as such. At a stage of analysis, process and value must be separated. They may, however, be later combined for practical purposes. An additional description of a reflective teacher was suggested in the student-teaching program at the University of Wisconsin (Zeichner and Liston, 1987). According to this description 'a reflective teacher is one who assesses the origins, purposes, and consequences of his/her work'. Accordingly, the process of reflection is a process of assessment. The image of a reflective teacher that these authors have in mind when proposing a program for the development of education teachers, is one who views knowledge as problematic rather than certain, the role of teaching as a moral craft rather than one of a technician, the curriculum as reflexive rather than received, and the milieu as a topic of inquiry rather than one that is determined in a hierarchical manner.

In 'New thoughts on teacher education' Solomon (1987) suggests that reflection mediates between past experiences, actions, personal theorizing, and understanding of received theories. It is a re-exploration of past experiences. Its value lies, according to her opinion, in the slow construction of personal knowledge and meanings.

An additional aspect of the reflection was proposed by Schon who described it as a tacit process: 'a person doesn't stop to tell himself — now I am reflecting . . . it is very often unconscious and can't be explained in words' (Schon, 1983, p.50).

In interviewing a group of student teachers' supervisors, Korthagen (1987) found that they had a relatively clear image of the 'most reflective teachers' but that they could not describe what they had in mind when referring to a 'least reflective teacher'. This finding is rather interesting as it raises two questions worthwhile of consideration: Assuming that the development of a reflective teacher is an important aim of teacher education and that the attempt to facilitate a tutee's growth has to start at the level of that tutee, but at the same time this level cannot be diagnosed, what will be the baseline to start from? Furthermore, is 'least' and 'more' reflective teaching a matter of quality or of quantity? Can levels of reflection be described along one continuum, or should they rather require several continua for this purpose? Gilbert Ryle (1949) proposes that 'what distinguishes sensible from silly actions is not their percentage but their quality'. Is this also true for reflection? As mentioned, the clarification of the concept of reflective teaching may shed some light on these questions.

In addition to the references made in relation to reflective teaching as a *process*, several *styles* of reflection have been suggested. In one categorization made by Van Maanen (1977) a distinction was made between three styles of reflection: technical rationality, linkage of assumptions underlying practical actions with particular value commitment, and incorporation of moral and ethical values into the discourse of practical actions. Following this categorization, Zeichner and Liston (1987) described several types of teachers: one is a technician who is interested in achieving goals that have been decided upon by others, another is a craftsperson who is interested in the rationale for conducting educational activities and in the quality of the achievements, and a third type of teacher is the moral craftsperson who is interested in the moral and ethical implications of educational activities. Schon (1983, p.68) used the term 'reflective practitioner' to describe one who is not dependent on the categories of established theory and technique, but constructs a new theory of the unique case. His inquiry is not limited to a deliberation about means which depend on a prior agreement about ends. He does not keep ends and means separate, but defines them interactively as he frames a problematic situation. He does not separate thinking from doing . . . reflection in action can proceed in situations of uncertainty or uniqueness, because it is not bound by the dichotomies of technical rationality.

On the other hand, some practitioners 'view themselves as technical experts' too skilful in their performance to detect problems to reflect upon. They use techniques to 'preserve the constancy of their knowledge. For them uncertainty is a threat, its admission is a sign of weakness'. Is this a description of the less reflective teacher? Is it a description of a dogmatic teacher? These are some questions that may have to be answered by further search. Whatever the answers to these questions may be, it is evident that Schon makes a clear distinction between two styles: technical rationality and reflection in action. Interestingly enough, Schon does not attach content values to his description of reflection in action, it appears that for him reflection is a value in itself.

From the analysis of the literature on reflective teaching several salient categories emerge:

A *Time Element* — pertains to the question of when does the reflection occur; in the present about past experiences (post-active thoughts), or in the present about on-going experiences (intra-active thoughts).

Level and Style of Reference — The differentiation between a *level* of understanding ('question and clarify why', Grant and Zeichner, 1984) and analytical thinking and assessment (Zeichner and Liston, 1987) suggests one category of reflection. The distinction between *styles*, illustrated by technical rationality and professional reflection in action, (the latter involving an element of inquiry and creativity and the former an adherence to a priori rules and norms), suggests another category.

Orientation — pertains to the different foci toward which reflection is directed and which are illustrated by the distinction between a perception of knowledge and of curriculum as problematic rather than certain; by the milieu as a topic of inquiry rather than imposed (Zeichner and Liston, 1987); by a practical versus a moral and ethical commitment (Van Maanen, 1977), and by a narrow versus broad context of reference.

This brief review of the literature on reflective teaching is summarized and analyzed into categories of reference in table 3.1. Following this review on processes of reflection in teaching some elaboration upon professional pedagogical knowledge, the content of these processes, is in order.

Table 3.1.
References to reflection in recent educational literature

Author	Year	Process description	Classification with regard to			Time perspective
			thought level	orientation	style	
Dewey	1933	active, persistent consideration of end and means	analysis	Broad context of social political and educational aspects	routine/reflection	retrospection
Van Maanen	1977	application, analysis evaluation	critical analysis	value commitment; social roles	technical/deliberative rationality	
McKay and Marland	1978	cognitive activities, thoughts on past experiences	general, not specified	—	—	retrospection
Shavelson and Stern	1981	assessment of plans accomplishments	analysis judgment	—	—	retrospection for future purposes
Schon	1983	taut, unconscious process interactive view of means ends, theory construction	analysis synthesis creativity	practical professional	technical rationality/reflection in action	retrospection present-intra-active

Grant and Zeichner	1984	questioning, clarifying,	analysis	ethical practical	—	—
Clark and Peterson	1986	post-active thoughts	general not specified	—	—	retrospection
Lowyck	1986	post-interactive thoughts information processing activities after teaching		—	systematic/ spontaneous; frequent sporadic	retrospection
Zeichner and Liston	1987	assessment of purposes and consequences	analysis synthesis judgment	view of knowledge as problematic, of teacher's role as moral craft, of curriculum as reflexive	technician craftsperson moral craftsperson	retrospection
Solomon	1987	mediation between past experiences, personal knowledge and theory re-explorations of experiences	analysis synthesis	situational context	—	—

Professional Pedagogical Knowledge

Attempts at understanding knowledge have a history too long to be cited here. For the present purposes only a glimpse into more recent studies is brought up to shed some light on the concept and to serve as background for the description of professional knowledge.

In a historical review of perceptions of knowledge written for educational purposes, Broudy (1977, p. 1) relates to the distinction made by Kant between *a priori* and *a-posteriori* knowledge and between *intuitive* knowledge of principles and *empirical* knowledge of facts. Similarly, Lampert (1984) makes a distinction between intuitive knowledge that each individual builds from personal experience and which is not necessarily explicit, and formal knowledge that is taught in a systematic manner in schools. A basic distinction between knowing *that* and knowing *how* was made by Ryle (1949). This distinction was followed by many, sometimes using different terms for the same meaning. For instance, Hoz (1987) used the terms *declarative* and *procedural* knowledge in a similar sense: the first kind of knowledge pertains to facts, organized either in small units or in large schemes, the latter pertains to the mental operations that occur with the declarative knowledge. This classification between knowing *that* and knowing *how* was enriched by Broudy (*ibid.*) who added a third category of knowing *with*, which furnishes a context within which a certain situation is perceived, interpreted and judged. Contexts can function without being at the center of consciousness or being recalled verbatim, they can be regarded as patterns, and as a form of tacit knowledge, they can be built of items that had once been at the focus of attention and have been learnt explicitly, they can be cognitive, affective, aesthetic, moral, social or religious. Another classification that Broudy elaborates upon is the one between *scientific* and *positivistic* knowledge on the one hand, and *humanistic* knowledge on the other. A *positivistic* theory will not accept conscience, anxiety, remorse, hopes as topics of research. Differences between scientific and humanistic knowledge engender a clash between two cultures and occur in debates about curriculum, *validity* versus. *utility*, between the quality of a body of knowledge — concepts, relations, theories, modes of inquiry — and usefulness. Broudy illustrates this difference by the following two questions: 'What is good physics?' 'What is physics good for?' However, these distinctions do not have to be viewed in an 'either or' manner, as dichotomies, but rather as a matter of extent, of more or less, of being characterized to a greater or less extent by a certain knowledge characteristic.

Novak (1977) brought up the issue of relativity. He proposed that the existence of a myth of scientific method is prevalent in the society at large. However, in view of changes that occurred in the perception of knowledge and in its sources, an attitude of relativity might serve well the purpose of knowledge analysis. A look into history may illustrate the point: the Greek and Roman writings that served for a relatively long time as sources of all knowledge in Western countries, were abandoned as a result of later thoughts expressed by

Copernicus in the sixteenth and by Galileo in the seventeenth centuries. Later, beliefs in experiential and systematic observations as sources of discovery of truth and the positivistic school of thought advocated by Comte gave way to different views of knowledge. More recently, a conception of the nature of the practitioner was suggested by Polanyi (1964) who introduced the concept of *tacit knowledge*. This kind of knowledge can be viewed on a continuum, with recognition clues which are almost ineffable, at the one end, and with cumulative understanding, which is usually non-verbal, but which can be retrieved with the aid of conscious reflection to test against another knowledge, at the other end. In sum, the translation of these views to the topic under study points to a distinction between two main orientations that are relevant to professional-pedagogical knowledge. The one connotes *structure, absolutism, positivism, rules and norms, validity*, the other connotes *fluidity, relativisn, humanism, utility*. Both orientations may be viewed along a continuum of tacit knowledge.

A more specific and operational description of pedagogical knowledge was proposed by Shulman (1987), in response to a call for a systematic enquiry into pedagogical knowledge that he himself made. An analysis of Shulman's propositions (*ibid.*) points to two main categories: *Content* and *Form*. Content was further classified into several sub-categories: 1) *Content Knowledge* of the field to be taught, the understanding of its structure and organization into concepts and principles at various thought levels. Several knowledge classifications made by Bloom, Gagne, Schwab, may be of help for this purpose. 2) *Pedagogical content knowledge* pertains to the application of the content knowledge to teaching and involves the representation of that content in a comprehensible, relevant manner, using a variety of alternatives to suit pupils' individual differences in various aspects, and 3) *Curricular knowledge* pertains to the familiarity with a variety of learning materials not only in one's own subject of teaching but in other subjects that the pupils are learning as well.

Form of knowledge was classified into: 1) *Propositional knowledge* that entertains research based principles, experience based recommendations organized in some theoretical framework, 2) *Case knowledge* that complements the former kind of knowledge by providing knowledge of specifics which are well documented and which are representative of an educational issue or phenomenon, and 3) *Strategic knowledge* that involves 'careful confrontation of principles with cases of general rules with concrete events... when two principles are in conflict or when two cases yield contradictory interpretations...' (*ibid.* p.13).

In some studies attempts were made at detecting differences in the perceptions of university teacher educators and school educators with regard to what constitutes crucial professional knowledge objectives. The profile obtained for the university educators entailed knowledge about students, about the social context of schooling, and about curriculum. The emphasis was on theoretical and general knowledge underlying the framework of teacher decision-making as well as on skills. The school educators' profile entailed an attached importance to knowledge about teachers and teaching strategies with an emphasis on particularistic knowledge that relates directly to immediate and daily decision-making (Schumacher, Rommel-Esham and Bauer, 1987). This and other studies (Gudmundsdottir and Shulman, 1987) refer to the same knowledge attributes that were mentioned by Shulman, even though they sometimes use other terms. The next examples may suffice to illustrate this point: The terms *theoretical* and *particularistic* knowledge used in the last mentioned study are parallel to the terms of *propositional* and *case study* used by Shulman (1987); the distinction made by Broudy between 'knowing that' and 'knowing how' is comparable to Shulman's distinction between *propositional* and *strategic knowledge*. Furthermore, in relating to the 'lights that teachers live by', Buchmann (1987) classifies knowledge into *folkways of teaching, local mores, private views*, and *teaching expertise*. Folkways refer to 'teaching as usual', practising half-consciously in ways in which people act in everyday life. Local mores are more variable and group related, and private views entertain an element of idiosyncracy. While the first three categories highlight sources and content knowledge, the fourth one — teaching expertise — refers to the ways in which knowledge is held and used. This distinction is also comparable to the one made between 'knowing that' and 'knowing how'. The distinction between folkways and private views may also be compared to the one between technical rationality and reflection in action.

Because of the broad scope and extensive analysis of pedagogical knowledge in Shulman's study, the present investigation will borrow mainly from its proposed categories.

Table 3.2 presents a summary and analysis of the various perceptions of knowledge in general and of professional-pedagogical knowledge in particular.

Table 3.2
Categories of knowledge derived from recent literature

Author	Year	Classification	
Ryle	1949	knowing 'that'/'how'	
Polanyi	1964	tacit/non-tacit	
Broudy	1977	knowing 'that'/'how'/'with' scientific/positivistic/humanistic	
Novak	1977	absolute/relative	
Schon	1983	positivistic/relativistic; personal	
Lampert	1984	intuitive/formal; systematic	
Shulman	1987	Content:	Form:
		1. subject-matter	1. propositional
		2. pedagogical	2. case
		3. curricular	3. strategic
Schumacher *et al.*	1987	general/particularistic	
Buchmann	1987	folkways/local mores/private view/ teaching expertise	
Hoz	1987	content	

The summary presented in Table 3.2 yields the following broad knowledge categories: *Content* — including subject-matter content, pedagogical and curricular knowledge, and *Form* — including propositions, cases and strategies. Each one of the content categories may be processed by each of the form categories and both kinds of categories may be viewed through each of the two main orientations mentioned above, one being relatively 'closed', that is, characterized by a positivistic attitude, by structure, rules and norms, and the other characterized by a more 'open' orientation and by an attitude of relativity, flexibility and fluidity.

Reflection and professional-pedagogical knowledge may now be juxtaposed to constitute a conceptual framework.

Reflection and Professional-Pedagogical Knowledge

The clarification of the concepts under study provides the basis for a systematic composition of a conceptual framework that will incorporate both concepts as well as the possible relations between them. Such a conceptual framework may be obtained with the aid of a mapping sentence, in which each concept component constitutes a facet, and the varying perceptions of that concept constitute an element of the facet. Facets are here used in the sense of classification criteria pertaining to a certain domain of content (Guttman, 1954). Such a mapping sentence, according to Guttman's theory, provides a conceptual framework and paradigm for further investigations and for the derivation of research hypotheses.

In view of the various attributes of reflection and of professional-pedagogical knowledge it is interesting to disclose the ways in which these two concepts coexist, and whether any composite concept structure may be detected. The mapping sentence illustrated in Figure 3.1 is proposed for this purpose:

The inner structure of reflection based on professional-pedagogical knowledge may be obtained with the aid of a questionnaire consisting of items that represent the elements of the various facets. The number of items will equal the product of the number of elements in facet A multiplied by the number of elements in facet B and in turn multiplied by the number of elements in each of the other facets.

A Smallest Space Analysis [SSA] (Lingoes, 1968) will point to the distances between all elements and thus provide profiles of various inner structures of professional reflective teaching, namely: how do the different elements interact with each other? Profiles built on data obtained from various groups of teachers are apt to point to the differences among them with regard to the characteristics of their professional reflection on teaching. Thus, questions such as the following may be answered: is the profile of reflective teaching of elementary school teachers different from that of high school teachers, and if it is, what is it? Is it in the level of reflection, is it on the type of knowledge that is reflected upon,

Figure 3.1.
Reflection and professional pedagogical knowledge — A mapping sentence.

FACET 1
A *reflection level* of:
- analysis
- synthesis
- judgment

FACET 2
with an *orientation* of:
- theory
- practice
- values

FACET 3
and *a style* of:
- technical rationality
- reflection in action
- subject-matter
- pedagogy
- curriculum

FACET 4
at *a time* of:
- post-active
- intra-active

FACET 5
within *a content knowledge*

FACET 6
in *a form* of:
- propostion
- case
- strategy

used

FACET 7
- intuitively
- formally

will yield a reflection profile of type X

etc. Similar questions may be answered with regard to teachers at various stages in their career, to teachers of varying personalities and in various circumstances and situations.

Theoretically, the suggested mapping sentence including its facets and elements may serve a conceptual framework for deriving hypotheses and for testing them. Naturally, not all facets must be used in any one single research. The facets to be used will depend upon the questions that the researcher is interested in.

Practically, the information gained on the profiles of reflective teaching may serve as a mirror for teachers' self-confrontation, which may arouse awareness to gaps and deficiencies in their perspective, and consequently motivate to fill in these gaps. Moreover, profiles of teachers at various stages of their career, in varying environments may guide the planning and implementation of teacher professional development programs at the pre- and in-service stages.

References

BERLAK, H. and BERLAK, A. (1981) *Dilemmas of Schooling, Teaching and Change*, London, Methuen.

BERLINER, D. (1987) 'In pursuit of the expert pedagogue', *Educational Researcher*, August–September, pp. 5–13.

BLOOM, B. S. (1956) *Taxonomy of Educational Objectives: The Classification of Educational Goals. Handbook I — Cognitive Domain*, New York, McKay.

BROUDY, H. S. (1977) 'Types of knowledge and purpose of education', in ANDERSON, R. C., SHAPIRO, R. J. and MONTAGNE, W. E. (Eds) *Schooling and the Aquisitions of Knowledge*, New York, John Wiley.

BUCHMANN, M. (1987) Teaching knowledge: The lights that teachers live by', *Oxford Review of Education*, 13, 2, pp. 151–64.

CLANDININ, D. J. and CONNELLY, M. F. (1986) 'What is personal in studies of the personal', in BEN-PERETZ, M., BROMME, R. and HALKES, R. (Eds) *Advances in Research on Teacher Thinking*, Lisse, Swets and Zeitlinger.

CLARK, C. M. (1986) 'Ten years of conceptual development in research on teacher thinking', in: BEN-PERETZ, M., BROMME, R. and HALKES, R. (Eds) *Advances in Research on Teaching*, Lisse, Swets and Zeitlinger.

CLARK, C. M. and PETERSON, P. L. (1986) 'Teacher thought processes', in WITTROCK, M. C. (Ed.) *Handbook of Research on Teaching*, Third edition, New York, Macmillan.

DEWEY, O. (1933) *How We Think*, Chicago, Regnery.

GAGNE, R. M. (1970) *The Conditions of Learning*, New York, Holt, Rinehart and Winston.

GRANT, C. A. and ZEICHNER, K. (1984) 'On becoming a reflective teacher', in GRANT, C. A. (Ed.) *Preparing for Reflective Teaching*, Boston, Allyn Bacon.

GUDMUNDSDOTTIR, S. and SHULMAN, L. (1987) 'Pedagogical content knowledge in social studies', *Scandinavian Journal of Educational Research*, Vol. 31, 2, pp. 59–70.

GUTTMAN, L. (1954) 'A new approach to factor analysis: The tadex', in LAZARSFELD, P. F. (Ed.) *Mathematical Thinking in Social Sciences*, Glencoe, Ill., Free Press.

HOZ, R. (1987) 'Dimensions of teacher knowledge structure and their identification by concept mapping', paper presented at the AERA annual meeting, Washington, D.C.

KORTHAGEN, F. A. J. (1987) 'The influence of learning orientations on the development of reflective teaching', Paper presented at the conference of the British Educational Research Association on Teachers' Professional Learning, Lancaster, July 2–3.

LAMPERT, N. (1984) 'Teaching about thinking and thinking about teaching', *Journal of Curriculum Studies*, 16, 1, pp. 1–18.

LINGOES, J. (1968) 'The multivariate analysis data', *Multivariate Behavioral Research*, 3, pp. 57–74.

LOWYCK, J. (1986) 'Post interactive reflections of teachers: A critical appraisal', in BEN-PERETZ, M., BROMME, R. and HALKES, R. (Eds) *Advances in Research on Teacher Thinking*, Lisse, Swets and Zeitlinger.

MCKAY, D. A. and MARLAND, P. (1978) 'Thought processes of teachers', CEDRS—ED 151328.

NOVAK, J. D. (1977) 'Representation of knowledge in program for solving physics problems', Proceedings of the 5th International Joint Conference on Artificial Intelligence, Cambridge, Mass., MIT Press.

PETERS, J. C. (1985) 'Research on reflective teaching: A form of laboratory teaching experience', *Journal of Research and Development in Education*, 18, 3, pp. 55–62.

POLANYI, M. (1958) *Personal Knowledge*, London, Routledge and Kegan Paul.

RYLE, G. (1949) *The Concept of Mind*, New York, Barnes and Noble.

SCHUMACHER, S., ROMMEL-ESHAM, K. and BAUER, D. (1987) 'Professional knowledge objectives for pre-service teachers as determined by school and university teacher educators', paper presented at the AERA annual meeting, Washington, D.C.

SCHON, D. (1983) *The Reflective Practitioner*, New York, Basic Books.

SCHWAB, J. J. (1964) 'Problems, topics and issues', in ELAM, S. (Ed.) *Education and the Structure of Knowledge*, Chicago, Rand McNally.

SHAVELSON, R. J. and STERN, P. (1981) 'Research on teachers' pedagogical thoughts, judgment, decisions and behavior', *Review of Educational Research*, 51, pp. 455–98.

SHULMAN, L. (1987) 'Those who understand knowledge growth in teaching', *Educational Researcher*, February, pp. 4–14.

SOLOMAN, J. (1987) 'New thoughts on teacher education', *Oxford Review of Education*, 13, 3, pp. 267–74.

VAN MAANEN, M. (1977) 'Linking ways of knowing with ways of being practical', *Curriculum Inquiry*, 6, pp. 205–28.

WITTROCK, M. C. (1986) (Ed.) *Handbook of Research on Teaching*, New York, Macmillan.

YINGER, R. J. (1985) 'Learning the language of practice', paper presented at the Symposium on Classroom Studies of Teachers' Personal Knowledge, Toronto, Ontario Institute for Studies in Education.

ZEICHNER, R. and LISTON, P. (1987) 'Teaching student teachers to reflect', *Harvard Educational Review*, 57, 1, pp. 23–48.

Chapter 4

Information Technology in Schools: Institutional Rewards and Moral Dilemmas

John Olson

I have been watching teachers use microcomputers for half a decade now and trying with their help (the teachers) to make sense of what I saw. At first it seemed odd to me that teachers were willing to put up with the inconvenience microcomputers seemed to cause them. My preliminary solution to this puzzle was to think that the microcomputer was a way for already avant-garde teachers to express themselves – a powerful symbol of their commitment to modernity. And thus the microcomputer is worth the trouble it causes.

But is it worth it? Looking closer it seems that teachers are caught up in something less benign – the enhancement of career in exchange for cooperating with school systems in the process of justifying vast expenditures on hard and software. Is the game worth the candle? Is the lure of technology seductive? How are teachers to respond? What is required of them? These are questions I ask in this chapter.

Teachers and Technology

To answer these questions we consider the case of one of eight teachers involved with us in a study of microcomputers in schools (Olson, 1988). We shall reflect on how institutional rewards can undermine good practice, hoping to contribute not only to debates about the value of microcomputers in education, but, more importantly, to those about the virtues needed to survive as a teacher in the perilous world of institution-driven innovation in schools.

Institutional rewards and practical problems are associated with access to information technology. In particular, pursuit of rewards may offer teachers career recognition and profile in school systems but may also, if taken up in an unreflective way, lead to injustices in the classroom and hinder achieving desirable social and academic goals. This peril is illustrated in the case to which I now turn.

Writing with the Computer: Question of Fairness

As one of the eight teachers who had been given computers in response to successful proposals to do research in their classrooms, Mrs E proposed an experiment in which writing using word processing was a 'treatment' intended to affect the quality of writing.

Mrs E used computers to help her students write better through student-student conferences and redrafting to improve writing. Access to computers encouraged these activities. In her project a selected group of students participated who had extra time at the computer and extra attention from her:

> I say to [the students]: 'How would you like to work on the computer a little more often than perhaps some of the other students? You'll be part of a group of ten kids who are going to work until about March. You will have to write a little bit more but the pay off will be that you will have a little bit more time on the computer and hopefully both of us will learn a little bit about yourself and writing and you will certainly help me. You'll be doing me a big service.' None of them wanted to decline . . .
>
> I want to find out if word processing contributes to better writing. One of the advantages of word processing on the computer is being able to move material around. However, some of the students are hesitant to do so, especially those who are not in the project and those who are not 'as quick'. They are afraid they don't know how to do it. Access to the machine motivates the students and gives them a sense that they're on their own.

Mrs E's practice has to be understood against the background of how middle school teachers teach language arts and what counts in that process. Student-student conferencing is not part of conventional practice, neither is the idea of having the teacher look at multiple drafts of writing. Other conventions form the social basis of middle school lessons. Her practice stands out as avant-garde because of the kind of relationship amongst students and between students and teacher she says she is trying to foster. It is against what normally happens that we can appreciate what she is doing.

However, her attempt to do something unconventional is itself conventional. The school system expects her to do unconventional things in order to win a pilot project for her classroom, but has conventional ideas about educational research and about change as being research driven. The pilot project format designed by the board, and her subsequent response to it, are entirely conventional approaches to change in practice through institutional intervention. These conventions, rituals if you like, part of bureaucratic life in school systems, do not encourage critical reflection of practice. Rather, they trade on the technical part of practice and ignore the ethical. How is this so?

What does the institution (school system) require of Mrs E? She has to convince them she will do something 'research-like' and 'psychological' in order to gain access to a scarce resource. The competition emphasizes the collection of data about the *instrumental* efficiency of the microcomputer:

> You know you're looking at slight changes in the group. It will be interesting to see how, not just the superficial types of revisions in terms of spelling corrections or the conventions [change]. You can hopefully try to raise their level of thinking, because they have to conference with two other students at least and then at least once with me.

She has to win an experimental trial with the computer as a research treatment within a certain framework for construing her work. She is expected to maintain a ritualistic approach to research (the horse race study) and a formalistic view of the object of her research ('levels of thinking'). Neither approach encourages attention to ethical matters. Her attention to form at the expense of substance can be seen in her odd failure to ask for a printer and a second disk drive, both of which would make it easier for students to use the word processing software.

More importantly, the experiment means that only certain students are given extra attention. These students are encouraged to participate through the offer of more time at the computer and not only for the possibility of better writing, but the opportunity to become more competitive in the job market. This is how she 'sells' her project to her student volunteers. It is how she values the computer:

> Looking back, I think that the students in the project have had the intensive feedback while the rest have increased their 'hands-on' computer time. I have learned more about how students revise their work. The students are glad to increase their knowledge of computers with a career in mind.

Only some students will have this benefit. The students who volunteer, who do not include less able students, receive extra attention and extra computer time in return for cooperating in the pilot project.

How does Mrs E deal with this question of fairness as she distributes access to the computer? She admitted that she did not distribute her time in a fair way, but that the experimental nature of the project justified this unfairness. What were the consequences of this decision?

Take the case of Sally, one of the students not granted extra access. The disappointment she suffered because of her print-out of a geometric poem she had constructed on the screen (she did not know how to use the return key) did not engage Mrs E's sympathies. Sally must struggle on on her own, she said, because this is one way that she will become a better person. But Sally, a student with learning difficulties, on the face of it deserved extra attention as much as the project students did. Why not accord to Sally what the other students were given? These basic matters of fair play were not part of what Mrs E was encouraged to assess within the framework of the pilot project approach she was caught up in.

Similarly Mark, who wanted to keep his work private, was treated as a rogue. But privacy is an important issue in the use of microcomputers. Why does she find it strange that Mark might want to keep his work private?

When Mrs E reflected on the students' experience of microcomputers, she returned to the computer literacy argument – computer experience is good for careers, which is the conventional view about computers in the school system and beyond. Even so, she has doubts about the value of computers as an aid to writing, and she does worry about the fairness. Yet she wants to continue the same activity next year by extending her pilot project to maintain access to the computer in her room.

Given the problems with the computer, it is odd that she would want to repeat the experience. How are we to understand her apparent satisfaction with what seemed to us to be very problematic results in a situation she recognized as unfair? Let us pursue these questions in more detail.

Competition for Scarce Resources: Reward in the School Culture

In our case study of eight teachers using computers, one of whom was Mrs E, we found that although the teachers had promised to pursue certain innovative activities using the microcomputer in their classroom, in no case did they feel that much progress had occurred in achieving promised goals — yet they all wanted to go on as before. Even though many difficulties were encountered, teachers wanted to continue with the same activities under much the same conditions. On the face of it their experience did not justify going on. Why then did they want to persist?

To answer this we need to look closely at the culture of these teachers — at what is conventional and unconventional in their practice. Practice is, after all, a social construct, and if we are to understand the nature of the practice we have to understand the common meanings of the group which are intersubjective (Geertz, 1973; Taylor, 1979). The imaginative universe of the teacher has to be understood if we want to understand what teachers are up to and especially the ends which constitute their practice. What are these teachers up to?

How are we to understand the thought that would lead these teachers to persist with what looked to us an unrewarding technology? The clue lay in what these teachers were doing before they took up with computers. When we examined how they taught before they had computers we found that these teachers all had experimented with various teaching innovations: simulations in geography; the use of film making in the classroom; analysis of student writing from a linguistics point of view. We concluded that in every case their practice had been avant-garde. Why then move to computers? And why move to this common form of teaching from such different avant-garde practices?

These teachers, we think, obtained a powerful language for communicating their interest in innovative methods to university people, others involved in new developments, and to administration looking for centres of innovation (see Jackson, 1968). In their competition for scarce resources in order to draw attention to their avant-gardism, they used information technology as a means to speak about what they valued — they drew on a culturally approved symbol to signal their avant-gardism.

The very capacity of this technology to symbolize their commitment to new practices, while its greatest strength, is also the wellspring of its seductive power. New technologies, being rewards in themselves and keys to further rewards, tempt teachers to pursue ends other than those which give their practice worth. MacIntyre (1981) calls such goods 'external' to practice.

> It is characteristic of . . . external goods that when achieved they are always some individual's property or possession. . . . [T]he more someone has of them, the less there is for other people. This is sometimes necessarily the case, as with power and fame. . . . External goods are . . . objects of competition. It is characteristic of [internal goods] that their achievement is a good for the whole community who participate in the practice. (pp. 190–1).

What was seductive about the new technology? Gaining access to it provides teachers with an expressive tool with which they can signal their avant-gardism. But are these technologies helping them practise better? Are these technologies worth competing for? Is it worth doing what the system wants done with these scarce resources in order to get them? Do teachers pay a high price to get hold of these symbols? There are a number of ways of looking at this. What do teachers have to promise and can they deliver? And even if they don't deliver what they promise, is what they actually do worthwhile? To answer these questions we have to understand the institutional framework in which these teachers practise.

Let us take the application process itself. First, the pilot project application form asked teachers to produce data useful to the institution – the school system. They were to see if, by using computers as a *treatment*, certain gains could be measured. The framework assumed that teaching technique was at issue, practice was uniform across levels of schooling, and that appraisal of computers in classrooms was a *technical* problem. Teachers thus were required to orient their projects to the political demands (external goods) of the institution for hard data about the outcomes of computer assisted learning rather than to pursue implications that emerged out of practice itself (internal goods), and to consider the value of the new technology in the light of their experience.

The competitive framework in which the pilot projects were run is not, however, one of the teacher's making. It is root and branch part of the bureaucratic institution in which they work.

The institutional process of giving access to scarce technologies, and asking for 'hard data' in exchange for recognition, made it harder for teachers to do what they ought to do — reflect on the value of the new technology, and thus exercise those *virtues* which enable them to make their practice worthwhile.

Had they been encouraged to exercise those virtues, their capacity to learn from the experience of microcomputer based teaching might have been otherwise. Let us pursue the matter of virtue further as a way of understanding how these teachers might escape the seduction of new technology and its blandishments.

The Character of the Teacher and the Seduction of Technology

The school system believes that parents want their children to have access to computers because jobs depend on computer literacy. However, there are only so many computers to place in classrooms. Thus a competition is held in which scarce resources are made available to computer oriented teachers who believe that computer literacy is needed for career enhancement. This system obtains from the teachers the kind of research it needs to justify the cost of information technology, and teachers gain access to system rewards. Both serve the cause of computer literacy. Computers go to those who share the idea that schooling involves the pursuit of external goods.

> Institutions are characteristically and necessarily concerned with what I have called external goods . . . . They are structured in terms of power and status, and they distribute money, power and status as rewards . . . . In this context the essential function of virtues is clear. Without them, without justice, courage and truthfulness practice could not resist the corrupting power of institutions. (MacIntyre, 1981, p. 194).

But what about the educational value of the computer based learning classroom and the classroom practices associated with it? What in this institutional process encourages critical thought about educational practice? Very little. The reasons are complex. School system approved research models stultify critical thought, career enhancement conflicts with educational values (Wilson, 1962) and the technology is itself seductive. What can be done about this? How are these pitfalls to be avoided and good practice sustained?

First, we have to say good practice can be explained in terms of *virtues* which sustain it. This is not a common way of looking at practice. Normally good practice is given not a moral basis for its discernment but a technical one (Berliner, 1987; Shulman, 1987). MacIntyre (1981) identifies honesty, courage and justice as the essential virtues of practice which act as reference points for explaining what teachers are doing in classrooms, as bases for identifying good teachers, and as norms which ought to be cultivated. How do these virtues feature in practice? What do teachers have to do?

> [Recognize] what is due to whom; [take] self-endangering risks; [listen] carefully to what we are told about our own inadequacies . . . in other words we have to accept as necessary components of any practice with internal good and standard of excellence the virtue of justice, courage and honesty. (MacIntyre, 1981 p. 191)

Practice is never just a craft or expertise – it is a socially based process involving virtues:

[Practice is] any coherent and complex form of socially established co-operative human activity through which goods internal to that form of activity are realized. Practice [provides] the arena in which the virtues are exhibited.... A practice involves standards of excellence and obedience to rules as well as achievement of goods. (*Ibid*, pp. 187, 190)

Practice (praxis) is, of course, not the same thing as craft (technique), because technique is aimed at the production of something, while practice is aimed at the exercise of virtue. In the former the activity is aimed at ends beyond the activity itself, while in the latter it is the activity itself which is the end (Aristotle-Nicomachean Ethics: Irwin, 1985). The practice of teaching is not essentially aimed at production of something, but at developing and exercising the virtues of the group to which teacher and student belong – it is a moral enterprise; not a technical one. Thus it is misleading to talk about the craft of teaching. There may be 'crafty' elements, but it is essentially not a craft.

Given that it is a moral enterprise, it demands critical appraisal of new forms of practice and of the institutionalization of change itself. While all educators are involved in this problem, major responsibility for worthwhile educational practice in schools falls to teachers who have to maintain an uneasy relationship with school bureaucracies. Yet those who work in administration must also reflect on their own role in this process of innovation so as not to yield to the seductive power of new technologies, of career enhancement, and of technological rationality (Schon, 1983).

Some might take exception to my analysis by saying: 'Why shouldn't teachers give some students access to experiences from which they are best able to profit? Really was Mrs E wrong in what she did?' The answer to this is not simple. Unfortunately there are not enough computers, not all students are equally able to profit, and some selection has to take place. Difficult choices are required in a situation of conflict in which wanting to do the best for everyone is not possible. Mrs E's dilemma was that by helping some she was not able to help others and indeed she had to take away from others. Seeing that dilemma for what it is and seeing how it arose is part of a morally based process of teacher education. It constitutes the path to good practice.

Teachers, like Mrs E, said that they found the project format constraining, that they knew it was a facade behind which competition for scarce resources was being conducted, but that they had to conform to the institutional plan, even if only later to abandon the declared project goals after they received the resources they had bid for. They did what they had to do to get access to system rewards.

What might teachers like these contemplate as they reflect on their experience of microcomputers in their classroom and in relation to the policies of school systems? I would say — look at what the computer symbolizes in your practice and your system and see if all of that squares with what you think worth doing as a teacher. Now this requires courage — a virtue — as we said at the outset. Courage, as MacIntyre (1981) points out, means being able to look critically at what you do.

The study of practice in education ought to be diagnostic in this way. Education is a practical, ethical process concerned about doing good things (Sockett, 1987). The practical point of its study is to assess the fitness of practice and to seek remedy where there is evidence of dysfunction. It takes courage to do that. Looking carefully at what teachers tell us about practice and about innovation is related: innovation ought to be a remedy for dysfunction, and reflecting on practice the way to diagnose it.

Those who practise do not always achieve the goods the practice sets out to achieve, for it is hard to avoid being 'seduced' by goods external to the practice, as we saw in the case of Mrs E. Thus the diagnosis of dysfunction – what causes practice to 'go off the rails' — is a crucial task for the student of practice, insider or outsider, because it is important to know where the perils lie.

Teachers work in an essentially conflicted institution about which, as MacIntyre (1981) suggests, we ought not to ask what end or purposes it serves, but rather of what conflict it is the scene. He says, 'It is through conflict and sometimes only through conflict that we learn what our ends and purposes are.'

This is the reason why it is valuable to reflect on practice in relation to its institutional setting and why teachers must become alert to the ways in which the institutions of schooling can undermine their own practice. Thinking critically about those conflicts is a way to improve practice itself and build valid institutions in which practice can improve. Reflecting on practice aids in developing good schools through ethically justified innovation. This is the link between research on teacher thinking and the process of innovation that ought to be made.

References

BERLINER, D. (1987) 'Ways of thinking about students and classrooms by more or less experienced teachers', in CALDERHEAD, J. (Ed.) *Exploring Teacher Thinking*, London, Cassell.

GEERTZ, C. (1973) *The Interpretation of Cultures*, New York, Basic Books.

JACKSON, P. (1968) *The Teacher and the Machine*, Pittsburg, University Press.

MACINTYRE, A. (1981) *After Virtue*, Notre Dame, University Press.

OLSON, J. (1988) *Schoolworlds/Microworlds: Computers and the Culture of the School*, Oxford, Pergamon.

SCHON, D. (1983) *The Reflective Practitioner*, New York, Basic Books.

SHULMAN, L. (1987) 'Knowledge and teaching', *Harvard Educational Review*, 56, pp. 1–22.

SOCKETT, H. (1987) 'Has Shulman got the strategy right?' *Harvard Educational Review*, 57, pp. 208–19.

TAYLOR, C. (1979) 'Interpretation and the sciences of man', in RABINOW, P. and SULLIVAN, W. (Eds) *Interpretive Social Science: A Reader*, Berkeley, University of California Press.

WILSON, B. (1962) 'The teacher's role: A sociological analysis', *British Journal of Sociology*, 13, pp. 15–32.

Chapter 5

Lies Teachers Tell and the Politics of Language

Alan F. Brown and Michael F. Kompf

The word lies carries a connotative look that draws attention much as does a traffic accident: a glimpse tells the spectator that something is out of order but the horrific potential of investigation serves as a deterrent to all but the morbidly curious. In this chapter we attempt to set aside morbid curiosity with lies and discover them as integral parts of teachers' repertoires of educational constructs. We were fortunate in securing the cooperation — and candor — of forty-eight classroom teachers. These persons wrote down verbatim accounts of very recent and evidently quite normal statements-other-than-fact made by themselves and also made by others. Luckily, too, our participants provided detailed data about themselves, the 'audience' and the setting of the utterances recounted. From this it became possible to develop a threefold model of the usage of lies in organizational life. Considering one's professional security, personal awareness of actions and status relative to target audience, lies are possibly seen as an apparently acceptable mode of interaction, one that may well be construed as necessary to operate within the unwritten political structure.

Interpersonal Communication and School Culture

Interpersonal communication is essential to complex organizations' operations and day to day life. Much is researched and more is written about staffing patterns, work flow and other administrator-oriented concerns. Little attention has been directed to the ways that members of an organization communicate personally with each other. Interpersonal communications, both verbal and semiotic, are the means whereby members gain or maintain their function and, as a result, their patterns of communication frequently become as imaginative and resourceful as possible so as to maintain favorable interaction norms. Indeed the patterns may become as esoteric as the nature of the culture within which they originate. This study attempts to understand several patterns of interpersonal utterances among members of teaching staffs. We are most concerned with verbal discourse that is other-than-fact or at least can be construed as somewhat different from fact. Knowledge of factual dissonance and justifications purported for discrepancies by the purveyor of lies form the purpose of this study.

In trying to understand the factors that make a school lively and successful, organizational studies usually start from unspoken assumptions that lie within an administrator's range of convenience. This is an error, it is argued, because the most significant set of interpersonal actions in a school — however much a principal may be shown to affect them — remain those of the teacher.

The lot of teachers as professionals has long been undergoing a process of change and development that challenges the grasp of knowledge as a basis for action. What is less encouraging is our questioning of the validity of this as a basis at all. Schon (1983) for example, notes that 'Even if professional knowledge were to catch up with the new demands of professional practice, the improvement in professional performance would be transitory' (pp. 14–15). Such organizational press viewed in concert with the contradictions inherent in the practice of education presents ample justification or rationalization for a lessening or easing of the rigid confines of what has been held traditionally to be specifically correct or true.

The actions of interpersonal communication being analyzed in this chapter, that of statements-other-than-fact, were chosen because of their potency for confusion or disruption of organizational patterns on the one hand and, on the other, for their promise of contributing to the vibrancy and authenticity of organizational culture. Lies, once accepted and understood, provide definition and distinction from other organizations within the general culture; they create a sense of identity.

Bok (1978) discusses lies as products of dilemmas experienced by persons in ordinary life. There are persons 'who think that their lies are too insignificant to matter much, and others who believe that lying can protect someone or benefit society' (p. xxi). She goes on to say that 'We need to look most searchingly . . . at those cases where many see good reasons to lie' (p. xxi).

The cases which concerned us most in this research were examples of teachers' lies for 'good reasons', as Bok put it. This, as our lies data reveal, was a fortunate finding: misrepresentation of factual events or situations was not imbued with the connotation of doing harm to another, but rather to facilitate the passage of problematic encounters.

Examples of constructive statements other than fact are not hard to find. Indeed, there is the case of a teacher becoming gleeful when telling how the principal told a teacher one thing, a parent another thing and was heard telephoning the superintendent yet another. In fairness, the glee is less in the incongruency of it all than in the discovery that no matter what was said, all got the right message. It worked. Professional literacy means understanding the unwritten languages and being able to translate them across an organization's several dialects.

The Construction of Lies

According to Ekman (1985) there are two main ways to lie: by concealment and by falsification.

> In concealing, the liar withholds some information without actually saying anything untrue. In falsifying, an additional step is taken. Not only does the liar withhold true information, but he presents false information as if it were true. Often it is necessary to combine concealing and falsifying to pull off the deceit, but sometimes a liar can get away just with concealment. (1985, p. 28)

Ekman goes on to say that liars tend to prefer concealment to falsification because it is easier. Nothing has to be made up or accounted for by memory later on. Concealment is passive and causes less guilt than falsification. Hidden knowledge can be attributed to the lie-recipient causing reassurance and less guilt for the liar. Concealment lies can thus be covered more easily afterward as they can be attributed to ignorance or to the intent to reveal or to later memory failure and the like.

Events may be misrepresented for a variety of reasons and in a variety of ways. Bok (1978) discussed the pattern set by St Thomas Aquinas which distinguished three kinds of lies: 'the officious or helpful lies; the jocose lies, told in jest; and the mischievous, or malicious, lies told to harm someone' (p. 34). The last category of lies were considered by Aquinas to be mortal sins and therefore the most grievous. Such lies are representative of lies of falsification and as such are of less concern to us in this study. Lies of concealment appear to be the lies of choice in education. This lesser form of lie, because of the ease with which it is constructed, tends to fall outside of any moral imperative which guides teachers' thoughts and actions. If, for example, a teacher has a lie-construct that has proved to be successful in assisting them to avoid confrontation with parents of difficult children, the success afforded by that lie-construct will ensure its being called into play at future moments of similar events. Such a lie-construct may become situationally real for that teacher. Kelly (1955) asserted that what a person believes to be real is real for them even if it does not correspond to external reality. A person may thus misrepresent his or her reality and act in a manner consistent with perceptual interpretation.

The Study

The title of the study is intentionally provocative; 'lie' is both stronger and more ubiquitous than needed. Yet it is used here to emphasize the weight of the problem that practice places before those who must learn to 'read' several idiosyncratic patterns. It appears as though persons who are responsible for keeping a school going must of necessity acquire some very unique literacy skills. That is, they must not only learn to read the meanings of the idiosyncratic words and other symbols of each member of a staff, but also they must learn how these symbols possess different meanings in different contexts. Worse still is being certain they themselves are able to articulate at least to oneself, what it is that is going on in the school. It is a question, as analyzed and discussed previously (Brown, 1986), of professional literacy.

From forty-eight teachers and principals at all grade levels, utterances that were statements-other-than-fact were analyzed. That the substance was other than fact was established by the research design requiring (a) first person data of periodic notations of reflecting both immediate and long-range, together with contextual descriptors and (b) second person data of periodic notations of validation or verification of utterances of other persons, again with contextual descriptors.

Responses were analyzed first for statements-other-than-fact disjunctions and second to construct several sets of patterns or structures for understanding this fairly common practice. Statements from our teachers were elicited by reflection, by projection and by conversation. All initially made written notations and later aided with the developing classification system and their place within it.

Findings as Format and Frequency

After several attempts to develop a system of categories — a lie taxonomy — the one that best represented the intentions behind these utterances was one that views them from three quite different dimensions. These three patterns (and there may be more) consider the utterers' (a) degree of awareness, i.e. extent to which they are cognitively conscious of their disjunctive statement, (b) security within their profession, i.e. where they are now in stages of professional growth (not administrative status) and (c) perceived status of target audience, or the intended receiver's rank relative to the utterer. Within each pattern are three or four levels so that one could imagine a forty-eight-cell cube. This, in turn, suggests a model or a set of guidelines to the tricky task of reading the patterns of interactions that characterize a culture. It is a task faced not only by every administrator but especially by every newcomer to a staff.

Both our 'lie model' and our frequency findings so classified are presented as Table 5.1 below. Rather than present our laborious definitions of each category, we let our participants define by examples which follow. Note, however, that a disjunctive utterance usually exemplifies one level in each of two or three patterns, not only the one used here.

Examples of these categories developed with help of participants are as follows: 1.1 Told friend I was going to be out near his town so I'd like to come out and see him — I actually drove there to see him specifically. 1.2 An acknowledgement that I had read a memo that I had not. 1.3 Requested additional lead time when making a decision of accepting a job opportunity. 1.4 stating 'getting on with the kids' is most important to teaching when I actually

Table 5.1.
Frequencies of disjunctions made by self, by other.

Pattern 1: Degrees of Awareness	Self	Other
1.1 Carefully deliberated disjunctions	11	16
1.2 Automatic routine responses	13	8
1.3 Confusion of intentionality	5	3
1.4 Unwitting disjunctions	2	2
Pattern 2: Stages of Professional Growth		
2.1 Uncommitted novice	3	3
2.2 Ambiguous career path	10	8
2.3 Securely established in profession	10	10
Pattern 3: Perceived Status of Audience		
3.1 Superordinate e.g. principal	6	5
3.2 Colleague e.g. teacher	12	11
3.3 Subordinate e.g. pupil	2	3
3.4 Outsider e.g. parent	1	1

found I rated most highly those that got on with me (administrator). 2.1 This final staff meeting is a waste of time. 2.2 Agreement with a teacher's problem 'Yeah that's too bad', even though I feel the teacher's own action caused the problem. 2.3 Request for classroom cupboards turned down because of 'budget restraints'. 3.1 'Excuse me, do I have to fill out all these forms?' 3.2 A person complaining about an administrator, while I was nodding my head implying assent although scarcely listening to this complainer. 3.3 Student asked, 'Did anyone fail assignment?' I responded 'I don't know', smiled and winked. He ran off happy telling everyone 'Lots of us failed the assignment.' 3.4 Agreement to attend a baseball game when in fact I had no interest or desire to attend.

Frequencies here may be difficult to analyze: they had limited opportunities for some categories (e.g. 3.4) and would be almost unaware of others (1.3, 1.4) even though we know from other studies (see Brown, 1986) they are alarmingly frequent. Certainly they freely report carefully thought-out lies and also those routine things that get uttered *pro forma*, especially from the comfortably experienced.

Whereas the stated purpose of the study was to understand reasons for lies, our meta-purpose has more to do with the professional development of both the teacher and the administrator. Politics is taught in the pre-service of neither. The politics of language, it appears, becomes learned with the length and variety of experience, if at all. For that reason, imaginative career seminars for school principals frequently attempt experience-intensifying programs such as simulations, facsimile creations and clinical projects. If the politics of language cannot be taught, the argument runs, we can at least provide the vehicle for learning. For teachers such vehicles have yet to be designed.

References

BOK, S. (1978) *Lying: Moral Choice in Public and Private Life*, New York, Vintage Book.

BROWN, A. F. (1986) 'Professional literacy, resourcefulness and what makes teaching interesting', in BEN-PERETZ, M., BROMME, R. and HALKES, R. *Advances of Research on Teacher Thinking*, Berwyn, Swets, North America. pp. 142-51.

EKMAN, P. (1985). *Telling Lies. Clues to Deceit in the Marketplace, Politics and Marriage*, New York, Norton.

KELLY, G. A. (1955) *The Psychology of Personal Constructs*, New York, Norton.

SCHON, D. (1983) *The Reflective Practitioner*, New York, Norton, Basic Books.

Chapter 6

Teacher Thinking Studies: Bridges Between Description, Prescription and Application

Joost Lowyck

It is not very original to be troubled by the complex relation between theory and practice in the domain of teacher thinking research. For almost a century, scholars in the field of teaching have tried to answer the persisting question of what 'teaching' looks like, and how 'effective teaching' can be defined. Their sophisticated endeavours obviously contrast with the popular wisdom of millions of practitioners, as reflected in the description of teaching by Montaigne more than four hundred years ago: 'du bon coeur, du bon sens et quelques petits trucs' ('a warm heart, a sound mind and some handy tricks'). In some way, Montaigne already anticipated the cognitive approach by including the mind in his definition. But any concept is dependent upon place and time and, thus, not directly transferable from a practical toward a scientific endeavour, nor from a sixteenth toward a twentieth century conceptualization.

Introduction: Research Versus Practice?

The very concrete practice of teaching follows its own rules of systematization: the progressive accumulation of supposedly effective behaviours which are transmitted from one generation to another in terms of concrete advice, metaphors, real life experiences, and realistic descriptions. The criterion of effectiveness is 'that' it works here and now, rather than 'why' or 'how' it works in many places and at different times. Already long before Jackson (1967), Stolurow (1965) and Zahorik (1970), educators knew that lesson plans are possibly relevant instruments for effective teaching, but they did not reveal the different types of planning nor the many influencing variables. Though a common-sense definition reveals what teaching could be, researchers are usually not inclined to accept its vagueness, nor the lack of empirical validation. On the contrary, they lean on theoretical frameworks, theories, models, and methods to discover how — at least in their conception — teaching and teaching effectiveness could be identified.

Described in this way, the relation between research and practice seems determined by the systematic and controllable versus the experiential knowledge base, or by general results versus concrete advice. This point of view, however, is not accepted by all researchers. In a publication of the Council of Europe (1980), a group of outstanding researchers in the field of educational technology raised the problem whether the present state of scientific educational knowledge provides a sufficient base for a technology: 'We think not, and accordingly hold that the knowledge base of educational technology requires scientific knowledge supplemented by experiential knowledge, i.e. knowledge generated by current practice' (Council of Europe, 1980, p. 9). This statement resembles the position of Gage (1978), who distinguishes between a science of teaching and a scientific basis for the art of teaching. 'The former idea, a science of teaching, claims much more and is in the end, I think, erroneous. It implies that good teaching will some day be attainable by closely following rigorous laws that yield high predictability and control. Practical enterprises, those conducted in the real world rather than in the laboratory, have both artistic and scientific components' (p. 17). It appears that the relation between description, prescription and practice is far from clear, and we have to look more closely at the theoretical struggle about theory and practice.

A well established method in research is to falsify an acceptable hypothesis. As we are mainly interested in teacher thinking research, we have chosen the following statement from the first ISATT publication as our hypothesis, namely 'Looking from a teacher thinking perspective at teaching and learning, one is not so much striving for the disclosure of "the" effective teacher, but for the explanation and understanding of teaching processes as they are' (Halkes and Olson, 1984, p. 1). In this quotation the authors suggest a dichotomous choice between explaining and understanding teaching on the one hand and looking for effectiveness on the other. But can we really be interested in teaching as it is, without any perspective on improvement?

Let us explore some avenues of thought in order to underpin our reflection. First we will examine some reasons for a shift toward a more descriptive approach: is it exclusively determined by the fundamental choice between description and prescription, or could we find other intervening arguments? Second, is it possible to gain purely descriptive knowledge about teaching? Third, can so-called descriptive knowledge be transformed into knowledge with a prescriptive value, thus making it suitable for practice?

The Unclear Status of 'Descriptive' Research

One could easily assert that there is a profound need for more descriptive research on teacher thinking: equally, one can advance enough arguments for claiming the contrary. Rather than start with the answer, we shall circumscribe more precisely some constraints for the argumentation. Indeed, we will not limit our exploration to teacher thinking research alone: it is stimulating to understand how colleagues in other fields have struggled with the same question and, in the end, formulated their tentative solutions. Furthermore, through a precise exploration of the problem we avoid a myopic view by looking too closely at a very familiar domain.

Description, Prescription and Application in Educational Psychology

Questioning the relationship between description, prescription and application evidently is not new, nor is it restricted to the field of research on teaching. On the contrary, it still remains an important impetus for lasting reflection within educational psychology in general. Glaser points to this as follows: 'In recent years, ... there has been increasing interest in and social pressure for the development of professional techniques for the application of what knowledge there is of learning, cognitive processes, and human development. It appears that some linking of theory and practice needs to take place' (Glaser, 1976, pp. 1–2). And, though many researchers in the field agree with the need for elucidating the connection between description, prescription and practice, they nevertheless disagree in many ways as to the solution. Hilgard (1964) for example, perceives the relation between learning theory and educational practice as the contrast between a pure science and its technological applications. Application, at least in his opinion, involves something more than the theory. Because the dichotomy of research endeavours in 'fundamental' versus 'applied' knowledge systems cannot contribute to the solution of the problem, Hilgard suggests a continuum with on the one side the 'purest' research in learning with no regard for its educational implications, (for example, animal studies, physiological, biological investigations) and on the other technological research and development where anything found in the previous stages is 'packaged' for wider use. This way of categorizing research into well-defined types is in line with three different kinds of research orientations as described by Ausubel (1968), namely basic science research, extrapolated research in the basic sciences, and research at an applied level.

In his thinking, however, Glaser (1979) rejects any dichotomy between basic and applied research within the cognitive paradigm, since it is 'apparent that research now being directed toward educationally relevant areas is both fundamental in character and, at the same time, directed toward practical understanding' (Glaser, 1979, p.6). His argument claims that 'one major influence in the development of present-day cognitive theory was work on applied problems, stimulated by practical applications required from human skills and performance in World War II and its aftermath. The analysis of human performance in man–machine systems, coupled with developments in other fields, shifted emphasis away from the unanalyzed correlation of input and output toward consideration of complex internal processes' (ibid). But, if we adapt Glaser's argument for teacher thinking studies, we have to remember the crux of his argumentation, namely the intrinsic applied character of the study object. If this is the case with our research topics, then the walls between pure and applied research in our domain are already cracking.

Description and Prescription in Teaching Research

Although the discussion between learning theorists about the status of their research is inspiring, the many arguments for bridging the gap between learning theories and education are not sufficient to clarify the inherent tension between description and prescription in the very specific domain of teaching. While psychological phenomena could be labelled as being 'natural', teaching is, unlike animal learning, a cultural and social activity with a moral dimension and an intrinsic orientation towards the optimal development of people. Teaching is an autonomous field of research (see Smith and Ennis, 1961), and it has to tackle the 'descriptive-prescriptive-application' problem in its own way. Gage and Unruh (1967) in their contribution to the theoretical formulations for research on teaching mention a dividing force between two main approaches of research on teaching, namely describing, or concern with the way teaching *is*, and improving, or concern with the way teaching *ought to be*. Despite these differences, Gage and Unruh nevertheless perceive some strikingly similar 'formulations' in the work of both Jackson (the descriptive line) and Stolurow (the prescriptive approach). For in their analysis of the teaching task Jackson (1967) as well as Stolurow (1965) distinguish between the pre-active and the active phase of teaching, and in Jackson's study, teachers — at least in some classes — typically followed a way of teaching similar to that of programmed instruction as advocated by Stolurow. These convergences recognized by Gage and Unruh, however, are purely conceptual and consequently do not build an empirically validated bridge between description and prescription. It is not intellectually sound to take one partial resemblance as an argument, and we have thus to examine more precisely the complex relations.

Some twenty years ago, Jackson (1967) in 'The way teaching is' formulated strong reasons for a shift toward a descriptive approach in research on teaching. Though he fully recognized the moral aspects of the teaching profession, aimed at improving things, he nevertheless rejected a direct connection between the need for improvement and research on teaching. The two arguments for his stance are the poor results of teaching effectiveness research on the one hand and the lack of knowledge about the complexity of teaching on the other. However, he immediately reduced the possible polarity between description and prescription, since 'the fact that some researchers seem to be chiefly interested in describing conditions as they are does not mean that they no longer care about what should be' (Jackson, 1967, p. 9). In our opinion, however, this claim says more about the moral sanity of researchers than about the validity of the argument. Clarke takes a totally opposite position stating that 'Because teaching involves intent it is not a value-free activity; hence, teaching theory must be normative, i.e. prescriptive' (Clarke, 1970, p. 411) and he subsequently formulates the prescriptions that apply in general to all teaching. Notwithstanding the enumeration of some peculiar characteristics of the teaching phenomenon, the complex relation between description and prescription is not yet clarified, and further scrutiny is needed.

The Shift From Prescription to Description

The difficulty lies in the question whether the arguments for the choice between description and prescription, or for a shift from one approach to another are intrinsically independent and equally valuable. Let us briefly review the different phases in the history of research on teaching, in order to discover possible reasons for a reorientation.

Shifts in the underlying theories Research on teaching heavily depends upon the perceived power of the available theories for understanding and influencing human behaviour. In times of the *test psychology*, human behaviour was described in terms of the specific 'structure' of the personality, consisting of a set of identifiable stable 'traits'. Within this view, behaviour was not directly studied since it 'emanated' from the personality characteristics. As a consequence, research on teaching aimed at the discovery of good 'traits' or 'characteristics' of teachers as predictors of effective teaching (see Domas and Tiedeman, 1950; Getzels and Jackson, 1963; Ryans, 1970). Prescriptive knowledge was sought not for training, but for selection purposes.

As a reaction against the vague and uncontrollable trait theory, *behaviouristic psychology* claimed a direct study of observable human behaviour. Within this paradigm, teaching behaviour was no longer a dependent variable of the personality, but an independent variable, influencing learning outcomes. Moreover, the analytical approach allowed fragmentation of the (too) complex human activity into behavioural particles suited for conditioning. Such analytical approach was advocated by Gage (1963) for research on teaching, when he argued that 'many scientific problems have eventually been solved by being analyzed into small problems, whose variables are less complex.' However, behaviourism failed as the exclusive interpretative framework for all complex human functioning. It concentrated too heavily on a person's reactive behaviours toward external stimuli, rather than on his active construction of a meaningful reality.

Cognitive psychology, in line with the older European tradition of the psychology of thought ('*Denkpsychologie*'), views human functioning as the construction of a unique reality through gathering and processing complex information. The complexity is situated not merely outside the subject but inside his enormous capability to process and use information. In line with this shift toward a cognitive science, teaching has been defined as 'hypothesis testing' (Coladarci, 1959), 'decision-making' (Shavelson, 1973), 'clinical information processing' (National Institute of Education, 1975), and 'problem-solving'

(Fattu, 1965). The focus is more on the way teachers think than on their classroom behaviour and learning effects. A brief overview of the evolution in psychology and of its reflection in teaching research could suggest a complete parallelism between the 'basic sciences' and their applications within the study of teaching. More concretely, one could ascribe the shift in research on teaching exclusively to the changing approaches in psychology. Are there no other arguments available?

Disappointing results of empirical research The shift in a paradigm is caused not only by shortcomings or evolutions in the referential theories, but by the (lack of) results in empirical studies as well. In the case of disappointing research outcomes, researchers tend first to attribute the failure to inadequate concepts or methodological shortcomings, but after a period of time the deficiency of the approach itself is recognized.

In line with the dominant psychological theories and available methodologies, research on teaching produced a vast quantity of results. Looking successively at the conclusions of each paradigm, the myth of Sisyphus comes to mind: the king of Corinth condemned forever by the gods to roll a stone up a hill in Hades only to see it roll down again on nearing the top. Let us briefly review this accumulation of pitfalls and question why there is no myth of continuity, like that of a snowball steadily growing and becoming visible to practitioners even at some distance.

For the *'teacher characteristics'* paradigm, Getzels and Jackson (1963) reviewed 800 studies after 1950 and more than 1000 before that date. Their scrutiny led to the disappointing insight that there is very little output, at least if one expects concrete and useful knowledge. One of the predominant reasons for this lack of productivity was that the personality traits used as measures for concrete teaching behaviour were too broad. The suggestion that teachers should be pupil-centred, friendly, enthusiastic or psychologically balanced, applies to all people in interaction with others. It hardly reveals any specific teaching characteristic. Moreover, the knowledge was gained by a correlational approach. On the one hand, teachers were submitted to test batteries measuring intelligence, attitudes, feelings, etc., on the other, some criteria for measuring the quality of teaching were used, such as opinions of supervisors, superintendents, school leaders, students and colleagues, and thus again depending upon some kind of 'popular wisdom'.

One approach in the study of teaching, looking at the specific behaviours of teachers and pupils in classrooms, is better known as the *'leadership tradition'*. Launched by the research of Lewin, Lippitt and White in out-of-school situations (see Lippitt and White, 1943), a number of studies in real classrooms have been conducted about authoritarian, democratic and *'laissez-faire'* leadership. The almost exclusive concentration on the democratic type of leadership was, of course, in line with the need for improving the democratic quality of schools, and from there, of society. It was clearly a prescriptive point of view. Anderson (1959) reviewed thirty-two studies on the effectiveness of leadership styles and concluded that: 'We were not fortunate enough to find that one method (style) is consistently different from the other; thus we are forced to explore new avenues. In short, the authoritarian-democratic construct as far as education is concerned at least has far outlived its usefulness either as a guide to research or as an interpretation of leadership behavior' (p.212). This and other criticisms against these studies led to the abandonment of the paradigm in favour of a more specific and controlled way of studying classroom climate, better known as the interaction-analysis approach, of which Flanders (1970) was one important representative. This approach was better known as the *process-product paradigm*.

The ultimate aim of this approach is to discover effective classroom behaviours and, by doing so, to generate prescriptive knowledge. The variables in teaching (here called 'process' variables) are practised in more or less observable behaviours, as grouped in a prolific number of observational systems (see Simon and Boyer, 1970). However, they reflect the many underlying conceptualizations of the 'optimal' teaching process. The criterion is the gain in learning (the 'product'). Teaching effectiveness, then, is defined by the correlation between the process and the product variables (Shavelson, Webb and Burstein, 1986). According to the paradigm, 'a teacher is effective if, within the time period studied, students, averaged over the whole class, answered more questions correctly on multiple-choice standardized achievement tests than expected, based on the pretest performance' (p.52). This paradigm clearly reflects a prescriptive position, because the teaching behaviours which appear to be effective, are norm-setting. Rosenshine and Furst (1973), for example, reported the following nine 'powerful' process variables: clarity, variability, enthusiasm, task orientation, criticism of the teacher, indirectness, student opportunity to learn criterion material, structuring comments, and use of different levels of questions and cognitive activities.

Despite these results, the paradigm has been the object of strong criticism. Heath and Nielson (1974) revealed fundamental weaknesses because the studies were *content-proof* and *pupil-proof*. Moreover, almost all observational systems register only the 'classroom teaching' situation, excluding individual settings and group work so that the results are *method-proof* too. Thirdly, teaching is perceived as a unidirectional activity of teachers, neglecting the influences of the situation, and in this way it is *context-proof*. Fourthly, because of the emphasis on observable behaviours, no information is gathered about the 'inner life' of teachers and pupils. Consequently, the process-product studies are *cognition-proof*.

The recognition of all these shortcomings led to a solution in two totally different directions. On the one hand, protagonists of the effectiveness paradigm sought new solutions within the process-product paradigm. Examples are the well known BTES 'Beginning Teacher Evaluation Studies' (see Fisher, Filby, *et al.*, 1978; Fisher, Berliner, *et al.*, 1978; Jones and Romberg, 1979). These studies do not concentrate on the separate bits of teaching behaviours, but on the patterns of teaching, as reflected in more encompassing teaching functions, like diagnosis, prescription, presentation, evaluation and feedback. More attention is paid to individual and group settings, and even the 'mediating variables' (Doyle, 1978) are considered. On the other hand, a more radical solution is sought in a switch from the process-product approach to a cognitive paradigm (Clark and Peterson, 1986).

Although the *cognitive line of research* emerged only recently, there is already a clear intrinsic evolution. At the beginning, emphasis was laid on the more formal and rational aspects of teachers' cognitive functioning. In many studies the process of teaching was described: how teachers plan lessons, make decisions, solve problems and process information. After some time, however, this process description was complemented by new insights. More and more attention was paid to the content of teacher thinking (cognitions, schemata, naive theories, personal constructs, concerns). And even the impact of the domain knowledge was claimed, as Shulman (1986) labelled it 'pedagogical content knowledge' and 'curricular knowledge'. Moreover, the possible link between cognition and action entered the focus of many research endeavours. Examples are the 'interactive thoughts' (see: Clark and Peterson, 1986), the expert-novice studies (Leinhardt, 1986; Berliner and Carter, 1986) and the theoretical effort to integrate teacher thinking and professional action (see: Lowyck, Clark and Halkes, 1988). It seems as if the cognitive paradigm on teaching will definitely avoid all the existing 'proofs' from the previous paradigm.

This overview of research on teaching, as presented above, could offer the wrong impression that the many disappointing outcomes within one approach immediately and exclusively caused a shift in research on teaching. There are, however, two main reasons for recommending caution: First, negative outcomes can stimulate conceptual refinement, methodological adequacy and meaningful grouping of results by meta-analyses without leaving the existing paradigm (see: Dunkin and Biddle, 1974; BTES studies). Second, the initiation of a new paradigm does not always depend upon an appreciation of the value of a paradigm, but can result from a fresh and unexpected way of looking at teaching. Examples are the alternative conceptualization of teaching (Jackson, 1967), the ethnographic approach (Smith and Geoffrey, 1968), symbolic interactionism (Delamont, 1976), and educational connoisseurship (Eisner, 1975). Overall, the shift from a prescriptive toward a descriptive approach is a rather complex phenomenon and surely not deductable from a limited set of factors.

The Supposed Impossibility of Pure Descriptive Knowledge in Research on Teaching

Despite the researcher's claim to generate descriptive knowledge about teaching as a universal phenomenon, it is not an easy task to describe reality 'as it is'. Even if we strive toward a well functioning apparatus of concepts and models, the divergency of approaches in research on teacher thinking — as often happens in complex human affairs — is much higher than one would wish and hinders our understanding of the phenomenon. We do not have *the* description of teaching complexity (as advocated by our hypothesis), but an enormous range of individual perceptions of teaching complexity. The vagueness of the conceptual framework, the babel of unclear, idiosyncratic definitions, the proliferation of models, the isolation of paradigms, and the suggested incompatibility of quantitative and qualitative methodology, all hinder the consolidation of thousands of research outcomes. How can we further the understanding of teaching in its complexity, if the concepts of teaching are apparently more complex than the teaching reality itself; and how can practical advice be deduced from a mix of non-compatible information.

Epistemological Difficulties

If we look for an understanding of the relationship between description, prescription and application, we should understand the type of epistemology produced in the different types of research.

In his book *The sciences of the artificial*, Simon (1970) makes a clear distinction between the natural sciences and the sciences of the artificial. As to the former, researchers have found a way to exclude the normative and to concern themselves solely with 'how things are'. An important question, however, is if one can or should maintain this exclusion of norms when moving from natural to artificial phenomena. Simon's distinction between natural and artificial sciences seems to fertilize our reflection upon the status of a science of teaching. Education and teaching are cultural artefacts and not natural phenomena. Egan (1982) argues that 'there is no such thing as a natural educational process out there which we should be trying to find, describe and explain. An educationally useful theory cannot sensibly be an attempt to describe and explain — it should describe an ideal or a good aim for the process and prescribe practical steps for bringing it about. An educational process exists only as we bring it into existence'. This quotation may sound somewhat offensive to an audience interested in describing teaching. But if we take the expert-novice approach in teacher thinking studies as an example, we will acknowledge its intrinsic tendency toward an understanding of 'good' teaching.

But the distinction between sciences also refers to the systematic way of gathering knowledge since both types of research have a distinct logic. Natural sciences can use the ordinary systems of logic: the standard propositional logic and the predicate calculi. Artificial science, on the other hand, is concerned with how things ought to be (ends) and with artefacts (means) to attain goals. A normative, deontic logic for handling 'shoulds', 'shalls', and 'oughts', however, has not been well elaborated until now. Simon offers the following example: 'In ordinary logic, from "Dogs are pets" and "Cats are pets", one can infer "Dogs and cats are pets". But from "Dogs are pets", "Cats are pets" and "You should keep pets", can one infer "You should keep cats and dogs"?' This rather amusing example illustrates the difficulties encountered with the logical validation of our descriptive knowledge of teaching.

Cronbach and Suppes (1969) distinguish between 'basic research' and 'applied research' emphasizing the possibility of each type of research to isolate subsystems and variables. Basic research aims at the generation of laws in the natural sciences, which is facilitated by the fact that the subsystems under study can almost always be perfectly isolated. The social sciences, on the contrary, had very little success in isolating subsystems. There is no doubt that the intrinsic impossibility to isolate the many variables in research on teaching worries researchers in this field. If they isolate the subsystems, the meaning of the study outcomes is strongly reduced, but if they try to integrate all the possible variables, the investigation is no more manageable. In our opinion, the solution of this fundamental and inherent problem is to alter the unit of analysis by starting with a level of meaningful functioning and to work further in a top-down approach, trying to understand more profoundly the details of the prior outcomes. For example, studying teacher planning during the pre-active phase of teaching is not very relevant if there is no knowledge about the impact of planning on interactive teaching. And it seems difficult to understand cognitive processes if there is no insight in the context in which the cognitions operate or in the specific subjects in which the cognitions are embedded.

Summarily, there is no argumentation for the acceptance of a direct transposition from descriptive outcomes to prescriptions in teacher thinking studies. Teaching is not a natural phenomenon, understandable with the usual logic. It is a social and moral enterprise in which values and norms are embedded. Moreover, there is no sound philosophical argument for the transition from 'is' to 'ought', because they are epistemologically isolated systems of knowledge. The transition from 'is' to 'ought' is only possible if no additional information is needed during the transitional operations. Briefly, there is no philosophical ground for claiming the intrinsic transition from 'is' to 'ought'.

The Lack of Conceptual Consistency

Within a specific research domain, the shift from one approach to another often leads to fresh metaphors and unusual concepts. Scheffler (1960) and Snow (1973) noticed that metaphors can provide new perspectives on old problems, but at the same time they embed some peculiar values and assumptions which often unknowingly influence the way in which the objects under study are interpreted. And, though metaphors enable researchers to explore a few key features of a phenomenon in line with the analogy, they are rarely precise enough to encompass all the necessary and sufficient characteristics of the object of study.

When taking the metaphor of the 'teacher as problem-solver' as an example, it is obvious that investigators in the field of teacher thinking gradually recognized its restricted value in understanding the complexity of the teaching activity. First, it is impossible to define precisely all the components within the 'task environment' of teaching itself. This observation contrasts with the problem-solving tasks as used in psychological experiments, entirely controlled by the experimenter. Teaching remains more complex and sensitive to diverging interpretations. Second, in contrast with the problem space of the problem solver, 'powerful influences outside the control of individual teachers play parts in defining the problem space' (Clark, 1986, p. 9). Metaphors have their limited interpretative power. Third, it became clear that the metaphor of problem-solving can only be applied to some degree. Teaching is not the exclusively rational activity of a teacher, but encompasses many routines and reactions to unpredictable situations.

Along with metaphors, many unusual concepts are introduced within a new paradigm. Examples from the teacher thinking approach are 'intention', 'planning', 'constructs', 'concerns', 'anticipation', 'reflection', 'personal theory', 'pedagogical knowledge', 'cognitive representations', 'knots', 'dilemmas', etc. However, the proliferation of specific concepts proves neither a systematic application of the metaphor nor a semantic consolidation. On the contrary, researchers often seem to conceptualize their investigations distinctly from the work of colleagues or predecessors. Referring to Carroll's (1963) distinction between denotative and connotative concepts, researchers on teacher thinking tend to lean more heavily on the connotative meaning of their concepts than on the denotative one. Their idiosyncratic way of wording often blurs the definitions already at hand.

After the initiation of new concepts and along with the progress of empirical research, the experienced one-sidedness of the concepts often leads to the use of a second, but opposite concept. In research on teacher thinking, a lot of 'dual concepts' are used, like 'thinking–routine', 'intention–action' 'planning–performance', 'pre-active–interactive'. But here again, some lasting problems are present. It namely depends highly on the definition of the first concept whether the second one is meaningful. Let us take the example of the concept 'routine'. If routines are defined as what all teachers do when not thinking (Morine, 1973), all the possible cognitive aspects of routines are excluded from research. However, psychological research on skills (Bartlett, 1964; Fitts, 1965; Welford, 1968) revealed that in almost all routinized activities cognitive processes, like anticipation, coordination, use of feedback, are extremely important. What then, is the relevance of the dual concept 'thinking–routine' if both refer to cognitive aspects?

The Transition From Description to Prescription

As has been elucidated in the previous part of this chapter, there is no direct link between natural or pure sciences and the artificial or applied sciences. It seems as if this observation excludes any utility of descriptive knowledge for the practice of teaching. Or, as Cronbach and Suppes (1969) assert, 'Most fundamental knowledge, indeed, cannot be "applied"; it does not prescribe a suitable practice. It can only stimulate the investigator facing a practical problem to manipulate some new aspects of the situation and to appraise effects he might hitherto not have considered' (p. 123). If we search for knowledge which could serve specific practical ends or guide decisions, not as much conclusion-oriented but decision-oriented inquiry is needed. Here, a subtle distinction has been made. Cronbach and Suppes (1969) refer to conclusion-oriented research 'when it is intended to have a general significance, whereas decision-oriented research is designed for its relevance to a particular institution at a particular time' (*ibid.*, p. 25). In this quotation, I think, we find the core of the problem about the relation between description and practice. Fundamental knowledge is only valuable for practice if it is supplemented by other kinds of knowledge which we can call 'value added', significant for practice, and useful for the practitioner in taking the right things into account.

Is this a sufficient argument to defend the practical value of descriptive studies? As will be explained in the remainder, several modes of transition between description and prescription are at hand. They refer not only to the supposed status of the research, but equally to the conditions for a meaningful transition. While scrutinizing the literature on descriptive and prescriptive teaching knowledge, some different conceptualizations came to mind.

Transitions Made by Researchers

Researchers can differ at least in their intention to describe or to prescribe. And, though a direct transformation from 'is' to 'ought' is not possible purely on epistemological grounds, the question is if and how we can use descriptive knowledge.

Description equals prescription For one reason or another some researchers who have gained descriptive knowledge, often change its status from description to prescription. Prescriptions, then, are descriptions often packaged together with some implicit criteria, and formulated in an action-oriented way. Within the process-product approach, the empirically validated effective behaviours of teachers have been used for a direct translation into prescriptions. Gage (1978), for example, formulated his so-called 'teacher-should' statements, mainly derived from the BTES tradition, like: 'Teachers should have a system of rules that allow pupils to attend to their personal and procedural needs *without* having to check with the teacher', or 'In selecting pupils to respond to questions, teachers should call on a child by name before asking the question as a means of ensuring that all pupils are given an equal number of opportunities to answer questions'. This immediate translation from correlational knowledge into prescriptions for behaviour appears to be legitimized at least by the use of empirically validated 'effective' teaching behaviours.

However, in many writings of researchers in the field of teacher thinking, the transfer of descriptive knowledge into prescriptions is also apparent. When taking the studies on expert-novice teaching as an example, we can detect some underlying expectations. Researchers expect from experts that they reflect 'effective' thinking and teaching. Expert behaviour becomes the end, and novice behaviour the starting point. But in almost no studies has the bridge between the novice and the expert been clarified, nor is it clear what the explicit criteria are to qualify an expert as an expert. It is as if we enter a vicious circle, having to define expert behaviour without a secured list of criteria to define expert behaviour. The usual solution of many researchers is to start with a provisional definition of the expert and to neglect further on to test the validity of the criteria used. In our study (Lowyck, 1980) we intended to select 'good teachers' whom we call 'experts' nowadays in order to trace a number of process characteristics of skilled teaching behaviour. Further analysis of the criteria used by the inspectors for the selection of a population of sixteen 'good' teachers revealed that they were 'experienced' but not unequivocally 'experts'. Consequently, we could describe cognitive processes of teaching, and not of 'good teaching'.

Description as a source of inspiration for prescription Descriptive knowledge can be used as a framework, a mirror in which the features of good practice can be reflected. In this way, descriptive outcomes can reflect the theoretical shortcomings of practice. For example, when in the process-product studies the 'hidden activities' of teachers during both lesson preparation and empty classroom situations remained in the 'black box', most systematic training programs of teachers did not focus on the planning, nor on the impact of the teacher's conceptual framework on his actions. It is since the descriptive studies on teacher thinking, that teacher education programs offer an opportunity to enlarge and adjust the cognitions of students.

But, even within the descriptive approach, it seems unclear whether the object of study is purely descriptive, or if the researchers already have an image of 'good' teaching in mind, which intrudes upon the descriptive concepts and models. It could be a challenging topic to investigate the reasons why researchers choose a concrete topic or a specific population for research. Apart from some more practical or pragmatic arguments, such as the accessibility of some kinds of teachers or students (why do we frequently study student teachers from our own institutions, or elementary teachers in schools?) or the suitability of a concrete (hot?) topic, like pre-interactive planning, are there no choices as to the 'relevance', of the object of study? I believe there are. Borko and Niles (1987) open their article with the statement: 'To teach successfully, one must plan successfully', and they assert that 'several recently conducted research studies have made a contribution to our understanding of teacher planning. And what we are learning about planning has the potential to improve instruction' (p. 167). At least the choice of the research object is justified by its expected relevance to practice.

Transitions Made by Teachers and Teacher Educators

Clark (1988) distinguished the following ways to characterize the relationship between research on teaching and teacher education. First, there is no relationship due to the isolated position of teaching research. Second, there is a direct relationship, such as the direct use of process-product outcomes in teacher training programmes. Third, the relationship between research on teacher thinking and the practice of teacher education exists only in potential. The researchers act as consultants to the community of teacher educators. It is this last relationship which has been further elaborated by Clark. In his opinion, the power of research on teacher thinking depends upon its possibility to penetrate the existing teacher preparation programmes. Moreover, the knowledge gained in descriptive studies allows no well-defined prescriptions as to how to educate teachers, but is rather a source of inspiration providing examples of concepts, methods and 'food for thought'.

One of the main problems in transferring research outcomes to real life situations is the centrifugal effect of most research endeavours. General descriptive knowledge is gathered by transcending the unique and individual thoughts and actions of teachers. And it often seems problematic to revitalize the 'generalized' and abstracted knowledge for practical purposes.

The practitioner as 'researcher' Research models are not only used by researchers, but can also offer inspiring ways for practitioners. Pope and Scott (1984) refer to the theoretical perspective of Kelly in addressing the importance of teachers' perspectives on the nature of knowledge. The metaphor used by Kelly is 'man-the-scientist', and he invited us to entertain the possibility that looking at people as if they were scientists (i.e. view their scientist-like aspects) might illuminate human behaviour. 'Kelly's philosophical position as that of "constructive alternativism" suggests that people understand themselves, their surroundings and anticipate future eventualities by constructing tentative models and evaluating these against personal criteria as to the successful prediction and control of events based upon the model' (Pope and Scott, 1984, p. 113). This way of perceiving the relation between research and practice is in line with the position of Day (1984), who claims that 'if research is to make a significant contribution to teacher learning and change, researchers must move away from the notion of themselves as prime designers and interpreters of the motivations, thoughts and actions of others towards a more independent role in which collaboration, consultation, and negotiation are first principles' (Day, 1984, p. 73).

The time lag between research and its applications in the reality. If, however, descriptive research outcomes should function as sources of inspiration for practitioners, there is a need for the dissemination of relevant knowledge. And, though teacher thinking studies mostly use concepts deduced from the real life of teachers, the transcoding of the information inside scientific models and paradigms often leads to one or another kind of alienation. Apart from the necessary translation of research findings, there is another problem. It often happens that there is a time lag between the production of scientific knowledge and its implementation into reality. Glaser (1979) makes an interesting observation. In present psychological research, the cognitive psychology is dominant, as were the behaviouristic S-R learning theories until recently. In contrast to this scientific shift, much of the application of psychological theory currently going on in schools represents the earlier behaviouristic approach. A nice example of this time lag is the definition of teaching skills. During the sixties and seventies, the concept of teaching skill was mainly defined by the analytic approach as advocated by Gage (1963). This interpretation parallels the use of skills in microteaching settings (Allen and Ryan, 1969). They were a number of simple and easily trainable 'techniques' deduced from the process-product research. This conceptualization strongly differs from what was already known in psychology about the cognitive interpretation of skilfulness (see Bartlett, 1964; Fitts, 1965; Welford, 1968), focusing on an adequate selection of information, anticipation, control of behavioural elements, decision-making and use of intrinsic feedback. And even within the cognitive approach, the idea of 'skilfulness' is not well recognized.

Perhaps, one of the main reasons for the loss˙of time in implementing research outcomes is the parallelism between the approaches in research on teaching and the teacher training models. It rarely occurs that one will use teacher thinking research outcomes within a competence-based teacher education model, and most teacher thinking adepts refuse to implement some interesting findings of the process-product paradigm. We can only refuse the integration of thousands of research endeavours into teacher education programs, if we continue to perceive the approaches in research on teaching as perfectly isolated ways of studying the complexity of teaching.

Conclusions

The rationale behind all research on teaching does not seem to be limited to the pure description of teaching, but to optimize — at least in the long run — the structures and processes of teaching and learning. However, scholars within this field can invent an almost unlimited number of research topics, methods and designs, solely from a sense of legitimate curiosity in the teaching and learning phenomenon itself. They restrict their responsibility to a profound or broad description of assumed relevant aspects of the teaching reality and envisage a self-fulfilling process of implementation of their findings into the practice of the daily classroom. They refuse to take into consideration the linkage between the generation of new or systematic knowledge and the moral task of stimulating the improvement of education. Is this a kind of intellectual schizophrenia?

The possibility for description is endless, not only because of the complexity of the phenomenon itself, but mainly due to the wide range of frameworks, paradigms, methods, and idiosyncratic approaches. The problem is, then, to discover descriptive categories which are important for a certain number of goals. In short, without a clear statement of the goals to be reached by research on teaching thinking, we can accumulate an enormous host of knowledge. Consequently, the amount of knowledge will be negatively correlated with its functionality. Hence, consolidation of research programs is needed as well as the definition of 'stop rules' for both the diversity (i.e. anarchy) and the amount of valuable knowledge.

The bifurcation between description and prescription is the consequence of the short term view on research on teaching. The relation between description and prescription cannot be a unilateral one. Descriptive theory is often the base for a prescriptive theory, which again could become a strong way of testing descriptive theory. This idea of the cyclical way of progressing in research is clearly formulated by Nuthall and Church (1976) who recognize four phases in research. First, during the descriptive phase, the necessary variables have to be discovered as the base for further investigation. In the second phase, the correlational one, relations between variables are studied. The third phase is the experimental one, in which possible causal relationships are detected. The outcomes of the second and third phases can serve as a base for refining the descriptive categories. In the fourth phase, a theory is elaborated in which the output from the prior phases is integrated. And, though this cumulative, recurrent and cyclical approach of research undoubtedly sounds very attractive, it rarely leads to the consolidation of research endeavours, even in a relatively young domain like teaching thinking.

If the several traditions in research on teaching have no integrative power, we have to accept our initial hypothesis, namely that there has to be made a dichotomous choice between description and prescription, or between the 'effectiveness' paradigm and the description of teaching as it is. Before leaving the scene, we can sympathize with Sisyphus, the king of Corinth...or write a new scenario for an integrative way of looking at the way teaching 'is' and 'ought to be'.

References

ALLEN, D. W. and RYAN, K. (1969) *Microteaching*, Reading, Addison-Wesley.

ANDERSON, R. C. (1959) 'Learning in discussions: a resume of the authoritarian–democratic studies', *Harvard Educational Review*, 29. pp. 200–15.

AUSUBEL, D. P. (1968) *Educational Psychology: A Cognitive View*, New York, Holt, Rinehart and Winston.

BARTLETT, F. (1964) *Thinking: An Experimental and Social Study*, London, Unwin University Books.

BERLINER, D. and CARTER, K. (1986) 'Differences in processing classroom information by expert and novice teachers', in LOWYCK, J. (Ed.) *Teacher Thinking and Professional Action. Proceedings of the Third ISATT Conference*, Leuven, Leuven University.

BORKO, H. and NILES, J. A. (1987) 'Descriptions of teacher planning: ideas for teachers and researchers', in RICHARDSON-KOEHLER, V. (Ed.) *Educators' Handbook: A Research Perspective*, New York, Longman.

CARROLL, J. B. (1963) 'A model of school learning', *Teachers College Record*, 64, pp. 723–33.

CLARK, C. M. (1986) 'Ten years of conceptual development in research on teacher thinking', in BEN-PERETZ, M., BROMME, R. and HALKES R. (Eds) *Advances of Research on Teacher Thinking*, Lisse, Swets and Zeitlinger.

CLARK, C. M. (1988). 'Asking the right questions about teacher preparation: contributions of research on teacher thinking', in LOWYCK, J., CLARK, C. M. and HALKES R. (Eds) *Teacher Thinking and Professional Action*, Leuven, Leuven University Press.

CLARK, C. M. and PETERSON, P. L. (1986), 'Teachers' thought processes', in WITTROCK M. C. (Ed.) *Handbook of Research on Teaching*, New York, Macmillan.

CLARKE, S. C. T. (1970) 'General teaching theory', *The Journal of Teacher Education*, 21, pp. 403–16.

COLADARCI, A. P. (1959), 'The teacher as hypothesis-maker', *California Journal for Instructional Improvement*, 2, pp. 3–6.

COUNCIL OF EUROPE (1980) *Educational Technology for Permanent Education: A Critical Reappraisal*, Strasbourg, Council for Cultural Co-operation.

CRONBACH, L. J. and SUPPES, P. (1969) *Research for Tomorrow's Schools: Disciplined Inquiry for Education*, London, Macmillan.

DAY, C. (1984) 'Teachers' thinking intentions and practice: an action research perspective', in HALKES, R. and OLSON, J. (Eds) *Teacher Thinking: A New Perspective on Persisting Problems in Education*, Lisse, Swets and Zeitlinger.

DELAMONT, S. (1976) *Interaction in the Classroom*, London, Methuen.

DOMAS, S. J. and TIEDEMAN, D. V. (1950) 'Teacher competence: an annotated bibliography', *Journal of Experimental Education*, 19, pp. 101–18.

DOYLE, W. (1978) 'Paradigms for research on teacher effectiveness', In SHULMAN L. S. (Ed.) *Review of Research in Teaching*, Itasca, Peacock.

DUNKIN, M. J. and BIDDLE, B. J. (1974) *The Study of Teaching*, New York, Holt, Rinehart and Winston.

EGAN, K. (1982) 'On the possibility of theories of educational practice', *Journal of curriculum studies*, 14, pp. 153–65.

EISNER, E. W. (1975) *Applying Educational Connoisseurship and Criticism to Educational Settings. A Proposal for the Spencer Foundation*, Stanford, Stanford University.

FATTU, N. A. (1965) 'A model of teaching as problem-solving', in MACDONALD, J. B. and LEEPER, R. R. (Eds) *Theories of Instruction*, Washington, Association for Supervision and Curriculum Development.

FISHER, C. W. *et al.* (1978) *Teaching and Learning in the Elementary School: A Summary of the Beginning Teacher Evaluation Study*, San Francisco, Far West Laboratory for Educational Research and Development.

FISHER, C. W. *et al.* (1978) *Teaching Behaviors, Academic Learning Time and Student Achievement: Final Report of Phase III-B, Beginning Teacher Evaluation Study*, Washington, National Institute of Education.

FITTS, P. M. (1965) 'Factors in complex skill training', in GLASER, R. (Ed.) *Training Research and Education*, New York, Wiley.

FLANDERS, N. A. (1970) *Analyzing Teacher Behavior*, Reading, Addison-Wesley.

GAGE, N. L. (Ed.) (1963) *Handbook of Research on Teaching*, Chicago, Rand McNally.

GAGE, N. L. (1978) *The Scientific Basis of the Art of Teaching*, New York, Teachers College Press.

GAGE, N. L. and UNRUH, W. R. (1967) Theoretical formulations for research on teaching, *Review of Educational Research*, 37, pp. 358–70.

GETZELS, J. W. and JACKSON, P. W. (1963) 'The teacher's personality and characteristics,' in GAGE, N. L. (Ed.) *Handbook of Research on Teaching*, Chicago, Rand McNally.

GLASER, R. (1976) 'Components of a psychology of instruction: Toward a science of design', *Review of Educational Research*, 46, pp. 1–24.

GLASER, R. (1979), 'Trends and research questions in psychological research on learning and schooling', *Educational Researcher*, 8, pp. 6–13.

HALKES, R. and OLSON, J. K (Eds) (1984) *Teacher Thinking: A New Perspective on Persisting Problems in Education*, (Proceedings of the first symposium of the International Study Association on Teacher Thinking, Tilburg, October 1983), Lisse, Swets and Zeitlinger.

HEATH, R. W. and NIELSON, M. A. (1974) 'The research basis for performance-based teacher education', *Review of Educational Research*, 44, pp. 463–84.

HILGARD, E. R. (1964) 'A perspective on the relationship between learning theory and educational practices', in HILGARD, E. R. (Ed.) *Theories of Learning and Instruction, (The Sixty-Third Yearbook of the National Society for the Study of Education)*, Chicago, The University of Chicago Press.

JACKSON, P. W. (1967) 'The way teaching is,' in ASSOCIATION FOR SUPERVISION AND CURRICULUM DEVELOPMENT AND CENTER FOR THE STUDY OF INSTRUCTION OF THE NATIONAL EDUCATION ASSOCIATION. *The way teaching is: Report of the Seminar on Teaching*, Washington, National Education Association.

JONES, G. A. and ROMBERG, T. A. (1979) *Three 'Time on Task' Studies and their Implications for Teaching and Teacher Education*, Madison, Wisconsin Research and Development Center for Individualized Schooling, University of Wisconsin.

LEINHARDT, G. (1986) 'Math lessons: a contrast of novice and expert competence,' in LOWYCK, J. (Ed.) *Teacher Thinking and Professional Action. Proceedings of the Third ISATT Conference*, Leuven, Leuven University.

LIPPITT, R. and WHITE, K. (1943) 'The "social climate" of children's groups', in BARKER, R., KOUNIN J. S. and WRIGHT H. F., (Eds) *Child Behavior and Development*, New York, McGraw-Hill.

LOWYCK, J. (1980) *A Process Analysis of Teaching*, (report no. 21) Leuven, Leuven University.

LOWYCK, J., CLARK, C. M. and HALKES, R. (1988) *Teacher Thinking and Professional Action*, Leuven, Leuven University Press.

MORINE, G. (1973) 'Planning skills: paradox and parodies', *Journal of Teacher Education*, 2, pp. 135–43.

NATIONAL INSTITUTE OF EDUCATION (1975) *Teaching as Clinical Information Processing (Report of Panel 6, National Conference on Studies in Teaching)*, Washington, National Institute of Education.

NUTHALL, G. and CHURCH, J. (1976), 'Experimental studies of teaching behavior', in WOLFSON J. (Ed.) *Personality and learning*, Vol II s.l., Hodder and Stoughton.

POPE, M. L. and SCOTT, E. M. (1984) 'Teachers' epistemology and practice', in HALKES R. and OLSON J. (Eds) *Teacher Thinking: A New Perspective On Persisting Problems in Education*, Lisse, Swets and Zeitlinger.

ROSENSHINE, B. and FURST, N. (1973) 'The use of direct observation to study teaching', in TRAVERS, R. M. W. (Ed.) *Second Handbook of Research on Teaching*, Chicago, Rand McNally.

RYANS, D. G. (1970) *Characteristics of Teachers. Their Description, Comparison and Appraisal: A Critical Study*, Washington, American Council of Education.

SCHEFFLER, I. (1960) *The Language of Education*, Springfield, Charles C. Thomas.

SHAVELSON, R. J. (1973) 'What is the basic skill?' *Journal of Teacher Education*, 24, pp. 144–51.

SHAVELSON, R. J., WEBB, N. M. and BURSTEIN, L. (1986) 'Measurement of teaching', in WITTROCK, M. C. (Ed.) *Handbook of Research on Teaching*, New York, Macmillan, pp. 50–91.

SHULMAN, L. S. (1986) 'Paradigms and research programs in the study of teaching: a contemporary perspective', in WITTROCK M. C. (Ed.) *Handbook of Research on Teaching*, New York, Macmillan, pp. 3–36.

SIMON, H. (1970) *The Sciences of the Artificial*, Cambridge, Massachusetts, The MIT Press.

SIMON, A and BOYER, E. G. (Eds) (1970) *Mirrors for Behavior: An Anthology of Classroom Observation Instruments*, Philadelphia, Research for Better Schools.

SMITH, B. O. and ENNIS, R. H. (Eds) (1961) *Language and Concepts in Education*, Chicago, Rand McNally.

SMITH, L.M. and GEOFFREY W. (1968) *The Complexities of an Urban Classroom. An Analysis Toward A General Theory of Teaching*, New York, Holt, Rinehart and Winston.

SNOW, R. E. (1973) 'Theory construction for research on teaching', in TRAVERS, R. M. (Ed.) *Second Handbook of Research on Teaching*, Chicago, Rand McNally.

STOLUROW, L. M. (1965) 'Model the Master Teacher or Master the Teaching Model', in KRUMBOLTZ, J.D. (Ed.) *Learning and the Educational Process*, Chicago, Rand McNally, pp. 223–47.

WELFORD, A. T. (1968) *Fundamentals of Skill*, London, Methuen.

ZAHORIK, J. A. (1970) 'The effects of planning on teaching', *Elementary School Journal*, 71, pp. 143–51.

Part II
Case Studies of Teachers' Practice

Chapter 7

Curriculum Stories: Four Case Studies of Social Studies Teaching

Sigrun Gudmundsdóttir

Experienced social studies teachers know their subject matter differently than novice teachers do. They have developed pedagogical content knowledge in the subject they teach. Central to the pedagogical content knowledge of experienced social studies teachers are the curriculum stories they use to organize content in their curriculum. This study describes and compares the pedagogical content knowledge of experienced and novice social studies teachers. Especially, the study focuses on the curriculum storymaking of experienced teachers and the novice teachers' attempts at creating such powerful curriculum devices. Data analysis draws on Shulman's (1987) 'Model of Pedagogical Reasoning and Action' and Applebee's (1978) modification of Vygotsky's (1962) stages of development. It illuminates dimensions in the curriculum storymaking of experts and novices that ranges from the simple, concrete and factual to the more inclusive, powerful and economic ideas.

Introduction

Teaching is transformation of knowledge and skills into a form that students can understand. This is a complex process that involves the creation of meaning out of texts. This process often includes the making of a *story* in the curriculum, a 'curriculum story'. Such a story is embedded in the curriculum and organizes content for pedagogical purposes. Curriculum storymaking is a process that novice teachers find problematic, but experienced teachers find so natural and easy that they may not always be aware of it. The ability to create and communicate curriculum stories is an important element of experienced teachers' pedagogical content knowledge (Gudmundsdottir, 1988). This study investigates how two novice social studies teachers, Cathy and Chris, and two experienced teachers, Harry and David, use the idea of a story to create meaning in the curriculum they teach.[1] The novice teachers are struggling to create and tell their stories and only attempt to do so for small units within the curriculum. The experienced teachers use several stories to communicate to students the ideas they feel are important in the curriculum.

Methodology

The four teachers teach high school social studies in the same school district in Northern California. This study focuses on the curriculum in one of the courses each of them taught. Data collection involved interviews that were tape recorded and transcribed verbatim, classroom observations, and collection of relevant documents in the field. For the novices, data collection covered a period of twelve months during the 1984–1985 academic year when Cathy and Chris were enrolled in a teacher education program. As part of their teacher education program, they taught freshman social studies[2]. They were interviewed seven times in one and a half to two hour interviews and participated in planning cycles that consisted of a pre-observation interview, observation, and post-observation interview.

The experienced teachers teach in the same high school. Harry and David are considered excellent teachers by colleagues and students.[3] After spending four intensive months in their classrooms, I tend to agree. They teach junior students American history. Harry teaches general track students and David teaches advanced placement students. They are veterans, having taught social studies for thirty-seven and twenty-eight years respectively. Data collection covered a period of four months during the 1984–1985 academic year. Harry and David were interviewed five and six times respectively, with each interview lasting between one and a half to two hours. They were observed twenty-two and twenty times respectively. Classroom interactions were tape recorded and transcribed verbatim.

Interview questions for all four teachers emerged from Shulman's (1987) model of the knowledge base of teaching. Questions focused on their content knowledge, pedagogical knowledge, their curriculum, and students in their class.

Theoretical Framework

Experienced teachers often have a unique understanding of the content they teach, called *pedagogical content knowledge* (Shulman, 1987). This way of knowing means that content has been restructured for pedagogical purposes. The curriculum story plays an important function in this process since it is one of the devices teachers use to organize content into a form that is meaningful for them and accessible for students.

The idea of a 'curriculum story' is similar to the common meaning of the word. A story has a beginning, a middle and an end. It has characters, plot, or plots, and sub-plots. The story is a device that helps teachers unify theory and specific events or ideas. Research on teacher planning supports the idea that teachers use an organizing principle in the curriculum. Yinger (1977) calls a similar process 'major idea' and Ben-Peretz (1975) 'curriculum potential'. These conceptions recognize the fact that curriculum materials include far more ideas than the developers intended. The idea of a curriculum story, however, goes beyond identifying a potential or an idea in the curriculum. It develops and dramatizes this idea through characters, plots and sub-plots.

Teachers probably spend their entire careers developing their stories as they encounter different kinds of courses and students. Most teachers are unaware of the stories they use, at least the teachers in this study did not know they used this mode of organizing the curriculum. Harry and David only discovered they had curriculum stories when they had to explain their curriculum to someone who has had a limited experience with American high schools. Experienced teachers are probably aware of the ideas they feel are important in the curriculum and how they are connected. Unlike Athena who leaped out of Zeus' head as a mature woman, the curriculum stories have taken years to develop, a process that will never end as long as the teachers continue to grow professionally. Each year teachers modify and shape their stories to take into account new understanding or insight. Some aspects of each story are found to be successful and they may grow stronger. Others are not successful and they grow weaker or disappear altogether. In this way the curriculum stories become representations of the teachers' experiences — representations that communicate their pedagogical understanding of the discipline they teach. Representing knowledge in this way is not unique to teachers since people of all ages and from all over the world function by constructing representations of experiences (Bruner, 1966).

The four teachers in this study constitute a continuum in the development of curriculum stories. The teachers' stories relate to Vygotsky's (1962) stages of concept development as elaborated by Applebee (1978). Applebee's model was developed for analyzing children's stories. It has six categories that progressively show the development of children's ability to construct stories. While the data in this study does not allow for such detailed analysis, a modified version of Applebee's framework can be used to illuminate dimensions in the story making and story telling of adults, who are novice and experienced teachers (see Figure 7.1).[4] The three key elements in the structure focus on relationships between shared attributes (shown as straight lines), central idea or core (parallelogram centers), and incidents or elements in the story (circ. t). Applebee's theoretical

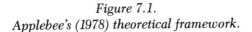

Figure 7.1.
Applebee's (1978) theoretical framework.

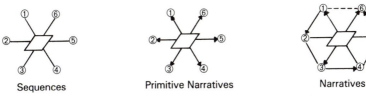

| Sequences | Primitive Narratives | Narratives |

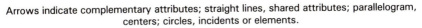

Arrows indicate complementary attributes; straight lines, shared attributes; parallelogram, centers; circles, incidents or elements.

framework shows how the structure of teachers' curriculum stories develop and unfold, from the simple to the more complex.

The simplest idea of curriculum storymaking used in this study is the *sequence*. It relates incidents to a central idea in a concrete and factual way. In terms of curriculum stories this involves teachers simply following the textbook using its structure or creating one that is similar to the way topics and ideas are covered. Each topic or page in the book is treated on its own and there are no attempts at connecting ideas and events over time. The emphasis is on covering the book or worksheets. This means that teachers have to keep the core constant. Topics and pages are related to the core individually 'on the basis of perceived similarity' (Applebee, 1978, p.68). The 'perceived similarity', in this case, is the organization of topics and ideas in the textbook. This modest structure both simplifies the task of organizing the curriculum and provides a method of dealing with future and unknown classroom events. With the *primitive narrative* further complexity is added to the structure. Now, complementarity strengthens the links with the core. This new structural element further simplifies the complex task of managing facts, ideas and pages in a book. At this stage the parts of the story hold together from the beginning to the end. The last stage of storymaking, as proposed by Applebee is the *narrative*. The plot is reversible in that the ending is entailed within the plot. Incidents are linked both through chaining and to a central idea. The story now has unity and focus that enables teachers to connect ideas across the curriculum and effectively communicate them to students.

From the theoretical perspective of Applebee and Vygotsky one would expect the experienced teachers' curriculum stories to be characterized by the last stage, narratives, and the novices' stories can be expected to be related to the earlier stages. The case studies of the four social studies teachers show that there are differences among them in expertise and style in curriculum storymaking.

Curriculum Stories

Novice Teachers

Cathy and Chris have degrees in anthropology from a private college that is renowned for its anthropology department. They consider themselves to have an excellent background in their respective specializations within anthropology. Both of them have found that their specialized content knowledge not only needs adjusting for pedagogical purposes, but is also of limited use when teaching high school social studies. Their efforts at curriculum storymaking have been central to the process of developing their pedagogical content knowledge.

As a part of the teacher education program, Cathy and Chris taught first year social studies in the same high school district in Northern California. Cathy considers herself to be an archeologist. Her areas of expertise are the methodological and scientific aspects of archeology, and ancient Greece. The official title of her course is 'Geography and cultural anthropology', but she calls it 'world cultures' and teaches it as such. She follows the textbook closely, and tries to use the idea of 'change' as a way of connecting the chapters. However, this does not work out since Cathy has not elaborated what kind of 'change' she is concerned with.

Observations of Cathy's teaching did not reveal any signs of her using this idea. Instead, she adopts the textbook's structure. It begins with a unit on geography and then moves to different regions of the world. Cathy thinks of this course of study 'in small pieces, region by region'. Geography is the starting point for each region because '(the students) have got to know where the place is'. The unit on Japan is an example of this approach. She began the unit with physical geography, emphasizing the causal relationship between geography, industry, and culture. After describing to students the lack of land and natural resources in Japan, Cathy moved to industrialization. She asked questions like: Why did they become industrialized? Students were invited to draw on the work they had just completed in physical geography to explore the answers. From industrialization they moved to culture: family, writing, haiku poetry and negative space in Japanese painting.

Geography was not part of Cathy's undergraduate education, consequently her knowledge in this area was limited before she taught the course. However, she learned about geography by having to teach it. Gradually, she began to integrate in her teaching this new knowledge with her content knowledge in anthroploogy. For example, the unit of Africa began with physical geography. Then she moved on to the Bushmen of the Kalahari desert. She told students about the Bushmen, describing the place they lived and their lifestyle. She then gave them a map of a site where Bushmen had lived in and a list of artefacts found. With this exercise she tried out with her class a typical archeology exercise that she had tried as a student in one of her favorite college classes. However, now the exercise had a strong geographical element.

Chris is the second novice social studies teacher. He is an anthropologist with expertise in cultural anthropology and human evolution. His special interests within anthropology are anthropological research methods, like those used by cultural anthropologists and researchers investigating human evolution. Early in the teacher education program, Chris realized that his specialist knowledge in human evolution did not translate immediately into something he could teach. He found that he was unable to make his content knowledge pedagogical. Later in the year Chris is able to do so in a limited way. He tries to transform his expert knowledge by creating a 'story' in a unit. He succeeds only when the content is close to the anthropology he knows. His stories only last for one unit. The following unit has to start afresh with a new story. Chris does not have a story for the whole curriculum. He has vague ideas about 'Man' as central to the course of study. This idea, however, does not influence or shape the stories for individual units.

Chris is working on his stories and he gets help from the teacher education program. In one of his teacher education classes, Chris comes across Schwab's (1961/1978) idea of the syntactical and substantive structures of the disciplines. The idea of substantive structures makes Chris think about cultural anthropology and human evolution in terms of different conceptions of anthropology. He uses the substantive structures of anthropology to conceptualize the stories, and he uses ideas from the curriculum class to structure them into units to teach. When he teaches topics that are outside anthropology, he cannot turn to the discipline for stories so he follows the textbook.

If the substantive structures help Chris conceptualize stories, then the syntactic structures help him finding effective ways of telling them. The syntactic structures of anthropology are evident in classroom activities. He simulated the ethnographic interview with his class where he played an informant and students were anthropologists. He also taught the theory of evolution by using skulls as evidence for the theory. He likes to give his students materials that resemble the kinds of experiences anthropologists have doing field work. He shows them movies and pictures of exotic cultures and has the students reacting as anthropologists. The ways of the anthropologist as a researcher making sense of data permeate all activities Chris has his students engage in.

Experienced Teachers

David and Harry teach juniors American history in the same school. David teaches an advanced placement class. The curriculum in his class reflects the official aim of the class. David's aim is to help his students pass the AP exam and at the same time he wants to provide them with an experience that is equivalent to a college freshman course.

The course curriculum begins with the Age of Jackson. David has divided the curriculum into historical periods that reflect a traditional chronological organization. David structures the course content with curriculum stories. He tells four stories that start with the Age of Jackson: *Women, Reform, Supreme Court Cases,* and *Wars.* The stories cover the whole curriculum, and are told throughout the school year. At different times, David calls upon the stories to explain and illuminate the topics he wants to cover.

One of David's stories, the *Story of Supreme Court Cases,* can serve as an example of how he uses his stories (see Figure 7.2). It's a useful story, according to David, because it reflects the mood of the country during each period. Sometimes, it is ahead of both public opinion and the administration in Washington, sometimes it lags behind. This story begins during the Age of Jackson. David captures the mood of pre-Civil War American society by covering the Dread Scott case. This case, according to David, captures in a nutshell the conflict between the North and the South that eventually exploded in the Civil War. This story is not called upon during the next historical period, the Civil War. David's other stories step in and interpret ideas and events. In the

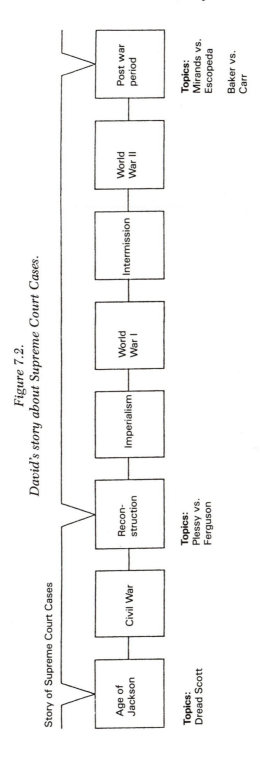

Figure 7.2.
David's story about Supreme Court Cases.

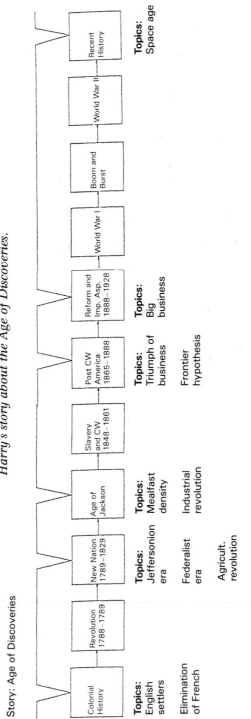

Figure 7.3.
Harry's story about the Age of Discoveries.

following period, Reconstruction, the story of *Supreme Court Cases* becomes important again. He uses this story to explain the civil rights blacks enjoyed for a short time. In the following four periods: Imperialism, World War I, Intermission, and World War II, this story is not called upon to explain ideas in the curriculum. Other stories take to the stage, and the story of *Supreme Court Cases* is in the wings waiting its 'grand appearance' in the last period of the course, Post War Period. During this period the story of *Supreme Court Cases* is very important since it helps explain the key ideas in the Civil Rights Movement.

Harry is the second veteran teacher. His knowledge of American history is impressive. He majored in history and has a masters degree in the subject. He teaches American history to a general track class. The curriculum covers the period from Columbus' Discovery of America to the present day. Like David's curriculum, it is a chronological progression that tends to emphasize political and economical history. The curriculum is divided into periods, some of which correspond to the textbook, but most of them are Harry's idea.

Harry has developed four stories that he communicates through the curriculum: *The Growth of Opportunities, The Age of Discoveries, Clash of Cultures,* and *Transformations of Cultures and Institutions.* Each story highlights different topics in the curriculum and connects them to similar ideas previously covered. One of Harry's stories, the *Age of Discoveries* serves as an example of the ways in which he uses his curriculum stories.

Figure 7.3 shows how the story about the *Age of Discoveries* highlights events and ideas during several periods in the history of the United States. Initially, this is an important story since it highlights several topics during the first period covered in the course, colonial history. Among those topics highlighted during this period are the English settlers and how they eliminated the French in the new world. During the next period, the American Revolution, Americans were occupied with other issues, so this story does not highlight any ideas. The story about the *Age of Discoveries* becomes prominent again in the period called Jacksonian Era. The topics highlighted are manifest destiny and the industrial revolution. The *Age of Discoveries* is now westward expansion that takes the boundaries of this story to the Pacific Ocean. During the Civil War this story is not called upon to highlight any topic. However, it takes on new dimensions in the period called post Civil War when Harry covers the frontier hypothesis and the triumph of capitalism. Discoveries are no longer new land, now they are foreign policy, that are highlighted in the period's reform and imperial aspiration. The story about the *Age of Discoveries* steps to the sidelines until the last period in the course of study where it highlights explorations in space.

Discussion

Curriculum stories are probably important characteristics of expertise in teaching. The stories demonstrate a command over the subject matter that enables teachers to see the 'big picture' in the curriculum. Research on teaching has shown that teachers' subject matter competence is not always related to student achievement. The curriculum stories, however, represent a different way of subject matter competence, called pedagogical content knowledge. This body of knowledge is probably not approached by traditional teacher competency tests. Curriculum stories have important similarities to elements of expertise as described by Berliner and Carter (1986), Carter and Doyle (1987) and Carter, Sabers, Cushing, Pinneger and Berliner (1987). These researchers identify the ability to perceive the 'big picture' and the ability to distinguish between relevant and irrelevant data as critical elements of pedagogical expertise. The curriculum stories enable teachers to perceive the big picture of the content in the curriculum and hold it for a full school year, and at the same time sort out important ideas from less important ones.

The curriculum stories of Harry and David are both economical and powerful (Bruner, 1966). The stories are economical because they enable the teachers to hold in mind large items of information. This is important, because in teaching good stories simplify the steps teachers need to take in processing information to show students how ideas or events are related to a larger set of issues. The curriculum stories are powerful because they enable teachers and their students to connect ideas and facts that on the surface seem to have very little in common. Powerful stories enable teachers to move back and forth between classroom activities and their story to illustrate a point and move the story plot along.

The differences in the storymaking and storytelling of novices and experienced teachers are highlighted when the accounts of Cathy, Chris, David and Harry are examined using Applebee's categories of storymaking. Cathy can be placed within the category called 'sequences'. She emphasizes coverage and follows the textbook closely, teaching world cultures region by region. She has a method that links information in a concrete and factual way: she teaches physical geography first, then causal relationships between geography, industry and culture. Her idea of 'change' as a unifying idea is not strong enough to influence the development of the ideas in the curriculum. Her method works with what Applebee calls 'perceived similarities'. She moves through the pieces in the order they are presented in the textbook without activating ideas that move beyond the 'surface' (Buissis, Chittenden and Amarel, 1976). She has reasonable mastery over the individual pieces, or the chapters, and frequently she is able to add information from other sources. A change in her conceptual or theoretical understanding is needed before she is able to go beyond the pieces and perceive or create the deeper structure that connects the chapters.

Chris, on the other hand, seems to be functioning within two categories, the primitive narrative and sequences. He tries to construct stories for individual units that have a central idea that he is able to communicate to students. His stories represent a mastery over content that enable him to move beyond perceived similarities, or the surface, to the ideas that connect the content he has to teach in individual units. In a way, he is drawing on the 'deep curriculum'

(Buissis *et al.*, 1976). The stories integrate content in a meaningful way, and at the same time relate classroom activities and assignments to his goal for the unit. Creating stories, however, is hard work for a novice teacher. When Chris is unable to formulate a story he defaults to the textbook, or the sequence category. His teaching style changes and he begins to talk about covering pages in the book or doing exercises at the end of chapters.

The case study of Chris demonstrates the importance of content knowledge in constructing curriculum stories. He has good stories for the units where he is able to draw on his content knowledge. In the stories he attempts to restructure his content knowledge for pedagogical purposes. Chris' problem is, however, that he is unable to maintain his stories across units.

The ability to maintain stories over a period of time distinguishes him from Harry and David who not only maintain a story throughout the school year, but they use several stories to account for the complexities of ideas they want to communicate to students. Chris seems to have a curriculum that is more like an 'anthology of short stories' rather than the 'extended novels' of the experienced teachers (Gudmundsdottir, 1988). His stories do not have the grand plots that hold the curriculum together over an extended period of time. But, Chris recognizes that a unifying idea is needed, for individual units. Cathy and Chris have vague ideas about an extended novel: Cathy's novel is going to be about change, and Chris' about Man.

David's and Harry's curriculum stories have all the elements of a narrative. Their stories have central ideas that shape the plots and at the same time move it along, connecting current events ideas covered earlier in the year. The experienced teachers' stories enable them to move between individual historical events, major historical ideas and classroom activities and assignments. The stories represent a unique interaction between their personal theory of the teaching of history and the practice of teaching.

Storytelling is not new to education. Some of mankind's greatest educators were storytellers. Storytelling as a way of instructing youngsters is older than the idea of organized education. It seems fitting that such an ancient and efficient teaching method should be one of the key ingredients in the developing pedagogical content knowledge of novice teachers.

Conclusion

Curriculum stories help teachers manage complex ideas and make them accessible for students. For the stories to function effectively they need a central idea that is strong enough to shape the events that contribute to the development of the plot. The experienced teachers have such stories. The curriculum stories are central to their pedagogical content knowledge. The novices are in the process of building their pedagogical content knowledge. Their attempts at storymaking and storytelling demonstrate the importance of their content knowledge in the development of pedagogical content knowledge.

Notes

1 All names are pseudonyms.
2 Chris and Cathy are subjects in 'The Knowledge Growth in Teaching' project.
3 Harry and David are subjects in a dissertation study at Stanford University School of Education, 'Knowledge Use Among Experienced High School Teachers', Gudmundsdottir (1987).
4 Cathy, Chris, Harry and David are part of two projects that did not set out to investigate curriculum stories. The discovery of the curriculum stories was part of those delightful surprises that characterize qualitative research. A study specifically focusing on curriculum storymaking would probably benefit from a detailed analysis using all of Applebee's categories.

References

APPLEBEE, A. (1978) *The Child's Concept of Story*, London, Cambridge University Press.

BEN-PERETZ,, M., (1975) 'The concept of curriculum potential', *Curriculum Theory Network*, 5.

BERLINER, D. and CARTER, K. (1986) 'Differences in processing classroom information by expert and novice teachers', paper presented at ISATT, Leuven, Belgium.

BRUNER, J. (1966) *Toward a Theory of Instruction*, New York, W. W. Norton and Company, Inc.

BUISSIS, A., CHITTENDEN, E. and AMAREL, M. (1976) *Beyond the Surface Curriculum*, Boulder, Colo., Westview Press.

CARTER, K. and DOYLE, W. (1987) 'Teachers' knowledge structures and comprehension processes', in CALDERHEAD J. (Ed.) *Exploring Teachers' Thinking*, London, Holt, Rinehart and Winston.

CARTER, K., SABERS, D., CUSHING, K., PINNEGAR, S., and BERLINER, D. (1987) 'Processing and using information about students: a study of expert, novice, and postulant teachers', *Teaching and Teacher Education*, 3, 2.

DEWEY, J. (1904/1964) 'The relation of theory to practice in education', in ARCHAMBAULT, R. (Ed.) *Dewey on Education*, Chicago, University of Chicago Press.

GUDMUNDSDOTTIR, S. (1988) 'Knowledge use among experienced teachers: Four case studies of high school teaching', Unpublished doctoral dissertation, Stanford University School of Education.

SCHWAB, J. J. (1961/1978) 'Education and the structure of the disciplines,' in WESTBURY, I. and WILKOF, N. (Eds) *Science, Curriculum, and Liberal Education*, Chicago, University of Chicago Press.

SHULMAN, L.S. (1987) 'Knowledge and teaching: Foundations of the new reforms,' *Harvard Educational Review*, 57, 1, pp. 1–22.

VYGOTSKY, L. (1962) *Thought and Language*. Cambridge Mass., MIT Press.

YINGER, R. (1977) 'A study of teacher planning: Description and theory development using ethnographic and information processing methods'. Unpublished doctoral dissertation, Michigan State University.

Chapter 8

Teachers' Classroom Activities and Certainty/Uncertainty Orientation

Günter Huber and Jürgen Roth

The orientation towards aspects of uncertainty vs. certainty of situations seems to be of great importance for teachers' planning and decision-making, and especially for those activities which generally are called educational style. By choosing more direct instructional methods teachers can avoid confrontation with their students' various, often conflicting ways of thinking; more indirect or open teaching methods on the other hand offer teachers the chance to learn more about their students' views of the world.

In this study three elementary school teachers, who participated in the pre-service training of eighteen student-teachers, reported about their educational goals, strategies, and orientations. The teachers' uncertainty/certainty orientation was measured by objective instruments, and they were observed during their lessons. In a seminar, the student-teachers later analyzed their experiences in these teachers' classrooms. Thus we can compare teachers' orientation style, their thinking about classroom activities, direct observational data from their classrooms, and student-teachers' reflections about classroom activities.

In their classes, the teachers acted according to their orientation style. Uncertainty oriented student-teachers experienced challenges in classrooms of uncertainty oriented teachers; certainty oriented student-teachers felt frustrated and intimidated. As a reaction they rejected these teachers and their teaching styles.

Theoretical Background

Education and instruction are characterized foremost by their social nature. Teachers and students try to realize their intentions under given personal and situational conditions. Their actions in turn lead to distinct group processes and structures, which then again influence the actors' orientations. The orientation towards situations is a personal factor that seems to be of special importance for teachers' classroom activities. This factor can be located on the dimension of uncertainty/certainty (Sorrentino and Hewitt, 1984; Sorrentino, Short and Raynor 1984). Sorrentino and Short (1985) showed interindividual differences in uncertainty/certainty orientation, and they verified influence on the regulation of social behavior: persons cope with uncertainty regarding the effects of own actions differently but consistently in varying situations. While some persons tend to approach situations where outcomes are uncertain, others tend to avoid them. Whereas the former individuals are more interested in finding out more about themselves and/or the actual situation, the latter try to retain available opinions and knowledge structures. Uncertainty oriented persons tend to consider their interaction partners' perspectives, i.e. they analyze the quality of arguments more than the source of argumentation (Petty and Cacioppo, 1984), and thus they seek 'to attain clarity'. Certainty oriented persons on the other hand try 'to maintain clarity' by means of following the majority or joining the point of view of other socially important persons. In learning situations they prefer to work individually or competitively, in order to conserve or to carry out their own ideas. Uncertainty oriented learners, however, prefer cooperative arrangements which enable them to elaborate differing viewpoints or even to integrate them (Hüber and Maikler, 1987; Hüber, 1988).

The uncertainty/certainty dimension should be especially important for teachers' planning and decision-making for those activities which generally are called educational style. By choosing more direct instructional methods teachers can avoid confrontation with their students' various, often conflicting ways of thinking, analyzing tasks, solving problems etc. More indirect or open teaching methods on the other hand offer teachers the chance to learn more about their students' views of the world. Moreover, by knowing the interpretations and problem-solving strategies of their students the teachers can help them to gradually discover on their own the appropriateness/inappropriateness of their approaches. Clearly, direct teaching creates a climate of certainty both for teachers and students, whereas open learning situations demand the personal motivation of all involved individuals to attain consensus among controversial ideas and behaviors.

Empirical Study

Hypotheses

Teachers try to realize specific goals by specific modes of teaching/learning according to their orientation towards certainty vs. uncertainty in classroom situations. Certainty oriented teachers prefer to structure classroom activities as precisely as possible, uncertainty oriented teachers at least tend to give way to ideas, suggestions, needs of students in social interaction. In correspondence to their orientation style, interdependence between teachers and students in social relations is more limited or more open.

Subjects

Subjects were three elementary school teachers. The teachers participated in the pre-service training of eighteen student-teachers. One day every week the student-teachers (in groups of six members) observed the activities in the three teachers' classrooms. The teachers and the student-teachers additionally met every week during a seminar in order to analyze and reflect upon their activities/observations.

Procedures and Materials

The second author, who organized this part of the pre-service training, and who ran the accompanying seminar, observed the classroom teaching by turns every week.

Orientation style of the teachers was assessed by two rating scales, one measuring the amount of uncertainty/openness for ambiguity, the other the amount of certainty/structure favoured by the subjects. A procedure described by Sorrentino, Short and Raynor (1984) led to a U/C-O score. Results of a former study with ninety-one subjects (teachers and student-teachers) served as the basis from which we determined our subjects' specific orientation styles. This was done by the first author; the second author was not informed about the teachers' orientations until he had written down his observations and conclusions.

In order to get access to teacher thinking the teachers were asked to describe (in written form) their educational goals in the classroom, teaching/learning modes used in their classrooms, and their own experiences and/or aspirations.

Classroom activities were observed directly by the second author, who took notes during his visits in the classrooms. He also gathered indirect information about classroom activities by taking notes of the student-teachers' descriptions of their experiences as observers in the classrooms.

In this way we can compare (1) teachers' orientation style, (2) their thinking about important professional actions (subjects' perspective), (3) direct observational data from their classrooms (investigator's perspective), and (4) student-teachers' reflections about classroom activities.

Results

Teachers' Orientation Style

The three teachers Christine, Birgit and Anna, were located on the dimension of U/C-O by comparing the resultant measures of their openness for ambiguity and of preference for structure with the results of a former study (Hüber and

Maikler, 1987) including teachers as subjects. Figure 8 shows the three present subjects' U/C-O scores as well as the arithmetic mean from the former teacher sample, which we used as criterion for placing the three subjects on the dimension of uncertainty/certainty. Thus we found that Christine was highly uncertainty oriented, Birgit was moderately uncertainty oriented, and Anna was clearly certainty oriented.

Figure 8.1.
Teachers' U/C-orientation.

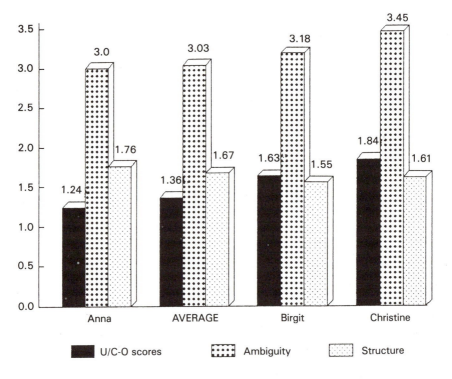

Teachers' Self-Descriptions

The teachers were asked to describe their educational style with regard to their goals, the strategies used to realize these goals, and their general pedagogical orientation. In the following we report the most important contents of the three teachers' self-descriptions.

Anna

Goals:

— students should like to go to school, and they should come trustingly;

— students should come to me with their problems, I will try to help them;

— students should learn about values and norms;

— readiness for tolerance and non-aggressive solving of conflicts should be promoted in school.

Strategies:

— intensive cooperation with parents . . . ;

— stimulate students to come to terms with each others' ideas;

— start with the children's experiences.

Orientation:

— I take the children's present and future very seriously;

— learning should be fun.

These statements were quite formal; their formulation is in some ways similar to the preambles of the official syllabus.

Birgit

Goals for students:

— students should gain self control;

— students should develop initiative, civil courage, and responsibility;

— children should become sensitive and aware of threatening authorities;

— they should not believe everything but view things critically;

— that the subject matter is appealing to children, and that they use their heads as well as their hands.

Goals as a teacher

— At least once a day I'd like to be totally immersed in harmony;

— I'd like children to demand that the teacher's task is to help and to explain . . . ;

— I'd like to be able to keep things better organized . . . ;

— I'd like to be able to speak in a lower voice and be more relaxed;

— I'd like to be able to be more differentiating . . . ;

— to be able to use more games in the classroom.

Strategies:

— I would prefer if there was no sharp distinction between school and life;

— I would like to behave in such a way that everybody likes me.

Orientation

— I'd like to be as I am now, but at the same time I'd prefer to be as systematic and perfect (with respect to the administrative demands of teaching) as a teacher getting an 'A' by his or her supervisor should be.

Birgit explained that she wrote down these statements spontaneously and 'without considering' any consequences.

Christine

Goals:

— help my students to acquire substantial, basic knowledge, to avoid failures as much as possible, and to have the students experience success in order that they may enjoy learning . . . ;
— motivate those students who do not get much help at home.

Strategies:

— precisely planned lessons, well structured blackboard design, a quiet working atmosphere, and clearly structured assignments for my students;
— at first I try to achieve these working conditions by being friendly and if this does not work I apply management techniques . . . ;
— considering my students' feelings;
— as I don't dare to expose myself to totally unstructured situations, I now usually make decisions about the structure and content of my students' tasks, but I also try to allow the students more freedom in terms of their own work: more team work, more practical experience, more flexibility and individuality in structuring of individual active learning time, differential treatment according to ability; i.e. I as a teacher am only available for those students who need help, and I initiate student activity instead of simply distributing information.

Orientation:

— I have already become more tolerant!
— I experienced that my students are more engaged to their work and they have more fun, but student achievements in my classes seem to be lower this year. I feel uncertain, even intimidated and partially embarrassed when doing my work in front of observers (student-teachers, lecturers from the university), because my informal ways may give the impression that I am a lazy teacher, who has not prepared today's lesson well. I hope to become daring and assertive, and to continue along this new direction in the right manner.

These statements on the one hand are very open and spontaneous, but contrary to the other two teachers' statements they also contained remarks about doubts and uncertainty.

Observations of the Lecturer

The second author accompanied eighteen student-teachers in three groups of six members during one term every week for one morning to one of the classrooms of the three teachers. During this time he observed the ongoing classroom activities as well as the interactions between teachers and student-teachers. The following descriptions were formulated by the second author *before* he was informed about the teachers' and his student-teachers' scores on the U/C-O dimension. The first paragraph in every description contains summarized observations, the second paragraph gives a summary of the observer's field notes of his inferences during the observations.

The Teachers in Their Classrooms

Anna

This teacher planned her lessons very carefully: she started each session with a well-prepared introduction before she continued with the lesson. Matters of importance were written on the blackboard, and as teaching supplements she used transparencies as well as worksheets. Towards the end of each lesson she made sure that the pupils had written down all the necessary information. The overall impression of the observer was that this teacher employed systematic and formal classroom teaching-style procedures (in the sense of a predictable series of steps).

However, when the teacher was forced to change her style of teaching, she felt intimidated and assessed the situation as 'disturbing'. Consequently, she always tried to get back to the 'old and familiar situation' as fast as possible. She seemed to know what was appropriate and important for her students. She also seemed to be convinced about the appropriateness of her teaching style. For this reason the teacher avoided reflecting upon her influence on the students.

Birgit

This teacher tried to integrate the central components of the Freinet approach into her teaching style by allowing independent study in specified learning situations, discussion circles etc. She has been teaching like this for the last three years. The fact that every one of her students was unafraid to discuss anything with her that came to mind was principally noticed by the observer, as well as that the students in no way attempted to avoid conflicts. In conflicting or critical situations this teacher always tried to find out how much she contributed to the situation. However, on occasions when she felt that the Freinet method was too daring she would use 'real lessons'.

What was most impressive about this classroom situation was the atmosphere of spontaneity and creativity. This teacher seemed to be very convinced that new possible modes of teaching can open up a reservoir of yet untouched teaching potential. Moreover, she was fully aware of the effects she had on the class as a person.

Christine

Her lessons were planned very well i.e. they were carefully structured and each sequence was based on the previous one. This teacher preferred to teach her students in the form of discourse. Specific activities or social organizations (working with a partner, team learning, etc.) were conducted more or less along a formal criterion and did not always correlate with what the actual classroom events demanded. The teacher had firm control of the class, and not much 'idling' occurred during her lessons. This did not give the students much of a chance to spontaneously develop ideas on their own. The teacher-student interactions appeared controlled and detached, though emotionally warm.

The observer noted additionally that this teacher seemed to be convinced that the attitudes of students could be changed by teaching in a well planned way. This teacher did not reflect upon her personal effects on the class.

Interactions Between Teachers and Student-Teachers

These are notes taken by the second author when he observed how the teachers introduced the student-teachers to the practical aspects of teaching in the classroom.

Anna

The student-teachers experienced lessons that were minutely planned. The teacher's motto was: 'The more minutely and extensively a lesson is prepared, the better it is'. Moreover, she also demonstrated a broad spectrum of instructional possibilities. She always excused herself when she felt that she had not been thorough enough. The formal structure of the presentation made it easy for the student-teachers to take notes during the lessons. Nevertheless, sometimes they did find her lessons somewhat 'dry' and too 'teacher-centered'. But mostly they were grateful for the precise and clear structure of the lesson, and they expressed admiration for the teacher's honest and persistent striving to organize content of the subject matter in such a way that the pupils could understand the presented information more easily.

After watching this teacher model the student-teachers felt confident and ready to prepare a lesson and to teach it in the classroom. They were no longer afraid of being criticized, and they were willing to accept critical commentaries.

The interactions between teacher and student-teachers were cordial, but reserved, although the teacher did try to help every student-teacher to become a 'good' teacher, regardless of how much time she did have to invest.

Birgit

Generally student-teachers liked to go to this teacher's classroom because they were always able to observe something new, i.e. classroom activities following the pedagogical thoughts of Freinet. But at the beginning they rarely dared to teach a lesson or even part of a lesson on their own. The student-teachers preferred to teach pre-structured lessons step by step, although they did accept the teacher's alternative teaching style — which on the one hand made many of them feel insecure. After a short time the student-teachers were divided into two factions, one group who was enthusiastic and the other who rejected the teacher's style. Later the student-teachers started to take responsibility and to teach on their own for limited periods of time. Some student-teachers were willing to accept the fact that the personality of a teacher influences his/her mode of teaching. Again other student-teachers behaved in a rejecting and sometimes defensive manner. They continued attending as student-teachers, since it is part of the required curriculum for teachers' pre-service training, but they exchanged remarks like 'This isn't a lesson!' or 'We are wasting our time!'. The teacher does not succeed in convincing these student-teachers otherwise. The more she tried to communicate with them in a very open manner, the more she was hurt by their rejection.

The teacher would have liked very much to interact with the student-teachers as she did with her students — such as inviting them to her home. Sometimes she had difficulties differentiating between students and student-teachers. She suffered if she noticed that some student-teachers were unable or unwilling 'to tune in on her wavelength'. Other student-teachers, however, discovered that her teaching style offered the students opportunities to develop other than usual abilities, that the social interactions between students were more friendly - and that the students still were successful in their studies.

Christine

Here the student-teachers were offered clear structures in every respect possible. The teacher's lessons, the occasions for observation, opportunities for student-teachers' practising teaching in the classroom, discussions after the lessons all were clearly structured, and they did not confront the student-teachers with 'surprising' events. The student-teachers also had to prepare their lessons formally, structuring their activities step by step. A meeting took place after the student-teachers had taught a lesson. Here everything was discussed in great detail and specific emphasis was given to problems of subject matter.

The relation between the teacher and her student-teachers was cordial but clearly reserved and differentiated: I am the teacher, you are the student-teachers. I can teach you how to teach well. If you are able to do what I am showing you, and if you do it in the way I demonstrate, you will succeed.

Student-teachers back in the university

Following classroom observations and teaching, the three groups (altogether eighteen student-teachers), three teachers, and the second author met for a seminar at the university. Compared to the teachers, the average student-teacher was less in favour of controversial situations, and s/he wanted more structure, thus attaining lower U/C-O scores, i.e. this sample of student-teachers on the average was more certainty oriented (see Figure 8.2).

Figure 8.2.
Student-teachers' U/C-O.

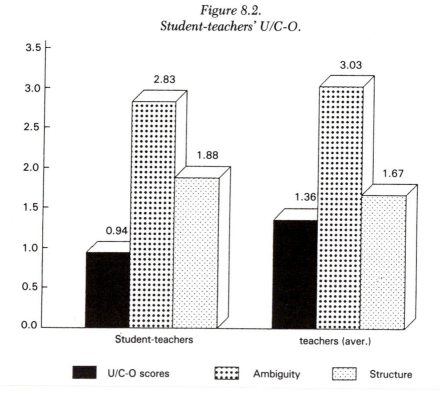

Two very different types of situations always characterized the beginning of the seminar sessions. Both atmosphere and processing of content problems were highly dependent on the participants' experiences during the preceding morning in the classrooms.

There were student-teachers who witnessed lessons without 'frictions'; now they expected theoretical information from us to use for reflection and elaboration of their classroom experiences. Mostly these students had observed carefully preplanned lessons, and they had developed a feeling of security in this type of educational environment. They expressed their overall impressions with remarks like 'I would like to be able to teach in the same way!', 'This teacher was really good!', or 'If I get enough out of these lessons, then I'll be a good teacher, too!'. It seemed that these lessons met strong needs of student-teachers regarding the general idea of teaching, for availability of procedures, and malleability of products. The student-teachers developed solidarity with the teacher they observed and identified with her as well.

On the other hand there were students who brought a great amount of emotions, even aggressiveness into the seminar, due to the uncertainties and contradictions they had to overcome during the morning hours spent in the classroom. Those teachers who based their lessons on their students' everyday reality and their subjective points of view could not avoid being exposed to their own limits, doubts or even their weak points. This type of teaching soon forced student-teachers to understand that structured lessons just create an artificial pedagogical climate of certainty, with smoothly flowing argumentations and mildly dosed, 'didactized' controversies. Many student-teachers participating in lessons tailored to the students' subjective experiences and conceptions began to feel intimidated; they no longer were 'fed', they no longer just consumed the 'goods' of teaching, but were forced to make up their own minds. Sometimes they not only expressed their uneasiness about this way of teaching, but also their anger: 'How shall I ever learn teaching!', 'We don't have equal chances — nobody shows us how to teach!' or 'There is no order at all!'.

The interaction during the seminar thus reflected the group dynamics among those student-teachers that attended Birgit's lessons. Student-teachers whose needs for structured experiences were fulfilled by what they had observed during the morning in the classroom rejected every information or discussion during the seminar that could disturb their opinions. They reacted most negatively to every approach to analyze more closely or even to address latent or manifest emotions of the other participants in the seminar. They evaluated those discussions as disturbing or as a waste of time. Student-teachers, on the other hand, who were intimidated by what they had observed during the morning began to envy those participants who seemed to have received something that had been 'denied' to them.

Discussion

Teaching Style and U/C-Orientation of Teachers

The documented thinking of the teachers corresponded clearly with their specific orientation style. Christine, the most uncertainty oriented teacher in this sample, strived to integrate open learning situations with constrictive conditions at school. At the same time she reflected on her own capabilities/incapabilities to bridge these contradictions in her daily routines. Birgit was less ambivalent in her statements; she wanted students to be able to act on their own, to develop responsibility, to become aware of threatening influences of authorities, to demand explanations and help from their teachers. She wanted to be independent, and at the same time fulfil her supervisors' expectations. Finally, Anne, a more certainty oriented teacher, made rather formal statements which could have been taken from the official syllabus.

The relation between teacher thinking and actual classroom behavior was more complex in this study. The expectations from the perspective of uncertainty-certainty theory were confirmed in the cases of Anne (certainty oriented/direct teaching) and Birgit (uncertainty oriented/indirect teaching). The activities of Christine, however, were somewhat more difficult to explain in the light of our hypotheses. Her teaching was fairly structured, and did not leave much freedom for spontaneous student behavior — as long as she felt confined by school regulations. As soon as for instance the university lecturer suggested alternatives in classroom proceedings she did not hesitate to arrange learning situations that provoked controversies among her students and forced them to make up their own minds.

Following a suggestion by Sorrentino (personal communication, July 1988), the structure component in the measure of U/C-orientation may be more appropriate than the resultant score in explaining these differences between classroom behaviors of our three teachers. As a matter of fact, the data in figure 8.1 can explain this: though Christine had the highest scores for preference of controversial situations (3.45), she exceeded Birgit in her structure score (1.61 vs. 1.55). By structure alone Birgit and Christine could change their positions on the U/C dimension; from these indications we would be able to forecast that Birgit will try to design open learning environments whenever possible, whereas Christine would be inclined to do the same, but take the risks only if she can rely on an authority to take responsibility.

This is exactly what has been observed: Christine's 'regular' lessons were highly structured, and she mostly tried to guide the students' learning processes. But whenever she was offered the opportunity to allow more freedom for student interactions and subject matter, i.e. if the lecturer, who represented a source of formal competence, took part of the responsibility, then — due to her high preference for controversial situations — she felt free to create and master much more open teaching/learning situations. When she was aware of a backup like this, especially if the person whom she evaluated as being competent, was present in her classroom, she presumable delegated responsibility and realized learning situations that came closer to her 'ideals' of teaching.

Relations Between Teachers' and Student-Teachers' U/C-Os

Uncertainty oriented student-teachers evaluated certainty oriented teachers as 'boring', 'dry', and 'fatiguing'; certainty oriented student-teachers on the other hand became supportive and gained assertiveness by observing these teachers. Uncertainty oriented student-teachers experienced challenges in classrooms of uncertainty oriented teachers; certainty oriented student-teachers felt frustrated and intimidated. As a reaction they rejected these teachers and their teaching styles.

Due to the small number of classrooms and student-teachers involved in this study, these findings are preliminary at best. However, within the limits of this study they are highly consistent.

Seminar Style and U/C-O of Student-Teachers

For an efficient organization of the seminar dealing with the student-teachers' classroom experiences we had to cope with a dilemma: student-teachers who observed teaching according to a style that matched their own U/C-O were open to reflect upon their experiences under the perspective of pedagogical-didactical theories. This approach however was totally unsuited for student-teachers who observed classrooms where learning was not organized in accordance to their certainty/uncertainty needs. Neglecting their controversial observations and feelings would mean not to take their contributions seriously. If nevertheless the seminar only would have considered theoretical problems, they would have withdrawn their attentiveness, resigned or they would have tried to permanently change the topic of discussion. The opposite would have been to start the seminar with an analysis of the other student-teachers' frustrated expectations and discuss the reasons for their intimidating experiences. This approach, however, would imply a totally different style for the seminar: no longer would the discussion be detached on subject matter and teaching methods, but focused on highly personal questions, on problems which could cause high ego involvement. From communication about content the seminar would switch frequently to the level of metacommunication. Exactly this type of person-centered approach the first group of student-teachers would reject, because such discussions would mean a waste of time in their eyes. To solve this dilemma, alternative techniques for seminars related to practical experiences of student-teachers will have to be designed and studied.

Conclusions

The findings from observations in classrooms and seminar sessions led to the conclusion that issues of personal development are highly influential for teacher education. Supposing that every teacher is eager to mediate her/his knowledge and experience to student-teachers, and every student-teacher is eager to accept this information, then the probability of positive results (in the sense of modifying teaching behavior, attitude change etc.) of observing lessons and trying to teach would be much greater, if student-teachers are confronted less with experiences that contradict their expectations of how a good lesson should be organized. Instead they should be exposed to finer dosages of discrepancies. In other words: teacher education should not only relate to person-environment interaction as a topic of theoretical interest, but should try to take those interactions into account which comprise the organization of learning situations for student-teachers.

Considering these conclusions for planning a practice-oriented seminar in teacher education, we first have to teach student-teachers that there is a broad variety of differently structured teaching methods; there are not just good or bad methods. The criterion is the goal of teaching/learning: there are objectives that can be reached faster or more precisely by structured approaches, whereas others need more open, less structured methods. The goal of teacher education should be to enable teachers to choose from a broad repertory of methods available. Nevertheless, there will be teachers who are more in favour of one approach than the other. Those differences will become quite obvious on specific occasions like observing a classroom as a member of a group of student-teachers or discussing teaching problems with colleagues. These situations will be suited for successful learning only if teacher education can establish a positive attitude towards the variability of teacher behavior: nothing is good or bad on its own by definition, but only in relation to the factors influencing classroom activities. A good teacher should be able to look at the problem of teaching style from the point of view of complementary approaches.

References

HÜBER, G. L. (1988) 'Preferences for learning situations and uncertainty orientation: A cross-cultural comparison', paper presented at a symposium 'Motivation by content and interest — an European approach in learning motivation?' at the annual convention of the AERA, New Orleans.

HÜBER, G. L., and MAIKLER, M. K. (1987) *Bereitschaft zur Kooperation und Gewißheits-/Ungewißheitsorientierung bei Studenten*. Bericht Nr. 19 aus dem Arbeitsbereich Pädagogische Psychologie der Universität Tübingen.

PETTY, R. E., and CACIOPPO, J. T. (1984) 'The effects of involvement on responses to argument quantity and quality: Central and peripheral routes to persuasion', *Journal of Personality and Social Psychology*, 46, pp. 69–81.

SORRENTINO, R. M., and HEWITT, E. C. (1984) 'The uncertainty-reducing properties of achievement tasks revisited', *Journal of Personality and Social Psychology*, 46 pp. 884–99.

SORRENTINO, R. M., and SHORT, J.-A. C. (1985) Uncertainty orientation, motivation and cognition, in SORRENTINO, R. M. and HIGGINS E. C. (Eds) *The handbook of motivation and cognition: Foundations of social behavior*, New York, Guilford, pp. 379–403.

SORRENTINO, R. M., SHORT, J.-A. C, and RAYNOR, J. O. (1984) 'Uncertainty orientation: Implications for affective and congnitive views of achievement behavior', *Journal of Personality and Social behavior*, 46, pp. 189–206.

Chapter 9

Perspective, Evangelism and Reflection in Teacher Education

Don Massey and Charles Chamberlin

The chapter presents case studies of fourteen elementary school teachers who had recently graduated from the University of Alberta describing their perspectives. Using Werner's (1977) conception that perspective provides 'presuppositions on the basis of which men structure their experiences, select their projects, and construct their multiple realities,' (p. 52), Kent's and Sarah's perspectives are described, their ideal and technological realities are inferred, and the roots of their views on teaching are examined. The tacit, unreflective nature of these perspectives seemed to be rooted in early learning in home, school, church and community, and later initial teaching experiences in schools.

Implications for teacher education follow from the apparent unreflective acquisition of teachers' perspectives. Suggestions by Tom (1984), Zeichner and Tabachnick (1985) and Schön (1987) point toward more emphasis on critical reflection about teaching and teacher socialization.

Finally, the moral base of teaching is noted, with particular concern for the political and social implications of teachers' relationships to their students. The effect of the hidden curriculum in Kent's and Sarah's classrooms suggests more emphasis by teacher educators on morality and ideology.

In 1977 Walter Werner extensively examined the concept of teacher perspective and its pervasive effect on daily teaching decisions and thinking. Werner described the breadth and power of perspective as being our natural attitude, with which 'we order, interpret and act within a life-world which is taken for granted by us' (pp. 14–15). Unique human perspectives provide 'presuppositions on the basis of which men (*sic*) structure their experiences, select their projects, and construct their multiple realities' (p. 52). The various forms of these internal realities shape thinking and acting, whether ideal realities, about what teaching is or should be, or technological realities based on need for control, efficiency and predictability of outcomes. As teacher educators plan their university programs, they need to consider the roots of these perspectives, ideal realities, and technological realities. This chapter reports on a research project which

133

used Werner's conception of teacher perspective to help examine the relationship between fourteen beginning teachers' daily teaching decisions and thinking, their underlying perspectives, ideal realities and technological realities, and the roots of those perspectives in the socialization effects of family, school and church, later university teaching, and finally experiences with teaching colleagues. The chapter concludes with some implications for teacher educators.

Procedures

This study of the impact of teacher perspective was carried out over a four month period employing a naturalistic observation research methodology with follow up interviews after each observation. Beginning teachers were observed weekly as they taught.

Teachers were interviewed an average of fourteen times over the research period. The interviews gave the teachers an opportunity to talk about their life-world, opinions, and acts, in their own words. Additional documents, such as lesson plans, report cards, and school policies were also collected.

The teachers included twelve elementary school teachers and two recent graduates working as interns under the supervision of experienced teachers.

In September 1986, eight professors and six graduate students began four months of classroom observation and interviews with fourteen recent graduates of an elementary school teacher education program. The study was conducted for the purpose of determining how beginning teachers define and interpret their teaching world, make decisions, and construct their actions. This study of teacher perspective was to be used for refining and redesigning teacher preservice and inservice programs.

Werner (1977) suggested that perspective is a broad world view which people develop from reflection on their own experience in their own culture. He believed perspective was intended to mean an active ordering of perceived reality.

These goals directed the study:

1   To identify the kinds of perspectives held and the decisions made throughout the year by teachers who were recent graduates of the teacher education program of the University of Alberta.
2   To identify the factors affecting teacher perspectives and decision-making.
3   To gain insights into redesigning or refining the teacher education program.
3   To provide understanding in redesigning inservice programs.

Validity concerns for the study were guided by Guba's (1981) concept of naturalistic research.

1 Prolonged engagement at a site to overcome, so far as possible, distortions produced by a researcher's presence and to provide the researcher with the opportunity to test his or her own biases and perceptions, as well as those of his or her respondent.

2 Persistent observation, in order to identify pervasive qualities as well as atypical characteristics.

3 Peer debriefing, to provide the inquirer with the opportunity to test his or her growing insights and to expose the researcher to searching questions.

4 Triangulation, whereby a variety of data sources are used to cross-check data and interpretations.

5 Collection of referential adequacy materials, whereby documents or 'slice of life' data items are collected against which findings and interpretations can later be tested.

6 Member checks, whereby data and interpretations are continuously tested as they are derived with members of the various audiences and groups from which data are solicited.

A unique feature of this study was the meetings held by the research team. Initially meetings were held to orient and train the team. Guba's work on the trustworthiness of naturalistic inquiries, Wolcott's (1975) writing on the importance of detailed field notes, and a list of questions on perspective adapted from Werner's (1977) study were used.

Regular meetings were held to discuss the methods of data collection, interviews, and emerging themes. Guest researchers and outside professors were included in these meetings serving in roles of clarifiers and critics. When the case studies were completed, project meetings were devoted to data interpretation, writing, and formatting the final report. As the fourteen case study authors discussed the themes from their individual case studies in these meetings, consensus was sought on major conclusions to be included in the final report. Each of the fourteen case studies was included in the appendix of the final report.

One of the strengths of this study was that it collected data from fourteen teachers. A limitation of this report is that it draws primarily from the case studies of the two authors. For a complete report see: Blakey *et al* (1987) *Sources of Teachers' Perspectives and Decisions: Implications for Preservice and Inservice Education*.

Brief descriptions of the case studies of Kent and Sarah follow to illustrate the relationships among some of their decisions, thinking, perspectives, and the roots of those perspectives.

Kent Reed's Decisions

Kent Reed taught a fifth grade class at Robertson Elementary–Junior High School. Located in the inner-city, the number of students in his class varied almost daily from fifteen to twenty. The context in which Kent made his daily decisions was dominated by his concern with the need for student control.

Activity Centres

One of the first decisions Kent made early in the year was to try to move to less teacher centred classroom instruction. He intended to increase the use of activity centres with his class. In our first interview, prior to school start up in September, he stated:

> I want to try and develop centres this year and really develop one centre at a time. I want to develop a really good meaningful centre for them. That is currently what I am playing around with. (Massey, 1988, p. 14).

> I want to try and get them, like the one with social studies, I would like it subject based but also activity based . . . there is a kit there that is map and globe reading skills . . . I want them to try and continue that on their own as well as for me to provide some instruction and provide guidance to help them work through much of that kit. The other two, this one is the listening centre. I don't know if I am going to have to start off with to provide some free time activity which will reinforce their reading habits and listening skills. The third area I am not quite sure. I would like to develop a Math centre that will be all hands on to reinforce what they will be doing in the classroom. (*ibid* p. 17)

In spite of the desire to move to student-centred instruction, Kent continued, for the most part, to use a teacher dominant model of instruction. Whole class instruction and individual work was the order of the day. Student desks remained in rows and the usual physical changes to the classroom which accompany the use of learning centres failed to appear.

Student Groups

The second decision in an effort to provide less teacher dominated instruction was to use a variety of student groupings. Kent articulated the benefits of such groupings as:

> Well just the socialization . . . that's part of it. I think it makes it a more enjoyable experience for them because they have fun. They can work with someone and they can do their work. (*ibid* p. 19)

However his groups were established in an effort to assist students with academic problems. Reading, for example, was the reason he had children work in pairs. This meant that he had to control which students worked together, and his choices were not always to the liking of students who had their own ideas as to whom they would prefer to work alongside. Kent recalled:

> After the initial shock of who they were paired up with . . . there was an awful lot of moaning and groaning but it has to be that way I think. Otherwise it just wouldn't work at all . . . some kids (would) be totally frustrated. I am sure that some are frustrated (now). At least they had someone with them who knew the answers or could get the answers . . . and share with them . . . . They were sitting quietly kind of contributing to the pairing up so you know hopefully it works out. I have to have them paired up with someone who can read, for sure, you know at this level. (*ibid* p. 22)

It was clear that Kent's ideal for students to have fun and enjoy the social interaction of peers was not being met.

Program Content

Content decisions in Kent's classroom were left to others. Program decisions were, for the most part, defined outside the doors of his classroom. Although he indicated at some point that he would modify programs, he tended to take the program as a given, and non-problematic.

> I'm, I guess, a type of teacher . . . if I'm teaching a grade, I use strictly all the curriculum books and I use everything, and I kind of go right in order until I know it.

> I want to know what the full program is, just what the whole is about until I understand everything that I'm supposed to be teaching, everything that's in the books and you know . . . next year, or even some months, or weeks I relax and say: 'Gee, I'm going to try this next . . . and it's not really there but it might be a really good idea to try it'. (*ibid* p. 28).

This was further exemplified by his reaction to a question about the social studies kit he was using.

> I didn't really choose it, it was in place when I came in and, uh, whatever was there I just . . . took over. (*ibid* p. 29)

Classroom Management

By far the most prominent in import and number were the decisions Kent made regarding classroom management. Classroom control was a constant concern and Kent had put in place a number of strategies to deal with what he considered inappropriate student behavior.

I have ... simple rules that I informed all the students of .... One person talks at a time, you raise your hand um ... when you want to speak, no walking around during the lesson. (*ibid* p. 23)

All that I ask is that everyone else listen and that they put their hand up and that one person talks at a time. It takes a while for them to realize that this is the system in my classroom but that is the only one you know I can deal with without going crazy myself. And usually it does work but mind you in the afternoon it does get a little bit noisier. (*ibid* p. 24)

In response to a question about penalties, Kent explained that he kept a chart on the front chalkboard which listed the students' names.

They have two free warnings. The first two check marks are like free ... just to warn them in case they have forgotten and every one after, fifteen minutes .... There is a maximum of forty-five minutes and then they get a pink sheet. There was a boy in here yesterday who during social studies class had four check marks, the second warning and three fifteen minute detentions and I sent him at recess down to Ralph (the assistant principal who filled out a behavior contract on a pink sheet.) That is a five step part that the school has. (*ibid* p. 23)

What Perspective Seemed to Underly Kent's Decisions?

Elements of Perspective

Why did Kent make the decisions he made? Kent's classroom decisions and action can be better understood when viewed through Werner's framework of perspective.

As an important part of perspective Werner identifies reality co-ordinates which he calls *paramount reality, technological reality*, and *ideal reality*. Paramount reality deals with the teacher's everyday world. It includes the stocks of knowledge, hopes, fears, motives and logics which are in use. Ideal reality would redefine what teaching is or should be under controlled conditions. Within technological realities the emphasis is related primarily to the way of doing things, in procedures, methods, treatments, remedial acts, and rules. These techniques are based upon the interests of control, certainty, efficiency and predictability of outcomes. Werner indicates that some realities are more important and powerful for teachers than others. For Kent, the ideal and technological realities were both concerns.

Ideal realities were important to Kent. In many ways Kent articulated the kind of ideal he sought for his classroom. This ideal appeared to be a classroom in which the pattern of teaching was student-centred. Students would work in clusters rather than rows. They would be involved in individual and small group activities. Learners would take on responsibility for tasks and their own behavior. He said:

I know I want to move from the way I am now teaching to a certain way I've got in mind. I use that one teacher who I was student-teaching with in grades 1 and 2 who had centres as a model. (*ibid* p. 16)

Kent, for the most part, appeared to take for granted the values of a more student-centred approach. Little time was spent talking about the merits of such instruction, although he considered it had social benefits for students as well as benefits for the teacher.

I think it takes a lot of strain off of teaching if the kids are doing their work instead of the teacher doing the work for them . . . . You know you are not going to get so fatigued . . . if they are in groups and they are doing the work instead of you standing at the front . . . . It's easier to go around and monitor, find out where a group is having a problem instead of going around to each individual when they get stuck. This way they can help each other . . . I like them to kind of solve their problems, work together to solve their problems, and then come to me if they are having difficulty. (*ibid* pp. 19–20)

An important question, and one unanswered by Werner, is where Kent's notions of the ideal classroom were rooted? Why did the technological reality co-ordinate dominate his planning? The explanation, in part, probably lies within the profession itself. Cuban (1984) outlines the shift from teacher-centred to student-centred classrooms as a major historical trend in the schools of North America. One might expect that Kent, as a product of a teacher education program, would have been exposed to this historical trend. He was also part of a school staff where several teachers used learning centres as the basis of their classroom organization. And, in particular he had been exposed during his student-teaching to a teacher who successfully used learning centres with young children.

If ideal realities dominated Kent's planning, then technological realities dominated his actions. When faced with a classroom decision Kent opted for alternatives which would produce control and certainty in the classroom. Here is how he felt about it.

I have to have tight control in the classroom and strict discipline. But people say, but you do it in a low-key manner. You don't like (shouts) 'Hey! Sit down!' or that type of thing . . . but (quietly) 'sit down'. (*ibid* p. 23)

What I learned in the teacher effectiveness (program) is you have to use a system. They give you guidelines and they give you advice, but you have to have a system that's going to cut down on any frustration or anxiety on your part so that you will not be negative with the students. (*ibid* p. 26)

In the morning you get in the car and are thinking all the way, like O.K. what if she (a particular difficult student) does this and what happens if she does that . . . like I would have twenty set plays in my mind of what I would have to do if so and so . . . acted up and if her two allies came in. It would just be a real circus if you didn't clamp down. (*ibid* p. 26)

Again, the technological reality with the focus on the ways of doing things and the concern with control came in conflict with ideal reality.

With the type of students that we have here, I am wondering if it is worth it because they haven't got that kind of control . . . but, maybe I should stick (to it), put one (learning centre) out and just stick with it and just keep hammering away until they do get used to it and know how to treat a centre. (*ibid* p. 20)

The domination of technological reality consistently prevented Kent from moving toward the more ideal student-centred classroom he sought. Five months into the school term he was still talking about wanting to establish learning centres.

Kent's preference for acting upon technological reality concerns helps to explain his approach to content. Using programs designed by others, sanctioned by the authorities and prepackaged for his use provided him with the certainty that he valued. In his words:

And that's it . . . I think . . . I want to be safe and secure first, and then I'll go and try to experiment. (*ibid* p. 28)

All these things are done by specialists and consultants and boards and everything, and it's all approved by . . . you know . . . the Province of Alberta so . . . if there is something wrong, then it's not my fault and I . . . everyone tries to struggle through so I have no qualms whatsoever, because it's all been approved. (*ibid* p. 29)

Reality Sources

An important question is why did Kent consistently give up ideal reality for technological reality? The answer, though not completely clear, appears in part related to the kind of experiences Kent had both in his own school life and in his teacher education program. He spoke glowingly of the primary teacher who had successfully involved him as a student-teacher in her student-centred classroom. It stood in sharp contrast to his own previous school experience. This one brief student-teaching experience and probably more generally, some of his course work had led him to believe that student-centred classrooms were desirable. What is also clear is that this notion of the ideal classroom had not been adequately developed for Kent to put it into action. In his words:

In the back of my mind I would like to see someone who has done it differently because I think it should be more the responsibility of the students . . . they would be getting a lot more out of it because it would be hands on as well. (*ibid* p. 20)

Kent's acceptance of the program in place is puzzling. Given the conventional wisdom in the field of elementary education one might have expected him to express some concern with program fit. Many areas of the program failed to meet the needs of his particular class. Often, the material was too abstract and frequently the topics were not even remotely related to the lives of these inner city children. However, again the need for certainty of outcomes and emphasis on procedures made the nature of the content a secondary concern. Until Kent was able to manage the routine of the classroom to his satisfaction, content was not a major concern.

Sarah's Decisions

Decision 1: Teacher Directed Math, Child-Centred Language Programs

Sarah taught a grade 1–2 split class at Purple school, for her second year. One of her key decisions was whether to stay with the child-centred, manipulation-of-materials based, discovery approach to math called *Math Their Way* which the other five experienced teachers in her grade level used, or to move to a teacher-directed, worksheet laden form of direct instruction a former classmate used.

> My math is different, I think I have my kids sitting down and doing more paper and pencil kind of work instead of letting them run, like, other teachers may not agree with me, but I just don't think they are learning, I don't know what it is they are learning when they are on the floor and playing with blocks constantly from week to week . . . I don't know, maybe it's just me, but I know I wasn't allowed to fool around with all that kind of stuff . . . . Like some teachers can handle that, they don't mind kids running all over the place, you know they think play is the greatest, and that is how kids learn, but that is just their philosophy, but it's not mine, I can't stand the noise, and I can't stand people throwing elastics and throwing blocks, and not doing what they are supposed to be doing, not on task. (Chamberlin, 1988, pp. 49–50)

Not only did Sarah reject the noise and chaos, but she had no faith in discovery learning:

> I have a friend teaching at another school and she had taught her kids the facts to five already by Christmas. I'm going, 'God, here I am!' And then I kind of really panicked, so then I went home and said, 'Well, I've got to teach them something. And I don't think they're gonna learn this $1 + 2 = 3$ by themselves. I'm gonna have to teach them . . . I had to struggle to get my facts taught to 10 as it was'. They needed practice and

practice and practice . . . I didn't think that they were gonna look on the floor and, like, start playing with red and green and decide, 'Oh my goodness, look at this, 1 and 2 is 3.' Like no way . . . I gave them directions instead of letting them discover . . . . When it came to adding, I didn't do it their way, I did it my way! So I gave them more sit-down and-fill-in-the-blank kind of sheets and like practice sheets. (*ibid* p. 51)

Sarah also felt unneeded in the discovery approach.

I think more kids will know if I tell them than if I don't tell them . . . I mean teacher-directed . . . I'm not here just to watch them learn and watch them struggle. Like I should help them. Watching them play, I just feel like I might as well not even be here. Like, my little brother could sit here. My mom could be here. They wouldn't be doing anything that I'm not doing. Maybe that's the feeling. I think they should need me. I want to feel needed. (*ibid* p. 53)

However, Sarah's skepticism about child-centred learning in math was in contrast to her confidence in language growth through child-centred methods. Sarah explained 'our' language program this way:

It might not be spelt right but it sounds right because that's how they are writing, they are writing the way they speak, they've got ten spelling mistakes or whatever because I encourage them to inventive spell, like spell how you think it sounds . . . . We read and read, you read and you do Morning Message and you do that spelling that we are doing, when they are ready they are going to realize that 'r', it's not just 'r' at the end of the word, its 'er' when you say October, so it'll come, you just have to have faith. Like I had trouble at first thinking, 'oh, these kids are going to grow up to be illiterate, they are not going to know how to spell or anything.' But they do, like they catch on to these things . . . . It's just a patience thing, like you just have to trust that it's going to happen, it's going to happen in spite of me, that's how kids learn to read and write . . . . You just do all these things and it just happens, it does. (*ibid* p. 53)

Sarah saw no contradiction in these two approaches to math and language teaching, arguing that you have to try different things to see what works best for you. In the next section, as we look at the perspective underlying these decisions about teaching methods, Sarah's meaning of 'what works' will become clearer.

Decision 2: Teaching Good Manners and Respect

An observer in Sarah's classroom would quickly realize how important good manners were to Sarah. Sarah explained it this way:

Now this might not sound like very much but manners, some of those children I don't know what goes on in their houses, but they come to school, they burp, they don't put their hand up, they're interrupting people, they push people, they grab things out of people's hands, throw things, like can you pass me the scissors please . . . they just throw it at you. And you think where have these people been. Like just simple things like that is something I'll have to spend a lot of time on with some of these children. (*ibid* p. 56)

Sarah felt these children should have learned good manners at home, but clearly parents had not taught their children to sit still, be polite, and show respect. She asked:

How can you expect them to go to the gym and sit there like a good audience? They don't even know what that means. You know, they're so used to just jumping up and doing their own thing. Maybe I'm wrong but . . . even when you go to church these days, you see little kids. They don't sit down quiet. They're playing. They're talking loud. They're driving trucks all over the place . . . . And where is that coming from? Well, one thing, home. They probably never have to sit still, maybe not even to eat dinner. Probably eat in the living room watching TV or whatever. But still, like they've got to learn it somewhere. So, I just think school might be a good place for them to start for some of them. (*ibid* p. 58)

Again, this decision to emphasize learning proper manners and respect reflects an underlying perspective rooted in Sarah's life history, as will be discussed in following sections.

Decision 3: Positive Reinforcement

Sarah used lots of praise and positive reinforcement with her students, but with some students more than others. When asked about her decision of who to praise how much, Sarah gave the following example to illustrate:

First impression I had of his mom was when she came to talk to me at parent–teacher interview. Like I told her your son is a very difficult boy to handle . . . . And then he was chewing on his jacket and she slapped it out of his mouth and, 'Get that GD thing out of your mouth' and I thought no wonder he's like this and I thought I am not going to get any support from her, you can see where this poor kid is coming from. And she said that he had stole something from the store and that she caught him so she made him take it back so he took it back and she made him apologize. Well you couldn't tell a kid like him, 'Say sorry,' he would never do that, he has to do it on his own or forget it, so she said, 'say it RIGHT NOW' and he wouldn't so she goes, 'OK, you're kicked out of the house.' Can you imagine, a seven year old boy, she goes, 'Yeh I packed his bag and put it on the doorstep and I said I don't ever want to see your face again' and I thought no wonder this little boy comes to school and he's in such a bad way some days. You know, after I understood kind of his family situation like you just had to, anything that he did like you really (would say), 'that's great'. (*ibid* pp. 66–67)

Another child Sarah praised extensively also had problems at home, as Sarah explained:

I've got children with problems. Like this one mother said to me, 'Well like anything she does wrong you tell me right now because I've got a big belt at home and that solves it all.' I thought to myself, 'I am not going to say a word,' like you don't want to, every time the kid goes home like you are almost afraid to even say anything like in a little way negative because you are afraid what's going to happen to her when she gets home, like I don't know, it just goes beyond like teaching them they are so deprived in other areas that you just, you want to cry sometimes and you think, 'How can this happen to this poor person?' (*ibid* p. 44)

These decisions to use praise more generously with some children were based on Sarah's perspective also, and are rooted in her own upbringing.

Perspective Underlying Sarah's Decisions

Werner (1977) saw perspective as an active *ordering* of perceived reality, using 'presuppositions on the basis of which men structure their experiences, select their projects, and construct their multiple realities' (p. 52). For Sarah, the ideal reality about relationships among people, especially between children and adult parents and teachers, included the expectation that people should treat each other with respect, and specifically that children should show deference to adults in positions of authority. Indeed, the common element in her decisions about how to teach math and language was the concern for orderliness, quiet, and children's respect for the teacher's role in the classroom.

One major difference between the *Math Their Way* and whole language approaches was in the degree of disorder and noise associated with math. While students could explore language during journal writing time without much teacher direction, they did so quietly in their seats. Their need for assistance was little more than bringing up their dictionary for Sarah to write a word in when they got stuck and couldn't inventive spell, so Sarah did not feel 'pulled in 20 different directions' as she did when children were on the floor in small groups learning math through play. Sarah explained as follows:

You can't expect them to be quiet when they're throwing things around in those tubs, like it's just impossible for the ones who are trying to understand to think and for you to even explain with all this noise is going on. Like it was just a sanity thing. Like you can only take it for so long, and then you, 'Ahhhhhh, I can't take this any more.' (*ibid* p. 48)

Sarah also expected to have students who had learned manners and respect at home, but when she discovered they had not, she bent every effort toward teaching them the kind of manners she had been brought up to value.

Sarah's perspective on manners, order, and respect was clearly rooted in her own upbringing. Sarah always used courtesy words when speaking to her students, and this emphasis on please, thank you, and good manners came from her parents, Sarah said.

Similarly, Sarah contrasted her students' failure to accept parental authority to her own upbringing:

So her mother came in and we were just talking and I said, 'Oh, Janelle, now that your mother's going to have another baby, you're going to have to be a big help around the house, right?' Her mother said, 'She won't do anything around the house.' And so then I thought to myself, 'She won't. Who's in charge here, her or you?' So if her mother lets her get away with not helping around the house? Her mother says, 'Oh, she won't help!' I can imagine when I was a kid. I'm sure we all try it. 'You're gonna set the table.' 'No, I WON'T!' Like I'd never get away with that. (*ibid* p. 59)

This perspective of proper manners and respect which Sarah's parents had insisted upon was also reinforced by Sarah's teachers when she entered school. Sarah remembered:

Like when I was in Grade 1, boy, there were times, we were almost not really scared of the teacher but you wouldn't even dare to talk to her unless you said please or something, 'May I please go to the bathroom.' . . . I remember one time I was in Grade 3 I said to the teacher, 'Can I go to the bathroom, please?' and she just looked at me, 'Pardon?' And I think 'What am I saying wrong?' and finally I realized that I was supposed to say 'May I go to the bathroom please?' but she made me say it three times right in front of the whole class and then I realized I was supposed to say 'may' so that was kind of a hard lesson. (*ibid* p. 19)

Clearly, Sarah's grade 1 and 3 teachers not only insisted on proper manners, but also expected Sarah to respect the teacher's role in requiring those manners be shown. Sarah recalled that her teachers were successful in demanding that they be accepted as 'the boss'.

Like when I remember back when I was a kid, I wouldn't even dream of doing or saying . . . half of those things those kids do . . . . Like I look back at my teachers . . . they didn't have the problems that I seem to be having. Like I don't think they ever had to say five times to us 'Be quiet.' We just listened. 'Cause you knew when you go to school, the teacher's the boss and that's who you listen to. (*ibid* p. 20)

Sarah's abhorrence of today's children's noisy play in church suggests that her perspective on proper manners and respect was the joint product of family, school and church mutually reinforcing community standards during her childhood in a small town. That deeply rooted ideal reality seemed tacit, pervasive and powerful in shaping her teaching decisions.

In the same vein, Sarah's decision to provide more praise and emotional support for some of her students who came from homes lacking those elements reveals more of her ideal reality about desirable relationships among people, particularly between adults in authority and relatively dependent children. In recounting a story of one boy in her class whose mother had threatened him, Sarah contrasted this with her own relationship with her parents:

> I don't think I realized how much the home has an impact on kids. Like I guess because I came from such a supportive family that I thought everyone was like that, you know. Like my friends, they all seemed to have the same and then when you see kids like this and then you meet their parents you think, 'Holy smokes. Look what I'm up against here.' (*ibid* pp. 55–6)

The supportive family relationships she had experienced with her parents seemed to have been the roots from which sprang her perspective on desirable relationships.

These examples illustrate the connections among Sarah's classroom decisions, her underlying perspective, and the roots of that perspective in her family, school, and church upbringing, tempered by her growing experience as a teacher. Notably absent from the factors influencing these aspects of Sarah's perspective is her four-year university teacher education program, though the in-school practicum was powerful.

During Sarah's university program she came to Purple School for an eight-week practicum. She recalled how she had been socialized into the school norms:

> When I was student-teaching here this school was brand new, that was the first year it was open. The Principal that started this school had an idea in mind of how he wanted this school to operate and he interviewed all these people with this idea so that everyone would have the same philosophy when they got here. Language Arts was a major deal and everything else just comes out of that, without the child's language you might as well forget it, you can't teach the curriculum anyway. That was the kind of message I got. And so he had hand-picked all these teachers and they came here and they had a little retreat and they came up with all these kinds of things.... They had things pretty well set, like this is what we do here at this school kind of thing, so you just kind of learn how to fit in and that's what I did, I wasn't about to argue. They had me like streamlined or whatever into their way of thinking almost kind of, so that was fine and then I went back to university. (*ibid* p. 24)

During the eight-week practicum, Sarah's teacher, Susan, showed her how to teach, and explained why that was a good way to teach. Not only was Susan modelling a particular view of teaching, but most other teachers in the school were also. All of them used 'morning message', USSR (Uninterrupted Sustained Silent Reading), avoided basal readers and workbooks, had children write and publish bound 'books', etc. Staff meetings sometimes broke up into grade level groups where all six teachers of split grade one-two classes would develop common goals and plans.

Later, when Sarah returned as an intern, she worked with Max, a teacher in another split one-two class, who shared much of Susan's perspective and practices. All of these colleagues had taught for ten years or more, and Sarah felt intimidated by their experience and expertise. She was being socialized into the norms of the staff group, 'streamlined into their way of thinking'. She was more likely to accept those norms because she was being evaluated by her teacher, and because she was impressed by the amount of experience all the other staff had.

The situation at Purple School was unusual in its homogeneous staff, chosen for a common perspective on teaching, and consequently exerting a more powerful socializing effect on the neophyte seeking acceptance. Sarah held a strong respect for experience, and was most aware of her lack of it and how much experience other staff had. Consequently, she comments on the 'streamlining' saying 'so that was fine'. She had learned the philosophy, norms, and practices of this specific school staff, and had eight weeks to practise teaching in their manner. She was successful in using the Purple methods and had gained some acceptance into the group.

After Sarah completed her fourth year at university, she returned to Purple School as an intern in Max's split grade one-two class. In mid-August she came to help Max set up the room. Max said he emphasized 'getting a natural flow to the day', establishing a set of routines so students always know what comes next, making transitions easy, automatic. Morning message, calendar, and *Math Their Way* using tubs containing manipulable materials were daily activities to be established with students so there could be individual responsibility for getting ready, Max said. Sarah recalled:

> When I first started I was an intern with Max, so at the beginning of the year he'd say, 'This is what you have to do the first day of school.' And all the things he was preparing were the same things that I was doing when I was student teaching here. (*ibid* p. 26)

The socialization into the staff norms which had begun during her eight-week practicum was continued during Sarah's brief internship with Max. The unanimity of teacher-held norms was certainly an atypical situation in which to begin teaching, and prevented Sarah from hearing from teachers holding alternative views, or subgroups with competing norms. Rather, there seemed to be only one right perspective on teaching for anyone on the Purple staff. Seemingly, the principal and all the teachers shared a body of beliefs, philosophy, practices, and norms which Sarah acquired. Sarah came to see herself as part of that group with many views and methods in common, and talked about how 'we' do things.

> A lot of what we do in grade one and two are similar, all the grade one and two classes do the same things, some of the same things. We all do morning message, we all have calendar time, we all have journal writing time, we all have printing time, chanting poems, quiet reading time. It's just that when you do them during the day is up to the individual teacher, but they don't really vary that much I don't think. (*ibid* p. 27)

Purple School has won an international award for its whole language program, and the standardized components Sarah lists as common activities provide additional pressures on a new teacher to conform. This formal recognition of the quality of the Purple way of teaching is something Sarah is well aware of.

> When you find out all these teachers have been hand-picked and everything, you think 'Well, they must know what they're doing.' I mean, they're good. They wouldn't be here if they weren't. Like this school, it's really high profile. Like there were people coming in here nearly every week observing teachers. So I thought, 'They gotta be good. They gotta know what they're doing or no one would come and watch them.' Like why would a teacher from another school come here if they didn't think they were gonna learn something? So I did exactly what everyone else was doing. (*ibid* p. 27)

In contrast, Sarah felt that the university had had no influence on her perspective, her ideal reality, or her daily teaching decisions. She said:

> Really, I didn't learn . . . what did I learn there for those years? Except for my student-teaching. I didn't learn anything. Like really, about day to day, everyday classroom things. (*ibid* p. 33)

The members of the university community had failed to influence her perspective, her tacit beliefs, values, and practices, her ideal reality. Indeed, Sarah was critical of the university's program in light of what she had learned from her colleagues at Purple School.

One of the shortcomings of the university program which Sarah saw when she started using themes to organize her language, science, social studies, art, and music planning was that the university taught discrete courses in those areas, which did not prepare her for Purple School's integrated planning. Sarah recalled:

> Ya, everything all those CIs were distinct and that's the way they taught us the way we should teach. . . . Like maybe if those CIs were integrated or something then we could see what was happening but they weren't, they were, 'OK, now you are in Art, this is (art time)'. (*ibid* pp. 34–5)

The same criticism applied to other courses where Sarah had not felt membership in a group, acceptance of a group's values, or of the norms and practices flowing from those values. Consequently, Sarah had little to give up when she entered the new Purple School group and encountered their values, norms and practices. In fact, Sarah's peer group during university included several engineering students who belittled her Mickey Mouse courses, and reinforced her perception of many of her professors as uncaring, unrealistic, impractical, theoretical. Unlike Zeichner and Tabachnick's (1985) four beginning teachers who carried some of their university beliefs over into their teaching, Sarah felt she had to start from scratch when she arrived at Purple School. She more closely fits Lacey's (1977) conception of beginning teacher response to school socialization labelled 'internalized adjustment'. This response involves newcomers complying with the norms and definitions of the situation presented by the staff in the school, believing that these accepted positions are for the best.

In summary, Sarah's classroom decisions suggest a perspective and ideal reality emphasizing proper manners, orderliness and respect among people rooted in her childhood experiences with family, school and church in a small town. Her expectation that the authority of parents, teachers and principals should be respected also seemed to stem from her early experiences with those three institutions. Her more recent experience with university and school institutions' socialization efforts points to the failure of the university and the success of the school. Some attempt to probe the reasons for these effects will follow.

Socialization of Teachers: Perspective by Evangelism.

Sarah and Kent illustrate several of the relationships among teacher thinking, underlying perspectives, and sources of perspective. Many of their decisions were part of what Werner called our natural attitude. Janesick (1978) pointed to the source of perspectives, and to their consequent changing nature, in social interaction: perspective is 'a reflective socially derived interpretation which serves as a basis for the actions which he or she constructs, . . . a combination of beliefs and behaviors continually modified by social interaction' (p. 3). The social interaction with their family, their teachers, their church, their professors, and their colleagues plays an important role as beginning teachers select the elements of emerging perspectives.

Often the interaction with members of these institutions provides teachers-to-be with values, beliefs and practices being advocated by precept and example. We saw Sarah's parents using polite words with her from the time she was very little, reinforced by church and teachers where respect and politeness were also advocated. Similarly, at the university level five early childhood graduates in our study who used play as a major method were surprised to be asked why they believed that way was best. Answers such as the following indicate the tacit, unquestioned nature of perspective: 'Why is play valuable?'

Sandra asked. 'If you have an early childhood background . . . you *know* that play is valuable . . . It's in your brain' (McNay, 1988, p. 20). Sandra told of an early childhood fourth year class where they shared written philosophies, 'and everybody came up with more or less the same points because we went to the early childhood programs since our second year' (McNay, 1988, p. 16). Another early childhood graduate, Molly, said 'she had a firm belief that children learn through play, not just in kindergarten, but in the primary years as well' (Blakey, 1988, p. 3). This unquestioning acceptance of a perspective on teaching seemed to result from the ethos of the early childhood program, the way students were kept together as a class, organized into a club, prescribed a common program with two or three like-minded professors who used learning centres to organize course activities. Peter Grimmet (1988) described this approach as Jimmy Swaggert evangelism, and argued that university programs should place more emphasis on developing graduates prepared to be critically reflective, seeking alternative perspectives from which to develop their own ways of thinking about teaching. Several of our case studies (Chamberlin, 1988; Massey, 1988; Scott, 1988) pointed to the power of school inservice programs which took Madeline Hunter's teacher effectiveness approach as their Bible and taught teachers how to put into practice a bag of teacher control tricks. This also has had great appeal to beginning teachers, who often worry about others' perceptions of their ability to manage a class. The approach used usually fits what has been typified as 'selling snake oil', or offering a quick cure without consideration of costs or of alternatives. This non-reflective, perhaps even counter-reflective approach to socializing beginning teachers may poorly prepare teachers such as Sarah and Kent to work out solutions to their own problems, as they recounted laying in bed at night or driving to school with their minds a tumult of anxieties about students' learning and behavior.

Three Alternatives to Evangelizing.

Other researchers have addressed the question of university and school socialization of beginning teachers. Alan Tom, in *Teaching as a Moral Craft* (1984), emphasized the morality of the teacher-student relationship: Tom argued that, 'teaching involves a moral relationship between teacher and student that is grounded in the dominant power position of the teacher and that 'teaching is moral in the sense that a curriculum plan selects certain objectives or pieces of content instead of others; this selective process either explicitly or implicitly reflects a conception of desirable ends' (p. 78). Tom pointed out that 'the ultimate test of authority is who decides what the distribution of authority is, who decides what the distribution of authority will be, and this decision is the teacher's province' (p.82). Consequently, Tom saw teacher educators as responsible for fostering critical reflection using models of inquiry including the moral domain. Tom's craft emphasis, rather than the science approach of the Gage process-product school, reflects his recognition of the situational nature of teaching, where individual teachers, with their unique perspectives, make teaching decisions deemed appropriate for the special circumstances in which they help children grow. This fits Sarah's contention that no one but herself could solve her problems, because they would not know her class and her beliefs and abilities.

A second view of socializing beginning teachers is presented in Zeichner and Tabachnick's (1985) review of the case studies of four of their recent graduates and the roles of university and schools in their induction into teaching. They examined reasons why two of their beginners 'attempted significantly to redefine the range of acceptable behaviors in their schools' (p. 12) to enable them to retain the teaching perspectives developed during their teacher education program, while two other beginners adapted to the dominant norms, values and practices in their schools. Zeichner and Tabachnick suggest that a mixture of technical control by the school, the strength and homogeneity of the school culture, teacher skill in building support, and other factors affect teacher success in maintaining entering perspectives. They have developed a program to help students study school culture and means of socializing newcomers into that culture. Thus equipped with some conceptual tools and practice in analyzing the socializing process of school staffs, beginners may be more able to consciously choose between their entering perspectives and the dominant beliefs in their new school culture.

Third, Schön's *Educating the Reflective Practitioner* (1987) argues that professional education needs to place neophytes in field work where they will have to create new solutions to unique problems in a specific context. Professional education can *not* be just teaching context-free rules, but rather requires

> reflection-in-action through which practitioners make new sense of uncertain, unique or conflicted situations of practice assuming neither that existing professional knowledge fits every case nor that every problem has a right answer. (p. 39)

Lacking right answers, beginners need a set of broad concepts to help them understand their problems and help create solutions. Schön believes these concepts are best learned by working with a master professional in practice, perhaps like the Scottish teacher preparation programs of twenty years ago.

Tom, Zeichner and Tabachnick, and Schön all point to the role of the university in developing beginning teachers who are capable of critical reflection on whatever values, norms, and practices are proferred by universities and schools as induction into the teaching culture begins. Rather than evangelizing or selling snake oil, perhaps universities should provide students with school experiences in which they practise critical reflection on the morality of alternative perspectives and the teaching practices which follow.

Sociopolitical Analysis of Educational Perspectives' Morality.

If this conclusion concerning the need for practice in critical reflection is reasonable, then some consideration of bases of morality are suggested. In this regard, the political nature of schooling becomes significant. Analyses of the socio-political role of the school institution by Friere, Apple, Bruner, Aronowitz, Bernstein and others are helpful.

Paulo Friere in *Pedagogy of the Oppressed* (1972) describes a 'banking' approach to teaching in which 'the teacher talks and the students listen — meekly; the teacher disciplines and the students are disciplined' (p. 59). The effect of this teacher authority-student obedient relationship is to prevent any student questioning of existing social structure, as Friere explained:

> The more students work at storing the deposits entrusted to them, the less they develop the critical consciousness which would result from their intervention in the world as transformers of the world. The more completely they accept the passive role imposed on them, the more they tend simply to adapt to the world as it is. (p. 60)

Nor is Friere's analysis limited in application to his South American homeland. Goodlad's extensive 1984 study, *A Place Called School*, found teachers primarily using this same teacher-text authority teaching method. In his 1988 book, Goodlad argues that the university role in its partnerships with schools must be one which challenges this tradition, arguing for radical change because 'The role of education in enculturation is threatened by serious imperfections in the culture itself' where there are 'clear signs of pathology in the community and, indeed, the larger society' (Sirotnik and Goodlad, 1988, p. 34).

Apple (1983) has described the moral responsibility of educators to resist the technical control of schooling in the tradition of Gramsci where 'hegemony is always contested' (p. 162). Apple depicts schools in which ideologies of different social classes compete, but the controlling mode is one which prepares workers for industry and offices. Schools prepare student/workers to develop the habit of following the rules, of being dependable in performing a job at a consistent level, of being reliable and getting the job done, and of internalizing the enterprise's goals and values. So Sarah worries about how one of her disobedient students will ever be able to hold a job, rather than worrying about whether a critical consciousness is being nurtured. Kent uses a social studies kit which he acknowledges is inappropriate for his inner city students because it is approved by higher authorities. His challenge is to create solutions to the discipline problems which ensue.

In the same vein as Apple's and Friere's analyses, Aronowitz (1973) argued that the school teaches students the hierarchical nature of society, and 'impresses students as a whole with their powerlessness' (p. 75). The hidden curriculum becomes a key element in the moral craft of teaching as children learn to think of themselves as disempowered, and lower class children develop an external locus of control and a low sense of political efficacy. However, they do learn the values and norms Bernstein (1977) associates with good industrial workers: respect for authority, punctuality, cleanliness, docility, and conformity. Bruner (1973) also has demanded that the political concern about power and who has it must be consciously included in any instructional theory, for it 'is a political theory in the power sense that it derives from concensus concerning the distribution of power within the society — who shall be educated and to fill what roles?' (p. 115). Teacher educators would do well to listen to Bruner's warning that the 'educator who formulates pedagogical theory without regard to the political, economic and social setting of the educational process courts triviality and merits being ignored' (p. 115).

These analyses of the ideological stance of the hidden curriculum in schooling underscore Tom's view of teaching as a moral craft. They also point to the importance of teacher education in preparing beginning teachers for including in their reflection-in-action analysis of the hidden curriculum. The values and self-concepts children learn from the social relationships built into teaching methods need to be the subject of critical reflection if beginning teachers are to become aware of socialization by universities and schools.

Sarah needs to have some of the conceptual tools Schön suggested to help her to reflect on her decision to use math *my* way rather than math *their* way, and the disempowerment that decision and its underlying perspective suggests. Kent needs to be able to recognize the moral dimension to his craft when he decides to put off setting up learning centres in order to achieve his technological reality of control and predictability with its hierarchical power structure. Molly and Sandra need to be helped to analyze the morality and ideology of play-centred learning in comparison to more teacher-centred learning. Kent needs to be able to look at Madeline Hunter's teacher effectiveness methods for the impact on self-concept, sense of political efficacy, and internal locus of control.

Perhaps teacher educators, both preservice and inservice, need to use less evangelism and give teachers more experience in analysis of socialization and of the moral and ideological bases of the teaching perspectives they present. Perhaps researchers need to more extensively probe the roots of teacher perspective in home, school, church, university and teaching contexts.

References

APPLE, M. W. (1983) 'Curricular form and the logic of technical control', in APPLE, M. W. and WEIS, L. (Eds) *Ideology and Practice in Schooling*, Philadelphia, Temple University Press.

ARONOWITZ, S. (1973) *False Consciousness: The Shaping of the American Working Class Consciousness*, New York, McGraw-Hill.

BERNSTEIN, S. (1977), *Class, Codes and Controls*, 3. London, Routledge and Kegan Paul.

BLAKEY, J. (1988), *Learning to Smell the Flowers*, Edmonton, Alberta Education.

BLAKEY, J. *et al.* (1987) 'Sources of Teachers' Perspectives and Decisions: Implications for Preservice and Inservice Education', Report, Edmonton, Alberta Education.

BRUNER, J. (1973) *The Relevance of Education*, New York, W. W. Norton and Co.

CHAMBERLIN, C. (1988) *Sources of a Beginning Teacher's Perspective*, Edmonton, Alberta Education.

CUBAN, L. (1984) *How Teachers Taught: Constancy and Change in American Classrooms, 1890–1980*, New York, Longman.

FRIERE, P. (1972) *Pedagogy of the Oppressed*, New York, Herder and Herder.

FULLER, F. and BOWN, O. (1975) 'Becoming a teacher', in RYAN K. (Ed.) *Teacher Education: The 74th Yearbook of the NSSE*, Chicago, University of Chicago Press.

GOODLAD, J. I. (1984) *A Place Called School*, New York, McGraw-Hill.

GRIMMET, P. (1988), Personal communication on a doctoral dissertation.

GUBA, E.G. (1981) 'Criteria for assessing the trustworthiness of naturalistic inquiries'. ERIC/ECTJ Annual review paper. Reprinted in Educational Communications and Technological Journal, 29, (2), pp. 75–91.

JANESICK, V. (1978) *An Ethnographic Study of a Teacher's Classroom Perspective: Implications for Curriculum*, East Lansing, Michigan, Institute for Research on Teaching, Michigan State University.

LACEY, C. (1977) *The Socialization of Teachers*, London, Methuen.

MASSEY, D. (1988) *How He Would Teach: Kent Reed*, Edmonton, Alberta Education.

MCNAY, M. (1988) *The Rookie: A Case Study of Sandra, A First-Year Kindergarten Teacher*, Edmonton, Alberta Education.

SCHÖN, D. (1987) *Educating the Reflective Practitioner*, San Francisco, Jossey-Bass.

SCOTT, N. (1988) *Choices: A Case Study of a Beginning Teacher*. Edmonton, Alberta Education.

SIROTNIK, K. and GOODLAD, J. I. (Eds) (1988) *School-University Partnerships in Action*, New York, Teachers College Press.

TOM, A. R. (1984) *Teaching as a Moral Craft*, New York, Longman.

WERNER, W. (1977) *A Study of Perspective in Social Studies*. Unpublished doctoral dissertation, University of Alberta.

WOLCOTT, H. (1975), Criteria for an ethnographic approach to research in schools, *Human Organization*, 34, 2, pp. 111–27.

ZEICHNER, K. and TABACHNICK, B. (1985) 'The development of teacher perspectives: social strategies and institutional control in the socialization of beginning teachers', *Journal of Education for Teachers*, 11, 1, pp. 1–25.

Chapter 10

Adults Learning – Teachers Thinking

Pam Denicolo and Maureen Pope

In this chapter we review the continuing need for studies which adopt a qualitative-interpersonal approach in research on teaching which is concerned with teacher thinking (Pope and Denicolo, 1986). It is also part of our own professional commitment as researchers to illuminate the personal perspectives of individual teachers using a methodology which would afford the participants in the research an opportunity to gain from the process. In common with Boud and Griffin (1987) we would argue that researchers on adults learning need to 'adopt the learners' frame of reference . . . address the concerns which they think are important and respect their felt experience'.

We report here on some case studies using a biographical approach as one way of addressing teachers' 'felt experience'. The student participants are adults who are prospective teachers of adults while the technique is one which has previously been used within social skills training. This 'snake' technique helped participants to provide a commentary on 'critical incidents' in their life history which they perceived as having relevance to their current thinking about teaching adults. This formed the basis for follow-up sessions which encouraged further reflection on practice, demonstrating the value of the technique for the professional development of the participants.

Introduction

Understanding of other people and their expressions is developed on the basis of experience and self-understanding and the constant interaction between them . . . it is not a matter of logical construction or psychological dissection but of an epistemological analysis. (Dilthey, in Rickman, 1976).

The observation above dates from circa the turn of the century, pre-dating scientific behaviourism and psychometrics and the emphasis on the quantitative approach to educational research. It is not without significance to the content of this chapter that we reflect on this historical approach to human understanding as being congruent with our current research approach and concerns for the continuing need for studies of teacher thinking which adopt a qualitative-interpretive approach. This is despite its inherent difficulties in practice and in reporting as discussed in a previous paper (Pope and Denicolo, 1986). As researchers on the thinking of school teachers (Denicolo and Pope, 1987), we have been concerned to illuminate the personal perspectives of the individual teachers using a methodology which would afford the participants in the research an opportunity to gain from the process. The current work with student-teachers continues this commitment since we concur with Diamond (1985) who stresses the value of the student-teacher reflecting on his or her implicit theories as part of the staff development process.

The focus of this research is the adult learner/student-teacher whose professional role will be the teaching of fellow adults. As psychologists and teacher educators, we are only too aware of the relative lack of empirical work on the teaching of adults and that the adult learner is a somewhat 'neglected species' (Knowles, 1978), although:

> We have finally really begun to absorb into our culture the ancient insight that the heart of education is learning, not teaching, and so our focus has started to shift from what the teacher does to what happens to the learners. (p.52)

Indeed, Mezirow (1985) views self-reflective learning as having particular importance in adult learning. In common with Boud and Griffin (1987), we would argue that *researchers* on adults learning need to 'adopt the learners' frame of reference . . . address the concerns which they think are important and respect their felt experience'. (p. 8).

As our current project is a continuing one, the emphasis in this chapter will not be on the particular results of the joint explorations of the meanings that adult learners attribute to their experiences. Instead, exemplars of specific reflections on the past and present which contribute to visions of the future will serve as illustrations to highlight the implications of the method and the potential uses of the technique for the development of teacher thinking, and hence for professional development.

Method

In our day-to-day discussions with learner teachers about their professional practice, we note continued comparisons of what they do and what they seek to achieve as teachers with their previous experiences both as learners in formal situations and as developing human beings and professionals in 'normal' or 'life' settings. Frequently they evidence their choice of method, for instance, by reference to a formative experience of their own, whether it be a positive one which they seek to emulate for their students or a negative one which they strive to avoid reiterating for others. As Habermas (1974) writes:

> Self-reflection brings to consciousness those determinants of a self-formative process of cultivation and spiritual formation . . . which

ideologically determine a contemporary praxis of action and conception of the world . . . . Self-reflection leads to insight due to the fact that what has previously been unconscious is made conscious in a manner rich in practical consequences: analytic insights intervene in life, if I may borrow this dramatic phrase from Wittgenstein.

Thus our own daily experience as teachers of adult learners in conjunction with our interest in teachers' thinking, particularly in terms of professional development, led us to seek out a method of formally investigating the salience of particular life experiences for current and proposed practice.

While Zeichner *et al* (1987) note that:

Studies . . . clearly indicate that biography exerts a powerful influence on teacher development, but much work remains to be done to clarify the particular source of the influence. (pp. 25–26)

Butt (1984) makes a strong argument for the use of biographical methods for understanding of 'teaching *as experienced* by the teacher':

Through examining the transformational quality of significant experiences in personal and professional lives, we can apprehend a teacher's formation or development in an educative as well as a training sense. (p. 100)

He also writes that no particular biographical 'method' exists *per se*, but rather that the field should be explored with methods developed to be germane to the participants, the study and the context.

Our concern was to encourage our participants to focus on 'critical incidents' in their life histories which they perceived as having relevance to their current thinking about teaching adults and, indeed, to their decision to change their role from professional practitioner to practitioner teachers. As Murray (1985) puts it, in proposing a dramaturgical model, we had:

a desire to find concordances or themes which cohere life experiences into a meaningful structure. (p. 173)

This resonates with Dilthey's (1976, *op cit*) proposition that:

The person who seeks the connecting threads in the history of his life has already, from different points of view, created connections which he is now putting into words . . . . The units are formed by the conceptions of experience in which present and past events are held together by a common meaning. Among these experiences those which have special dignity, both in themselves and for the passage of his life, have been preserved by memory and lifted out of the endless stream of forgotten events. (p. 215)

While 'connecting threads' and 'stream of life' are evocative metaphors in this description of life events, we found a different analogy used in social skills training to be of practical value in our particular research project. (However, it is interesting to note here that one of our participants found it more fruitful to use her own analogy, 'a developing fish', to achieve the same aims.) We called this method the 'snake' technique, after Priestley *et al* (1978) and, as far as we are aware, it has not previously been used as a staff development or research tool in teacher education.

Our participants, who were already alert to our interest in personal constructions of life events in general and professional role in particular, were asked to participate in an exercise which would involve them in thinking back over their life experience to elicit particular incidents and experiences which influenced their career paths. They were asked to reflect in private, visualizing and drawing their lives as a winding snake in which each 'twist' in its body represented a change in direction of, or intention for, their career. Brief annotations were to be included, for each twist, about the experience or incident

Figure 10.1.
Snake: Student 9.

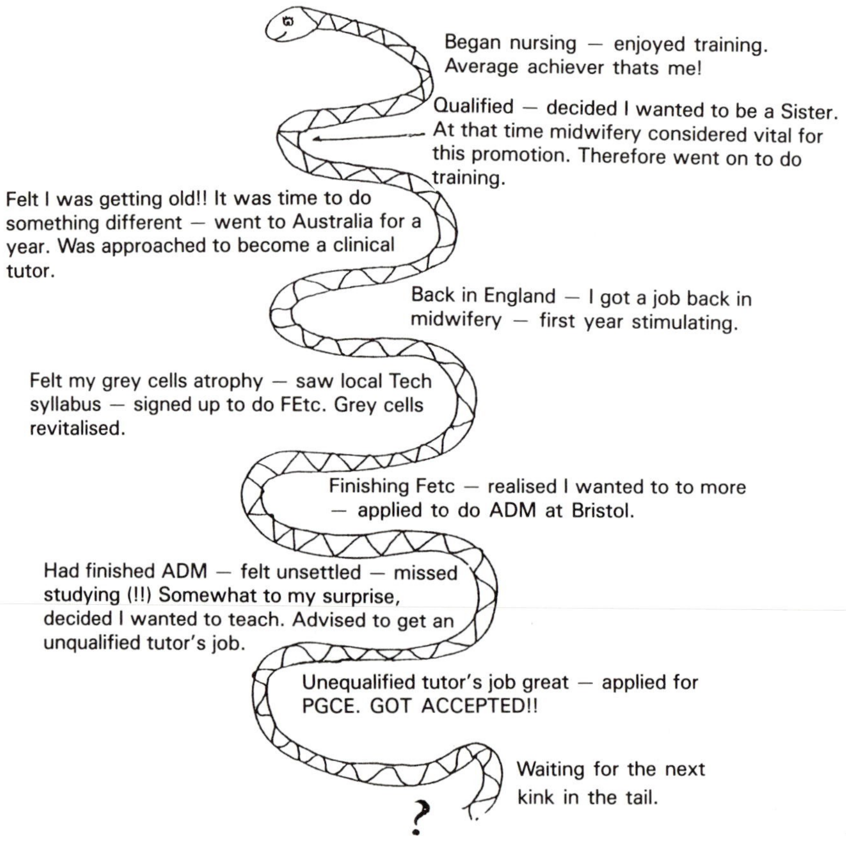

Began nursing — enjoyed training. Average achiever thats me!

Qualified — decided I wanted to be a Sister. At that time midwifery considered vital for this promotion. Therefore went on to do training.

Felt I was getting old!! It was time to do something different — went to Australia for a year. Was approached to become a clinical tutor.

Back in England — I got a job back in midwifery — first year stimulating.

Felt my grey cells atrophy — saw local Tech syllabus — signed up to do FEtc. Grey cells revitalised.

Finishing Fetc — realised I wanted to to more — applied to do ADM at Bristol.

Had finished ADM — felt unsettled — missed studying (!!) Somewhat to my surprise, decided I wanted to teach. Advised to get an unqualified tutor's job.

Unequalified tutor's job great — applied for PGCE. GOT ACCEPTED!!

Waiting for the next kink in the tail.

?

which precipitated the change. No instruction was given about *when* in their lives to start considering whether experiences influenced career and it is of interest to note that the majority of participants who subsequently submitted their 'snakes' to the researchers in conditions of confidentiality mentioned incidents from pre- or early school years which continue to contribute to the 'why' and 'how' of their role. Two of those whose snakes began later in life were among the original eight chosen for in-depth interview from those who expressed willingness to discuss their reflections in greater depth. In interview they recalled earlier experiences which at least acted as predisposing factors to later 'twists'. (See Figure 10.1 and also Appendix 1 to this chapter, part of a transcript from such an interview).

We were thus able to analyze twenty-five 'snakes' for recurring themes and similar 'critical incidents', and, to date, interview eight participants. It is noteworthy that many of the participants were so stimulated by these reflections, and the self-knowledge engendered by them, that they were eager to continue the process in more in-depth interviews. The general course of these interviews was to allow the participants to revisit their 'snake' to consider any omissions or changes, followed by an opportunity to focus on particular incidents, elaborating their significance as formative experiences for both career decisions and personal 'style' as a practitioner.

Although termed an 'interview', the procedure followed was more akin to a personal interrogation by the participant of their own reasons for isolating a particular incident and personal reflection on its import for and effects on their practice. Our own recollections and the transcripts of these audio-taped sessions reveal that only the barest minimum of intervention was required of the 'interviewer', that taking the form of non-critical encouragement to continue, for example, 'How did that make you feel?' 'How does that work out in practice?' Like Rogers (1986) we found variation in degrees of reticence, but the procedure of valuing this experience as determining their sense of professional identity did seem conducive to the sharing of intimate experiences which have a profound effect on 'being'.

The following poem, quoted by Rogers, conveys some of the essence of this experience:

Poem for Everyman*

I will present you
parts
of
my
self
slowly
if you are patient and tender.
I will open drawers
that mostly stay closed
and bring out places and people and things

sounds and smells, loves and frustrations, hopes and
sadnesses,
bits and pieces of three decades of life
that have been grabbed off
in chunks
and found lying in my hands
they have eaten
their way into my memory
carved their way into my
heart
altogether — you or i will never see them —
they are me.
if you regard them lightly
deny that they are important
or worse, judge them
i will quietly, slowly
begin to wrap them up
in small pieces of velvet,
like worn silver and gold jewelry,
tuck them away
in a small wooden chest of drawers

and close.

Wood, J. 'How Do You Feel? A Guide to Your Emotions', Prentice Hall.

The sessions concluded with a discussion of the appropriateness of the technique for both reflection and projection and as a potential developmental tool — speculation.

Segmented Reflections

There were several recurrent themes or similar types of critical incidents which were seen to be particularly generative of these teachers' images of their role and its conversion into practice. These fall into the following sub-headings derived from the data and used as a means of elucidating the data from all completed snakes although they are interlinked with each other within and across transcripts from interview participants.

Human potential
Importance of self-concept
Importance of challenge
Power of teachers
Teachers as models
Recognition of different ways of learning
Recognition of full human potential
Total experience of students

It is relevant to note here that all of the student-teachers involved were of mature years (between 28 and 45 years old) and had reached positions of responsibility in their previous profession, mainly in the Health Service, by means of promotion and in-service courses. There was an almost equal distribution of those who felt that they had previously chosen their original profession and those who felt that they had been coerced into it either by advice and pressure (socialization) from a significant other (parent or teacher) or had chosen it as the least unfavourable in a limited choice. However, many in the first group remarked on reflection that they now realized limits on their opportunities for development in their youth. What was significant overall was their current realization that they possessed skills and abilities previously unrealized and certainly untapped or even acknowledged in former years. This made them particularly concerned as teachers not to underestimate the *potential of their students*:

> I was laughed at by my teacher for wanting to be a nurse — I clearly remember that chap laughing — I'd like him to see me now. (Student 1)

> I see myself as someone who helps people to become what they want to become ... I am not a factory conveyor belt ... I feel strongly that we don't make enough effort to identify the needs and potentials of people and we don't work on that potential. (Student 3)

A closely related set of ideas was that involving *self-concept* and how others, particularly teachers, are instrumental either in its formation or its reinforcement or challenge it.

> One of the things I learnt about teachers was they don't value those who have to struggle. (Student 1)

> Failing my 11 plus was the begining ... I got turned down for all sorts of courses, I wasn't good enough. (Student 3)

> I remember on the first day of training we had to write down all our 'O' and 'A' Levels, and I hadn't got any — I felt quite inferior — but there was one tutor who recognized this in me and she boosted me up all along and made *me* believe in *me*. (Student 2)

Although some felt that a poor self-concept and the undervaluing reaction of others had delayed their development, there were some who took this as a challenge and thence as a stimulus to greater achievements. Appendix 1 to this chapter — a lengthy extract from one student — clearly demonstrates this influence as do the following short extracts.

> This 'putting down' stirred up in me the realization that I had to fight for what I wanted ... there's always been these barriers to fight against ... along with a need to prove myself ... I have to have a challenge still but I no longer feel the need to prove myself. (Student 4)

> It was scary but it gave me the opportunity to see my own potential and use it. (Student 3)

> I'm a very stubborn lady, if I'm told I *can't* that makes me all the more determined to go on. (Student 1)

Their own experiences, and that of fellow students, also gave them cause to acknowledge *diversity in approaches to learning* and how to handle it:

> I can remember being a student and not being ready for certain teaching/learning styles... sometimes it made us angry and bolshy as students... it took different people different amounts of time to get used to that (independent learning). (Student 4)

> I do try to pick out people and try to give them confidence — that there might be something in them even if they haven't got paper qualifications... not talking down to them. (Student 2)

> You need to build the trust gradually. (Student 1)

The preceding quotations could also be used to illustrate another reitereated theme, that of the *power of teachers*, as does:

> It makes me reflect on the power of teachers... my own power as a teacher is worrying. (Student 1)

> Looking back again, there was an English teacher who was at Canterbury... she said to come to Canterbury and she showed me the University. Again, she picked me out, not because I was terribly bright, but it just seemed as if I could respond... so she was important. (Student 5)

> The Domestic Science teacher lived round the corner and again she encouraged my interest in cookery... I think that when I'm encouraged and I'm doing well, I will do anything for that teacher and I will give as much as I can. (Student 7)

> ... she was my supervisor but she was lazy and left everything to me which was scary but it gave me the opportunity to see my own potential and develop it. It taught me how important it is to build people's confidence. (Student 3)

Similarly, it can be seen that these recollections of their own teachers served either as negative *role models* or, conversely, as models to emulate as with student 1:

> One particular teacher was very important to me... she was very dynamic... spoke in a language which I warmed to... not a very academic language... it showed me I could be *me* and be a teacher.

Most of the participants at some point highlighted their awareness that students come to learning with *many experiences* which, although not necessarily 'academic', nevertheless affect their learning:

> Each learner has a world outside the academic institution which affects how they are in the institution. (Student 1)

Being a lone parent has also been important — there are lone parents, people who are stuggling . . . I go out of my way . . . to realize that they are also living their own lives — not just going through an adult education system. (Student 2)

Some of this current awareness had deep roots:

I didn't excel at school. They're very deep, children's memories . . . it was a small seaside town and children came from a two parent family. Coming from a one parent family we didn't belong, not at that time even though it was after the war. If your father had died, that was fine, he was a hero, but if not then you didn't belong, and certainly if you were poor. You went to the headmaster and suddenly you had to have your school dinners free. (Student 8)

Throughout their commentary on their 'snakes', the students identified *developing confidence, taking on challenges, realizing the complexity and individuality of people, identification of needs and potential, developing trust between teachers and students* as aspects of the teacher's role. Some students recognized that they had undergone shifts in perspective regarding their role values and that a supportive climate was needed during such transitions. Commenting on initial experimentation with self-directed learning techniques, Student 6 said:

. . . because nurses are all essentially practical people anyway, they always feel it's a bit airy-fairy talking about self-directed learning and you do pick up the jargon and they turned off from that . . . I think you need a sort of mentor . . . when you experience failure and you know the students thought it was a failure . . . I get very down when things don't work and you need someone to say [as did her supervisor] . . . 'the one who used more experiential methods pushed them and challenged them and made them struggle to learn'.

Student 2 recognized her shift as significant learning (Rogers, C. 1961) and noted that her experiences were also reflected in those close to her:

I went in very conservative in my views — very authoritarian — they changed me but they gave no support for that radical change — it was very traumatic for me — I think if you are going to change people that much, you should also have a support system for the stress. My husband has changed along with me — he was once a very conservative factory worker but as I have grown and talked and questioned, so has he.

Kolb and Fry's (1975) 'learning cycle' suggests that learning is facilitated through experiencing events, reflecting on them, conceptualizing and experimenting in a continuous cycle. From our discussions with the adult learners about their thinking as teachers or would-be teachers of adults, they had reflected on many of their experiences and some conceptualization had taken place. All had indicated that reflection on these experiences had raised their awareness about their intentions as teachers and of their personal values:

> I used to be very radical and pessimistic you know — come the revolution! — now I'm more optimistic — now I'm thinking most people have got power, you don't need a revolution... you can let students know they have and can use it. (Student 2)

> I feel I have changed such a lot as a person. I've learnt more about me and people... about facilitating, about developing abilities not just in a formal teaching situation, about understanding why people get stuck and can't move on. (Student 4)

Robertson (1987), referring to the Kolb and Fry model and her own experience, noted that 'seeing oneself in a new light turned out to be one thing, but knowing how to put these insights into action... was even more difficult' (p. 76). This was echoed by Student 8 who recognized that she still needs to experiment with her conceptualization of teacher as helper.

> I see the teacher as a helper , I suppose facilitator is the correct word, but as a helper, not a fountain of all knowledge, sort of as a guide... knowledge which I can share if you want me to share and I'll be happy to share but it's no good me giving you my knowledge, you have to find your knowledge, and what I want to do is to help people find their knowledge. I think from my own education, I have knowledge given to me which when they put me into a situation where I had to function, I couldn't use it and I think that that, as a teacher, is what I don't want to do. I want the knowledge to come from them, and I don't know how to do that. I'm beginning to learn but I don't know how to do it... I need to feel and once I've assimilated that, then I'll digest that and then I'll learn and I've only got to the stage where I've done my feeling. (Student 8)

Teachers Thinking — a Tool for Research and Learning

So far in the chapter, we have presented but a few of the 'connecting threads' in the lives of the teachers who participated in our research. William James likened the mind and consciousness to a rope made up of many threads which if cut across would give a false impression of its construction. One needs to follow the threads over time to gain insight into the structure of the rope. We are well aware that the segments of the 'snake' as presented here give but a limited impression of the felt reflections and professional core of the participants in our study. Nevertheless we hope that they have demonstrated that the technique can be one more tool in the kit bag of researchers on teacher thinking, especially those who, like Torbert (1981), would advocate that educational research should be educational!

Adult educators have emphasized a person-centred approach to teaching

(Knowles 1978, Rogers, A. 1986). Qualitative-interpretative research is predicated on similar principles in that the participants (not subjects!) are seen as active meaning-seeking individuals whose views of the world are valued by the researcher. As researchers on adult learning and adult educators, it seemed appropriate that we should seek a tool which would be consistent with the principles of these two domains. Diamond (1985) remarked that 'if teachers can be helped to "open their eyes" they can see how to choose and fashion their own version of reality' (p. 34). Our experiences with the 'snake' technique suggest that by using it, the researcher can gain insights into personal meanings of the teachers and the participants are encouraged to view and review their personal theorizing regarding teaching and learning.

In being asked to consider their past and reflect on its influence, they confronted themselves with habitual responses to factors which may no longer be pertinant or were able to recognize and understand why they or their students behaved in particular ways in their role. This encourages them to address, evaluate and develop their performance with greater clarity of insight.

This particular process, in which the participants produced their own agenda, investigated each item to their own satisfaction with the researcher acting as an interested but non-evaluative partner was valued by all participants, not the least because it represented a seldom available opportunity in a life filled with 'what', 'when' and 'how' to reflect on the pervasive influence of 'why'.

Perhaps the last words should be left to the adult learners/teachers of adults.

First, the student who recognized that the tool could be useful with the teaching process itself, perhaps some way into the course when the students were less 'subject-bound' and trust had been established. She implied that we cannot advocate reflective learning to our adult learners unless as teachers of adults we do the same.

> I think that if we look at ourselves then perhaps we can help them to look at themselves and they'll know what they want instead of being told what they want. (Student 8)

And the students who held a mirror to themselves:

> I feel so enthusiastic now, I feel empowered — by coming to terms with my self, by reflecting on the theories in terms of my real life. (Student 2)
>
> One thing that did become clear by writing it all down as opposed to thinking, was how much my career had ruled my life. I know it has, but actually seeing it on paper, the Health Service has ruled my life. It's ruled where I've lived, it's ruled how much money I've had, it's ruled the fact that I've ended up in education. If anything . . . it's made me think is this really what I want out of life, is there more to life than this. For me, the Health Service has been a disease — you can't get rid of it. It is my life. (Student 6)

Appendix

Student 6

I wasn't born a teacher. I never thought from day one that I want to be a teacher. It's probably by accident as much as anything. I did always want to be a nurse but I didn't know why. No history of nursing or anything like that in the family or any friends or people that I knew, I just always wanted to be a nurse. I think the thing that drove me on is the fact that right from the age of 3, that's as long as I can remember wanting to be a nurse, people used to ridicule it really and say she'll not be a nurse. When I finally started nursing people would then say 'I'll give her a month'. That made me more determined. I put down that I left school without any qualification and that is because I didn't work hard enough at school. School was a social occasion, it were a time to go ladding. I went for the social life, I didn't go for learning. When I was very little, I didn't like school because I had to leave my mum. I felt very much imprisoned and the teachers seemed very strict, they hit you with rulers, so I didn't like it. Junior school — I had a few moves around to different schools and I just went coz I had to go. Senior school — well that was a social event — boys were on the scene and that was definitely it. Nevertheless I still wanted to be a nurse and we were given very little directives on what we needed, career-wise. We had one interview with the careers officer who said be sensible, don't be silly — you can be a shop assistant. I said I don't want to be a shop assistant. He sent me a form to go to work at C&A. I just tore it into pieces and sent it back by return of post. I was very arrogant like that. I know I had this particular teacher at school who tried to put me down all the time. She knew that school for me was a social event. It was a needlework teacher and I always used to cut corners — I would never pin and tack — I always got straight on to sewing. I'd produce things very quickly and at the end they were as good as what the others produced but I'd cut the corners and she didn't like that and so she said I'd never be a nurse — I'd be lucky if I got a job at Bassetts. I didn't actually leave school when I should have — I should have left at summer and I went on until the following Easter because I hadn't got a job as a nurse and I had no intention of leaving school until I'd got the job I wanted. I was very very arrogant and so I used to turn up every day at school — I never ever missed a day off school — I'd go if I were dying because it was such a social event. The teachers would say K — , why are you still here — you're off the register, you shouldn't be here and I said 'because I haven't got a job' — 'that's no excuse, get out, go to the DHSS'. I said I was waiting for a nursing post. 'Rubbish, you'll not get a nursing job without any qualifications', so all the time I felt 'I'll show them'. The required qualifications were equivalent to 3 'O' levels for SRN training at that time and I didn't have anything, but these were the days when they had cadet nurse schemes as opposed to pre-nursing schemes and the Northern General Hospital was advertising for cadet nurses, so I took an entrance exam and got in as a cadet nurse. I was a cadet nurse for two years and during that period you went to college and did all sorts of things, ballet, cookery, English, maths, all sorts of things. I loved it because you went two days to pre-nursing college and three days you spent in the hospital and you didn't just work on the wards, you worked in all the departments of the hospital, so I worked in the kitchens, I learned all about diets, I learnt about physiotherapy, occupational therapy, pharmacy, administration, you worked in a matron's office. I really got a good grounding with regard to the organization of hospitals and I loved the patient contact, I loved titivating things on the wards, generally being a cadet nurse. However, at the end of that two year period, if you didn't have 'O' levels, then you didn't have the opportunity to take them at college. If you didn't have them, you didn't have them. As a cadet nurse, if you had the 'O' levels to start with you were streamed into SRN, if you didn't you were streamed into SEN training which we were really brained washed then, but that was the nurse of the future, and if you wanted to be a nurse, that's what you did. So really I thought I did want to be a nurse, so I did that and that was the hardest nurse training I ever did, probably because of the area I worked in because the people were really ill, they needed to be there and we were given an awful amount of responsibility. Three months into training you were running wards on nights, with forty children on the ward. It was quite horrific. But that was twenty-three years ago and that was expected . . . .

I actually failed my SEN on the practical. The minute I failed I thought that's it I'm going to do SRN but of course everyone said if you can't pass your SEN you won't pass your SRN but I said I'm going to do my SRN. Then I got married, had the children and I worked part-time here, there and everywhere. It was then that I thought I need to do my SRN because I'm every bit as good as the SRN I was working with. Then I saw the need for further education and then we moved house, I couldn't get a job as a SEN, because I was at Sheffield, I was foreign. I thought I've got to go back to college, I've got to get the 'O' levels, I've got to get the SRN. That's when I went back into education and I went on one of these adult return-to-study courses and did 'O' levels, I did six 'O' levels in a year and also worked, I did two jobs at the same time, so I worked terribly hard, because I'd not done that sort of study for a long time and I didn't know what level to aim at. I got them and I'd really enjoyed it so much that I decided to stay for another year and do some more 'O' levels and 'A' levels which I did. Then I went on to do SRN training and lived away from home. I left my family because I didn't know what the amount of study would be like. I didn't know how high

I had to aim because if you take the SRN training with nothing and fail, you can get your SEN, if I failed I'd get nothing, so I had to pass. That was quite easy passing that. I then decided that I needed to live nearer home. By this time I'd got the urge for more study, I couldn't just go to work any more, I had to be studying something. I thought shall I do psychology, but I thought no, if I'm going to work, it may as well be in a qualification so that's when I did midwifery. I didn't work hard at all in midwifery, it was ever so easy, disappointingly easy. I did that back in Doncaster and by the time I'd gained my midwifery I immediately wanted to go on and do the advanced diploma in midwifery because I needed to learn. Up until recently, the education had been for me, it had been me that had been wanting to get the education as opposed to give it. I immediately started applying to do the advance diploma in midwifery. You must have practised as a midwife before you do it so I got straight into that as soon as possible. I had an awful battle, a political battle at hospital, a financial battle, terribly hard to actually get seconded for the course, but I did and I got that. Having gained the advanced diploma, this must now lead to promotion because my aim really as much as education is to change the midwifery service and I thought that by gaining these legitimizing certificates, that that would be one way to influence things, because you can't influence it from the low, you're too small a cog, so I needed to get up there, but I was much too outspoken in the hospital I was in. I was obviously a threat, so I couldn't get promoted so that's when I moved to Scarborough and that's when I really got involved in education because I've got the ADM. I intended not to waste that, I wanted then to go on and get the PGCE, and we've only got five years to get it, so it would have to be somewhere in the near future. Also the job in Scarborough, as well as being promotion, it involved teaching student nurses on the maternity care course which I saw as another challenge and really at the same time I thought that if I got a teaching certificate, I could then get the students, tomorrow's midwives and perhaps change things that way. I don't know that I ever will but that was the thought then, so really I suppose that education for me has been a tool to work my way up personally and now I see it very much as a tool to change the maternity services. It's perhaps not what education should be used for but as you go along, your views change as well, other things come in as well. I now see it, as well as being a tool to help me change things by using the students, I also see it as helping the profession, helping the students because I feel I understand how they're feeling and realize the support that they need, and that midwives in the profession need.

References

BOUD, D. and GRIFFIN, V. (Eds) (1987) *Appreciating Adults Learning: From the Learner's Perspective*, London, Kogan Page.

BUTT, R. (1984) 'Arguments for using biography in understanding teacher thinking', in HALKES, R. and OLSON, J. (Eds) *Teacher Thinking*, Lisse, Swets and Zeitlinger.

DENICOLO, P. and POPE, M. (1987) 'Perspectives on the teaching profession or relative appraisal', in *Proceedings of Third Conference on Teacher Thinking and Professional Action*, Leuven, Belgium, pp. 411–25.

DIAMOND, P. (1985) 'The altering eye', in BANNISTER, D. (Ed.) *Issues and approaches in personal construct theory*, London, Academic Press.

HABERMAS, J. (1974) *Theory and Practice*, London, Heinemann.

KNOWLES, M. (1978) (2nd edition) *The Adult Learner: A Neglected Species*, Houston, Gulf Publishing Co.

KOLB, D.A. and FRY, F. (1975) 'Towards an applied theory of experiential learning', in *Theories of Group Processes*, London, Wiley.

MEZIROW, J. (1985) 'A critical theory of self-directed learning', in Brookfield, S. (Ed.) *Self-directed Learning from Theory to Practice*, San Francisco, Jossey-Bass.

MURRAY, K. (1985) 'Life as fiction', *Journal for the Theory of Social Behaviour*, 15, 2, July, pp. 173–88.

POPE, M. and DENICOLO, P. (1986) 'Intuitive theories — A researcher's dilemma', *British Educational Research Journal*, Vol. 12, No. 2, pp. 153–65.

PRIESTLEY, P. *et al.* (1978) *Social Skills and Personal Problem Solving*, London, Tavistock Publications.

RICKMAN, H.P. (1976) (Edited and translated) *W. Dilthey — Selected Writings*, Cambridge, Cambridge University Press.

ROBERTSON, G. (1987) 'Learning and the hidden agenda', in BOUD, D. and GRIFFIN, V. (Eds) *Appreciating Adults Learning: From the Learner's Perspective*, London, Kogan Page.

ROGERS, A. (1986) *Teaching Adults*, Milton Keynes, Open University Press.

ROGERS, C. (1961) *On Becoming a Person*, New York, Praeger.

TORBERT, W. (1981) 'Why educational research has been so uneducational: The case for a new model of social science based on collaborative theory', in REASON, P. and ROWAN, J. (Eds) *Human Inquiry, A Source of New Paradigm Research*, Chichester, Wiley.

ZEICHNER, K.M. TABACHNICK, B.R. and DENSMORE, K. (1987) 'Individual, institutional and cultural influences on the development of teachers' craft knowledge', in CALDERHEAD, J. (Ed.) *Exploring Teachers' Thinking*, London, Cassell.

Chapter 11

Teacher Styles

Lars Naeslund

The content of this contribution about teacher styles is based on a four year research project about work conditions of teachers and principals.

The aim of my study is to describe and conceptualize the connections between teachers' task performance and 'working relations'.

The empirical data are divided into three parts:

- Teacher styles (shortly presented here)
- Coping strategies
- Organizational conditions

The concepts have been derived by induction from data according to the method known as grounded theory.

When grounded theory is applied the findings can be presented in a hierarchic form. Thus at the top level, four *dimensions* of teacher styles are identified viz. ambition types, routinization styles, individualization policies and competence profiles. At the middle level *categories* of teacher styles are discovered. In this chapter the ambition types are described. The main categories are called missionary, duty and survival orientation. To get a realistic picture of the implications, however, these categories are divided into more specific sub-categories. At the very concrete level *cases* illuminate how different teacher styles appear. In this chapter three teachers called Pete, Ben and Dave are contrasted. The task performance and its consequences — i.e. rewards, work loads and risk — of each teacher is penetrated.

Introduction

In research on teachers — like in psychology — it is possible to distinguish between a generalistic and a differential approach. The former is predominant in Sweden. Several contributions have demonstrated that a kind of pseudo-dialogue (question-answer-reaction) is predominant in the classroom discourse when lessons are analyzed by for example, Bellak's analytical chart. (cf. Gustafsson, 1977, Lundgren, 1977). However, the pseudo-dialogue pattern is neither a phenomenon typical for Sweden nor a contemporary finding. On the contrary, the well-known review by Hoetker and Ahlbrand (1969) states that this pattern is repeated in several studies in various countries and subjects during half a century. Thus Colin Power (1980) has concluded: 'A teacher is a teacher is a teacher'.

The differential approach often addresses teaching style and its consequences for the pupils' progress. In England the study by Bennett (1976) resulted in an intense debate about the efficiency of 'modern' and 'traditional' methods in teaching. Another investigation (Galton and Simon, 1980) that applied detailed observation, categorized teaching styles according to significant characteristics. Teachers practising different styles were labelled: individual monitors, class enquirers, group instructors and changers. (The latter was divided into three sub-groups viz. infrequent, rotating and habitual changers). Efficiency or loyalty towards state policy, however, seems to be the criterion taken for granted.

In this chapter the perspective is differential, but efficiency and loyalty are neglected. Our interest area is the teacher as a person, i.e. the question is: what does a certain style tell us about the teacher's possibilities to get satisfaction, cope with the task and remain sane. Thus the teacher — not the teaching process — is the objective of this study and our criteria are the internal rewards, work loads and vulnerability (risks) of the profession.

Method

Some thirty teachers in three schools have been investigated by the author. (Context: Swedish compulsory school, upper stage, pupils age 13–16). The teachers were not selected as 'successful' or 'burn-outs' etc. but chosen more or less randomly. The method could be called 'obserview' because the selected teachers were visited during lessons and breaks for one or two days on average. Finally a semi-structured interview (slightly over one hour) about the task, its performance and meaning to the teacher was executed.

The teachers did not know when they would be visited. Nevertheless they accepted this study probably because of its aim and design. (As a matter of fact the teachers' union did support this investigation very strongly). Neither the classroom activities nor the chat during breaks were recorded by a formal analytical chart. Our field notations have been collected and recorded in a free way similar to ethnological studies. The semi-structured interviews, however, were tape recorded. Afterwards individual cases, teacher portraits, were drawn. Later teacher styles were classified according to (dis)similarities between teachers.

Findings

Roughly, teachers differ according to what they want to achieve, what they can do and what they actually do. Thus the differences have been classified according to four dimensions, viz.

- ambition types (missionary, duty and survival orientation)
- routinization styles (strong and weak routinization)
- individualization policies (individualizers, coping-policy-teachers and border setters)
- competence profiles (generalists, specialists, mixed-practice-teachers and boundary pushers).

The last dimension will be explained for the reader. The generalists prefer to teach the same school class in many subjects in order to achieve good contact between teacher and class, i.e. they give priority to the social and psychological welfare of the pupils. The specialists, however, are identified with a certain school subject they master well, and prefer to teach many classes around this content, i.e. they give priority to cognitive goals. Mixed-practice teachers get bored by full-time teaching and try to increase their psychological rewards by mixing part-time teaching with other tasks. (A woman teaching domestic sciences in our pool solves her alienation problems by mixing half-time teaching and half-time consultation in home economic matters). Boundary pushers suffer from the narrow frames in ordinary school practice. Therefore they combine teaching with other duties in school which facilitate more flexible teaching for themselves and their colleagues.

The individualization policies and routinization styles will not be explained here. Hopefully they may be at least approximately understood by intuition. (They will be illuminated as well in the case studies of Pete, Ben and Dave below). The ambition types, however, will be presented in a more elaborated way.

As mentioned before there are three main orientations according to ambitions: missionary, duty and survival. Roughly speaking their intentions are to save the world (missionary), the school (duty) and own sanity (survival). For a more detailed analysis of the concrete implications it is necessary to differentiate the teachers into sub-groups as well. These styles have been identified.

However, categorizations of teacher styles are too abstract to give the reader a concrete conceptualization about authentic teachers. Some teacher portraits may illuminate the meanings and implications of individual differences. Three male teachers at the same school, teaching the same subjects (social studies) have one thing in common: they are, in one way or another, respected and successful teachers. The conceptualization and performance of the task is, however, quite dissimilar. Consequently the rewards, work loads and risk are *not* the same for Pete, Ben and Dave (pseudonyms).

Ben comes to his lessons pushing a trolley (with stencils), Dave pushes at least two trolleys (with e.g. self-made pamphlets and encyclopedia) and Pete only carries a textbook in his hand. These visible dissimilarities mirror different routines, but, beyond the level of appearance, there are important differences in philosophy and lifestyles as well. The differences can be summarized as follows:

Orientation	Style	Characteristics	Implications
MISSIONARY	Totally missionary	The teacher's mind and practice is characterized by commitment and a philosophy	+ Commitment gives meaning and results. – Unrealistic ambitions create frustrations.
	Partially missionary	The teacher's commitment is oriented towards a specific topic stressed in the practice (e.g. human rights, conservation, good literature)	+ Commitment gives meaning. The ambitions are realistic and can often be achieved. Challenge mixed with routine help the teacher to keep sane. – Frank priorities in content may create conflicts.
DUTY	Subject professional	The teacher stresses subject goals. The ambitions as a subject expert are counterbalanced against the duties to be a loyal civil servant	+ Responsibility gives meaning and results. – Subject orientation creates conflicts with integrative reform-policies.
	Conventional	The teacher's practice is routinized. Textbooks and other facilities may be used predominantly.	+ The pragmatic attitude prevents conflicts with people in the surroundings. – Monotony makes the teacher feel bored.
	Law and order	The teacher's worldview is oriented towards traditional ideals: order, obedience, diligence.	+ Order in classroom. Often moral support from parents. – Struggle with pupils from other classes (during breaks etc.). Conflicting norms with liberal colleagues.
SURVIVAL	Temporary	The teacher avoids energy consuming activities depending on either hard work load or life crisis.	+ Safe strategy for experienced teachers during short periods. – The longer crisis-period the more risky strategy.
	Permanent	The teacher's practice is characterized by loss of ambition, structure and planning.	– Lack of results, bad self-confidence, bad humour.

Aspect		Teacher	
	Pete	Ben	Dave
Classes	Mostly from the high-status villa district	Partly from the middle-status house district, partly from the rural periphery	Partly from the middle-status house district, partly from the rural periphery
Frequent instructional aids	Textbook	Stencils	Self-made pamphlets with information and tasks for the pupils
	Notes on the blackboard	Combination of several textbooks	
Individualization policy	Border-setting	Coping	Individualizing
Resources needed/used	Nothing extra	Resource teacher	Lots of extra instructional aids
Evaluation	Tests that demand genuine understanding	Tests with fixed standards for passing. Pupils who fail will be retested over and over	Tests that demand simple basic knowledge (rote learning). Little differences in scoring (ceiling effect)
Room for planning	School and home	School	Home
Content selected	Traditional school knowledge	Traditional school knowledge	Priority to projects regarded as important by teacher and class
Political message	Western democratic	Not consistent	Revolutionary commitment

The principal of the school was asked whether our teachers had got different classes by accident or on purpose. 'I feel in the air what kind of pupils suit them best' was the reply (with a mystic smile). The choice is appropriate because the rural pupils probably would object to Pete's lectures. (They are not used to it from the middle-stage because those classes were organized as non-graded instruction). Dave on the other hand 'gets sick' by teaching upper-middle-class pupils because they are too career-minded for him.

Pete regards individualization as utopic and has no idea how to handle it appropriately. Ben tries to cope with it by giving more (and more difficult) tasks to the fast and clever pupils. Dave's ambition is to adapt the tasks to individual differences in pupil interests etc.

Ben's need for an assistant teacher is related to his (weak) classes and his task performance. When pupils are supposed to answer paper-and-pencil questions they ask for help and in some classes it is not possible for one lone teacher to have sufficient time for everybody. Dave wants to be independent from other adults but needs a surplus of extra teaching aids to make the lessons more interesting.

According to content *Pete* is very aware of our cultural heritage from Athens, Rome and Jerusalem. When contemporary issues are studied he pays attention to political dilemmas. His professional creed seems to be: There are no easy solutions, but in a democratic society well-informed citizens can learn to make wiser decisions rather than badly-informed ones. *Dave* is anxious to devote much instructional time to issues that really concern the pupils. When the class (one single lesson) studied funeral rituals in an ancient culture the pupils got extremely interested in discussing life and death. Thus Dave decided to study 'life and death' for a whole month with this class. This kind of improvization, however, is difficult to master for a teacher who applies a rigid plan for a whole school year. Dave's custom of making his own pamphlets for his classes solves his problem of combining studies in time-consuming projects (e.g. life and death) and the pupils' need for general knowledge and basic facts. Besides, Dave regards the textbooks as useless because he considers them too smooth, abstract and dull. As a Marxist he pays more attention to social conflicts than consensus. Consequently he devotes most time to Finland when the Nordic countries are studied because conflicts between classes and languages are most apparent in the Finnish society. *Ben* is a pragmatic teacher with a juvenile charisma. His task performance is partly flexible because he adapts the instructional material and his oral message to the characteristics of each class. On the other hand his classification and framing (cf. Bernstein, 1977) is very strong. Every project lasts two weeks in each class. Planning and evaluation are carried out every second week. He works between eight and four at school but not at home. He likes to live far from school, because this separation helps him to keep work and leisure apart.

Every teacher is unique and Pete, Ben and Dave are interesting as a comparison as the internal consistency in each case is evident. Turning now to the category system developed (and introduced above): Pete is a typical duty teacher with a subject professional style. In fact he was the chief opponent when the principal of the school decided to cut down the expenses to subject matters in order to favour other tasks, e.g. coordination of pupils' care and administration. Ben is a duty-teacher as well but he does not suit perfectly a single style. Dave illustrates the 'total missionary' style perfectly well but his sense of humour and sociological insights save him from becoming frustrated. Successes make him happy as a teacher but failures make him fascinated as a sociologist. Thus his approach to failure is analytic, which saves him from depression.

Both Pete and Ben are routinized in their task performance but the content of the routines differ (Pete lectures and Ben assists the pupils when they are supposed to solve tasks).

The advantages of these routines may be that the work load decreases for the teacher and classes as everybody knows what to do thanks to the systematization. The monotony on the other hand is risky because it is not possible to perform Pete's lectures in every class at school. Dave is non-routinized and the advantage of this is that variation is rewarding to himself and probably to the class. Sometimes, however, pupils complain about the disorder in the classroom when the activities change too quickly or the management is not strict enough. His true individualization increases his rewards — and work load. None of the three teachers are extreme generalists or specialists.

Discussion

Teachers are different if we regard their conceptualization and performance of the task and its consequences for the teacher, i.e. rewards, work loads and risks. The teacher can, in one way, choose how to perform his task but he has not the power to decide the conditions of a task, i.e. class, subject, lesson time, resources. A principal or supervisor thus must know the teachers in his staff quite well to make *wise* decisions.

In Sweden the school authorities have argued for a collectivization of teachers' work. It has been claimed sometimes that teacher cooperation is *the* solution to improve school work for pupils — and the teachers as well. But teachers often resist the State's efforts to make the teaching staff more homogeneous. Regarding Pete, Ben and Dave it is quite easy to see why teachers often refuse to cooperate very closely. There are few 'traits' they have in common. Nevertheless, teachers can be successful in quite different ways.

Buchmann (1986) claims that teachers must become more role-orientated and less person-orientated. But the important question is: who can judge what is the adequate and realistic kind of role-orientation. At best Buchmann's idea is defensible if one imagines that it is possible to convert a 'survivor' into a 'duty teacher'. But would it be a wise ambition to change every 'missionary' to become a duty teacher? I don't think so, because commitment can raise the quality of instruction. According to Buchmann: 'Everyone likes to be comfortable, free of pain and bother. But the perspectives of psychology and profession are not the same' (*ibid.*). In my view there is a third perspective on teaching, viz. practising a *philosophy* which is the classical perspective on teaching. As a father of two I would gladly send them to Pete, Ben or Dave. But I would not be happy if the authorities in my country had the power to decide how Pete, Ben and Dave should perceive and perform their tasks.

References

BENNETT, N. (1976) *Teaching Styles and Pupil Progress*, Open Books, London.

BERNSTEIN, B. (1971) 'Class, Codes and Control', Vol. 3, *Toward a Theory of Educational Transmission*, London, Routledge and Kegan Paul.

BUCHMANN, M. (1986) 'Role over Person: Morality and Authenticity', *Teachers' College Record*, 87, 4, Summer.

GALTON, M. and SIMON, B. (1980) *Progress and Performance in the Primary Classroom*.

GUSTAFSSON, C. (1977) *Classroom Interaction*, A study of pedagogical roles in the teaching process, Stockholm Institute of Education, Department of Educational Research.

HOETKER, J. and AHLBRANDT, W. P. Jr. (1969) 'The Persistence of Recitation', *American Educational Research Journal*, 6, pp. 145–68.

LUNDGREN, U. P. (1977) *Model Analysis of Pedagogical Processes*, Stockholm Institute of Education, Department of Educational Research.

POWER, C. (1980) 'Classroom Research and the Problems of Teachers', (unpublished manuscript), Flinders University of South Australia.

Chapter 12

Teachers' Thinking about Professional Development: Relationships between Plans and Actions

Miriam Ben-Peretz, Moshe Giladi, Ben-Zion Dor and Ruth Strahovsky

It is widely accepted that the professional growth of teachers is a vital element in improving education in schools. There is evidence that teachers are more responsive to professional training after they are in service rather than before, and the profession is shifting toward the conception of inservice education as continuous professional development.

The goal of the present study was to investigate teachers' intentions, motives, and expectations of the sabbatical year, their views about possible modes of engaging in professional development, and the relationship between their plans and their actions.

More specifically the objectives of the study were:

— to identify teachers' motives and expectations for participating in studies during their sabbatical year
— to establish teachers' satisfaction with the study programs
— to investigate teachers' views about possible, alternative, modes of engaging in professional development in their sabbatical year
— to identify teachers' perceptions of their own teaching
— to search for relationships between different variables
— to identify relationships between teachers' plans about the sabbatical and their actual choices

The Ministry of Education in Israel has recognized the right of every teacher for a sabbatical year after six years of service in the public school system. A special sabbatical fund was established with the government setting aside, for each participating teacher, 8.4 per cent of his/her salary, the teachers contribute 4.2 percent of their salary each month. The participating member has the right to take a sabbatical leave in the seventh year. During that year teachers earn 66 per cent of their regular salary. If teachers wish to do so they have the right to work and earn the additional 34 per cent.

During the sabbatical year teachers are required to participate in professional courses of their choice, for no less than sixteen hours weekly, at an accredited university or teachers' college. Tuition is paid from the sabbatical fund. The sabbatical year has opened a new track of professional growth for Israeli teachers. They may use this year for accumulation of credits for a higher degree, as well as an opportunity to reflect on their work, and learn new professional approaches. Teachers may choose four hours out of the required sixteen for studies which are outside the professional realm.

Among the study options offered to teachers on their sabbatical leave one may find courses in the various subject matter areas, courses in pedagogy and instructional strategies, as well as courses aiming at widening the cultural horizons of teachers. Thus, teachers may choose to focus in four out of the sixteen required weekly study hours, on topics like drama, dance, foreign languages etc.

It is often claimed that the growth of professional knowledge of teachers is promoted by inservice studies (Lortie, 1975). Lortie emphasizes the necessity of devoting appropriate resources to staff development programs and to the evaluation of their impact on teachers. Goodlad's study (1983) showed that most inservice programs are sporadic, tend to focus on 'fashionable' topics, and that relatively few teachers participate in them. According to Goodlad it is essential to plan comprehensive inservice programs and to encourage teachers' participation. Jackson (1975) argues for the allocation of sufficient time for staff development so that teachers will have ample opportunities for professional reflection.

The Israeli model of a sabbatical for teachers provides these opportunities to all teachers.

Methods

In-depth interviews were conducted with teachers who were in the middle of their sabbatical year, and with teachers who had just finished their sabbatical. On the basis of these interviews, a questionnaire was constructed which dealt with the following issues: background variables, motives for sabbatical studies, satisfaction with the programs, preference for alternative modes of staff development during the sabbatical, teachers' perception of their professional activities.

Two populations of participants in sabbatical staff development courses responded to the questionnaire. One population studied at the inservice department of the University of Haifa, N = 23. The second population studied at the inservice department of Oranim, a teachers' college of the Kibbutz movement, N = 56.
The data were analyzed using SPSS computer program yielding frequency distributions, means, standard deviations, X^2, and correlations.

Characteristics of Participants

Of the fifty-six participants at Oranim, eight were men and forty-six women.

34 per cent were between the ages of 25 and 35
59 per cent were between the ages of 36 and 45
 7 per cent were between the ages of 46 and 55
65 per cent had a seniority of 11–20 years
27 per cent had a seniority of less than ten years
 8 per cent had a seniority of more than twenty years
82 per cent teach at general public schools
 8 per cent teach at parochial schools
10 per cent teach at other schools.

All of the twenty-three participants at the university were women.

26 per cent were between the ages of 25 and 35
30 per cent were between the ages of 36 and 45
44 per cent were between the ages of 46 and 55
About 50 percent have seniority of more than twenty-one years
About 50 percent have seniority of between 11 and 20 years
70 percent teach at general public schools and the rest at parochial and other schools.

Findings

Findings will be presented in the following order:

— Motives for joining staff development programs
— Satisfaction with programs
— Interest in alternative modes of staff development
— Perception of teaching
— Relationships between variables
— Teachers' enrolment in inservice courses

Motives for Joining Staff Development Programs

The major motives cited by participating teachers for joining the staff development programs during their sabbatical are personal enrichment, revitalization, and learning teaching strategies (See table 12.1).

It is interesting to note that teachers are not motivated by a wish to extend their knowledge in the content area they are teaching, nor do they perceive the inservice courses offered to them as leading to job promotion. Most participants in our study were middle-aged with a rather high level of years of seniority. It may well be that at this stage in their professional careers teachers are not

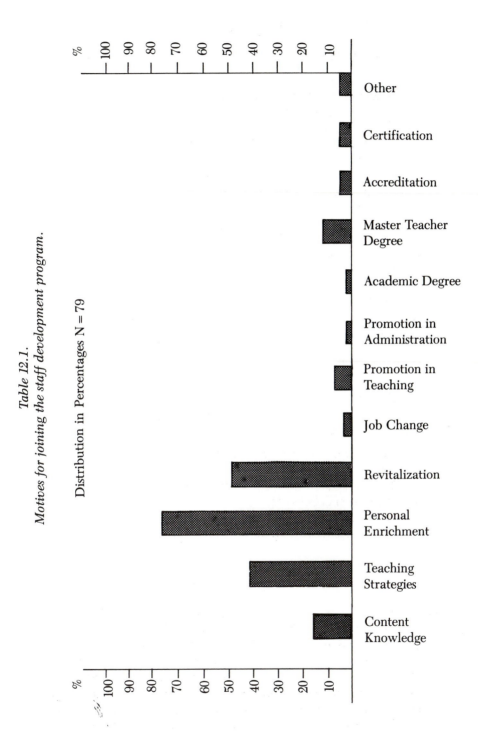

Table 12.1.
Motives for joining the staff development program.

Distribution in Percentages N = 79

interested in new subject matter knowledge, nor do they consider realistic possibilities of promotion. On the other hand, it is encouraging that these experienced teachers are still looking for new modes of instruction.

Satisfaction With Programs

In general all participants are satisfied with the programs (see table 12.2).

Table 12.2.
Satisfaction from staff development program.

Distribution in Percentages N = 79

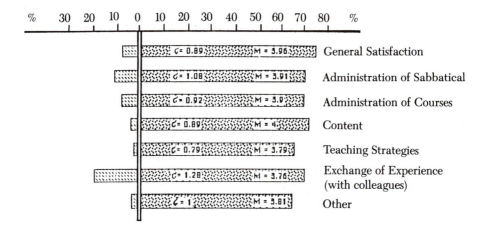

The only element of the programs which causes some significant dissatisfaction is the meeting with peers and the exchange of experiences. It may well be that the format of the courses does not provide appropriate and satisfactory opportunities for the desired exchange of ideas and experiences.

Interest in Alternative Modes of Self-Development

Some of the alternative modes of staff development which were included in the questionnaire were considered to be highly desirable by about 70 per cent of the participants (see table 12.3).

Table 12.3.
Alernative modes of sabbatical.
(in percentages) N = 79

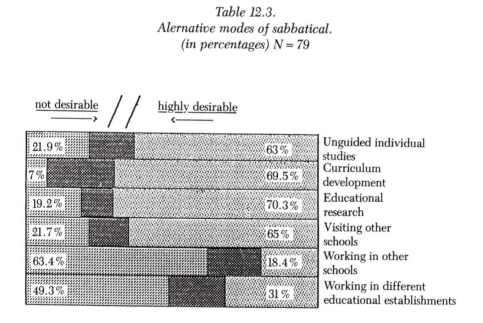

It seems that the teachers wished for a more active and independent involvement in activities leading to the enhancement of their professional abilities. Among these activities we find participation in curriculum development projects, and in educational research. Visits in other schools is also a possible mode of staff development desired by about two-thirds of the participating teachers. On the other hand, teachers are not interested in spending their sabbatical working in other schools, or in other educational institutions. This is an interesting finding when one compares teachers with other professionals, like physicians or psychologists, who often tend to work in other hospitals or counselling institutions, during their sabbatical, and consider these experiences as important for their professional development. It may be that in the teaching profession creative and unusual activities like research, which break the monotony of the regular teaching duties are preferred by teachers. Teachers may also be wary of meeting the challenge of unknown institutions, being used to their own environment, and to the security of their own classrooms.

Perception of Teaching

The participating teachers reveal a strong positive sense of their own professional competence (see table 12.4).

Table 12.4.
Perception of one's own teaching.

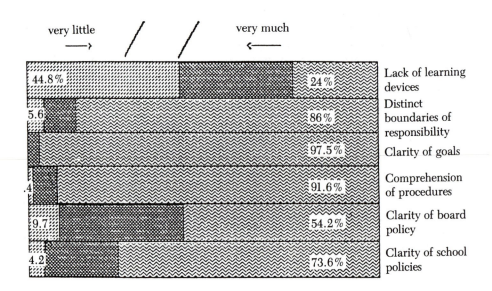

very little →		very much ←
44.8%	24%	Lack of learning devices
5.6	86%	Distinct boundaries of responsibility
	97.5%	Clarity of goals
.4	91.6%	Comprehension of procedures
9.7	54.2%	Clarity of board policy
4.2	73.6%	Clarity of school policies

Almost all the teachers claim that they are fully aware of the goals of their work and that they know how to fulfil their professional roles. There seems to be a gap between teachers' perception of their expertise in functioning in their classrooms, and their awareness of the policies of the educational establishment outside the school. Even their own school policies are less clear in the eyes of teachers than their own teaching goals. The self-confidence of teachers in their professional role may partly explain their relative lack of interest in gaining 'professional knowledge' in their sabbatical year.

Relationships Between Background Variables and Teachers' Views About the Sabbatical

Some interesting differences between teachers with varying background characteristics were noted. One significant difference related to the previous education of the teachers. Sixty per cent of teachers who had a teachers' college education, as opposed to 90 per cent of those who held university degrees, were not interested in gaining additional knowledge in the subject matter areas they teach. Teachers with more seniority (more than twenty-one years) were less interested in learning about new teaching strategies (85 per cent not interested) than their colleagues with fewer (less than ten) years of teaching experiences (50 per cent not interested). These findings raise some concerns. It seems that older teachers, who may be unaware of educational innovations would gain a lot of learning about new approaches. Teachers seem to rely on subject matter knowledge acquired years ago, during their university studies, and do not tend to learn about changes in their field. Participating teachers did not show enthusiasm for working in other schools. Department heads are even less interested in doing so than regular teachers. They may be extremely hesitant to give up the status they have earned in their schools.

Several insights into teachers' thinking about studies during their sabbatical year could be gained by examining correlations between variables. There exists a negative correlation between general satisfaction with the program and the preference of organized, fixed, learning groups according to teaching subjects. Teachers who are satisfied with opportunities for exchange of experiences with colleagues also reject stable and homogeneous learning groups. It seems that teachers prefer meeting new colleagues from areas other than their own in staff development courses. Positive correlations were found between preferences for individual and independent study and the wish to participate in curriculum development or research projects.

It seems that some teachers view their professional development as active involvement in learning situations and tend to prefer alternatives to the rather passive regular course work. Teachers also seem to value highly the opportunities for meeting new colleagues, and the exchange of experiences. This finding may be accounted for by teachers' usual loneliness in their classroom.

Teachers' Enrolment in Inservice Courses

We present some findings about teachers' thinking concerning their sabbatical year and its potential uses for professional development. What courses did teachers actually choose to study? We present the findings of their enrolment separately for Oranim, the Kibbutz Teachers' College, and for the inservice department of the School of Education at the university of Haifa.

At Oranim 48 per cent of the teachers on sabbatical leave study in courses which focus on subject matter, such as science, literature, computer studies. Another 12 per cent chose courses on teaching strategies or educational innovations such as 'teaching the disadvantaged', or 'teaching for democracy'. Forty per cent of the teachers chose courses which may be perceived as fulfilling their wish for personal enrichment and revitalization, such as art or drama courses.

At the university 42 per cent of the teachers on sabbatical leave chose courses in subject matter areas, like English, French, Arabic etc. Twenty-nine per cent enrolled on courses dealing with new educational strategies, such as 'education for family life' or 'critical use of television programs'. Twenty-nine per cent chose personal enrichment studies like drama, psychology etc.

Discussion

A sabbatical year for teachers, at all levels of the educational system, is one of the main routes for professional development in Israel. In our study we found that the participating teachers were by and large satisfied with their study programs. Because of the administrative specifications of the sabbatical year most teachers have a significant number of years of experience. This fact may account for some of the findings, such as the pronounced desire for personal enrichment and revitalization during their sabbatical. Their expressed motives for study are not to deepen their knowledge in the subject matter areas they teach, nor do they view the inservice studies as a road to promotion. The low level of preference for 'content' courses may be accounted for by teachers' intuitive understanding that 'pedagogical content knowledge' (Shulman, 1987) is more important than 'content' knowledge for the improvement of teaching. At present many inservice courses do not deal with 'pedagogical content knowledge'. The results indicate that the frame of inservice courses is too limited in its scope, and addresses teachers as rather passive consumers of knowledge in a great variety of domains. Yet, it seems that teachers may be interested in a more active learning mode, such as engagement in non-regular professional activities, like curricular development and research.

Planners of inservice programs could try to provide teachers with learning experiences in these areas and could seek to expand the format of their plans.

Teachers perceive their sabbatical studies as opportunities for exchange of ideas and experiences outside their own school and subject area. This finding seems to indicate that it is not advisable to organize school based inservice courses, contrary to the growing trend to enable teachers to participate in staff development in their own schools.

On the other hand teachers are not eager to spend time teaching in other schools than their own, as part of their professional growth process. In this respect school teachers differ from university teachers who tend to act as visiting professors in other institutions. One of the explanations for this difference may be that university faculty are rewarded for their efforts, both financially and from the point of view of academic status. It may be possible to create similar circumstances for school teachers as well.

Teachers seem to cherish the meetings with colleagues. This need is sometimes fulfilled by inservice courses. One of the courses at Oranim may serve as an example. This is an interdisciplinary course in 'studies of the country'. A variety of teachers choose this course which integrates lectures with a large number of trips to study history, geography, nature and culture of the countyside. These make up about 60 per cent of course time. The framework is informal and provides opportunities for many hours spent together outside of classrooms and buildings. In this context close interpersonal relations develop between teachers with different ethnic backgrounds who teach different subject matter areas in a variety of schools. Teachers who participate in this course tend to apply their new knowledge almost immediately in their own classrooms. Thus, the course fulfils needs for personal enrichment, for exchange of ideas and experiences with colleagues outside one's own area of teaching, while responding to the expectations of the educational system that the knowledge gained during the sabbatical year will serve to improve teaching.

It is important to note the gap between teachers' thinking about the sabbatical year, their perceptions and plans, and what they actually do during this year. In spite of their stated preference for personal enrichment courses, most teachers participate in courses extending their subject matter knowledge and aiming at improving their teaching skills. One of the main reasons for this discrepancy relates to the official requirements of the sabbatical studies. It would be interesting to investigate the impact of more flexible requirements on teachers' choices. It may also be the case that teachers view 'personal enrichment' as a luxury which will not contribute to their professional lives. Further research is needed to identify the possible impact of different staff development programs during the sabbatical year on teachers' perception of education, and on their teaching strategies.

References

GOODLAD, J. J. (1983) *A Place Called School*, New York, McGraw-Hill.

JACKSON, P. W. (1975) 'Old dogs and new tricks: Observations on the continuing education of teachers', in RUBIN, L. (Ed.) *Improving In-service Education: Proposals and Procedures for Change*, Boston, Allyn and Bacon.

LORTIE, D. C. (1975) *Schoolteacher: A Sociological Study*, Chicago and London, the University of Chicago Press.

SHULMAN, L. S. (1987) 'Knowledge and teaching: Foundations of the new reform', *Harvard Educational Review*, 57, 1, pp. 1–22.

Chapter 13

Teacher and Pupil Cognitions in Critical Incidents

Udo Hanke

In the behaviouristic paradigm it is presumed that interaction among teachers and their pupils is mainly guided by external stimuli.

Taking a cognitive point of view we presume that action is also guided by what individuals expect, fear or hope to attain. This 'epistemological approach' regards the teacher and his or her pupils as active, information-seeking and information-processing individuals who, especially in critical incidents, not only react in an everyday routine-type manner but act as conscious decision-makers, viewing their action as part of a meaningful framework established by the interpretations of the interacting partners (*cf.*Anderson, 1985; Brehmer, Jungermann, Lourens, and Sevón, 1986; Goldman, 1986; Groeben, 1986; Schön, 1983).

In a six-year research project, supported by the Federal Institute of Sport Science in Cologne and conducted at the Department of Physical Education, University of Heidelberg and the Heidelberg College of Teacher Education, a special method for the investigation of decision-making processes in critical incidents was developed. During the development, test and retest period the method of 'structured dialogues' was improved and evaluated in more than 200 interviews. This technique is theoretically based on a social interaction model first developed by Hofer and Dobrick (1978) and adapted for physical education by Hanke (1980, 1987; for a description of the model *cf.* also Huber and Mandl, 1984, pp. 59ff.).

Past research on teacher-pupil interaction has largely been teacher-centred with pupils being regarded as the passive, recipient element of the interaction process. Pupils' perceptions, intentions and evaluations have only rarely been the focus of analysis and even less frequently has research attempted to compare teacher and pupil cognitions during identical incidents. To provide comparable data the method of 'structured dialogues' was simultaneously developed for the investigation of teacher *and* pupil cognitions so that a comparative analysis was possible. A descriptive analysis of teacher and pupil congitions will give insight into their patterns of decision-making, especially when repeated interview data can be used.

Past research has shown that misunderstanding and conflicts in educational contexts are largely attributable to incongruent interpretations of situations and actions between the teacher and his or her pupils. From a more detailed knowledge about teacher and pupil perceptions, causal attributions, objectives as well as stimulus- and reaction-outcome-expectancies (Mischel, 1973) during educational interaction, an improvement in teacher training and inservice education may be achieved, but only when the methods applied are capable of giving a clear and unbiased description of those cognitive processes actually employed to generate observable behaviour.

Feedback to teachers about incongruent situation-perceptions, attributions or evaluations of outcome between themselves and their pupils can then serve as a valuable impetus to reflect on their teaching and to modify routine-type teaching practices. For this modification process special cognitive training materials have to be applied.

Method

The views expressed in papers by Nisbett and Wilson (1977a, 1977b) and Nisbett and Bellows (1977) which tried to propagate the general inability of subjects to create reliable and valid verbal reports for the use of scientific research have clearly been rejected by the contributions of Adair and Spinner (1981), Cotton (1980), Ericsson and Simon (1980, 1984), Kraut and Lewis (1982), Rich (1978), Smith and Miller (1978) and White (1980).

While Nisbett and Wilson used experiments that can be characterized by subject deception, information overload and confounding the description of cognitions with giving reasons for observable behaviour, the later study concentrated on critical incidents that were selected and characterized as reflective decision-making by the participating teachers.

This approach can be viewed in the tradition of recommendations made by Smith and Miller (1978):

> We advocate the direction of research attention to the issue of when (not whether) people are able to report accurately on their mental processes and suggest that tasks that are engaging and not overlearned are one promising area in which to look for evidence of such awareness (p. 316f.).

When using self-selected situations, memory problems are reduced and the probability of rationalization when using stimulated recall techniques is decreased, since subjects need not be confronted with the 'objective' outside view of the situation and thus do not have to synchronize subjective situation perceptions with the view of the observer fed back to them through technical media.

This study involved twenty-eight male and female PE teachers who taught in grades six to eight. The data are based on twenty-eight teacher and twenty-seven pupil interviews. One pupil could not be interviewed because during the investigated critical incident she had broken her arm.

Before each interview the PE teacher was contacted and informed about the purpose of the investigation. Possible apprehension was reduced and the non-evaluative character of the interview was pointed out. Selection of subject matter was not influenced by the researchers. Before the beginning of the PE class pupils were given general information about the presence of the researchers without mentioning the ensuing interview so as to avoid possible changes in attention and behaviour. Instruction during the PE class was videotaped and the researchers took notes on situations which the teacher might have selected as a 'critical incident'. Immediately after class the teacher was asked to choose a 'remarkable situation' that involved active decision-making, and agreement between teacher and interviewers was established on the identification of the situation and the pupil involved in it.

The interview techniques applied during the 'structured dialogues' included special focusing questions, which aimed at avoiding a confusion of cognitions before and after the incident with the actual decision-making cognitions during the incident. In addition to this the interviewers looked out for reported contradictions and justifications.

Teachers and pupils were encouraged to use 'don't remember' replies and were informed that the variety of interview questions does not reflect the researchers' view of an equally differentiated cognitive decision-making process. One interviewer asked the questions and applied the 'focusing technique' while the other coded the answers on an analysis sheet using categorial terminology. During the teacher interview these entries were discussed by the teacher and the two interviewers, following the criteria of 'communicative evaluation'. All interviews were audio-taped and reanalyzed to check entries that were made during the interview.

After the end of the PE class and the identification of the situation and the pupil involved, the pupil was interviewed first. Knowing the pupil's perspective enabled the researchers to conduct the teacher interview using the pupil's cognitions as a background and helped to sharpen the interviewers' awareness for teacher contradictions and justifications. The pupils were assured of confidential use of their data, especially that the teacher would not be informed about their perspective of the situation.

Results

On the basis of the eighteen cognitive elements which constitute the information processing model two groups of results were compiled:

— descriptions of frequencies of reconstructed teacher and pupil cognitions
— comparisons of teacher and pupil cognitions.

Frequencies of Teacher Cognitions

For half of the twenty-eight teachers the critical incident was 'unexpected', while the others considered the situations as 'common' but nevertheless demanding conscious decision-making. The situations were characterized as 'negative' for the teacher, the other pupils or the instructional process by twenty-five teachers. Twenty-four teachers reported being aware of the importance of the situation and rated the importance 'high' to 'very high' on a six-point scale. Replying to the question whether they had thought about reasons as to why the critical incident occurred, twelve teachers reported that during the time span between perception of the situation and their observable reaction they had not thought of any reasons at all, thirteen of the other sixteen teachers made the pupil responsible for the incident and only three attributed the situation to their own behaviour.

Only half of the teachers reported thinking about situation-outcome-expectancies (i.e. the development of the situation if they would not intervene), thirteen of whom thought the situation would develop negatively.

With regard to their choice of possible reactions it is striking that only one teacher reported that he had not reacted immediately but had attempted to gain additional information about the situation. Twenty-two teachers reported that they had not thought of any alternatives to the behaviour which they actually showed.

Since understanding and misunderstanding in educational contexts largely depends on the ability of the interacting individuals to change perspectives, in the final part of the 'structured dialogue' the teachers were asked if they had thought about the pupil's perception, attribution and emotions. Eighteen of the teachers reported that they had not thought about possible perceptions of the situation by the pupil involved, twenty did not think about the pupil's evaluation of the situation and seventeen spent no time thinking about the pupil's emotions during the incident.

Frequencies of Pupil Cognitions

The pupils were interviewed about their cognitions related to two different phases of the incident. The first part of the interview concentrated on their cognitions up to the time when their behaviour was observed by the teacher, and the second part dealt with cognitions after the teacher's intervention.

Twenty-three of the twenty-seven pupils reported that they had behaved 'spontaneously' and eighteen described their behaviour as 'negative' with regard to the teacher or class. The spontaneity of pupil behaviour is also reflected in the fact that twenty-six pupils did not consider the teacher's perspective and twenty-five had not thought of any alternatives to their chosen behaviour.

Comparison of Teacher and Pupil Cognitions

Because of the missing pupil, twenty-seven one by one comparisons of teacher and pupil cognitions were possible. In twenty-one cases teachers and pupils agreed in the description of the situation. There was, however, disagreement in nineteen cases with regard to its importance. When comparing the reported causal attributions about the origin of the situation disagreement occurred in nineteen cases. The comparison of the objectives expressed by the teacher with those perceived by the pupil showed disagreement in eighteen cases.

In a second step a cross-comparison of self-reported congnitions with the alleged cognitions of the other was conducted. Since the number of cases where teacher and pupil had changed their perspective was very small, only a few comparisons were possible. In these cases the picture was very clear: when a change of perspective was reported, the implications were incorrect.

Discussion

The results reported above indicate that by using the method of 'structured dialogues' a descriptive analysis of cognitive decision-making processes during self-selected critical incidents is possible. In addition to the results presented, an in-depth analysis of the data reveals that in the investigated sample of teachers certain cognitive constructs or decision-making elements are either missing or show a certain 'bias' favouring the teachers' position and neglecting the pupils' perspectives.

Missing cognitions do not have to be interpreted negatively if the teacher or teacher-educator view this omission as irrelevant for the choice of behaviour. In many cases the inability to report about cognitions also has to be seen as an indication of highly automated processes or sub-routines, which may be activated even in situations characterized as 'conscious decision-making'. If highly routinized action, however, results in a teacher behaviour being interpreted negatively for achieving desired objectives then these routines have to be modified by increasing the consciousness of the teacher during decision-making situations.

If teachers are informed about the results of several 'structured-dialogues' that were compiled in similar critical incidents with their pupils and accept that the reported cognitions actually were responsible for their observable behaviour and should they, in turn, consider this behaviour responsible for certain learning outcomes in the pupils, teacher-educators find themselves in a positive argumentative situation: together with the teacher they can then select training materials which aim at modifying the decision-making cognitions of the teachers.

For this purpose special cognitive training materials were developed which are described below.

Cognitive Intervention Training Materials

During a follow-up research project cognitive training materials were developed which can be used by PE teachers and coaches and are designed for self-directed analysis and modification, but which ideally are implemented in specially designed inservice modification programmes (Treutlein, Janalik and Hanke, 1989a, 1989b).

These materials consist of the following training modules:

1 Materials to sensitize teachers and coaches to their subjective perception of cognitive constructs
2 Examples and materials to improve cognitive discrimination abilities
3 Instructions about self-directed learning and working with training-partners ('tandems')
4 Audio-visual training materials ('video-simulation')
5 Materials to visualize 'cognitive switches' (*cf.* below)
6 Instructions for microteaching and role-playing
7 Information on the normative, didactic position under which the materials were compiled
8 Basic assumptions of the 'theory of action model' used for the reconstruction of cognitions
9 Perspectives of continuous learning and integration into everyday situations.

A prerequisite for the modification of cognitive decision-making is increasing subjective awareness in hitherto unreflective routine type reactions. For this reason the materials begin with a focus on the training of so-called 'stop-action techniques', which consist of internal and external vocalization of intervening commands and interspersed actions that are combined with special relaxation techniques. Together with increasing the subjective awareness of advance-signals for critical incidents these methods give the teachers time to reflect and to implement alternative cognitions. In most cases using 'stop-action techniques' does not slow down observable behaviour and therefore is not discernible for the interacting partner. The cognitive intervention approach is basically designed for individual diagnosis and training. This permits the teacher and teacher-educator to choose training modules which aim specifically at those needs and deficits which were diagnosed and which the teacher desires to modify. These decisions should be based on a subject-subject relationship between teacher and teacher-educator and should meet the demands of dialogue-consensual communication (Groeben, Wahl, Schlee and Scheele, 1988).

Multiple cognitive reconstruction of decision-making processes usually reveals certain patterns which can be visualized by using the 'cognitive switches analysis sheet' (see figure 13.1) which displays the results of the structured dialogues in a condensed form.

Reflection on patterns visible in the 'cognitive switches analysis sheet'

Figure 13.1.
Structured dialogues.

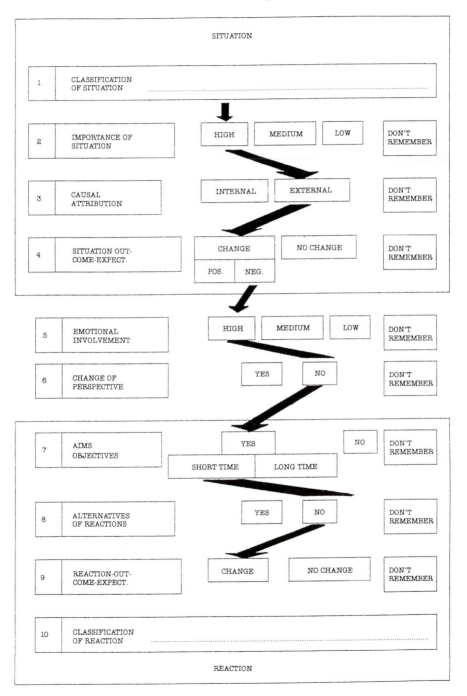

together with a comparison of research results on the relationship between teachers' subjective theories and observable teacher behaviour serves as a basis for selecting the cognitive training modules which are designed to modify these specific cognitions.

First results from cognitive intervention training seminars have shown that an individualized approach can effectively modify the subjective theories of teachers (Wahl, Schlee, Krauth and Mureck, 1983) and that the method of 'structured dialogues' is capable of giving a valid description of peri-actional cognitions responsible for generating observable behaviour.

From an evaluation study of the cognitive training materials described above, which is in progress, information about the feasibility of the approach is expected.

References

ADAIR, J. G. and SPINNER, B. (1981) 'Subjects' access to cognitive processes: Demand characteristics and verbal report,' *Journal for the Theory of Social Behavior*, 11, 1, pp. 30–52.

ANDERSON, J. R. (1985) *Cognitive Psychology and its Implications*, New York, Freeman and Company.

BREHMER, B. JUNGERMANN, H., LOURENS, P. and SEVÓN, G. (Eds) (1986) *New Directions in Research on Decision-Making*, Amsterdam, North-Holland.

COTTON, J. L. (1980) 'Verbal reports on neural processes: Ignoring data for the sake of theory?' *Personality and Social Psychological Bulletin*, 6, 2, pp. 278–81.

ERICSSON, K. A. and SIMON, H. A. (1980) 'Verbal reports as data', *Psychological Review*, 87, 3, pp. 215–51.

ERICSSON, K. A. and SIMON, H. A. (1984) *Protocol Analyis*, Cambridge, MA, MIT Press.

GOLDMAN, A. I. (1986) *Epistemology and Cognition*, Cambridge, MA, Harvard University Press.

GROEBEN, N. (1986) *Handeln, Tun, Verhalten als Einheiten einer verstehend-erklärenden Psychologie*, Tübingen, Francke.

GROEBEN, N., WAHL, D., SCHLEE, J. and SCHEELE, B. (1988) *Forschungsprogramm Subjektive Theorien*, Tübingen, Francke.

HANKE, U. (1980) *Training des Lehrverhaltens von Sportstudenten. Ein Vergleich zweier Trainingsverfahren auf der Basis des Microteaching.* Unveröffentlichte Dissertation, Institut für Sport und Sportwissenschaften, Universität Heidelberg.

HANKE, U. (1987) 'Cognitive aspects of interaction in physical education', in BARRETTE, G. T. FEINGOLD, R. S. REES, C. R. and PIÉRON, M. (Eds.) *Myths, Models, Methods in Sport Pedagogy*, Champaign, IL: Human Kinetics, pp. 135–41.

HOFER, M. and DOBRICK, M. (1978) 'Die Rolle der Fremdattribution von Ursachen bei der Handlungssteuerung des Lehrers', in GÖRLITZ, D. MEYER, W. U. and WEINER, B. (Hrsg.), *Bielefelder Symposium über Attribution*, Stuttgart, Klett. pp. 51–63.

HUBER, G. L. and MANDL, H. (1984) 'Access to teacher cognitions: Problems of assessment and analysis', in HALKES, R. and OLSON. J. K. (Eds) *Teacher Thinking*, Lisse, The Netherlands, Swets and Zeitlinger, pp. 58–72.

KRAUT, P. E. and LEWIS. S. H. (1982) 'Person perception and self-awareness: Knowledge of influences on one's own judgements', *Journal of Personality and Social Psychology*, 42, 3, pp. 448–60.

MISCHEL, W. (1973) 'Toward a cognitive social learning reconceptualization of personality', *Psychological Review*, 80 4, pp. 252–83.

NISBETT, R. E. and BELLOWS, N. (1977) 'Verbal reports about causal influences on social judgements: Private access versus public theories', *Journal of Personality and Social Psychology*, 35, 9, pp. 613–24.

NISBETT, R. E. and WILSON, T. D. (1977a) 'Telling more than we can know: Verbal reports on mental processes', *Psychological Review*, 84, 3, pp. 231–59.

NISBETT, R. E and WILSON, T. D. (1977b) 'The halo effect: Evidence for unconscious alterations of judgements', *Journal of Personality and Social Psychology*, 35, 4, pp. 250–56.

RICH, M. C. (1979) 'Verbal reports on mental processes: Issues of accuracy and awareness', *Journal for the Theory of Social Behavior*, 9, pp. 29–37.

SCHÖN, D. A. (1983) *The Reflective Practitioner: How Professionals Think in Action*, New York, Basic Books.

SMITH, E. R. and MILLER, F. D. (1978) 'Limits on perception of cognitive processes: A reply to Nisbett and Wilson', *Psychological Review*, 85, 4, pp. 355–62.

TREUTLEIN, G., JANALIK, H. and HANKE, U. (1989a) *Wie Sportler wahrnehmen, denken und fühlen*. Köln, Strauss.

TREUTLEIN, G., JANALIK, H. and HANKE, U. (1989b) *Wie Trainer wahrnehmen, denken und fühlen*, Köln, Strauss.

WAHL, D., SCHLEE, J., KRAUTH, J. and MURECK, J. (1983) *Naive Verhaltenstheorien von Lehrern*, Oldenburg, Universität Oldenburg.

WHITE, P. (1980) 'Limitations on verbal reports of internal events: A defutation on Nisbett and Wilson and of Bem', *Psychological Review*, 87, 1, pp. 105–12.

Part III
Innovations in Thinking and Practice

Chapter 14

Relations Between Thinking and Acting in Teachers' Innovative Work

Ingrid Carlgren

Teaching practice is mostly not considered to be reflective. It is governed by tradition and rules rather than by reflection on actions and causes of actions.

In Sweden a great number of teachers are taking part in school-based curriculum development. Innovative work in school-based curriculum development is expected to lead to new practices. Its objective is also to generate practices based on reflective thinking.

Will school-based curriculum development result in reflective practice? This chapter discusses the connection between innovative work and reflective practice in relation to some results of a study of school-based curriculum development. Different kinds of innovative work are described in relation to three dimensions: why the old practice was changed, the meaning of the new practice, and how the change was realized.

The author's conclusions are that reflective thinking is not necessary for change of practice. The shaping of the new practice seems, however, to be influenced by the relation between thinking and acting in the innovative work.

School-Based Curriculum Development as a Way of Making Teaching Practice More Reflective.

Since the beginning of the 1980s, school development in Sweden is supposed to take the form of school-based curriculum development, which is expected to be innovative work on a broad scale, where most of the teachers in the schools participate.

This is part of what Lundgren (1986) has called the second generation of school reforms based on the idea of decentralization and goal-directed rather than rule-directed teaching practice. It is expected that this will lead to a practice more based on reflection and less bound by tradition.

School-based curriculum development can thus be seen as a strategy for changing teaching practice — making it more professional and reflected upon.

Is this the case? What is the connection between school-based curriculum development and reflective teaching practice? What then is meant by reflective practice? In the rhetoric connected with the Swedish school reforms the meaning of reflective practice is that the intentions are formulated and that deliberate choices of procedures in accordance with the official goals are chosen.

An alternative way of understanding reflective practice is given by Schön (1983) who emphasizes 'reflection-in-action' which means reflection on 'knowing-in-action'. As a consequence practitioners do not operate in a real world but in a constructed representation of a practical situation. The possibility for teachers to be reflective in this sense has been questioned (see for example Jordell, 1987). The question of reflective teaching is connected with the question of the nature of teachers' knowledge as well as with the relations between thinking and acting in teachers' work.

The concept of theory has been used in relation to teachers' knowledge. Bromme (1984) argues that this concept is not a good metaphor for understanding teachers' expert knowledge, since it suggests analogies between teacher knowledge and scientific theories. Scientific theories are often in the shape of a hierarchy of statements which can be transformed into a technology for teaching.

An alternative metaphor for teachers' knowledge is the concept of image. According to Clandinin and Connelly (1986) teachers' personal, practical knowledge is in the form of images from which practical principles and rules can be derived. The images are 'the intellectual power' behind the practices. The relation between thinking and acting is dialectical. Thinking and acting are two sides of the same coin. (See also the chapter by Day in this section.) School-based curriculum development is expected to lead to reflective practice. The question of reflective teaching is, however, connected with the question of the nature of teachers' knowledge and the relations between thinking and acting in teachers' work.

These questions will be discussed in the following pages. But first I will present some results from a study on teachers' innovative work from a teacher perspective. Different kinds of innovative work are described in relation to three dimensions: why the old practice was changed, the meaning of the new practice and how the change was realized.

The concept of image as a way to describe teachers' knowledge and minded practice (Clandinin, 1986) to describe teaching practice means that thinking and acting are not separated, but one is a prerequisite as well as a consequence of the other. How then, is it ever possible to change practice in a radical way? How is this connected to the question of the relation between thinking and acting?

One aspect of innovative work that has been pointed out is that almost all innovations are changed when they are implemented (see for example Hoyle, 1970, House, 1974, Fullan, 1981). In what way is this connected with the different kinds of innovative work?

A Phenomenographic Study of Teachers' Innovative Work.

In order to describe the innovative work from a teacher perspective but not the teachers' own understanding of innovative work I used a phenomenographic approach (Marton, 1981). In this the aim is to find varying conceptions of a certain phenomenon, conceptions that are qualitatively different from each other. These conceptions are systematized and described.

Conceptions in the phenomenographic sense are not conscious. They are the taken-for-granted basis for conscious opinions. One basic assumption is that the same phenomenon might be conceived of in qualitatively different ways, and the intention is to describe these different ways of conceiving. The outcome of a phenomenographic analysis is thus a set of categories for descriptions of a phenomenon.

To achieve this outcome interviews are made with a number of subjects concerning the phenomenon in question. Since the conceptions are not reflected on, it is not possible for a person to express a conception directly, i.e. it is not possible to ask a person about his conception. It is, however, possible to study conceptions by having persons express themselves about a phenomenon. By analyzing several interviews expressing different conceptions, it is possible to discover the conceptions. The categories of descriptions are constructed to express the essential meaning of the conceptions.

In this study (Carlgren, 1986) the phenomenon was teachers' innovative work. My assumption was, however, that this phenomenon is not something you can ask teachers about as such. I therefore conducted interviews with teachers about their own work, which by others had been described as school-based curriculum development. Out of the teachers' descriptions and understandings of their own innovative work I constructed different categories of conceptions of innovative work.

Twenty-six teachers were interviewed about their innovative work. The interviews lasted 45–90 minutes. They were recorded, transcribed verbatim and then analyzed.

The resulting set of categories was developed into different types of innovative work. That is — the following description of types is based on teachers' descriptions of what they have done and how they understand it. It is further based on all twenty-six interviews, although I will only discuss thirteen here. Those thirteen were all about the same innovation, namely, about using literature in the teaching of Swedish (LBS for Literature Based Swedish in the following). It was one of the most common curriculum developments in the lower and intermediate stages of the comprehensive school in the years 1983–85.

Different Kinds of Innovative Work

All the interviewed teachers knew about and were inspired by a model where all the elements of the Swedish curriculum were connected with the reading of literature. This model was developed by a teacher and presented in a couple of booklets.

There were, however, only a few of the teachers who were able to put the model into practice by themselves. If we call these first generation innovators, the remaining innovative works were second or third generation. That is, when the first teachers had succeeded in putting the model into practice, they could present a more concrete model, which several other teachers could use. When LBS became more common it was spreading by itself. There was no longer a need for demonstration. At the same time the innovation was changed into a more traditional model than it was intended to be in the beginning.

Although only a few teachers could concretize the model by themselves all the thirteen teachers were very satisfied with the new practice after having tried it. As an innovation LBS was an extremely easy one to implement.

The reading of fiction was common to all projects, as was the building up of routines around this reading (different kinds of tasks, i.e. grammar tasks, writing reviews, spelling practices etc.).

There were, however, also differences between the projects. These differences are described not by the concrete details but by means of some categories which are developed to capture the underlying conceptions.

To illuminate the description of the categories some excerpts from the interviews are presented along with the descriptions.

Why Was the Old Practice Changed?
LBS as an 'Extension' of the Old Practice or an 'Alternative'

LBS as an Extension

In these cases LBS was added to the earlier practice through the innovative work. The content of the Swedish curriculum was in that way extended. To what extent the curriculum was changed varied. The innovation was carried through as a kind of gradual change, where new pieces were added and successively replaced old ones.

> The intention is that the children shall experience something more than the textbook....
>
> I still use textbooks and traditional instruction . . . but the kids must get an interest for literature. They must get used to reading books. They must read something else than what's in the textbook.

LBS as an Alternative

These were cases where LBS was replacing the earlier practice. The teachers were dissatisfied with the old practice. The children did not like it or learn enough. The teachers ascribed this to the form of instruction. The new practice (LBS) was seen as a solution to those problems.

> The teaching of Swedish has not worked on the intermediate stage . . . .
>
> The kids didn't like reading and writing . . . I started to think about the teaching of Swedish — how to make it more popular, how to get the kids to read . . . .
> Thanks to the model it was easy to change.

The differences between the two types of innovative work concerned the reason for the change of practice. When LBS was seen as an extension, no problem was experienced with the old practice. The reason to change was to extend the content of the Swedish curriculum . The change was gradual. LBS was not seen in opposition to the old practice. When LBS was seen as an alternative, the change was radical. The reason for change was that the old practice was seen as a problem. The unsatisfactory results were connected with the earlier form of instruction.

In that context LBS became a solution to the problems experienced with the old practice.

The Meaning of the New Practice

LBS as a 'Complement', a 'Method' or a 'Framework'

LBS was an innovation that was easy to implement. It was easy for the teachers to believe in it and the immediate effects were obvious and positive. On the surface the projects looked very similar but under the surface and at a closer look the differences were significant. Regarding several details the different projects were in opposition to each other. These differences concerning the details became intelligible in relation to the following categories:

LBS as a Complement

There was more time for reading literature and for making oral and written reports of what one had read compared to the traditional curriculum. The focus was on giving the children reading experiences, an inclination for reading and reading practice. The meaning of LBS was mainly reading of literature. To a large extent the forms of instruction did not change.

> You must give the kids a love of reading — they are to get used to reading books from the start. They must read something else than what's in the textbook.
>
> Sometimes we read in the textbook. Then it is not the experience of reading, but giving questions about what's read.
>
> It's a security to have the textbook. Different moments in the right order . . . . I want to be sure that everything is included.

LBS as a Method

All parts of the Swedish curriculum were connected with the reading of literature. The children chose books and tasks, and through the tasks in connection with reading the books all parts of the curriculum were included. Every child could work at his own speed and the teacher could follow which tasks the different pupils had accomplished and how. Since the pupils chose books on their own level of reading ability there was a natural individualization. The focus was on LBS as a form of instruction.

> Literature as textbook — the instruction can be individualized, love of reading created and grammar can be worked on . . . .
> We have a system around the reading of books that all kids know . . .

LBS as a Framework

The reading of literature was the foundation for the instruction but certain parts of the curriculum were disengaged. One reason for this was that the teachers saw that the reading experiences could be destroyed by always connecting tasks to the reading. Another reason was that the teachers had developed alternative forms of instruction concerning those parts. It is as if LBS served as a crutch for the teachers, to get away from the old practice and the dependency on the textbook. Gradually they did not need the crutch.

After having tried LBS for some time, problems were experienced — therefore the forms of instruction must be further developed. LBS was both a general form of instruction and reading of literature.

> The books must not be cut up and the reading experience destroyed. It is when the children have a total experience of reading that they develop a love of reading. Therefore I have only content-oriented tasks connected with the reading now . . . . I've isolated the grammar parts a bit . . . but I'm not guided by the textbook . . . . I think all parts are included in a more natural way now than I used to before . . . . The different parts of the subject are more separated now than before. The bringing in of the grammar again is not a 'bringing back'.

How Was The Change Realized?
Innovative Work as 'Development', 'Testing' or 'Adoption' of New Practice

Innovative Work as Development of New Practice.

This involved development of the new practice in relation to certain ideas of the purpose as well as the practice. As a result there was a development of the ideas as well. The development of the new practice was connected with a construction of a representation of the instructional practice. Conceptions regarding the means and the ends and the relation between them were developed.

> I found out that the origin of our problems were the textbooks that governed the life of the classroom. I didn't have the initiative — the textbook had it . . .
>
> I had been motivated to change the teaching for a long time but couldn't find the angle of approach . . .
>
> Today the situation is totally different. The three years have been hard work. . . . I've been on unfamiliar ground . . .
>
> But now I'm on solid ground in a way I have never been as a teacher before. I know every minute what we are doing and where we are going... And I can improvise — use the instructional moments that emerge in everyday life. Earlier the textbook decided and that did not have any connection with the life in the classroom.

The significance of the innovation was that problems in the old practice were solved and that the conceptions of what was done became more precise and differentiated.

Innovative Work as Testing of New Practice.

LBS was tested in relation to its intended ends. The results from this testing determined whether the new practice was to be adopted or not. LBS was seen as a concrete model that could be taken over as it was. Depending on the results of the testing it would be adjusted.

> You look at if it's working . . . if you are getting closer to the goals you have put up or if you are going in another direction . . . . If you reach the goals you can go further and decide new goals and go on climbing . . . . You raise the goals and try different means.

The significance of the innovation was that the results in relation to some specific goal were improved. The results were guiding the development.

Innovative Work as Adoption of New Practice.

This started from a belief in the new practice as a better practice than the existing one. The innovative efforts and the thinking aimed at getting the new practice to work. LBS was seen as the solution to the problems in the old practice or (if there were no experienced problems) as something good that would make the teaching of Swedish better. It was something the teachers believed in, their efforts were about getting it to work.

> I was looking for a way to teach the children without the boring textbooks... grammar was plodded through. Every child was supposed to do the same thing...
>
> Through this (LBS) the teaching can be individualized, love of reading created and grammar can be worked with starting from the books...
>
> We have talked and judged the results, changed and created new things.... You can feel when what you are doing goes well, if the children are interested and so on. No one of us has been hesitating. We all believed in it...
>
> We have got happy and self-governed children who like their school-work. Most things are impossible to assess.

The new practice was adjusted in accordance with the pupils', the parents' and the teacher's reactions. The significance of the innovation was that it led to more satisfied pupils and/or teachers.

The differences between the three kinds of innovative work can be summarized in the following way:

	The meaning of the improvement	*The ground for change*
Development of new practice	The teachers knew better what to do and why	Ideas
Testing of new practice	The outcome of the teaching was better	Results
Adoption of new practice	The pupils, parents and teachers were more satisfied	Reactions

Relations Between Thinking and Acting in Teachers' Innovative Work

Innovative work can be described as work aiming at changing the means to achieve certain ends. The difference between the three kinds of innovative work can be described as differences concerning the relation between the means and the ends.

In the 'development'-kind of innovative work (DIW), the innovative work included the development of the means as well as the development of the significance of the ends, the means and the relation between means and ends. In that way a representation of LBS was constructed and the means were formed in relation to that. The relation between means and ends was developed as a theoretical relation.

In the 'testing'-kind of innovative work (TIW), the innovative efforts concerned the establishment of an empirical relation between means and ends. The question for the teachers was: Will these means lead to the expected ends?

In the 'adopting'-kind of innovative work (AIW), the relation between means and ends was taken for granted. The teachers thought of the means as the only possible means. The innovative efforts therefore concerned getting LBS to function.

The relation between means and ends was in DIW a *theoretical relation*, in TIW an *empirical relation* and in AIW a *taken-for-granted relation*. In DIW and TIW thinking and acting were separated, in AIW it was not.

These differences were expressed in the way the teachers could talk about their innovative work. In AIW they could describe what they were doing and why (in terms of the ends). In TIW they could also tell if the ends were achieved. In DIW, finally, they could furthermore describe the significance of means and ends and the relation between them. In DIW a theoretical representation of the new practice was constructed.

LBS is a model for the teaching of Swedish. It is built up around an idea that a meaningful context for the subject must be created, and that this can be done through connecting the different elements of the curriculum to the reading of literature. This idea can, however, be understood in different ways.

To characterize the differences between the ways of understanding LBS, I will use a distinction pointed out by Dewey (1936), namely between the meaning of the words apprehension and comprehension. Apprehension is direct understanding, the object and the meaning of the object is the same. Comprehension is indirect understanding. The understanding is not immediate but delayed. The meaning must be constructed for the object to be understood. This construction work produces concepts through definitions and distinctions and other 'thinking tools'.

When an object is apprehended it is not meaningful to ask for the meaning of that object — the meaning is conceived of as obvious. When an object is comprehended it is, however, meaningful to ask for the meaning.

The way of understanding in DIW can be called comprehension, while it was more like apprehension in AIW.

Both DIW and TIW were characterized by separation between thinking and acting and in both kinds of work the teachers were interested in the results. But the meaning of the testing varies. In TIW the testing was in order to verify a connection. The relation between thinking and acting can be described as a process of trial and success. When there is success the connection is established, when the success fails to come there is no systematic way to change the methods.

In DIW the testing was in order to develop the connection. The relation between thinking and acting is then a process of trial and error. When there is error, the thinking has to go on. The constructed representation has to be developed. In that way errors will lead to better thinking. If the goals are reached, your knowledge will be confirmed, but not growing. If your goals are not reached, your knowledge will grow under the condition that your practice was the consequence of a way of comprehending the situation. Then the situation is 'experimental' (Peirce, 1966) — it has theoretical meaning. This difference between DIW and TIW is analogous to the discussion of verification or falsification as the most important prerequisite for scientific knowledge growth (Popper, 1963).

How is Radical Change Possible?

In everyday practice thinking and acting are not separated. What is done is seen as the only possible thing to do. It is based on common sense. It is not reflected on but seen as 'natural'. The acting is built on assumptions that are not questioned but taken for granted. (They are however not conceived of as taken for granted!) The means and ends are one. The means can be justified by the ends if the question is asked, but there is no experienced need for this.

What Makes Change Possible?

In my study two ways of change were described. When LBS was an *extension* of the old practice the change was gradual and when LBS was an *alternative* to the old practice the change was radical.

When LBS was seen as an extension, the thinking-acting totality of the old practice was not challenged. It was possible to go on with the old practice and at the same time introduce LBS.

When LBS was seen as an alternative there was, however, a breaking up of the thinking-acting totality. Problems were experienced and the relation between the means and the ends was questioned. Thereby the thinking could be separated from the acting and alternative ways of acting could be considered.

Translations of the Original Innovation

Attempts at curriculum change are often translated into something quite different from the original innovation as they are implemented in the classroom. How and why does this translation occur?

The description of the differences between the different kinds of innovative work can contribute to the understanding of how the translation occurs.

LBS was a model that worked on several levels. One level is that it gives every child something to do all the time. The individualization becomes natural, and the teacher is released from her monitoring and pacing activities. On another level it is a model that gives the children the possibility to be responsible for their own work, which they like. Besides it is more fun to read real literature than the textbook. Then there are more levels, which are not so easily described and demand constructive thinking to formulate. This is what the teachers in DIW did.

All kinds of innovative work realized the LBS-model on a surface level. In TIW the direction was towards deeper levels through a stepwise process. In DIW the teachers aimed at deeper levels from the beginning, and worked on the realization of these levels. This was possible through the construction of the representation necessary for comprehension.

An example of the differences: the writing of a review of the books was intended to be a meaningful task but the children did not seem to think so. In AIW some of the teachers kept the review tasks but admitted they did not function as intended, while others excluded the review tasks. In DIW the teachers created different means to make the review tasks meaningful to the children. That is — in DIW the teachers made the tasks function the way they were supposed to! This was possible by means of the theoretical representation of LBS.

This takes us back to the question of the connection between the means and the ends. If this connection is seen as a *mechanical* one the question of comprehension or not is not important. The connection does not have to be created — it is sufficient to introduce the means in order to get to the ends. Instead of seeing the connection as mechanical it can be seen as *possible*. This means that the connection may appear as an empirical connection (which is not the same as a causal connection), but in order to accomplish a possible connection the possibility must be realized. To be realized it must be comprehended. This, in turn, means that what is comprehended is possible to accomplish. The quality of the thinking and the relation between the thinking and the acting will thus determine what is possible to accomplish.

It has been suggested that teachers' constructs or subjective knowledge influences the translation of the innovation. What is the original innovation? Is it the actual manifestation of procedures or is it the idea behind the procedures? If the innovation is considered as theoretical as well as practical the question of translation of the innovation changes. It is not a matter of translation but of realization of an idea — and in order to realize the idea it has to be understood. When it is not understood the practice can be imitated and also 'translated' in accordance with the teachers' personal practical knowledge.

In the thirteen cases of LBS-innovation there was a connection between the realization of the idea and all three dimensions of the innovative work. The 'best' realization was accomplished when the old practice was questioned, LBS was seen as a framework and the new practice was formed in a 'development' kind of innovative work.

How Will Innovative Work Influence the Relation Between Thinking and Acting in Teachers' Practices?

In connection with school-based curriculum development the practice is expected to become more reflected upon. The belief in goal-directed practice as the way to reflective practice is a popular idea in Sweden today. My study of teacher innovative work shows, however, that this is not always the case.

The different kinds of innovative work are all goal-directed, i.e., the new practice is connected with a specified purpose. The ways to realization of the goals are reflective (in DIW) as well as unreflective (in AIW).

In DIW the construction of a representation of LBS was the ground for reflection. This representation, through which the practical situation can be comprehended, may be called an object of knowledge (Althusser, 1958; Piaget, 1977) for the situation. It is a theoretical representation of the situation. If the object of knowledge is formulated and made explicit the knowledge growth can be collective.

It seemed thus, as if innovative work as such was not sufficient for the practice to be reflective. The practice can be changed without reflective thinking. Instead the construction of a theoretical representation seemed to be the decisive prerequisite. There are two possibilities regarding the relation between innovative work and reflective practice.

Innovative Work as Theoretical as Well as Practical Construction Work

In everyday practice knowledge is not constructed, reality is conceived as an undifferentiated totality which is to be manipulated. This does not produce knowledge (Kosik, 1978). To produce knowledge there must be a dividing of the undifferentiated totality. A systematic relationship between theory and practice must be established. Innovative work can be seen as knowledge or producing practice. The outcome of innovative work is not only new practice but also theoretical representations of that practice. These objects of knowledge can continue to direct the forming of practice. In that way a practice based on reflective thinking is established.

Innovative Work as Forming of New Practice

In everyday work the methods are tools to bring about things. In innovative practice the tools are analyzed and developed. This can be done in a theoretical as well as a non-theoretical way. In DIW the object of knowledge serves as a tool during the innovative work so that a new practice can be developed. This practice will then become everyday practice and routinized. The object-of-knowledge will be part of the common sense and considered as natural and, consequently, a ground for apprehension rather than comprehension.

References

ALTHUSSER, L. (1958) *För Marx*, Stockholm, Bo Cavefors förlag.

BROMME, R. (1984) 'On the limitations of the theory metaphor for the study of teachers' expert knowledge', in HALKES, R. and CARLGREN, I. (1986) Lokalt utvecklingsarbete, *Göteborg Studies in Educational Science.* 56, Göteborg.

CLANDININ, D.J. (1986) *Classroom Practice. Teacher Images in Action*, Lewes, Falmer Press.

CLANDININ, D.J. and CONNELLY, F.M. (1986) 'What is "personal" in studies of the personal?' in BEN-PERETZ, M., BROMME, R. and HALKES, R. (Eds) *Advances of Research on Teacher Thinking*, Lisse, NL, Swetz and Zeitlinger.

DEWEY, J. (1936) *Människans natur och handlingsliv. Inledning till en social psykologi*, Stockholm, Natur och Kultur.

FULLAN, M. (1981) 'Research on the implementation of educational change', in CORWIN, R. *Research in Sociology of Education and Socialization*, Vol. 2, pp. 195–219.

HOUSE, E. (1974) *The Politics of Educational Innovation*, McCutchan, Berkeley.

HOYLE, E. (1970) 'Planned organizational change in education', *Research in Education*, 3, pp. 1–22.

JORDELL, K.O. (1987) 'Teachers as reflective practitioners? On the teaching profession in the light of Donald Schön's view of professionals as reflective practitioners', in STROMNES, L., SOVIK, N. (Eds) *Teachers' Thinking. Perspectives and Research*, Tapir.

KOSIK, K. (1978) *Det konkretas dialektik. En studie i människans och världens problematik*, Göteborg, Röda Bokförlaget.

LUNDGREN, U.P. (1986) *att organisera skolan. Om grundskolans organisation och ledning*, Stockholm, Liber.

MARTON, F. (1981) 'Phenomenography — describing conceptions in the world around us', *Instructional Sciences*, 10, pp. 177–200.

PEIRCE, C. (1966) 'What pragmatism is', in *Selected Writings. Introduction and notes*, WIENER, P. New York.

PIAGET, J. (1977) *Epistemology and Psychology of Functions*, Dordrecht Reidel cop.

POPPER, K. (1963) *Conjectures and Refutations. The Growth of Scientific Knowledge*, London, Routledge and Kegan Paul.

SCHÖN, D. (1983) *The Reflective Practitioner: How Professionals Think in Action*, New York, Basic Books.

Chapter 15

The Development of Teachers' Personal Practical Knowledge through School-based Curriculum Development Projects

Christopher Day

This chapter reports the impact on teachers' personal practical knowledge of their involvement in five school-initiated, school-based professional and curriculum development projects which took place at a school and community college in Lincolnshire, England during 1986–87. It describes the impact on the thinking of those teachers who participated actively, and raises issues for the management of school-based work which is designed to enhance the professionality of teachers and the quality of education for pupils.

Although the work described in the chapter is particular to one school, it is not untypical of many throughout England since financial devolution of in-service funds occurred under the Local Authorities Training Grants Scheme (LEATGS). Essentially it provides an example of the way in which new social and political contexts have caused an operational reconceptualization so that curriculum and professional developments are no longer ad hoc occurrences, but part of a managed system. As with any system of management which is initiated from the centre, it raises issues of commitment, motivation, and ownership in relation to changes in teachers' thinking and practices which are fundamental to those involved in promoting curriculum and professional growth.

The scheme reflected the belief that there can be no curriculum development without teacher development (Stenhouse, 1975). The involvement of teachers in a 'generative' role is both a valuing of their capacities to (actively) evaluate and design as well as to deliver the curriculum and a recognition of their resistance to (passively) implementing other people's ideas. This valuing has practical implications for all those who seek to provide opportunities for the development of teachers' personal practical knowledge, defined by Connelly and Dienes (1982) as:

a comprehensive view teachers have of themselves, their situations, and their role within a situation. It is composed of theoretical knowledge elements, elements of understanding of the teachers' practical curriculum situation, and of personal beliefs and values concerning what can and should be done in the teacher's circumstances (pp. 183–4).

The Context

The school had a recent history of school-based curriculum development. Three years previously three voluntary study groups had been formed through the initiatives of the previous (newly appointed) Principal and Vice-Principal to engage in cross-curriculum review. They had met after school over the course of a year, and then submitted their reports. However, the national industrial action by teachers had, in effect, hindered implementation of the recommendations contained in the reports, so that, for some members of staff, the exercise had been unproductive. Nevertheless it was the view of the overall project co-ordinator that:

> The climate in the school is good for this kind of action research. It's right for this school at this stage in its development . . . it's got a tradition for progressiveness and forward thinking. Here is a project which is central in that it is going to look at curriculum and curriculum delivery, and this is what many staff think their schools should be addressing themselves to now . . . in the light of all the initiatives and comments that have been made about school in recent years.

The research covers the period September 1986 to December 1987. The numbers of teachers involved actively in the projects on a voluntary basis constituted more than half of the total school teaching staff of seventy-three. Each group had a leader who was allocated two periods each week off timetable, and the groups themselves were allocated between ten and twenty days of supply cover to enable members to conduct their investigations. The key feature which underpinned the scheme was that:

> teachers themselves can be active in promoting changes of style or content which will lead to significant developments across the curriculum (Branston, 1986a).

In the spring term of 1986, the Principal of the school, as a result of meetings which he had initiated with the Director of Education, the Chief Inspector of schools and the local TRIST (Technically Related In-Service Training) director, and following a paper which he had written in support of school-based curriculum development, called a full staff meeting in school time. At this meeting support was sought and given for a written submission to fund a scheme for curriculum development which indicated both 'the Principal's perception of major areas for future development and his belief in Branston teachers as their own experts' (Branston 1986b). The Principal wrote the detailed submission which was approved both by the Academic Board, Heads of House and the governing body of the school. The submission gained support as 'a special pilot scheme to assess the effectiveness of timetabled INSET as a model for replication in the future' (Branston, 1986b). At this stage (May 1986) the Principal issued a 'Launch Pack' informing all staff that the scheme had gained financial support, outlining the rationale and methodology of the scheme, and seeking responses form individuals to their involvement in five project areas:

Project Areas

1   The curriculum (to become known as curriculum descriptions)
2   Teacher research into classroom phenomena (to become known as learning about learning)
3   The role of the tutor/tutorial structures
4   The modular curriculum
5   CPVE. (Certificate of Pre-Vocational Education)

The areas for investigation were selected by the Principal and agreed by the Academic Board prior to being 'offered' to the staff of the school; and the following criteria were established:

(a)   projects should centre on an important school issue (of curriculum or learning styles, and related organizational/structural implications);
(b)   projects should be collaborative. Paricipation in them, the process, should be regarded as an important outcome in itself, as a way of supporting the view that school self-analyses and self-renewal are key aspects of a teacher's professionality;
(c)   projects should lead to, or clearly prepare for, an actual change, or the central aim of TRIST proposal will not be achieved;
(d)   project teams should be deliberately and clearly linked to the normal, on-going processes and bodies which in theory 'manage' curriculum maintenance and review (for example, Academic Board or Heads of House or staff conferences) so that the danger of isolation is avoided, and so that the proposal has maximum status and impact. Every effort should be made to relate projects to other aspects of school development, including other school INSET, secondments, departmental curriculum development etc;
(e)   projects should clearly relate, immediately or less directly, but always, to classroom interactions. The stimulation of direct consideration of, or research into, what happens at the point of learning should be an aim. Teachers should be encouraged to become their own researchers into classroom phenomena. (Branston, 1986a)

Those who had expressed interest in team leadership/co-ordinator roles were approached and the staff common room bulletin indicated which individuals had been selected. This was a significant moment in the history of the development of the scheme, since it not only marked its practical launch — only six months after its inception — but also emphasized management support for principles of ownership and collaborative participation through the ways in which the process was organized. First, there was a deliberate move by the

Principal to distance himself from his initial 'ownership' of the scheme by placing control of its development in the hands of the individual project leaders (almost all of whom had 'middle management' positions in the school) and by appointing an overall co-ordinator whose role was 'to liaise with the teams and leaders, facilitate whatever they plan to do, promote the feedback from each project to everybody else, and keep an eye on the submission criteria...' (Branston, 1986b). Second, within this organizational structure, his intention that all participants should feel ownership was clearly indicated:

> Needless to say, the title 'team leader' implies nothing about where the ideas, plans for development come from. He/she is simply the focus/co-ordinator of the team effort.
> Lists of interested colleagues can go to co-ordinators, so expect to be approached by them this term or early next, or approach them first....
> (Branston 1986b)

The projects, it seemed, were to be pursued by communities of equals and success would therefore be the result of collaboration. Third, resource support was to be provided for all participants:

> Probably the best way to organize resources is to allow each group its own supply day budget, and let people concerned decide as they go along how to spend it. (Branston, 1986b)

The author's role was that of external evaluator. He was invited by the Principal of the school as a 'sympathetic outsider to tell us what is happening as we go along... and later to report our feelings as people, our perceptions as professionals, our achievements as educators' (Branston, 1986a). In effect, he was a researcher-evaluator, for in order to achieve an evaluation which was derived from the cultural perspective of the participants, 'how people see things from within' (House, 1981), it was necessary to seek insider information and respect indigenous definitions and values. In this sense the research is in the naturalistic, phenomenographic tradition (Guba, 1978; Bogdan and Taylor, 1975). The two basic assumptions were that the same phenomenon might be conceived and perceived in qualitatively different ways (Marton, 1981), and that, 'Fundamentally, the most important evaluations of professional services are those conducted (or commissioned) by the professionals themselves' (Stufflebeam and Shinkfield, 1985).

The methodology was that of case study, involving documentary analysis, attendance at selected project meetings, and a series of interviews with all the forty-six project participants, the Principal, Vice-Principal and co-ordinator, and eight staff who were not actively involved. Formal interviews were conducted over an eighteen-month period at four points before, during and after the formal ending of the projects. Interviews lasted between thirty and ninety minutes, were taped and transcribed. Drafts of the evaluation report were circulated to all participants for authentication. The research process and the evaluation report aimed to 'contribute both to the practical concerns of people in an immediate problematic situation and to the goals of social science by joint collaboration within a mutually acceptable ethical framework' (Rappaport, 1970).

The Branston Scheme in Action — Teachers as Experts: Teachers as Researchers

In keeping with the Principal's notion of 'teacher-as-expert' there was an assumption that the teachers in these projects already possessed a great deal of knowledge and understanding of the contexts which they were going to investigate. This view of teachers as experts represents an assertion by the Principal of the school and those who supported his initiative — taken only months after arriving at the school — of 'the creative power inherent in the group of teacher colleagues' in his school (Schmuck and Schmuck, 1974); and coincidentally reflects five principles for effective personal learning:

1   Learning requires opportunities for reflection and self-confrontation;
2   Teachers and schools are motivated to learn by the identification of an issue or problem which concerns them;
3   Teachers learn best through active-experiencing/participation;
4   Decisions about change should arise from reflections upon and confrontation of past and present practice;
5   Schools and teachers need support throughout processes of change.
    (Day *et al*, 1987)

Through the systematic analysis of a specific aspect of school life, they could now begin to articulate the principles underlying practices more clearly and so 'present them for critical self-scrutiny and for examination by colleagues' (Nixon 1987). With the exception of CPVE, which was an on-going project, all the work was innovatory.

Curriculum Descriptions Group

All teachers are concerned with the curriculum. It's fundamental to what we do . . . . What we all do is to close our classroom door and shut the school out.

The group of six teachers from across the disciplines, led by the then Head of English Department, aimed to produce a 'summary of the curriculum offered to Branston pupils, such that all staff could gain some insight into the experiences children were receiving in areas other than personal specialisms' (Williams, 1987).

The project was divided into two areas:
(a) discovering what the curriculum is, and how it is delivered;

(b) investigating a means of presenting a description of the whole curriculum in a comparatively immediate and accessible form.

The group had a total of twenty days of teacher time for its researches and meetings. During term one of the project members devised and administered a questionnaire, based upon elements of learning identified in Curriculum Matters 2 (DES, 1985) to discover and describe the framework of the curriculum, what overlap of subject areas and interests, and what complementary material and approaches were present.

Term two was spent in pupil pursuits in order to 'gather a flavour of the curriculum on offer'. In this exercise five members of the group observed the same class of first year pupils on each day of the same week in order to gain an overview of the curriculum in action. In addition, pupils were interviewed. The results were analyzed and discussed and provided the information on which a display which was to form the centre piece of the presentation of the groups was based. The group worked on the displays during term three and presented the results in terms one and two of the following year at two separate meetings. At these meetings issues were raised concerning the curriculum (balance of age and experience of staff; possibilities of gender stereotyping) and the relationships between the ways in which different subject departments 'delivered' the curriculum.

Learning About Learning Group (Entitled Originally 'Classroom Phenomena')

The support for this kind of project was fundamental to the Principal's belief in teacher-as-expert; and the purposes were described as being:

(i) to stimulate the teacher-as-researcher/analyst model
(ii) to emphasize classroom experience as worthy of primary, personal analysis by teachers themselves, as the obvious and in fact only possible 'experts' in promoting learning (Branston, 1986a).

The most important intended outcome was described as 'an increase in confidence among teachers that they can discuss, theorize about and be active in the management of learning (or the environment it happens in) and that they are the natural experts at analysis of its features' (*ibid*). This coincided with the group's aspirations for a heightened awareness of what they were doing which would 'rub off in conversation with other people'. None of the group had any previous experience of classroom research.

Members agreed to focus upon classroom interaction in their own classrooms, initially upon areas which were of particular personal interest. Impressions recorded at the end of the first term were described as 'striking, particularly the blinkeredness' and 'isolation of much pupil experience in the classroom'. As a result of discussion, the main areas of interest which emerged were: teacher questioning as an aspect of teacher/student exchanges; and how best to motivate students and encourage them to take greater initiative in their learning. A decision was made to focus first upon the volume and types of teacher questioning through the observation of colleagues' classrooms from within and outside the immediate project group. This was to fulfil the group's agreed secondary aim, 'to acquire experience of methods of research, especially of observing each other teaching'. An aim which was of equal importance, however, was 'to achieve a greater sense of team identity, greater ease of co-ordinating the group's work and ... being able to meet to discuss common ground'.

Below is an extract from the team leader's report on this part of the group's research.

Teacher Questions

Six members of the group each observed at least seventy minutes worth of lessons, recording the types of questions used by teachers on an analysis sheet adapted largely from the one described by Douglas Barnes . . . . The strongest impression formed by the group was of the sheer number of questions generated by teachers. This surprised both the observers and the observed. The most startling case involved a teacher who had been happy to have a lesson of hers observed though rather apologetic that the lesson would not involve many questions; in fact 110 were recorded in thirty-five minutes.

Observers were left with the impression that rather too often questions were just a method teachers had of controlling or dominating a discussion; rather than provoking thought they could in fact dull the student's receptiveness to the occasional really valuable question. (Laycock, 1988)

Whilst seasoned researchers from outside schools will find little to surprise them in this information it is worthwhile emphasizing that many of the teachers were learning this for themselves for the first time and were deeply affected by their discoveries.

As a result of this, the group decided to try to view the experienced curriculum from the pupils' viewpoint, and five members engaged in student pursuits each following a different student from the same mixed ability first year class (11–12 year olds) through a day's lessons on different days of the week.

The final report reflects the learning which occurred from the student pursuits:

One of the strongest impressions to emerge from this section of our research was of how isolated many of the students seemed to be — from their teachers and from their peers. In this context it seemed significant that observers commented on the very small amounts of time when students were expected to produce or discuss work in groups. This was corroborated by the findings of the Curriculum Descriptions Group

> which suggested that the first year spent more time engaged in listening than in any other activity and very little time learning through structured discussion. (Laycock, 1988)

This part of the work led on to investigating group work as a means of countering the sense of isolation noted in the student pursuits. Six members of the group volunteered to act as observers of group work in different departments. They found that, 'While there was some debate about whether group work could provide an appropriate teaching technique in all subjects and for all abilities most members of the group had their belief in its potential confirmed'.

The Role of the Tutor Group

> We've got a different job in that we've *got* to have done something by next September.

This statement illustrates the urgency of this group's task. Initially, the project had been described as having 'the potential for initiating major, whole-school review' of the pastoral curriculum, with the aim of providing 'examples of practice and some real lines of development for future teams of tutors'. By the time it was launched, there had been a 'statement of intent . . . on an eventual move to horizontal groups'; and by the end of the first term an 'imminent change from a vertical to a horizontal pastoral system' was reported. Ten staff were involved actively in the project, five of whom were Heads of House under the current pastoral system, and not all were committed to changing this. This project was unique within the context of the other projects in that it became clear during the first term that its role was not to conduct research in order to describe or make recommendations for change but rather to plan for the implementation of a policy decision taken by the Principal which did not have the unanimous support of staff: 'We felt that there was a need . . . to justify this change. There was no staff consultation on a major scale at all.' Although the Principal responded to this feedback by producing a paper and holding a meeting, as far as the progress of this group's work was concerned, 'a term had been lost'.

The first term had been spent by the whole group meeting together at two weekly intervals at lunchtimes to discuss the advantages and disadvantages of change, to assimilate literature about horizontal pastoral systems and to define the role of the tutor:

> But it's very difficult, because with a change like this, depending upon somebody's age and what job they have in the school and how settled in a rut they are, talk about change to them, especially people in middle management positions, if these people are facing change and reject that change they're in the working group . . . then it is a very, very difficult working position . . . so we're working under constraints of all sorts.

Additionally, the whole team attended a part-time externally directed in-service course. At the end of the first term there was still a certain amount of ambiguity and uncertainty perceived concerning the role of the project group. The parameters of its work had not yet been clearly defined:

> If you've not got a firm foundation to start with, all your preparation and hard work will be no good. We still don't think that the senior staff have taken on board the many day-to-day things — geographical, location of first year groups, reporting systems, sport and competition. Who's going to think about that? . . . . We're still worried because we think a lot of things that need doing will not have been done, and that might affect how effectively the tutor can operate from the start . . . . We're actively conscious that we need to have time to be together as teams as often as possible before next September . . . . At the start of the summer term we've got to be there ready to kick off our in-service training . . . the half term before Easter we've got to start packaging the course, ready for September.

During the second term members of the team visited schools already operating a horizontal pastoral system, but the bulk of the spring and summer terms were spent working in five pairs in devising tutor materials for use in each of the five school years. Although there had been reasonably effective liaison, it was reported that meetings of the whole project group, 'petered out like a car running out of petrol'. Nevertheless, despite 'conflicting views, attitudes, opinions within the team . . . I think we are working towards a common approach'; and in terms of implementing as distinct from recommending or initiating change it was clear that some success was achieved. Speaking in the term following the formal ending of the project, one group member stated that:

> I would certainly think that the . . . team now has benefited from it . . . there were one or two who were very dubious about tutor work, a little frightened of being involved in it, the methods . . . but through talking about it, looking at methods, the role of the tutor in tutorial work, they've overcome it.

The Modular Curriculum Group

> When you're looking at delivering the curriculum you've got to look at the needs of all the pupils . . . . The idea is to break two year courses into shorter units, separately chosen by students, and assessed individually . . . students could then achieve balance/breadth/relevance more easily — because they can bolt together smaller units, from a wider range, to achieve the same amount of certification. (Branston 1986b)

The modular group aimed to investigate 'how far such an approach could help solve the fourteen-sixteen curriculum problem of providing a broad, relevant comprehensive experience for all, of whatever ability or future speciality; and how far the team-based modular approach could facilitate improved curriculum planning in all years' (Branston 1986b). The underlying assumptions for this project, made explicit in the 'Launch Pack', were that all students have a right to be offered a 'broad, balanced, relevant and enjoyable' curriculum experience, but that the curriculum currently on offer was unable to provide this within the available time. Because the traditional patterns of choice and traditional syllabuses were 'hard to overthrow in order to fine tune the... individual student's curriculum, it was proposed that the modular curriculum might have something to offer'.

The group of fifteen teachers from across the science, CDT, languages, humanities, home economics, and business studies departments began its investigations by 'obtaining and assimilating the *theory* of this subject', through meetings in which individuals had been encouraged 'to discover areas of personal interest or responsibility'. There had also been a visit by an 'expert' who had spoken to a whole school 'staff conference' about the modular curriculum. During the latter part of the year members of the group visited schools which operated a modular approach to curriculum delivery in their own field. One common thread described as running through the schools which were visited was that 'a large number of staff are demonstrating a good degree of commitment and belief' to a modular approach. Among the members of the group itself, however, commitments varied, and opinions differed as to the validity of a modular approach for all subject areas. Additionally, a recurring theme perceived in the schools visited was that 'perhaps a lot of these schools had problems... and that they'd seen the modular thing as a way out' and that this contrasted with the relative success of the current Branston curriculum. The project was, therefore, very much exploratory and the value lay in the increase in understanding achieved by members. It was, nevertheless, a policy issue which was to be pressed by the Principal during the following year.

Certificate of Pre-Vocational Education (CPVE) Group

This project differed from the other four in that it had already existed during the previous year. Nevertheless, this specialist development of a certificate in pre-vocational education for students was described as, 'having potential messages... as regards team-teaching and student-centred resource-based, activity-led learning'. (Branston 1986b). The aims of this group of six, each from a different discipline, were to both evaluate an ongoing course and to develop it further through explorations into assessment and profiling, active learning and assignment development. Most of the twelve days of 'supply' time was spent by group members attending appropriate short courses outside the school. This was seen as a cost-effective method, 'not only in developing the CPVE approach and philosophy within the course but also because of the effect it has had on teaching (or managed learning) in other areas.... Staff have had to consider new classroom strategies as well as working closely with colleagues.' In addition two two-day in-house task-specific meetings were held during the year. The team leader described what made CPVE different:

> We are actually a team that's working... putting into practice what we're learning. We're doing the two things at the same time, we're practising and we're learning. The other teams are learning in order to practice... We're meeting all the time.

By the end of the year, the categories of learning experiences offered to students had doubled from two to four and the numbers of students opting for this had increased from eleven to twenty-two. This was attributed partly to 'hard work' which had given the course 'credibility' with students, and, significantly, partly to the scheme:

> I think being part of the programme... gave the whole thing some status... things would have happened ultimately, but we wouldn't have been at this stage now.

Professional Development Issues

Essentially, the projects had given the participants the opportunity to move from a normal mode of 'insider activity' (Ebbutt, 1982) in which they worked in isolation in their own classrooms, reflected on their own practice from time to time, incorporated the results of their reflections into their practice sometimes, but did not collect data systematically nor produce written reports, towards a teacher researcher 'classic action research mode'. Here the teachers worked in their own (and sometimes other) classrooms as part of a coherent group which met regularly. They systematically collected and analyzed data concerning their own and colleagues' practice, generated hypotheses and wrote reports open to public critique. In addition (the dissemination phase) they worked towards improvement by testing hypotheses at institutional level. In this very real sense they were involved in innovation, promoting confrontation (but not necessarily changes) of thinking and practice at both personal and institutional levels.

During the interviews, the participants and non-participants talked about their reasons for involvement or non-involvement in the projects, their hopes and fears, their achievements and the constraints that hindered these. Although interviews were conducted individually, there was a remarkable degree of consensus within each project group both in the early interviews, those conducted during the course of events and after the formal ending of the projects. Five issues in particular were raised which are pertinent for further consideration by those involved in encouraging the development of personal practical knowledge.

1   The climate — contextual constraints.

2 Self-reflection.
3 Peer support and collaboration.
4 Institutionalization of innovation.
5 Ownership and control.

The Climate

It is important in evaluating school-based work of all kinds to remember that it occurs within at least three major contexts — national, local (school) and individual (social-psychological) — and that these will affect attitudes of participants and non-participants to learning and change. One group leader had referred at the beginning of the project to the previous, 'two years of discontent' during which teachers' associations had been in dispute with central government over pay and conditions of service; and a member of another group had seen the projects as coming, 'at the end of a bad year as far as morale goes'. One year later, another pointed out the continuing burdens of coping with off-site initiatives promoted by central and local governments, so that, 'nowadays morale is so low that people would be reluctant to give up their time to do something like that again.'

Evidence has also been presented concerning curriculum development activities which had been initiated under a previous Principal and in which individuals had placed considerable time and energy but which had not been translated into action. A report on the views of thirty non-project staff conducted independently referred to *'The Branston Factor'*:

> Almost universally staff experience in this area had been bad. Most regarded them as ineffective talking-shops that produced little of merit. Others had reacted with considerable hostility to findings critical of their departments, calling into question the validity of methodology and findings. At the end of the day nothing was done with the findings of these groups . . . . Hence many dedicated and experienced members of the Branston staff, from management to scale 1 teachers, had no intention of repeating such an experience. (Hall, 1987)

Thus it was perceived as vital that the Principal 'persuade the staff that what's going on is actually going to be acted upon, that any initiative which he takes . . . has got to be clearly focused.'

This view was reinforced in interviews which were conducted with the majority of staff who were not project group members. Referring to the 'Learning to Learn' project, one had, 'doubts about what's going to happen to it . . . I can see the result being a lot of files and reports'; another was not against changes in the pastoral system, but, 'There's too many changes . . . and we're going to have to do most of it in our own time'; and another was in favour of a modular curriculum, 'providing that teachers are well trained for it'. The following statement is typical of those expressed by many non-participant staff about the speed and nature of the changes:

> Sometimes you feel as a member of staff that he's going along too
> fast.... There is a feeling generally in the school that he's going along
> too fast...we teachers are a bit jealous of things that we've already
> established, and are very wary of change...he's going uphill in a way
> because unfortunately the previous head did not always have the
> backing of the staff.... People need the human touch.... Someone
> to...be prepared to listen to people's criticisms...fears...you can
> sometimes forget that you need to talk to people.

Attitudes to involvement in changes (the conscious act) and changing (the
ensuing processes) will inevitably be affected by these and other more personal
factors. While most were positive about the ideas themselves, one had been
'seriously put off because it would have been tinkering with my time'; another
had, 'too much on my plate'; and a third had 'lost my missionary zeal'.
However, it was reported that, 'without doubt the biggest single factor in
deciding people that they would not get involved...was time' (Hall, 1987).

Self-Reflection

The projects had aimed to encourage participants to look at and reflect upon
their thinking and practice; and it was implicit that these same participants
would make decisions, where appropriate, to change. Rogers (1983) has argued
that where individuals are encouraged to revisit beliefs then personal growth
will occur and 'significant changes' will be implemented. Others have posited
that by being provided with opportunities to explore values, intentions, and
practices, teachers are more likely to question 'taken-for-granted' expectations,
perceptions, norms and beliefs. (Argyris and Schon, 1976; Nias, 1987). It would
seem that theory was borne out by practice:

> It was well worth doing...the chance to see what's actually going on in
> school...just to see what activities were going on has helped me. It's
> been an eye opener. We've enjoyed the tasks we've set ourselves...the
> minutiae of educational research...looking at the data and drawing
> conclusions. The very process we've enjoyed, as well as the final
> benefits.

The model of teacher professionality promoted by management in the school
explicitly recognized the importance to teachers' learning of the use of their
personal, practical knowledge (Elbaz, 1983) and, as a means of utilizing this, a
dialectical process of reflection both 'on' and 'in' action (Schön, 1983; Connelly
and Clandinin, 1985).

Participants across all groups spoke of personal gains that had been made as
a result of the activities of visiting other schools, discussing values and ideas with
colleagues, reading, looking at life in classrooms. The projects had provided

'... an opportunity to look at other people's ways of looking at things' and although in one group, 'a majority think that we didn't achieve as much as we ought ... all in all I'm glad I had the experience.' 'If nothing else comes of this ... approach, it will have brought me into contact with more pieces of material, and I've been made aware of other methods ... topic areas ... which cannot but help.'

Two gains in particular are worth highlighting in the context of professional development and change. The first concerns the changing of individuals' perspectives of their own work from a narrow departmental to a broader school context:

> I think it's helped us all to see the school as an organism, that whatever you contribute can inevitably only be a part of the whole. And it's been interesting to see how other parts of the organism work, what they contribute.

The second concerns the recognition — perhaps the re-recognition of the gap between intentions and practice:

> There's the inevitable problem that you have a vision of what you want to do, and what you actually accomplish is only going to be a fraction of that vision.

Finally, the provision of *time control* proved to be fundamental to the motivation and commitment of the participants. It was generally observed that a lot of people have given up considerable amounts of time' to the work. This theme was repeated through all the groups, as the comments below illustrate:

> I think I put in far more time than I was actually given ... so having an afternoon or morning session a year working on it (the project) wasn't a bonus, but it did make us feel that we were doing something which other people were going to look at.
> If you're given time to observe a lesson, then you're going to have to spend many times that to do anything meaningful with it afterwards.

It was observed in two of the groups that, 'People started getting fairly tired through the year', and we have read that one group's work began to 'peter out'. Additionally, when asked whether they would wish to continue to participate in school-based curriculum development work in the following year, a significant number of participants stated that they 'wanted a break from it'. This was not, it seemed, because they were no longer interested, nor, for the vast majority, because they had had negative experiences. One, for example, had been studying on his own for a number of years, and so wanted to 'tick over on my responsibility and enjoy my teaching'. Another said that he would probably continue what his group had been doing after a year's break; and a third stated that he 'felt it was detracting from my lessons quite a lot.'

It is worth reflecting on the issue of involvement in projects which require extra time and energy in relation to the notion of 'bounded' or 'containable' time. Here the problems of research fatigue and increasing lack of confidence by individuals in their ability to focus upon the central task of teaching would be taken into account at the planning stage of school-based curriculum and professional development work. Whilst it has been noted that, 'The best way to improve practice lies not so much in trying to control people's behaviour as in helping them control their own by becoming more aware of what they're doing' (Elliott, 1977), and whilst adults undoubtedly benefit most from those situations which combine action and reflection, it is nevertheless incumbent upon those who manage school-based curriculum and professional development to ensure also that 'commitment' does not become associated with 'stress'. Perhaps teaching should not be regarded purely or even predominantly as teacher-pupil contact time:

> There should be an in-built time to discuss teachers' problems and things that happen in the classroom, because we tend to keep problems to ourselves, or discuss them with perhaps one to two close colleagues . . . I think a lot more time ought to be devoted to it.

It will be clear, then, that the opportunities had enabled teachers to reflect systematically on and confront their thinking and practices; and provided active support for them both in their learning processes and in the planning, implementation and evaluation of curriculum development in school which arose through the school-based action research which, with the learning networks, formed the central core of each project. The processes by which this was achieved are represented in figure 15.1. Deliberative reflection and inquiry,

Figure 15.1.
An in-service professional development process (based on Day, 1987).

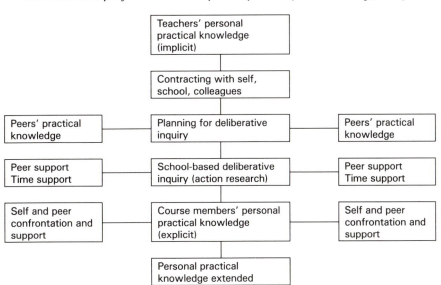

contracting (with self and others), self and peer confrontation, and the sharing of insights gained from this are posited as essential ingredients in developing teachers' personal practical knowledge.

Peer Support and Collaboration

It is sometimes assumed that schools are social and sociable places. Writing after the project had ended, one member made this comment:

> I think that in a big place like this the weakness is that staff don't know each other. They pass like ships in the night . . . We began to appreciate people far more, and . . . working together like that you get a greater appreciation of people. You get to know them better. And I think the better you know somebody, the better the opportunity of achieving things working together.

A gain identified by participants related to the value of work which brought teachers from different disciplines together. Two comments, in particular, illustrate the perceived value of this:

> The biggest value is just opening communications between groups of teachers who would otherwise not necessarily talk about teaching . . . I've never done that before . . . It's valuable not just to confirm hunches that you may have had yourself, but to share those with other people and see that they too share them.

and

> I think it was important that we did spend time together as a group in school time. I think that adds a greater kudos to what we do . . . that the school thought it important enough to give it time.

However, not every member of every group will necessarily provide the same level of commitment, and this may have adverse effects upon the dynamic and learning processes of groups. One leader spoke of the need to 'reconcile' himself to people's individual commitments — which ranged from one who, 'just stopped coming to meetings with five seconds notice each time', to others who, 'after Friday night's meeting which finished at five o'clock . . . spoke for a further twenty minutes about it'.

The roles played by group leaders are crucial to the degree of success of the various enterprises, and in view of this it is surprising that no leadership training and team building programmes were provided prior to the beginning of the projects. Team leaders' commitment and credibility were not questioned by colleagues, and while some were viewed as 'middle management' figures and others as 'very much grass roots' this did not seem to be an issue in the functioning of the groups. One member of the senior management team was 'impressed by the methods employed for getting the teams together, and the quality of the debate'. Nevertheless, it is clear from the reports of the projects that leadership knowledge and skills are essential prerequisites for the management of school-based curriculum development.

Institutionalisation of Innovation

In an interview after the project had ended, the Principal stated that:

> At the moment what's important to me is that kind of (open) attitude and awareness and openness, especially in view of the fact that teachers do feel kicked about and treated as menial (a reference to the national context of centrally initiated change through legislation). It's more important to me that their sense of professionalism has been increased . . . than that any specific change has been achieved.

Evidence that individual project members had changed has been presented already and change in two areas — the pastoral system and CPVE — had occurred. The pastoral system change had been serviced by rather than resulted from the work of the 'Role of the Tutor' group. So to that extent its work was disseminated and utilized (although it is too early to judge how effective this has been.) The CPVE group's work was self-contained and its report attests also to its successful adoption and implementation by its members. Both these projects had prepared for change. The members of the 'Modular Curriculum' group had examined the issues and no policy recommendations had been made at that time. Two of the departments involved were, however, making further investigations with a view to designing modular curricula. Both the 'Curriculum Descriptions' and 'Learning about learning' groups had entered the projects with expectations that they would share their findings with their colleagues in the school. Both hoped that their work 'will affect the work of the school' and that the information would, 'enable people to understand what they are doing . . . what's happening in the school . . . then decide is this the right thing, is this the right way to do it? What changes do we need?' One member stated that 'it is very important in a large school with so many different subjects that the left hand should know what the right hand's doing and when and how; and another envisaged it as 'an exercise in information sharing which then could be used department to department . . . as a means of breaking down subject barriers.'

Evidence of the participants' perceptions has already been provided, and it is clear that overall the scheme had been valued. It had 'made people feel that there is life after their classroom lessons'. It had been welcomed as being important in 'making people aware of issues in education . . . because it means that we are looking at ourselves to see what we are doing with children . . . which will either confirm or help people to look again at some of the ideas'. The scheme itself recognized that 'as teachers we want to do something about our own profession, about what's going on here. We want to examine it . . . to look objectively at what we are doing.'

Hall's (1987) report confirmed the data gathered during the evaluation that 'those significantly involved believed quite firmly that the scheme overall had benefited the school, even if they had doubts about their own particular sub-group'; and the perceived gains for the participants themselves have already been enumerated. It is worth recording, however, that 'those who had no or little involvement felt they had not benefited at all.' (*ibid*).

In effect, the hope for adoption or use of the findings was in part based on an act of faith, a belief that if they had intrinsic merit and were perceived as being 'valid', then acceptance by others could be achieved through traditional modes of dissemination (for example a report and presentation).

Miles (1983) reveals the naivity of this belief in a paper which seeks to investigate the mystery of institutionalization of innovations. He concludes that:

> past research — and conventional wisdom — has tended to suggest that a 'good', well-mastered innovation that its users endorse or support will somehow just stay around. There has been an overemphasis on user ownership, involvement and technical skill; the organization-level structural and procedural changes required for institutionalization have stayed vague and mysterious.

Investments made in planning for processes of curriculum development could, therefore, be ineffective for those not directly involved unless accompanied by deliberate attention to the institutional steps that lock an innovation into the local setting.

> New practices that get built into the training, regulatory, staffing and budgetary cycle survive; others don't. Innovations are highly perishable goods. Taking institutionalization for granted — assuming somewhat magically that it will happen by itself, or will necessarily result from a technically mastered, demonstrably effective project — is naive and usually self-defeating. (Huberman and Crandall, 1982)

In the Branston scheme the school management ensured that the new practices which were necessary as part of the imminent change in the pastoral system were planned through the 'role of the tutor' project teams; and the CPVE team were throughout linking theory and action within a committed and relatively self-contained group.

The findings of both the 'Curriculum Descriptions' and 'Learning about Learning' groups (and to a lesser extent the 'Modular Curriculum' group) were not accompanied by structural and procedural changes. Whilst these groups planned for dissemination by producing, and in one case presenting, their findings, no detailed consideration was given to the very principles of participation, collaboration and ownership which had characterized their own learning throughout the projects. One is led to conclude that perhaps the expectation in the scheme that participants would act as agents for change for others' as well as their own thinking and practice was a worthwhile dream, but a reality which remained out of reach.

It seems then that school-based curriculum development which meets institutionally perceived needs can be successful providing that these coincide with those of the individuals involved and that they do not and are not perceived to affect the structure of the organization or curriculum of others in the school.

Ownership and Control

The Principal's underlying intention was to engage colleagues in collaborative activities for the 'common good' of the school (Lewin, 1946) so that there was a moral imperative implicit in his selection of the projects. The assumption (untested until the projects got under way, though implied by the operative principle of voluntarism) was that this would be shared by the project members. A related assumption was the expectation that the results of the investigations — whether descriptive or in the form of recommendations — would be disseminated to colleagues in the school and an aspiration that change could result.

This raises an important issue for those who seek or are offered resource support for professional and curriculum development, for inevitably there will be an 'institutional needs' dimension which will have to be taken into account and may conflict with the personal or group needs dimension. In any need identification procedures and staff and curriculum development programmes, this matching between felt individual and institutional need is bound to be potentially problematic. The Branston scheme implicitly recognized this, but did not fully account for it, although the Principal did see the scheme as being the first of three one-year phases which would account for differently perceived needs. Nevertheless, as this chapter has indicated, some problems arose in the course of particular projects in 1986–87 in which changes in school policy which were perceived as necessary by the Principal and senior management colleagues conflicted with the views of some of the staff members involved.

Much attention, particularly in England (Elliott, 1980; Simons, 1979, 1987; Day, 1981) and also Australia (Kemmis *et al*, 1981; Smyth, 1987) has been given to establishing a particular ethical framework for the control of teacher research, so that, for example, 'involvement should be voluntary and teachers should retain a high degree of control over the direction of the teacher research and the confidentiality surrounding their contributions' (Wallace, 1987). In this conception the primary focus is upon groups of teachers using action research frameworks (practical and ethical) to support the improvement of their own practice. Kemmis (1981) has distinguished between 'practical' and 'emancipatory' action research:

Action research . . . can be practical (i.e. deliberate groups decide the best ways to act within existing constraints) or emancipatory (the process of reflection leads to action based upon a critique of the social milieu). Just as the patient is emancipated from the oppression of his psyche through the process of self-reflection, so also in social theory, the act of self-reflection within critical communities is emancipatory. The emancipation of participants in the action . . . from the dictates or compulsions of tradition, precedent, habit, coercion, or self deception.

Whilst the *process* of action research which occurred in the project groups was emancipatory in the sense that their participants were free to opt in, design and implement, and evaluate, the emancipation of the mind and spirit did not always lead to empowerment in terms of the ability to change individual and collective practices and policies. For example, in the case of two of the project groups emancipation was circumscribed by the knowledge that in the former case the Principal had taken a policy decision to change pastoral systems and in the latter case that he valued modular approaches to curriculum planning and delivery groups. Both of these were investigating areas of school life which were controversial. It was not, perhaps, surprising that even the project groups themselves were characterized by occasional dissension and conflict. The *'role of the tutor'* was particularly controversial, since it became clear during the first term of the project that a decision had been taken by senior management to change the pastoral 'house' system to a horiztontal 'year group' system.

One of the group commented that 'It's like building your house on poor foundations'. Many staff were not committed to the planned change 'even in our own team', and there was initial and continuing resentment that 'there had been no staff consultation on a major scale'. It was 'very difficult early on to get a nice climate at meetings', because 'there's a lot of ill feeling and a lot of dissension'. A member of the group summarized the difficulties that, ultimately, caused the project group to split into year group pairs in order to set the scene for the new system:

> Every meeting we have, somebody puts a spanner in the works about something. If we'd all been committed we'd probably have got our ideas together now . . . I think there's a feeling at the back of people's minds that, 'I'm keen, but am I wasting my time? Will the things that we have suggested be taken up.'

Clearly, the project members felt that they were being denied the opportunity to conduct a 'reconnaissance' of pastoral systems and to consider relative merits before reporting on these to colleagues. 'We were overtaken by events . . . so that the work of the group, in the summer term, seemed to stop, because we were so busy trying to get everything ready for the tutors to operate in September.' Commitment to the process of investigation was not universal and, far from being empowering, this project appeared to frustrate many of its participants. The decision on change had already been taken, and it took some time for members to adjust.

The *'modular curriculum'* group members also held different opinions about the value of a modular approach, but (perhaps because no management decision had at that time been taken) appeared to co-exist in relative harmony.

Although 'it's not a coherent group' its intention was to 'up its awareness of modules and their purposes and how successful they could be'. There were 'some people who are fairly antagonistic' ('Basically we've got quite a lot of reservations against') to the notion; others who were 'hesitant' ('I find it a threat'); and others in the group who were 'committed'. Some who were concerned to 'defend' the position of their department ('Practical subjects are becoming expensive') and, where appropriate, 'fight for its development'. The ethos of the group is aptly summarized:

> I think people feel that we're going to modular whatever happens, but it's not as cut and dried as that. You've *got* to look at it in depth before you do it, and if we look at it in depth, and feel that with the present resources it's not fair to do it, then we won't do it.

In three of the groups, however, it was clear that members had similar interests, motivations and prejudices, and that school and individual needs coincided.

For one member of the '*curriculum descriptions*' group involvement in the project was a 'natural extension' of work in a particular subject area in which a curriculum had been designed and developed for years 1–3. He anticipated that this would help him to look at 'broader issues'. Another had 'always been interested in cross-curricular links' and had tried to build these up in his previous school. His 'prime motivation' was to 'try and find out what is being done elsewhere'. A third member was keen to 'learn more that will help *me* develop, help me be a better teacher' and he too wanted 'a lot more cross curriculum activity to take place'. The fourth project member expressed similar sentiments, feeling that 'there should be a tie up between what we're doing and other departments.'

'I always do reflect a lot on what I do. I always have done. I'm that sort of person really' seemed to characterize the backgrounds of those ten teachers (all but two of them from the English and maths departments) involved in '*learning about learning*'. The key activities of observing classroom action, whether from the viewpoint of the teacher or the pupil (as in the pupil pursuit tasks) suggested that this was a 'doing' group. 'It's all very well to sit and philosophize about education, but unless it's going to do something then . . . I've got 101 things I can be doing . . . The reason that a lot of people are doing this is that they're at the heart of it . . . We're deciding what we're doing as we go along'.

Yet despite this, much of the group's time was spent in designing observation schedules, analyzing results and hypothesizing on the processes and outcomes of teaching and learning.

Perhaps the key feature of the work of these groups is that it did not threaten the existing order in the school. Similarly, the *Certificate in Pre-Vocational Education* group had already been in existence prior to this project. Its work was not, therefore, regarded as affecting significantly the existing order in the school. The team had 'identified itself'

We are actually a team that's working . . . putting into practice what we're learning. We're doing the two things at the same time . . . the other teams are learning in order to practise.

The team members 'would have been doing this anyway' and the project had provided additional support for them to meet together regularly and to work on the design and documentation of a developing course for a minority of school students.

In a real sense, then, work undertaken which attempts to support professional development through teacher-generated research runs the risk of being seen ultimately as an instrument of control rather than empowerment, where the research is proscribed by curriculum needs or policies defined by an individual or group of staff who hold senior positions within the management structure of an institution. Teachers recognized this and commitment by those who did not share this value position was adversely affected. Managers of schools need to take account of principles of ownership and change when taking an initiating role in school based curriculum development.

The Conditions for Change

So far the author has sought to establish the context for this study and to provide insights to the reader regarding the processes and outcomes of each project. The final part of the paper focuses upon the conditions for learning and change which underpinned the projects, and planning considerations for those engaged in promoting the development of teachers' personal practical knowledge within the context of school-based professional development work. The central features of the model of curriculum and professional development which had been presented to the staff by the Principal were that teachers were to be active participants in their own learning, that resource support would be given through funding and the establishment of peer group support networks, and that teachers should only opt in if a project had a personal significance for them (Shumsky, 1958). Figure 15.2 summarizes the planning considerations and takes account of the variables which were identified as a result of the research and evaluation process.

It recognizes that 'need' may be identified by any individual or group or by collaborative need identification procedures but that the key to progress is in contract building, contract making and the provision of resources. It is at this stage that the kinds of responsibilities and answerabilities (by management to teachers and vice-versa) for the duration of the work may be clarified, established and negotiated. The model avoids making judgments upon the effectiveness of particular management stances, so that the opportunity exists for 'pro-tem' power and authority relationships to be negotiated. However, it is implicit that where the culture or ethos of the institution is expressed through antagonistic management-staff relationships, then success will be difficult to achieve. Essentially, principles of collaboration based upon an affirmation of

Figure 15.2.
Planning considerations for supporting the development of teachers' personal practical knowledge through school-based curriculum and professional development.

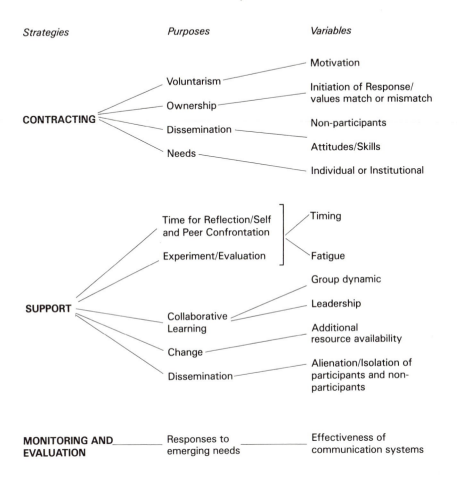

teachers' ability as learners and partners (if not equal partners) within continuing professional development programmes must be adopted if these programmes are to succeed.

Summary Issues

What, then, may be learnt from the experiences of this scheme that may help in promoting more effective and efficient learning structures for professional development in the future? This final section presents a summary of issues which are derived from the experiences of the participants and those of the researcher/evaluator. They are presented in the form of propositions for developing teachers' personal practical knowledge.

Propositions for Developing Teachers' Personal Practical Knowledge

Proposition 1: Curriculum development as the servant of continuing professional development. Research in teaching and curriculum development is integral to professional development. Curriculum research and reform should be viewed as activities which serve the needs of professional development rather than vice-versa. School-based developments must be continuing and systematic rather than sporadic and *ad hoc*.

Proposition 2: Motivation, commitment and ownership. Tension between individual, school and externally identified needs must be recognized. Whoever initiates an idea, it is crucial that those involved in pursuing it are, and perceive that they are, able to adapt and adopt so that it ultimately belongs to them. If this is recognized and acted upon then motivation and commitment to the idea are more likely to be achieved.

Proposition 3: Collaborative planning. A hallmark of successful development is the extent to which there is shared decision-making between teachers and management and teachers who work in the same team.

Proposition 4: Contracting and team building. Teams must be given the power to make decisions and to participate fully in the planning, processes and evaluations of their work. The parameters for decision-making must be negotiated initially and, where appropriate, renegotiated. Programmes must be available which enable team leadership and team building skills to be acquired.

Proposition 5: Voluntarism. Voluntarism is a basis for action rooted in faith and personal feeling. It is developed through dialogue and thought and is a *sine qua non* for successful professional and curriculum development.

Proposition 6: Reflection, analysis and participation. Learners must be active participants in their own learning. Successful professional development is that which assumes that the experiences and intuitions of practitioners, their personal knowings gleaned from personal experiences are of prime value. It consciously employs reflection, analysis and experimentation by providing active opportunities for participants to move from intuition to the disciplined collection of experiential knowledge. In this way vicarious experiences may be evoked which lead to further experiential and propositional knowledge, and hence enhanced information upon which decisions may be taken for changing practice.

Proposition 7: Horizontal relationships. Relationships are likely to be more effective when based upon the notion of 'professional community' rather than 'hierarchical direction'. Lateral rather than hierarchical structures within organizations will be more effective. Peer groups are the best bases of influence.

Proposition 8: Problem identification and individualism. No two departments or schools are exactly alike. Therefore the judgments made about curriculum and action taken by those in them must not lightly be supplemented, ignored or dismissed. Problem identification must be both systematic and situation specific.

Proposition 9: The use of human resources. There should be a prime but not exclusive reliance on the use of internal rather than external human resources (ref. Proposition 6 above).

Proposition 10: Support of management. Institutional support of a material and psychological-moral kind is essential in order to provde time, energy, a sense of task and teacher being valued, and a mutually acceptable time-frame. Planning must take account of the need for interim adjustments in the kinds and levels of support to take account of individual affective factors (for example, fatigue, lessening of commitment).

Proposition 11: Knowledge dissemination and utilization. Decisions concerned with the dissemination and utilization of knowledge outside the individual participant or participant group must be made at the planning stage and appropriate support built into the processes of any professional and curriculum development scheme. To be effective, dissemination must be founded upon principles of ownership, negotiation, collaboration and shared decision-making. It may be enough that scheme participants themselves have gained from their involvement. Dissemination must be recognized as a complex process which may be inappropriate in this kind of work.

Proposition 12: Harmony. An underlying variable which is critical for effective implementation of structural and procedural change is teacher-principal harmony:

> Working relations between administrators and teachers had to be clear and supportive enough that the pressures and stresses of incorporating something new could be managed together. The message of our own model is that both teacher mastery/commitment *and* administrative action are critical for institutionalization — and that linkage between them can be achieved. (Miles, 1983)

Perhaps the final voice to be heard should be that of the person who initiated the idea, who had been passionately convinced of the necessity for professional research and development to be seen as an 'utterly natural part of every schoolteacher's role' within his own institution; and who had undertaken considerable searching and lobbying for resources from outside the school to support the project:

> Only the future will tell whether school-based research and development will become as natural as breathing here, but I am confident . . . From an LEA view school-based work certainly proves to be very cost-effective in terms of 'activity generated per pound of resource', but of course it needs *some* funding.
>
> Overall, despite our imperfections we have, I believe, shown that there truly is an appetite for school-based, teacher-centred collaborative research. I also believe that this school is healthier and stronger because of the activity its members have participated in than it would otherwise have been. I intend to continue to pursue the 'Teachers and Experts' approach.

References

ARGYRIS, C. and SCHON, D. (1976) *Theory in Practice: Towards Increasing Professional Effectiveness*, Jossey-Bass.

BOGDAN, R. and TAYLOR, S. (1975) *Introduction to Qualitative Research Methods*, New York, John Wiley.

BRANSTON (1986a) *TRIST The Branston Proposal*. Draft for Discussion at Academic Board, 14 April.

BRANSTON (1986b) *Branston TRIST (Teachers as Experts)*, Launch Pack, May.

CONNELLY, M. F. and DIENES, B. (1982) 'The teachers' role in curriculum planning: A case-study, in LEITHWOOD, K. (Ed.) *Studies in Curriculum Decision Making*, Toronto, OISE.

CONNELLY, M. F. and CLANDININ, D.J. (1985) *On Narrative Method, Personal Philosophy and Narrative Unities in the Study of Teaching*. Paper presented at annual meeting of NARST, Indiana.

DAY, C. (1981) *Classroom-Based In-Service Teacher Education: The Development and Evaluation of a Client-Centred Model*, Occasional Paper, No. 9, University of Sussex.

DAY, C., WHITAKER, P. and WREN, D. (1987) *Appraisal and Professional Development in Primary Schools*, Open University Press.

DES (1985) 'The curriculum from 5 to 16', *Curriculum Matters 2: An HMI Series*, London, HMSO.

DES (1986) *Local Education Authority Training Grants Scheme: Financial Year 1987-88*, Circular 6/86, London, HMSO.

EBBUTT, D. (1982) 'Educational action research: Some general concerns and specific quibbles', *Teacher-Pupil Interaction and the Quality of Learning Project, Schools Council Programme 1*, Cambridge Institute of Education.

ELBAZ, F. L. (1983) *Teacher Thinking: A Study of Practical Knowledge*, London, Croom Helm.

ELLIOTT, J. (1977) 'Conceptualizing relationships between research evaluation procedures and in-service teacher education, *British Journal of In-Service Education*, 4, 1 and 2.

238

ELLIOTT, J. (Ed.) (1980) 'The theory and practice of educational action research'; *Classroom Action Research Network Bulletin No.4*, Cambridge Institute of Education.

GUBA, E.G. (1978) *Towards a Methodology of Naturalistic Inquiry in Educational Evaluation*, Centre for the Study of Evaluation, Los Angeles, University of California.

HALL, R. (1987) *An alternative assessment of the Branston School and Community College TRIST Scheme 1986/7*. Unpublished M.E.d assignment, School of Education, University of Nottingham.

HOUSE, E. (1981) 'Three perspectives on innovation', in LEHMING, R. and KANE, M. (Eds) *Improving Schools: Using What We Know*, London, Sage.

HUBERMAN, A. M. and CRANDALL, D. P. (1982) 'Implications for action', *Vol. IX of People, Policies and Practices: Examining the Claim of School Improvement*, The Network Inc.

KEMMIS, S. (1981) *The Professional Development of Teachers through Involvement in Action-Research Projects*, Geelong, Deakin University.

KEMMIS, S. *et al.* (1981) *The Action Research Planner*, Geelong, Australia, Deakin University Press.

LAYCOCK, P. (1988) *Branston TRIST: Learning about Learning*, Report, March.

LEWIN, K. (1946) 'Action research and minority problems', *Journal of Social Issues*, 2, pp. 34-46.

MARTON, F. (1981) 'Phenomenography — describing conceptions in the world around us', *Institutional Sciences*, 10.

MILES, H. (1983) 'Unravelling the mystery of institutionalization', *Educational Leadership*.

NIAS, J. (1987) *Seeing Anew: Teachers' Theories of Action*, Geelong, Deakin University Press.

NIXON, J. (1987) 'Only connect: Thoughts on stylistic interchange within the research community', *British Educational Research Journal*, Vol. 13, 2.

RAPPAPORT, R. (1970) 'Three dilemmas in action research', *Human Relations*, 23.

ROGERS, C. (1983) *Freedom to Learn for the 80s*, Columbus, Ohio, Charles Merrill.

SCHMUCK, R. A. and SCHMUCK, P. A. (1974) *A Humanistic Psychology of Education*, Mayfield, National Press Books.

SCHÖN, D. A. (1983) *The Reflective Practitioner: How Professionals Think in Action*, London, Temple Smith Ltd.

SHUMSKY, A. (1958) 'The personal significance of action research', *Journal of Teacher Education*, 9, pp. 152–5.

SIMONS, H. (1979) 'Suggestions for a school self-evaluation based on democratic principles', in ELLIOTT, J. (Ed.) 'School-based evaluation', *Classroom Action Research Network Bulletin No.3*, Cambridge Institute of Education.

SIMONS, H. (1987) *Getting to Know Schools in a Democracy: the Politics and Process of Evaluation*, Lewes, The Falmer Press.

SMYTH, J. (1987) *A Rationale for Teachers' Critical Pedagogy: A Handbook*, Geelong, Deakin University Press.

STENHOUSE, L. A. (1975) *An Introduction to Curriculum Research and Development*, London, Heinemann.

STUFFLEBEAM, D. L. and SHINKFIELD, A. J. (1985) *Systematic Evaluation*, Boston, Kluwer-Nijhoff.

WALLACE, M. (1987) 'A historical review of action research: Some implications for the education of teachers in their managerial role', *Journal of Education for Teaching*, 13, 2.

Chapter 16

The Influence of Teachers' Thinking on Curriculum Development Decisions*

Lynne Hannay and Wayne Seller

Curriculum development, especially if conceptualized in a deliberative mode, requires an individual to make decisions that partially arise from their practical knowledge and to share their meaning with other participants involved in the process. Through examination of this process, researchers have an opportunity to explicitly examine both the thinking process and the relationship to subsequent action.

The study reported in this chapter investigated how teachers went about making curriculum decisions, the nature of the process, and the influences on the curriculum development process (Hannay and Seller, 1987). This chapter focuses on the deliberations of one committee with specific reference to how the practical knowledge of the participants influenced the development process and how their practical knowledge was reciprocally influenced by their involvement.

Theoretical Framework

Several different theoretical frameworks were applied to the data collected. First, the authors applied curriculum deliberative theory to the process observed. Curriculum development based in a deliberative framework suggests that curriculum making is not a theoretical enterprise but is choice and action emanating from the practical (Schwab, 1969). Deliberation, according to Reid (1978) is 'The methods by which most everyday practical problems get solved' (p. 43). As individuals make practical decisions, they formulate alternative problems and solutions.

Throughout this process, the curriculum orientations or values of the participants are actively involved. As Scheffler (1973) suggests:

*Funded by the Social Sciences and Humanities Research Council of Canada, Grant # 410–85–0531.

> Practical thought attempts to answer such questions as 'How shall I act?' 'What should be done?' 'What course of action ought to be followed?' . . . it is clear that the aim of practical thought is not only the implementation, or even the expression, of specific decisions, but the formulation of more general intentions and prescriptions, embracing practical and moral principles. Such expressions and formulations guide decisions, and thereby action. (p. 188)

The role of an individual's personal and professional beliefs, therefore, are an integral component of the curriculum deliberation process. For instance, Reid (1978) refers to the stock of knowledge that deliberators bring to the deliberative process while Walker (1978) emphasizes the importance of platform in the process. Elbaz (1981) provides a framework to identify components of practical knowledge: rules of practice, practical principles, and image. Rules of practice are recipes of what to do in certain situations while principles are broader philosophical views. Clandinin and Connelly (1984) suggest that:

> Image, for us, is a kind of knowledge, embodied in a person and connected with the individual's past, present, and future. Image draws both the present and future into a personally meaningful nexus of experiences focused on the immediate situation which called it forth. It reaches into the past gathering up experiential threads meaningfully connected to the present. And it reaches intentionally into the future and creates new meaningfully connected threads as situations are experienced, and new situations anticipated from the perspective of the image. (p. 3)

As curriculum deliberation explores 'what is' in order to examine 'what should be', the practical knowledge of the individual is an integral component of the process. Practical knowledge will certainly be brought to bear through individual problem framing, suggested alternatives and habits. Further, the rules of practice, principles, and image that a participant brings to the process interacts with those brought by other participants. We need to further understand the impact that practical knowledge and interactions between the developers might have on the development process (Ben-Peretz and Tamir, 1986).

Methodology

This chapter focuses on the deliberation of one school-based curriculum development committee. The committee met for eight full day sessions over the course of one school year. The teachers involved in this project were required to develop the curriculum to meet external requirements. Each teacher involved had approximately twenty years of experience teaching geography.

Role of the Researchers

The research design of this study was embedded in a collaborative research mode. The researchers were participant observers (Gold, 1969) in the sense that they participated in the development process. However, the roles of the two researchers pertaining to the data reported in this chapter were very different. One researcher, Lynne Hannay, was a participant observer and was actively involved in facilitating the actions of the committee studied. She had been asked by the school Principal to work with the geography committee. The relationship between a school and an OISE (The Ontario Institute for Studies in Education) Field Centre is such that development services are provided free of charge in exchange for the opportunity to conduct on-going, field-based research. In her OISE field development role, the researcher performed what Gold has classified as a participant-as-observer. In this role 'an observer develops relationships with informants through time, and where he is apt to spend more time and energy participating than observing' (Gold, 1969, p. 35). The decision to assume a more active participant role was based on the researcher's conscious attempt to implement the curriculum leadership role prescribed by Schwab (1983) and her OISE field development responsibilities. In addition, this form of participating observation had the potential of providing greater insight into the curriculum development process. As Schubert (1986) suggests:

> The method of practical research is experiential interaction with situations. Knowledge that illuminates situational problems is deeply embedded in the fabric of those situations. Researchers who wish to provide such knowledge must also become embedded in those situations. Otherwise their insights will be more superficial than substantive. (p. 140)

However the second researcher acted in a purely observational role. He was able to review the verbatim transcripts of the committee meetings to examine the role of his co-researcher in the project. In such a manner, the researchers were able to gather the insight from participation advocated by Schubert (1986) while maintaining a more objective focus.

Data Collection Techniques

As the intention of the study was to document the development process as it emerged, several naturalistic techniques were employed. Field notes were maintained for each session. Each meeting of the committee was audio-taped and then transcribed. Consequently, data analysis was based upon a verbatim record of the development sessions. The participants were also interviewed. The taped interviews were of a conversational, open-ended nature. The audio-tapes were then transcribed.

Certain credibility techniques were embedded into the research design.

Triangulation of data sources and collection devices were employed. Specifically, this included district correspondence and handouts regarding the development process, taped observations of committee meetings, and taped interviews with the participants. Member checks were conducted on a continuing basis throughout the different phases. The observation period, one school year, meets the criteria of persistent observation.

Data Analysis

The meeting and interview transcripts were analyzed for instances where the practical knowledge of the participants influenced the curriculum development process. The data were also coded to indicate how the participants changed their personal practical knowledge throughout the development project. Constructs evident in the literature on personal practical knowledge guided the process and, in addition, the patterns emerging from the data were used to clarify the literature.

Findings

The overall purpose of this study was to examine how decisions are made in a curriculum development process (Hannay and Seller, 1987). This chapter investigates the influence of the participants' personal practical knowledge on their decisions while developing a school-based curriculum. The data analysis revealed the powerful role that the participants' personal practical knowledge played in the curriculum development process. Conversely, involvement in the process impacted on the participants' practical knowledge as they began to reconceptualize their teaching methodology, their role in the classroom, and the role of their students.

The framework developed by Elbaz (1981) is used to conceptualize the role of personal practical knowledge as indicated by the actions taken by the committee. The following sections outline the images, the rules of practice and general principles pertaining to the development process.

Image

The past images of the participants influenced their curricular decisions. Of particular importance were their images of themselves as geography teachers, the role and capabilities of students, and the curriculum development process itself. As noted earlier, their images were modified through their involvement in the curriculum development process. The following section describes how the initial images held by the committee members influenced the curriculum development process and how those images became modified through their involvement.

Image of Teaching

Generally, the five experienced teachers involved in developing this school-based geography curriculum saw themselves as subject-matter specialists. They were not teachers, they were 'geography teachers'. Additionally, each teacher advocated a specific area of geography such as physical or human geography. Their past image involved sharing their geographical knowledge with their students by giving a lecture.

Particularly during the first two meetings, committee members struggled with what constituted geography and lobbied for their particular interests. As one teacher stated very early in the first meeting:

> I'm thinking the same way you guys are right now. I don't want to be hooked in with human geography, I don't like it . . . . How in the hell can he [another committee member] teach physical geography if you don't like it? (Meeting One, p. 6)

It was not only a matter of personal interest, but the changes in content advocated by the Ministry of Education guideline also required a shift in what constituted geography as a subject matter. A committee member, Mark, voiced his concern:

> What you are saying is that sometimes you get sort of airy-fairy and you end up not teaching geography because the bottom line about geography, I think, has to do with man's relationship with the earth's surface, and it's a spatial thing. If you are starting to talk about the causes of World War Two, which you could twist it around so that you did, you're not teaching geography any more, you've slipped over the edge somewhere. (Meeting Two, p. 33)

During their second full day meeting, the geography committee began to re-form their image of geography, at least in terms of the curriculum document. They selected five major themes which incorporated their several different conceptions of geography with that of the Ministry document. The past ascendancy of either human or physical geography was abandoned in favour of integration and they also added a cultural and economic focus to their curricular framework.

By the third meeting, the committee would no longer accept content selection based solely on past practice but now required a defendable position. For example, one participant asked:

> If a kid came away from your class and he's taken economic geography, what would you like him to have touched upon or know? You've taught him economic geography, now what? (Meeting Three, p. 49)

Changing from a factual content to a focus on concepts and skills was the second major shift contained in the Ministry of Education guideline. Adapting their past image of themselves as a source of knowledge to that of a facilitator required a great deal more effort for the committee. Committee members had a great deal of trouble in conceptualizing their role as being anything other than a teller. The following comment by Mark was representative of their image of geography teaching:

> When you say a geography lesson, do you mean like a lecture sort of thing? Where you make a few points and then they go and do something with that kind of information? (Meeting Three, p. 50)

Accepting the dominant role of skills and concepts rather than factual content required the participants to revise their image developed through their twenty years of teaching geography. Assisted by an external facilitator, the committee members adapted the growth chart contained in the Ministry of Education geography guideline to meet their particular needs. Through their efforts at matching skills and concepts to their content choices, the participants began to accept the changing role of factual content. Although the committee had designed a list of concepts and a skills growth chart by the end of the fourth meeting, they still struggled with this changing image of teaching geography. Ralph summarized their dilemma:

> I think because we're subject specialists, by and large, that we have a tendency in the secondary level to be more content oriented than in the elementary level. Maybe what Mark is saying is that we are so content conscious that if we develop this format and force ourselves to go with skill objectives and that sort of thing, that hopefully, as you say, we come out with a happy medium. (Meeting Five, p. 109)

However, during the last three meetings of the committee they incorporated skills and concepts into their curricular decisions. By now, at least on a theoretical level, committee members had revised their image of teaching geography to include a concept/skill focus. The following extracts from these meetings display the role of their revised image:

Jack: I think that's where the skills come in, eh? When it comes to Futures we should be teaching the kid where he can find the information rather than what the information is, because the information is mind-boggling. What you teach them today, nine months from now is nothing.

Archie: So I think that's kind of what the idea of the Futures program is, to prepare these people not with content but with the skills to get or to find what they need. (Meeting Seven, p. 8)

Ralph: So a skill to develop would be to develop a map of language areas, right?

Jack: So that goes to the bottom there.

Ralph: And case study . . . origin of the English language. Then you're going to investigate the origin spread of one of the major languages? That would be another skill. (Meeting Eight, p. 53)

Image of the Student

As the committee members began to change their image of teaching geography, they also had to cope with their images of students. Initially, they perceived the ability and interest of the student in very negative terms. The teachers assumed that if students were bored and disinterested or performing poorly in their work, the fault lay with the students rather than any aspect of the teaching process. This image did not change very much through their involvement in the curriculum development process. Committee members did not invest a great deal of time in considering the relationship between the curriculum being developed and their students. The student was perceived very negatively, as represented by Jack's comment early in the first meeting:

> You know the calibre of students we have nowadays. They come to class because, maybe, they are poor students. (Meeting One, p. 11)

Later in the same meeting, Mark described how he thought students would react to a problem-solving activity:

> This is human geography: 'What are you going to do with the Indian problem?' You know just throw it [problem] out to them [students]. A lot of kids are going to say, 'give them more money', and other kids will say, 'shoot them all', but other kids will say, 'fix up their reserves' or say, 'get rid of them'. (Meeting One, p. 54)

Mark still evidenced a similar attitude towards the ability of students during the seventh meeting of the committee:

> This idea of having everybody research every question and so forth, or taking an attitude, I think you often end up with nothing. (Meeting Seven, p. 9)

The major difference evident in the meeting transcripts was an increased willingness to accept that students could accept some responsibility for their own learning and were capable of some degree of problem-solving. Consequently, while the participants did not vocalize a change in how they perceived student abilities or interest levels, they did design more student-centred activities. This suggests they were considering the students in an alternative light.

Image of the Curriculum Development Process

The most overt change in the images of the geography committee was in their perception of the curriculum development process itself. The committee members entered into the process because of provincial government legislation which required that each secondary school had a course of study for each course taught in the school. The school administration had decided to use this policy to facilitate teacher growth through their involvement in the development process.

Consequently, the committee members perceived they were involved in the committee because of external mandate:

> I mean [the Department Head] is just pushing the pressure down the ladder. He's getting pressure from the [Assistant Principal], and he'll [Assistant Principal] claim he's getting pressure from whomever . . . I believe it is the Ministry of Education that says you have to have all these nice concise little documents in your office when we [Ministry of Education] come around. (Meeting One, p. 8)

The initial intention of the geography committee members, then, was to develop a paper product to satisfy this external pressure:

> What we have to do is come up with a curriculum, sort of a general statement, as to what is going on in grade eleven. And then we can each go in our own direction, quite frankly. (Meeting One, p. 5)

They suggested that committee members divide the task up and construct components based on their past practice:

> I think the best bet is that you gentlemen prepare your physical geography [course], I'll prepare the human for the general [grade] elevens and Archie can prepare his for the advanced [level] . . . You can have copies of ours, we'd like a copy of your physical [geography course]. (Meeting One, p. 3)

Very quickly, committee members expressed concern with this proposed practice; not because they were dissatisfied with dividing up the curriculum task or with existing pedagogy but because of declining enrolment in geography. A decrease in student enrolment in their subject area might result in a cancellation of geography courses and their re-assignment to other teaching areas. They decided a revised curriculum might attract student enrolment. Consequently, during the second meeting, the committee formally opted to work together to complete one curriculum that would encompass not only their past major focus of human and physical geography but also such new themes as economic, 'Futures', and cultural geography.

As the committee continued in their development work, their perceptions began to change from resisting participation to perceiving some value in the process. As one committee member stated in an interview conducted halfway through the year:

> What does the curriculum mean to me? It means getting down on paper the things that you're supposed to be doing within a course throughout the year, analyzing it and seeing whether you're doing the right thing and thinking about it. Thinking about what you're doing in the classroom. I think that is the real value to it anyway.

By the end of the eight meetings, held over the course of the school year, members of the geography committee had a different image of the curriculum development process. They now perceived the document produced as being a valuable tool to assist their teaching not just as a paper product to satisfy the school's administration. They summarized their feelings in the final session:

> *Jack*: We learned a lot from [the process] so I think that is the important thing.
>
> *Archie*: By doing it yourself, you're going to write a document that you can use. By doing it collectively, you're going to use the document. All of us can use it.
>
> *Ralph*: You have sources of interest that we all have. Like I have my stash of goodies, okay? And then all of a sudden it comes out, 'Geez, I never thought of using that.' You get a whole different perspective than you get doing it on an individual basis or two guys that are teaching the course . . . And you get a pride of ownership, too. (Meeting Eight, p. 114)

One aspect that influenced this change of attitude was an increased sense of teacher empowerment. In the early committee meetings, participants often expressed concern that a written curriculum document would result in a decrease in the personal autonomy of the teacher, Jack expressed his concern:

> That's why I say I hope the office doesn't come in and say, 'Now, God darn it, I thought you should be in Africa today and you are in China'. (Meeting Two, p. 37)

By developing the curriculum they felt comfortable with the product and by organizing that curriculum around concepts and skills rather than discrete factual content, these teachers gradually developed a sense of control over their classroom practice. Both the knowledge they had of and the ownership they felt for the finished product created the empowerment they evidenced.

Rules of Practice

The development of revised and new rules of practice was intertwined throughout the process of changing images. Indeed, it was often through struggling with alternative teaching methodology that the committee members envisioned their new images. The relationship between classroom image and rules of practice is natural given that methodology, not a curriculum document, is the practical for teachers. In this case study, two major areas dominated the teachers' search for alternatives and new rules of practice: teaching strategies and the use of resources. The following section describes their efforts at developing such alternatives.

Teaching Methodology

As documented in the previous section on image, the studied teachers had primarily employed lecture or Socratic instructional methods in their everyday teaching. Generally, they had not used more interactive activities such as group work, simulation games, role-playing, or problem-solving.

However, the shift from their past emphasis on factual content to a focus on concepts and skills as the basis of their new curriculum required that the committee investigate alternative teaching strategies. This process began halfway through the curriculum development process when the committee members realized their past rules of practice were incongruent with their new images. At this point, they cautiously began to discuss alternatives:

Mark: Do you ever do role-playing?
Archie: I have, maybe once.
Mark: I never have. Well, I've sort of toyed with the idea. How do you do it?
Lynne: [provides examples]
Mark: I'd like to see that, quite frankly, because I don't really know that much about role-playing. I mean I know the general drift of it but I stop and think to myself, 'mmhm I can't'. Maybe I don't give enough thought to it. (Meeting Four, p. 48)

In this first discussion of alternative teaching strategies the teachers evoked several different past images. First, they questioned what this might mean for themselves as teachers, with a special concern for their work load:

Archie: I think role-playing and most of those types of strategies demand a heck of a pile of preparation because the better they're prepared, in my mind, the more successful they'll be in the classroom. I find I just don't have that kind of time. (Meeting Four, p. 49)

Second, they searched through their past experiences both as students at teachers' college and as teachers:

Archie: I've never seen an example in my teaching career. You know, say in teachers' college or something like that . . . I think that is why I tend to stay away from it. (Meeting Four, p. 49)

Third, the committee members questioned whether such a teaching strategy would work with their image of students:

Mark: See, what I always wonder is, how do you motivate them [students]? How do you get them to care that much [about role-playing]? I mean you do it, I do it, for fun but some of the kids they don't want to spend the effort. (Meeting Four, p. 50)

After the external facilitator provided some practical examples of how role-playing might be incorporated into the high school curriculum, the committee members discussed specific aspects involved in using role-playing and other similar interactive teaching strategies:

> *Mark*: How often do you do all these things? Like you know, how to do them and so forth? You don't do them mainly on the account of it's easier to do it the other way. I mean the old Socratic style is easy. You could walk in and say, 'Well, here we go.' There's no preparation really. You know the course and so forth. You just go in there. There's not a lot that is absolutely necessary and I think that so often you might do it, not because this doesn't work or anything like that, but just because it is so much more work. (Meeting Four, p. 54)

> *Archie*: I think one of my greatest, I can't say it's fear, but I think it's one of my greatest reasons for not doing this kind of stuff in the past was I never felt comfortable when it came to an evaluation. How do you evaluate? (Meeting Four, p. 56)

As the committee members struggled with their past images and rules of practice, they contemplated trying out the alternative strategies in their classroom:

> *Archie*: Just sitting here talking about it [role-playing], I think I'm going to try it with my [grade] elevens coming in the next semester. (Meeting Four, p. 52)

The committee also incorporated alternative teaching strategies into all subsequent curriculum planning. Through this process they still searched for an image of what these strategies would mean for their classroom practice. Several extracts from the transcripts exemplify the process.

> *Mark*: Jigsaw grouping. I've never done it before but I always mean to. Do you ever do jigsaw grouping?
>
> *Ralph*: No.
>
> *Mark*: You know, guys are sort of responsible for different things. (Meeting Five, p. 10)
>
> *Archie*: In other words, we're looking for skills . . .
>
> *Mark*: Skills, yeah, skills.
>
> *Archie*: Do something besides your Socratic method here.
>
> *Mark*: Yes.
>
> *Archie*: What else do you do? Well, there's something you can do. You can have them make population pyramids later on here under the models . . . So I mean they're getting a skill. If they can construct one, they're going to be able to read one. (Meeting Six, p. 28)

The completed curriculum document included numerous examples of interactive teaching strategies. In fact these techniques dominated the document. Interview data gathered from the school's administration also suggests that the teachers involved were experimenting with alternative strategies in their classroom prior to the introduction of the new curriculum. However, the data only supports the assertion that involvement in the curriculum development process had resulted in some new rules of practice applied to the curricular decision-making process itself.

Resources

As the members of the geography committee investigated alternative teaching strategies congruent with the skill and concept basis of the curriculum, they also encountered the need to re-conceptualize their use of resources. Of particular importance was how they used textbooks in their classroom. When they started the development project, the evidence suggests they considered the textbook as the curriculum:

> Mark: In fact, I give the kids that thing right out of the book in the grade twelve geography [course]. I say, 'These are the units. This is the kind of things we're going to be touching upon.' (Meeting Three, p. 32)

The teachers involved were so grounded in the use of textbooks that initially they had copied the tables of contents from several different books to guide their curriculum decisions. As the teachers revised their image of teaching geography and developed the five themes as their major organization, the textbook chapters could not be employed in this manner. With their theme organization, only portions of the chapters were applicable and they sought alternative sources of knowledge to support their curriculum. The committee became selective with their choice of textbook usage and questioned the validity of using textbooks as the curriculum.

The committee members also envisioned alternative resources to support more interactive teaching strategies including topographical maps, on-site visits to local areas of geographical interest, and audio-visual materials. More importantly, however, they started to view each other as a source of knowledge. They moved to a much more collegial support model:

> Mark: Pool our knowledge. That's one of those things you always say you're going to do and then you find yourself doing the unit again and you think, 'Uh, I was going to do this last year. I was going to get all organized and I didn't.'
>
> Archie: I think that, Mark, gathering materials, to get it done, you'd almost have to say, 'Okay, next meeting, boom.'
>
> Archie: To me, the only way you're going to get hands-on material is to set it up so that that's going to be our goal. We are expected to

come in with our hands-on material to share. If we did that a
couple of times a year...

Lynne: You'd get some neat stuff.

Archie: You could come up with some good stuff.

Jack: We'd have an interesting course, that's right. (Meeting Four,
p. 23)

General Principles

It is difficult to ascertain if the curriculum development process had facilitated
any major shifts in the general principles for the members of the geography
committee. As outlined in the previous two sections, the evidence documents
that the participants modified their images of teaching and the curriculum
development process, and sought out rules of practice to support their emerging
images. However, general principles are more deeply embedded beliefs
regarding the learning process, teaching methodology, the worth of certain
knowledge, and student characteristics.

Certainly, through their curriculum development work, the participants
deliberated on each of these facets. They struggled with perceiving the learning
process as one that individuals negotiate for themselves through solving
problems and developing skills, as opposed to having someone (usually a
teacher) organize and deliver factual knowledge. The participants also
investigated alternative teaching strategies that differed from their past reliance
on the lecture or Socratic methods. Perhaps the most difficult factor addressed
by the committee members was re-conceptualizing what constituted
knowledge. In their past experience, knowledge was factual content. In their
developing image, knowledge of worth became concepts and thinking skills.
Theoretically they had made this adjustment as the finished curriculum
document emphasized thinking skills, problem solving and concepts, with
specific factual content as only the vehicle to achieve these goals. The changes in
what constituted knowledge of worth and teaching modifications necessitated
changes in how the teachers viewed the characteristics of their students. The
participants did not vocalize a change in their negative perceptions of student
characteristics but they did design activities that would require more active and
self-actualized students.

While the participants struggled with each of these components through
their deliberations on the grade eleven geography curriculum, modification of
the beliefs themselves might have to wait until they have implemented the
curriculum in the classroom. Recent research suggests that a change in beliefs
follows, not precedes, a change in behaviour (for example, see Fullan, 1985;
Guskey, 1986). This research suggests that teachers change beliefs as they
identify changes in student behaviour, achievement or attitudes that they can
attribute to the innovations. Perhaps, as the geography committee members
taught their new curriculum they would have gradually adapted their general

principles to fit with their new images and rules of practice. However, this remains conjecture as the research study only documented the curriculum development process itself.

Discussion

The data presented in the previous section provides insight into the influence of teachers' practical knowledge on the curriculum development process. The data also clearly documents how involvement in the process influenced the teachers participating in the project. The evidence suggests that the participants revised their image of teaching and their image of the curriculum development process itself. Additionally, they explored alternative rules of practice concerning teaching methodology and the use of resources. This concluding section of the chapter examines what factors influenced the process experienced by the geography committee.

The Experienced Process

An analysis of the transcript data suggests that the geography committee experienced three phases in making their curricular decisions: 'cut and paste'; cognitive dissonance; and assimilation. Each of these phases will be briefly reviewed in the following paragraphs.

Phase One: 'Cut and Paste' When the teachers began the curriculum development process, they intended to 'cut and paste' from existing curriculum documents, their current practice, and textbooks to create a document satisfactory to the administration. They envisioned having the document completed in two days. The curricular decisions were to be based on the participants' past experience of teaching geography. At this stage, they interpreted the new Ministry of Education guideline through their image of teaching as that of presenting factual content. Committee members failed to recognize the major shifts in philosophy contained in the guideline. Consequently, their discussion regarding the new guideline primarily involved identifying the changes in content. Most likely, a curriculum document produced in this stage would have mainly focused on shifting content, with little revision, from one grade level to another. The Ministry emphasis on problem-solving and thinking skills would not have been a major focus of their document. The status quo would have been preserved, through default not by a reasoned decision.

Phase Two: Cognitive Dissonance The committee members began to be dissatisfied with the status quo because of the declining enrolment in geography courses. Initially, they intended to make cosmetic changes to their current practice by combining physical and human geography into one curriculum. The changes envisioned by the participants still just involved shifting and re-organizing content. The committee had no intention of making major changes to their existing way of teaching geography because they did not perceive a problem with their existing practice.

However, as the committee developed the integrated curriculum, they opened a Pandora's box of changes. During the second and third meetings, committee members started to question the purpose of content knowledge and, through more careful analysis of the new Ministry guideline, explored concepts and skills as the basis for the curriculum. This discussion necessitated a consideration of the teachers' images of students and teaching. By the fourth meeting the committee was deliberately reviewing their existing practice and searching out alternative methods of teaching. The committee no longer accepted past practice as a justification; they now required a reasoned argument to support a decision.

As the committee members moved away from a tacit acceptance of their past practical knowledge, they became dissatisfied with their existing practice. They asked themselves such questions as 'How should I teach?', 'What other strategies could I use?', 'What resources would I need?', and 'How could I obtain these resources?' Consequently, they started to question their past practice and their images of teaching. This, in turn, led to an investigation of new rules of practice that might be more congruent with their developing images. Through this process, the participants made their existing curriculum and practice problematic.

Phase Three: Assimilation The cognitive dissonance phase gradually became the assimilation phase. By the fifth meeting, the committee had established their new images of teaching and new rules of practice. They now had a criterion from which to make their curriculum decisions. In the remaining meetings, the participants applied their new images and rules of practice. The committee reviewed earlier decisions to ensure congruency with their new criterion. They questioned the material presented by other committee members as to whether it fitted the new images. The curriculum document they had completed by the eighth meeting reflected the images and rules of practice that had emerged during the curriculum development process.

Members of the geography committee had acted on their revised images and rules of practice while making their curricular decisions. However, these changes must be implemented in the practical reality of the teachers' world. New ideas about the role of content and alternative teaching strategies have to be incorporated with the world view of the teacher which involves classrooms, administration demands, and students. Implementing their curriculum document will require that the teachers involved assimilate the new concepts into their practical world and into their general principles on what constitutes good teaching practice and learning activities. Unfortunately, the movement from acting upon curriculum decisions to acting upon classroom practice remains beyond the scope of this study.

Factors Facilitating the Curriculum Development Process

Several factors seemed to facilitate the curriculum development process experienced by the geography committee. First, the curriculum process leader employed a deliberative curriculum process to guide the project. Second, the process leader provided facilitative leadership. Third, a supportive climate was developed that allowed individuals to take risks.

The Deliberative Process

The deliberative curriculum process is based on several tenets. First, curriculum problems are practical not theoretical problems (Schwab, 1969). Second, those problems should be conceptualized as uncertain, not procedural problems (Reid, 1978; Knitter, 1985). Uncertain problems concern questioning whether something 'should' be taught rather than just 'what' should be taught. Third, according to deliberative theory, curriculum decisions involve generating alternatives and selecting an alternative based on reasoned judgment (Reid, 1978). Fourth, the curriculum development process itself can best be represented by a spiral, not a linear, process (Schwab, 1983; Roby, 1985). These tenets can be used to enhance the curriculum development process through the adoption of appropriate strategies and actions such as those described in the facilitative leadership section.

When the geography committee began the curriculum development process, they intended to focus on 'what' content should be taught. The process itself was viewed as a procedural problem — to produce a document to satisfy the administration. Through their deliberations, the committee questioned their past practice. This questioning eventually changed the nature of the problem from that of a procedural to an uncertain problem. They began to generate alternatives and demanded that a reasoned argument be the basis of their eventual decision. The committee members focused on whether something 'should' be taught and 'how' that might be best accomplished. Through this process, the committee moved from perceiving curriculum development as a theoretical activity necessary to satisfy legislated policy and administrative mandate to a practical activity useful to themselves as teachers.

Facilitative Leadership

Facilitative leadership was the second factor influencing the curriculum development process experienced by the geography committee (Hannay and Seller, 1988). The committee had two leaders. A teacher was the designated leader and assumed a leadership role pertaining to subject-matter decisions. The external researcher, in her role as field developer, assumed the process leadership of the committee with the agreement of the participants. It is this later leadership role that was particularly germane in facilitating the deliberative process.

Two components influenced the ability of the process leader to guide the curriculum development project: knowledge and facilitative strategies. The process leader brought into the project a knowledge of the curriculum development process itself and a knowledge of the philosophical changes underlying the new Ministry of Education guideline.

The process leader envisioned the purpose of curriculum development not only as document production but as a growth opportunity for the participants. Consequently, she stressed the importance of reflective dialogue over the need to quickly produce a written product. The process leader had an understanding of the nature of deliberative curriculum development and encouraged a back and forth dialogue that allowed individuals to express their ideas or concerns. She also believed that the curriculum development process was a circular not a linear process with a major emphasis on a reasoned approach.

The process leader also had an understanding of the philosophical changes in the new Ministry geography guideline. She realized that the initial images held by the geography committee members were incongruent with the image underlying the new guideline. Consequently, she was able to use the techniques outlined below to help the participants internalize a sense of cognitive dissonance.

Two strategies were employed by the process leader to facilitate the curriculum development process: questioning and 'gentling'. The leader modelled an acceptance of alternative views and gently guided the committee members to question their past practice. The leader posed the questions in tentative terms such as 'I'm wondering . . .' rather than stating a direction or a viewpoint. Frequently, the leader asked questions that would foster a discussion pertaining to the images, rules of practice and general principles held by the committee members. By answering the questions, the committee members explored alternatives to their past practices of teaching geography.

The process leader also employed a strategy that might best be described as 'gentling' to help committee members gain the confidence to take risks and share their professional expertise. Rather than challenge the teachers with an abrupt change in practice, she initially introduced issues that reflected the current beliefs of the members. Gradually as the process unfolded, the leader raised more complex concepts that encouraged the teachers to question their past practice.

Through the questioning and gentling strategies, the process leader helped the committee members develop a sense of cognitive dissonance. As they addressed the issues raised, they became dissatisfied with their past images and rules of practice. Consequently, the cognitive dissonance was internalized by the participants and was not imposed. The committee members sought alternatives, not because of an administrator or a policy document, but because of their personal and professional needs.

Supportive Climate

A climate supportive of reflection and risk taking was essential to allow the committee members to question their past practice. Facilitative leadership was crucial in creating and maintaining this climate. By guiding the process through questions and tentative suggestions, the leader facilitated the development of a questioning climate where reflection was accepted and encouraged. Additionally, the leader encouraged a climate that supported an exploration of and a respect for alternative ideas. A respect for both the personal and professional knowledge of the teachers involved was an essential condition to the development of a supportive climate. The personal questioning of past images and practices that has been documented in the findings section of this chapter, could only have occurred in a climate that supported personal reflection and growth.

Conclusion

As the teachers involved in this study made their curricular decisions, they reflected on how they had taught in the past and how they should teach in the future. The growing critical awareness influenced the development process in several different ways. Each new image explored or new rule of practice considered added a new dimension to be included in the completed curriculum. The production of the new document was no longer regarded from a 'cut and paste' perspective, but became an educative experience for the participants. As the tensions inherent in their past teaching practice were resolved, a curriculum document was produced which the members felt proud of and excited to have created. The curriculum development process was appreciated as an enjoyable, if a difficult and an exhausting experience. The result was a sense of ownership rather than a product-driven exercise.

This study provides insight into the dynamic nature of the practical knowledge of one group of experienced teachers and the influence of this knowledge on the curriculum development process they underwent. Involvement in the deliberative process broke down the teachers' isolationist past experience and provided an opportunity for reflective collaboration on professional matters which the teachers found stimulating and rewarding.

References

BEN-PERETZ, M. and TAMIR, P. (1986) 'What do curriculum developers do?' *Curriculum Perspectives*, 6, 2.

CLANDININ D. J. and CONNELLY, F. M. (1986) 'Teachers' personal practical knowledge: Image and narrative unity, Unpublished paper, University of Calgary and The Ontario Institute for Studies in Education.

ELBAZ, F. (1981) 'The teacher's "practical knowledge": Report of a case study', *Curriculum Inquiry*, 11, 1.

FULLAN, M. (1985) 'Change processes and strategies at the local level', *The Elementary School Journal*, 85, 1, pp. 392–421.

GOLD, R. (1969), 'Roles in sociological field observation', in MCCALL, G. and SIMMONS, J. (Eds) *Issues in Participant Observation*, Reading, Mass., Addison-Wesley.

GUSKEY, T. (1986) 'Staff development and the process of teacher change', *Educational Researcher*, 24, 5, pp. 5–12.

HANNAY. L . and SELLER, W. (1987) *Decision-Making in Curriculum Development*, Social Science and Humanities Research Council of Canada, Grant No. 410–85–0531.

HANNAY, L. AND SELLER, W. (1988) 'The curriculum leadership role in facilitating curriculum deliberation'. Symposium presentation at the Annual Meeting of the American Educational Association, New Orleans.

KNITTER W. (1985) 'Curriculum deliberation: pluralism and the practical', *Journal of Curriculum Studies*, 17, 4, pp. 385–95.

REID, W. (1978) *Thinking About the Curriculum: The Nature and Treatment of Curriculum Problems*, London, Routledge and Kegan Paul.

ROBY, T. (1985) 'Habits impeding deliberation', *Journal of Curriculum Studies*, 17, 1, pp. 17–35.

SCHEFFLER, I. (1973) 'The practical as a focus for curriculum: Reflections on Schwab's view', in *Reason and teaching*, London, Routledge and Kegan Paul.

SCHUBERT, W. (1986) 'Curriculum research controversy: A special case of a general problem', *Journal of Curriculum and Supervision*, 1, 2, pp. 132–47.

SCHWAB, J. (1969) 'The practical: A language for curriculum', *School Review*, 78.

SCHWAB, J. (1983) 'The practical 4: Something for curriculum professors to do', *Curriculum Inquiry*, 13, 3, pp. 239–65.

WALKER, D. (1978) 'A naturalistic model for curriculum development', in GRESS J. and PURPEL D. (Eds) *Curriculum: An Introduction to the Field*, Berkeley, McCutchan.

Chapter 17

Teachers Never Stop Thinking About Teaching: Sharing Classroom Constructs With Expert Volunteers

Michael Kompf and Donald Dworet

In research conducted over a four month period, a case study method was devised to provide a basis for examining the practical use of expert volunteers (i.e. inactive teachers with experience and certification) in an elementary school setting. At the same time we wished to examine, from a more theoretical basis, the constructs classroom teachers have when placed in a situation requiring a posting and sharing of their constructs. The volunteers in this study agreed to participate two or three half-days per week and carry out in-class instructional activities assigned to them by a host teacher.

Questions were asked of both host teachers and expert volunteers to conversationally elicit their constructs regarding: anticipated and actual benefits and problems of teaching; workload effect; and classroom effectiveness regarding student outcomes.

Responses given in semi-structured group interviews and individual report forms indicated that host teachers had high levels of confidence in the ability of expert volunteers to carry out assigned classroom duties responsibly and effectively. Extra time became available for individual student consultation and special needs. Host teachers indicated that more was able to be accomplished as these volunteers were like 'extensions of themselves'. The school board in which this pilot study was conducted has indicated an interest in carrying on beyond the proposed time frame for the project and is considering adoption of this program on a board-wide basis.

Our conclusions indicate that not only were former teachers' constructs about teaching able to be reactivated and used in a manner consistent with existing classroom constructs, but that host teachers were able to share what had been their own professionally-oriented system of constructing the classroom. Once the beneficial aspects of sharing duty-related constructs became obvious and common classroom constructions were recognized, any levels of discomfort experienced by the host teacher or expert volunteer decreased substantially. Thus by *learning* to share constructs, host-volunteer teams were able to work together effectively and efficiently.

Objectives

In this study we looked at the impact of introducing five expert, inactive teachers acting as volunteers, matched with host teachers, into an elementary school to assist in classroom routines in their area of expertise for two or three half-days per week.

As Kelly (1955) discussed, persons have relatively stable sets of core constructs that remain so over time. One of our considerations in this study was that inactive former teachers would have, in a latent or submerged form, core sets of educational constructs that would come into play when required. It may be argued that a teacher's concept of self-as-teacher is the product of construct generation, testing, and revision that accumulates over a lifetime of educational work. Constructs are person or situation specific, but the generalizability of any accumulated system is dependent on the successful anticipation of events managed by that system. We considered that teachers' constructs about teaching would incorporate preactive, interactive and postactive dimensions. Any discrimination between these modes of thought would remain sharply in focus even for practitioners having had interruptions in their professional careers. The daily effects of practice on commonly used educational construct systems may well act as a hone providing a basis for ongoing sharpening, i.e. testing and development of constructs, or, what Schön (1987) referred to as reflection-in-action. Conversely, those latent constructs of non-practising teachers may be more typically viewed as having foundation in what Russell and Johnston (1988) called reflection-on-action thus taking into account the historical basis of construct development. That which Schön (1987) describes, without reference to the large body of constructivist work, is clearly the developmental processes persons undergo in construct development and revision. Schön (1987) prescribes a reciprocal relationship with the self that acts in a diagnostic manner focusing on the *how* and *what* of that which is taught and the manner in which it is received and acted on by students and the subsequent effect it has on teacher behaviour. According to Dewey (1938) teachers do not act in a vacuum. Their classroom actions are dependent not only on their own previous actions but on the actions of those who have taught before them. Teachers develop a sense of educational purpose or what Dewey called a formation of purpose by:

> (1) observation of surrounding conditions; (2) knowledge of what has happened in similar situations in the past, a knowledge obtained partly by recollection and partly by information, advice and warning of those who have had a wider experience; and (3) judgment which puts together what is observed and what is recalled to see what they signify. (p. 69)

Of relevance and value in thinking about teacher action is the sense of historical and conceptual continuity which may be visible in the posting, use and development of educational constructs amongst persons sharing instructional responsibilities (see Postman, 1979). We anticipated that host teachers able to take full advantage of the program would be willing to share their constructs of teaching and communicate same to volunteers while the volunteers would share the reactivation, testing, validation or revision of their latent constructs once called into play. Of concern to us was the visible, explicit sharing of constructs-in-practice and the effect of this sharing on teacher behaviour and instructional delivery.

Theoretical Framework

Because of the potentially broad implications of this research, a pilot study was undertaken to discover what phenomena merited closer examination and more precise measurement. For the purposes of this chapter we have chosen to formulate our understandings with the positions of Dewey (1938), Kelly (1955), Schön (1987) and Russell and Johnston (1988).

Dewey (1938) felt that the educational process was a lifelong venture of learning for all persons. Teachers, in this view, would ideally see themselves as playing an interactive role of both student and teacher, simultaneously teaching and learning as an educational experience unfolds. An openness and willingness to learn and thereby reconstruct experiences into more meaningful and influential guides for practice forms the core of Dewey's advice for teachers.

A reliance on Kelly's (1955) theoretical premises allows us to infer much about the ways in which people develop, maintain, preserve, enhance, and test their personal constructs through personal theory as an outcome of practice and personal theorizing as a developing cognitive process. Dewey (1938) argued for 'one permanent frame of reference: namely, the organic connection between education and personal experience' (p. 25). He felt that events which are personally meaningful are, through their heightened relevance, contributors to the *quality* and *effect* of the associated experiences. According to Dewey, both educating and becoming educated are lifelong experiences complete with purpose and an end-view. Schön (1987) connects much of Kelly (1955) and Dewey (1938) by stating that:

> This view of the practitioner's reflection-in-action is a *constructionist* view of reality with which the practitioner deals — a view that leads us to see the practitioner as constructing situations of his practice, not only in the exercise of professional artistry but also in all other modes of professional competence (p. 36).

It is our belief that the constructivist view taken by a teacher to develop his personal view of teaching does not end with professional withdrawal. It may be assumed that such a heightened level of cognitive awareness is not solely dependent on the daily exercise of such professional prowess, thus endowing inactive teachers with the propensity for latent educational constructs arising from reflection-on-action. If this is the case, then inactive educators, when placed back in the classroom situation should quickly rise to a proficient level of competence. The dormant educational constructs of inactive educators when reactivated, should facilitate acclimatization not only to the classroom but also to the broader, current educational milieu.

Methodology

A methodology such as the one undertaken in this study is an attempt to gain understanding by making a dynamic ongoing process momentarily visible by capturing teachers' willing disclosures about their contextual feelings regarding teaching actions. Our concern deals with how teachers have not only chosen teaching actions, but chosen from among them those constructs on which they will act and how related constructs may be shared. *'Teachers are assumed to make choices among dichotomous alternatives*: to promote equality or excellence . . . . These choices are thought to enable teachers to avoid dilemmas in their everyday practice' (Lampert, 1985, p.190). With the prospect of another qualified professional in a teacher's classroom the choices may not only serve to avoid dilemmas but to extend possibilities about practice by the sharing of constructive alternatives.

In order to attain the quality and type of information required, we used a semi-structured interview format to elicit conversational constructs regarding: the anticipation of the host-volunteer interaction, the actual interaction and subsequent evaluation by both involved parties and its effect on practice. In addition to interviews we collected information from open-ended questionnaires.

Recent advances in Personal Construct Theory (PCT) research on the value of conversationally elicited constructs versus grid elicited constructs has avoided the thorny issue of which may be better and focused on the products of either method of elicitation. High face validity may be attached to conversational elicitation as persons are able to represent their realities (Kelly, 1955).

Attempts at understanding the interconnected nature of constructs and communication have extended possibilities for more and deeper information to be extracted from conversationally elicited constructs. Loos and Epstein (1989) argue that the provision of a conversational context in which problems and issues may be most effectively understood and resolved is dependent on the *continuance* of conversation. They refer to conversations as emergent, co-developed, co-constructed realities. The therapist, or researcher, is therefore a partner in the co-creation of communicative systems in which the goal is clarity of constructions. Yorke (1989) argues that the character sketches developed by Kelly (1955) represent a 'far freer process, since respondents would be encouraged to give expanded construals rich in intonation, choice of syntax, metaphor and exemplification — for which repertory grids allow little scope' (p. 14). Epting (1988) reminded PCT workers that Kelly (1955) in considering his theory of experience was concerned with the content of statements as well as the structure of statements. In his work with children, Epting (1988) implies limitations with the formal approach held by many PCT researchers. He states that more experientially oriented studies explore 'further constructive alternatives such as person-as-child person-as-storyteller, or person-as-philosopher' (Epting, 1988, p. 3), none of which would appear to preclude or lessen the utility, validity or reliability of conversationally elicited constructs. Whether or not constructs are shared or held in common, as we wished to determine, becomes a matter of content analysis and evidence of similar sentiment in utterances which are treated as constructions.

Methods

An elementary school (kindergarten to grade 8) was designated as a study site. Eight teachers volunteered to act as hosts and specified the duties they would assign to an expert volunteer and described the type of person with whom they felt they could work effectively.

Two methods to elicit expert volunteers were used. First, we contacted recently retired teachers by mail. Second, we advertised in a local newspaper for inactive teachers willing to do volunteer work. We were able to match five volunteers with the host teachers. In two cases one volunteer was shared by two teachers.

At an initial meeting in Mid-October, 1987, volunteers met the host teachers and discussed the terms of their volunteer services. We met approximately every two weeks thereafter for three months and sought answers to the following questions through both questionnaires and interviews with host teachers and volunteers:

What benefits were anticipated from having/being an expert volunteer?

What were the actual benefits of having/being an expert volunteer?

What problems were anticipated from having/being an expert volunteer?

What actual problems occurred as a result of having had/having been an expert volunteer?

Were there any difference in workload, i.e. greater or lesser?

What was the effect on the students in classes with volunteers?

What differences are there between expert and non-expert volunteers?

Would you wish to continue this program? If so, why? If not, why not?

Volunteers and host teachers were matched by examining the experience, qualifications and preferences of volunteers and considering these factors in light of the requests of the host teachers. Our instructions beyond providing introductions over lunch and a simple explanation of what we were up to were simply: the volunteers must commit themselves to at least two or three half-days per week for one school term, the host teachers must use the volunteers in a way that would take maximum advantage of their professional experience and training. Orientations to the school, programs and students were left in the hands of individual host teachers and the school Principal. We held lunch meetings every two weeks throughout the project for oral and written feedback.

Results

As one of the purposes of this study was to determine the efficacy of using expert volunteers, it was essential that these volunteers be perceived by host teachers as possesssing different qualities from the traditional non-professional volunteer and would be used accordingly. It was anticipated that the expert volunteers would be given professional responsibilities, i.e. performing actual instruction rather than the usual volunteer role of marking papers, cleaning up or designing bulletin boards.

Though both the host teachers and the expert volunteers were quite enthusiastic about this project we were concerned over the difficulty of having two certified teachers in one class with one being both part-time and subservient to the other. Examination of the comments obtained from our questions to both the teachers and the expert volunteers showed that the above concern was not necessary. This finding, along with several others to be discussed, reveals that the use of an expert volunteer is a most appropriate use of one's inactive professional talents.

Host Teacher and Expert Volunteer Constructs

Although the host teachers were well accustomed to having volunteers in their classrooms they were not experienced in being part of a team-teaching situation, nor were they provided with any training in how such a situation should be treated. It was our intention to determine the constructs in regard to working with another adult and what positive and negative aspects they saw in such a situation.

The host teachers believed that the expert volunteers would: provide more teacher attention to special needs students; assist in the assessment of individual students and therefore detect problems in student learning; allow the teacher to spend more time with the whole class. The expert volunteers believed that by participating in this program they could contribute something 'worthwhile to the development of children'. They expressed the view that this volunteering opportunity would allow them to update their skills and educational philosophy without being responsible for a whole class five days per week.

On the side of caution the host teachers believed that expert volunteers would create more work for them because of the additional planning they anticipated would have to take place. Additional teacher concerns included:

extra time required to be adequately prepared for the classroom presence of an 'expert volunteer'; additional class distractions due to individual students seeking the volunteer's attention at inappropriate times; concern regarding the volunteers' knowledge of current curriculum and student learning objectives; adjustment of the student to appropriate use of another adult in the classroom.

The expert volunteers had related concerns over whether or not they would be able to 'get along' with the host teacher and his/her students. They were apprehensive over whether their educational approaches would be acceptable to the host teacher and whether students would take advantage of their presence by behaving in a manner that would be contrary to the expectations of the host teacher. One expert volunteer expressed concern over being given 'joe jobs' requiring no expertise rather than assignments which required being knowledgeable about professional teaching practices.

It is clear that both the host teachers and expert volunteers had similar concerns, or if you will, constructs, anticipating the involvement of an expert volunteer in a classroom. Both groups had common constructs about teaching capabilities, classroom management capabilities and adjustment capabilities of the students to the new situation.

The actual benefits as expressed by the host teachers appear to have exceeded the expected benefits. One associate teacher wrote:

> ... has done much more than I expected. She has planned a reading lesson and provided reading materials from the public library. She has also volunteered to make charts and change bulletin boards. Because she is capable of working with a group, I have more time to spend with the other pupils.

Further comments from the host teachers suggest that the presence of an expert volunteer helped the students in two significant ways. First, it gave them another adult to whom they could relate. This allowed the teacher to have more time to help individual students without being interrupted. Second, the expert volunteers, being both competent and confident in their instructional capabilities, were consistently able to take individuals or small groups and provide professional instruction. This allowed for students to better understand new material or permitted students requiring remedial assistance to receive additional help from a knowledgeable professional.

In response to our question regarding the effect on the class of having an expert volunteer present two or three mornings a week, the teachers believed that the effect was very positive with no particular disruptions. The teachers wrote that acceptance by the class was immediate and that the students easily approached the expert volunteers for assistance. One teacher commented that her class needed to learn that the behavioural expectations of the expert volunteer were the same as hers. This last point was not commonly expressed but is something which may need to be more closely examined when pairing expert volunteers with host teachers.

The host teachers were asked about the effect on their workload due to the presence of the expert volunteer. In all responses the teachers indicated that their workload had been affected. The teachers suggested that though their load during the day had been reduced, this reduction was offset by the additional time required to plan additional student activities which were now possible due to the presence of the expert volunteer. In addition, the teachers also believed that they had to spend more time planning to be adequately prepared for the expert volunteer's presence. In all cases the teachers reported that their students reacted very positively and eagerly went with the expert volunteer whenever requested to do so. There apparently was no extensive adjustment period required. The students appeared to enjoy relating to another adult who was not their regular teacher. It should be noted, however, that this school has had a variety of non-expert volunteers (parents and high school co-op students) for several years. This reaction to the expert volunteer may be the result of the students being used to the presence of other adults in their classrooms.

Overall, the teachers evaluated the use of expert volunteers very highly. One teacher referred to the expert volunteer as 'a welcomed colleague.' Another teacher wrote that this experience was 'positive for all parties — volunteer, teacher, and student'. One teacher believed that a parent volunteer would have done similar things, but would not have done as good a job. She believed that there was a qualititative difference as a result of the expert volunteer having actual experience in professional teaching. The teachers suggested that in-service sessions be provided to ensure that expert volunteers are used appropriately, i.e. in a team approach, one that implies a working with rather than a working for. After spending several weeks participating, the volunteers believed that their expectations had been fulfilled. In addition to the beliefs expressed above, the volunteers found that they felt tremendous satisfaction knowing that they had helped someone, they liked the challenge of planning meaningful lessons and they enjoyed being involved in something new and different. One volunteer expressed the view that by working part-time, she enjoyed her spare time more. In every case, the volunteers believed that the actual teaching experience provided in this program was essential to their continued involvement. They would not have been as strongly motivated had they been assigned traditional non-professional responsibilities. They believed their talents and abilities were put to use effectively and they were challenged by the experience.

Before starting the program, the volunteers had several reservations. One was concerned over the title 'expert volunteer' because, though she had taught elementary grades for many years prior to her leaving teaching, she did not perceive herself as an 'expert' in any particular school subject. After the program began the expert volunteers believed that all of their concerns were not justified. In every case the teacher and the volunteer cooperated in a friendly and professional manner. Appropriate tasks were assigned, there was no conflict over educational approaches (in fact, the host teachers complimented the expert volunteers on their effectiveness), and the students did not 'play one teacher against another.' The only difficulties encountered by the volunteers were quite minor. One was concerned that she had inconvenienced the teacher due to their having to share teaching manuals and another believed that she had been taken advantage of by one student who, when asked about books he had read in the reading centre stated that he had read all of them. The volunteer did not learn until the following week that this could not have been possible and then had to get the student to select an appropriate book for his book report.

Students in each of the five classes used were reported to have responded very favourably to the presence of the expert volunteer. The children quickly accepted the volunteers as their teachers and were very open and communicative. One volunteer commented that the students in her class responded very slowly at first but then a feeling of trust developed. She went on to write 'I like them, and I think the feeling is mutual.'

We were concerned about how the expert volunteers' personal workload might be affected by their commitment to this pilot study. The volunteers reported that the adjustment to their personal schedules and commitments had been negligible except for one volunteer who had to cut back on physical fitness activities. They were particularly pleased that under this program they were not required to bring work home with them and that all the planning was done for them by the classroom teacher. In one case a volunteer did some lesson planning over a weekend but it was her choice to do so and it did not interfere with any other plans.

Overall, the expert volunteers were very enthusiastic about their experiences. They believed that volunteer teaching was a very 'stimulating way to spend a few hours each week.' It provided them with a chance to be of assistance to both pupils and teachers while being free from responsibility. The volunteers also saw their involvement as fun while still being provided with an excellent learning experience. They were treated as professionals and made to feel very comfortable by the staff. They suggested that there is a definite need for this type of program and were very pleased to have been able to take part.

The volunteers also suggested that more time be provided to allow the teacher and the volunteer to meet and discuss the students and the program before actual teaching commences. They believed this additional initial knowledge would have been most beneficial. Our results indicate that none of the expected problems or difficulties materialized. In fact the only problem indicated by our host teachers was their guilt over the fact that they were no longer 'doing it all.'

Conclusions

The results of this study were encouraging. Host teachers found they could spend more time with individual students' special needs. Their level of confidence in the volunteers, once established, remained high throughout the study period. Little direction was necessary as compared with non-expert volunteers. The expert volunteers were quickly perceived by the host teachers as being competent and confident. They had no difficulty in allowing the expert volunteers to take over the instruction of individuals or small groups thus allowing more students to receive the additional assistance they required in order to better understand new material. In all situations, the expert volunteers provided excellent assistance in marking, assessing student skill level and providing instruction without any direction from the host teacher.

The volunteers believed that their presence in the classroom was valuable for two important reasons. The primary reason was that individuals and small groups of students were able to receive remedial assistance from a knowledgeable professional (which is how the expert volunteers saw themselves). The second reason was the flexibility that the presence of the expert volunteer accorded the host teacher. This flexibility allowed the host teachers to work with certain students that they normally would not have had time for without the presence of another competent adult in the classroom. The volunteers believed that their involvement and capabilities decreased both the teachers' workload and stress.

During and after the experience, constructs about teaching were similar for both groups. Once all the participants understood that the assigned tasks were not onerous to arrange or to carry out, a mutual understanding of complementary roles took place. This mutual understanding was based on evidence that expert volunteers were indeed highly capable of teaching effectively, managing groups and classes in a professional manner and working alongside the host teacher in a cooperative and friendly style. Many of the anticipated problems did not materialize but rather a professional approach to practice was taken by both parties leading to more efficient and effective instruction. The expert volunteer was perceived by one host teacher to be 'an extension of herself', a phrase we believe is most appropriate in our concern over understanding the nature of shared professional constructs about teaching. Evidence and application of these common constructs were again appropriately described by one teacher who wrote:

> Mrs P. has done much more than I expected. She has planned a reading lesson and provided reading materials from the Public Library. She has also volunteered to make charts and change bulletin boards. Because she is capable of working with a group I have more time to spend with other pupils

This quotation describes an individual who was given no direct training by the host teacher and yet fulfilled a role which closely approximated that of the host teacher. The information from the host teacher perspective indicates that, in their view, expert volunteers were sharing teacher constructs about classroom action.

Expert volunteers indicated a high level of satisfaction from their involvement. One volunteer continued to be involved until one week before giving birth. Another volunteer found a renewed interest in teaching and intends to search for a full-time position. One retired volunteer found that a less demanding form of classroom commitment had not only given her something to do, but that she was also spending extra time, joyfully, going to the library searching for materials.

The volunteers believed that the three month commitment they made to be part of this program was reasonable. They did not want to extend their volunteer service any longer at that point in time, although several of them thought they would be willing to do it again at a later date. Despite much initial enthusiasm, the volunteers felt that if they were to remain involved they would lose this enthusiasm and their volunteering would become a 'job'. They suggested that for this program to remain effective, limited blocks of time for volunteer service should be maintained.

The aforegoing point has several implications for the commonality of constructs teachers develop for their professional tasks. Despite evidence that both volunteers and teachers had similar constructs in regard to how and what students should be taught, the degree to which they feel enthusiastic is related to the feeling about the tasks being a 'job'. This view of teaching as a 'job' may be held and transmitted by the host teachers and thus lessen their (and others) enthusiasm. Such an affective component may impinge on teachers' constructs about teaching and have an effect on performance. The affective component and its influence on teaching constructs and performance needs to be more fully exposed.

From a constructivist perspective, all teachers, hosts and volunteers, were able to successfully communicate the essence of their classroom constructs and monitor the ways in which volunteers were able to incorporate them into their adjunct role. Success, *per se*, became defined by a new cooperative definition of shared constructs about classroom interactions and the splitting of duties. All participants felt that successes were due to the existence of, and reactivation of volunteers' former constructs about classrooms. The sole negative comment was from one host teacher who indicated that she 'felt guilty about not doing all teaching.' It is our opinion that in-class observation may provide more insights to the actual nature of the benefits and a more acute perspective of any hidden drawbacks.

Educational and Theoretical Importance

As we have shown, sufficient constructs-in-common existed among the teachers we studied. Our suspicion is that all teachers may share in a widespread construct pool which assists them in anticipating and resolving ongoing and novel educational events. Kelly's (1955) theory helps us to consider the experience of volunteerism as we have described it in a meaningful way. Teachers as social beings appear to have many constructs in common. We would also argue that, from a cognitive perspective as relates to classroom action, teachers have common constructs pertaining to language and interaction, instruction and assessment which can be held in common by current or inactive professionals.

This pilot study may well mark the existence and availability of an untapped resource that could provide many benefits for educators. Obvious advantages aside, there exists potential for the inclusion of a permanent corps of expert volunteers within interested boards of education. As the inclusion of volunteers affects neither jobs of full-time teachers, supply teachers, nor non-expert volunteers, all persons participating would receive the benefits of volunteers over and above programs currently in existence. The minimal training and instruction required by expert volunteers because of their existing constructs about teaching lessened the impact of 'new' persons in the classroom.

Although, as shown above, strong arguments for this type of program can be made from a theoretical perspective, the most compelling reasons are in terms of classroom effectiveness and desirable learning outcomes.

We wished to circumvent the traditional problems associated with the use of non-expert volunteers by drawing a special emphasis on the exclusive use of non-practising teachers with qualifications similar to their employed counterparts, i.e. individuals who, in other circumstances, would have been fully acceptable as practitioners to all supervising agencies. In order for this to be successful, it had to be demonstrated that inactive professionals not only maintained their constructs about teaching, but that these constructs were also in agreement with teachers who were trained at a different time and were teaching in a different place.

The responses of both host teachers and volunteers to this program, were positive beyond expectations of all concerned. All three groups with a stake in this study, i.e. students, teachers and volunteers, benefited positively from the experience.

Utilizing these untapped resources presents an exciting alternative that may be a truly appropriate response to classroom dilemmas of the 1980s. In a time of fiscal restraints and teacher shortages methods must be found which allow for an increase in teacher effectiveness without additional burdens being placed on the system.

It is important to note that the alleviation of curriculum delivery problems and temporary lowering of pupil-teacher ratios for the purposes of individual instruction is not intended to affect the teachers' ultimate professional responsibilities for their classes nor in any other way affect the legal, contractual arrangements between the profession and the governing bodies. This utilization of expert volunteers is based on the premise that expert volunteers would not replace the classroom teacher, substitute teachers, teacher aides or current volunteer programs.

References

DEWEY, J. (1938) *Experience and Education*, Collier, New York.
EPTING, F. R. (1988) 'Journeying into the personal constructs of children', *International Journal of Personal Construct Psychology*, 1, 1, pp. 53–62.

KELLY, G. A. (1955) *The Psychology of Personal Constructs*, 1 and 2, Norton and Co., Chicago.

LAMPERT, M. (1985) 'How do teachers manage to teach? Perspectives on problems in teaching', *Harvard Educational Review*, 55, 2, May.

LOOS, V. E., and EPSTEIN, E. S. (1989) 'Conversational construction of meaning in family therapy: Some evolving thoughts on Kelly's sociality corollary', *International Journal of Personal Construct Psychology*, 2, 2, pp. 149–67.

POSTMAN, N. (1979) *Teaching as a Conserving Activity*, Dell Publishing Co. Inc., New York.

RUSSELL, T. and JOHNSTON, P. (1988) 'Teachers' learning from their own teaching: Analyses based on metaphor and reflection', paper presented at AERA annual conference, New Orleans.

SCHÖN, D. A., (1987) *Educating the Reflective Practitioner*, Jossey-Bass, San Francisco.

YORKE, M. (1989) 'The intolerable wrestle: Words, numbers and meanings', *International Journal of Personal Construct Psychology*, 2, 1, pp. 65–76.

Chapter 18

Polytechnic Careers: Development in Instructor Thinking

Hugo Letiche

In this chapter I try to identify the zone of proximate development of polytechnic instructors by studying how they *understand* their own work situation.

This goal puts two demands on the research. On the analytical side I have to develop criteria to identify levels in career development. I have approached this question by comparing William Torbert's theory of personal professional development with my theory of situational development in professional frames of understanding. On the empirical side I have collected and analyzed career history data, in order: (1) to demonstrate the differences in appropriateness of Torbert's and my analyses, and (2) to indicate threats and opportunities that exist to polytechnic lecturing.

I conclude that the lecturers studied do not experience the link between individual career experience and the challenges facing their profession, proactively. Lecturer awareness of the polytechnic career is limited to isolated, individual observation. A flight-from-teaching is taking place, fueled by a lack of dialogical inclusive insight [i.e. shared professional self-awareness which takes social/cultural/historical factors into account]. A broader form of professional self-definition is a prerequisite for further career development.

Introduction

From the perspective of the investigation into professional education and development, one wants to know if effective instructors *use certain patterns of making meaning* in their work. This knowledge can potentially be used to facilitate professional growth. This theme is, in this chapter, developed on the basis of research into careers of polytechnic lecturers.

My involvement in the ethnological study of polytechnic lecturers began when I experienced that the *ideal representation* available to me by reading the literature on polytechnic careers, and the *actual work I did*, seemed to be totally different. The question *Why bother with career histories?* was not posed. I asked *What is the real nature and mission of polytechnic lecturing?* without considering the possibility that the question cannot be adequately answered. I tacitly assumed that the work I did was meaningful and purposeful. I never doubted that it was worth expending the energy demanded; I never asked myself if one could sensibly refuse to make the effort.

Confronted by the data presented here, and an ever growing distance to the subject matter (I last lectured at a polytechnic eight years ago), I am now less sure what purpose the struggle and suffering have. I do not believe that the policy makers are concerned, nor that the public at large much cares. Even the lecturers do not cry out all that strenuously, though those I interviewed did caste their story in a negative discourse, i.e. I was told [*discourse*] what polytechnics were *NOT*: what the relationship with colleagues did *NOT* amount to, how the individual's teaching was *NOT* typical of the institution, why the Deans did *NOT* have any real authority, how the department was *NOT* at the forefront of new developments, and how the lecturer did *NOT* have chances to develop further intellectually. The *ME* and the polytechnic were continuously at loggerheads. Every career was described in terms of institutional negation.[1]

The research is reconstituted here in the reverse order to which it occurred:

— I began empirically with the career history interviews to see if the data collected would corroborate or falsify my previous observations. I had written a longitudinal study of my own lectureship, based on a phenomenological, auto-analysis of my polytechnic career with students as co-researchers.[2] This form of triangulation was open to methodological criticism as was my choice to study my own career. Therefore the choice to re-examine the issues with a greater distance between the researcher and the researched.

— At a minimum, the rules of method to be clarified include: how lecturers were chosen to be interviewed and what was the method of interviewing.

— Career history data can only tell us something about in-service teaching if it gets addressed by interesting and/or important questions. Interviewing for interviewing's sake will only produce a flood of uninteresting and/or uninterpretable data. The categories of analysis used to address the data make the reasearch effort worthwhile or not. I have assumed that career histories are discourse or text, and can thus be appropriately studied with the use of ethnomethodological discourse analysis.

Analysis

How have I analyzed my career history data? What can such data be used for?

I have identified ways polytechnic lecturers understand themselves in their specific work contexts. I try to reveal how the interviewees construe their work/social reality. I identify intructor logic in use: what are the crucial criteria employed to understand in-practice reality? The analysis focuses on the frames of understanding that the instructors use.

The product of the in-depth interviewing is text, i.e. transcripts of interviews. This text is analyzed to understand what frames of comprehension are employed by the interviewees to describe their work situation. Thus the focus is on the frames of understanding and not on the object of description (here, working at a polytechnic). The level of analysis emphasizes meta-level issues — not what is said, but the logic behind what is said, is under study. The career history data is analyzed to reveal the mind frame that the practitioner has used to understand the immediate work circumstances. The speech acts of practitioners need to be studied for what they are: various ways of framing and verbalizing in-service experience.

The analysis of career history data can emphasize issues drawn from: (i) the sociology of education, (ii) organizational behavior [guaging practitioner efficiency, pro-activeness, maturity], or (iii) the situational [phenomenological] reflection on career development [leading, for instance, from immediate subjectivity to contextual/societal relevance]. In the sociology of education the emphasis is on career structure and social position; in theories of personal development it is on the sorts of action which lead to personal and organizational success; in the situational perspective it is on the results of interaction.

Since I am interested in the developing effectiveness of personal action, or the evolving insight into how learning can be supported, the sociological focus of the teacher role which makes short shrift of matters such as situational and process factors, or tacit learning strategies, or the experiential research approach falls outside my focus.

Theories of personal development provide an interpretative perspective on teacher careers which is relevant to my concerns because they stress the link between individual maturity and professional effectiveness. Social psychologists use, as their point of departure, the insight that people develop, an inner self or core, through contact with significant others as they mature. This substantial self is highly resistant to situational changes and comprises the individual's most salient and valued perceptions of the ideal and real self.[3] Nias (1985) has used career history data to investigate the importance of reference groups in this process of ego anchoring; her results:

> I have described the varying self-perceptions and types of commitment which characterize the teachers' substantial selves.
> Teachers who failed to find referential support within their schools — that is, who had no-one to whom they felt they could talk (about their political, cultural, religious views) — came progressively to deny the social reality of adult life... those who found confirming responses within school from at least one other person gained the confidence to continue behaving consistently with their sense of self-image.[4]

What I believe to be the three crucial elements to a theory of personal development are introduced here. Firstly, the 'I'/'me' relationship, wherein the tension between the actor as behavior — as initiator of events, as involved in occurrence — and the actor as reflection on him/herself — in self-image, in an ideal-self — is examined. Secondly, the 'self'/'other' relationship, wherein cooperation and community are shared or rejected is studied. Thirdly, the tension between beliefs and reality, wherein goals and values — the career mission or dream — can or cannot be sustained, is observed. A theory of personal [career] development shows how individuals cope with the varying demands and challenges posed by the three levels.

The professional self-description found in the interviews provides me with autobiographical texts wherein I can identify the speaker's tacit assumptions about interaction, authority, and expression. I analyze the teacher belief systems on the basis of the tensions between the 'I'/'me', 'self'/'other' and beliefs/reality levels. This analysis takes place firstly on the basis of William Torbert's social psychological grid — a theory of personal development inspired by organizational behavior.[5] Secondly, I analyze the data on the basis of my own situational (phenomenological) grid.

In Torbert's analyses career development is examined on the basis of a six phase scheme, advancing from the individual ('I/me'), to the social ('I/Other') and ultimately to a teleological ('beliefs and reality') perspective.[6] The developmental line moves from the lowest, most basic forms of career awareness, to more complex and inclusive forms of insight. In the first four phases the person sees personal and social reality through the specific lens of the phase; s/he has to act impulsively, opportunistically, diplomatically, or as a technician. These phases are characterized by their inside out [one's acts are compulsive] use of the logic; the last two phases make an outside-in [one chooses from a repertoire of possible behaviors] use of the logic. The six stages of development:

1   **Impulsive:** An impulsive teacher is virtually a contradiction in terms. The 'I' totally terrorizes the 'me'; the behavior is randomly impulsive, functioning is chaotic and unorganized.

Behavior which seems impulsive is probably a reaction to a conflict with significant others, or is a temporary outing of uncertainty, or results from the observer not understanding the behavior involved.

2   **Opportunistic:** The first assumption to this stage is that things are made to be manipulated unilaterally. This is the world of action oriented, flexible persons who are fixated by short-term, narrowly self-interested gains. People are seen as external to oneself and are meant to be manipulated. The 'I' is stronger than the 'me,' but a fragile sense of identity does exist.

Because education does not offer much immediate gratification, opportunists do not do well in it. Opportunists are to be found on the lowest job levels, and disproportionately in the prison population.

3   **Diplomatic:** The diplomatic lecturer is capable of appreciating the others' preferences as well as his/her own; s/he can exercise control over his/her own behavior as well as over the outside world. Selfhood (for instance, the teacher role) is discovered by conforming to group norms

(the 'proper teacher'). The diplomatic phase is characterized by the possession of an other-directed personality wherein loyalty and group harmony are all-important. Potential conflict gets smoothed over, masking true feelings and any unwelcome facts. A spurious appearance of harmony is maintained. Public conflict and the loss of face are avoided at all costs. The 'me' predominates over the 'I'. 'Reality' (the status quo) dominates beliefs; what the group defines as appropriate behavior is what one adheres to. It is assumed that conformity to group norms leads to approval and happiness. The diplomat is essentially past oriented — wanting to master a code that already exists.

Many observers interpret teacher career histories as representative of this phase. I contest this assertion.

4 **Technician**: The individual identifies with his/her skills. Career development manifests itself in the mastery of an external system of professional norms. Pedagogic expertise and the mastery of didactic principles are such norms. Social conformity has been superseded by intellectual awareness; expertise and ability are crucial. Technicians are not aware of their role in the overall functioning of an organization; they focus on the internal logic of their expertise. Technicians identify so strongly with their expert ability that it, to a significant degree, possesses them. In their pursuit of competence, there is an effort to achieve independence.

Technicians are open to expert learning and populate advanced university courses. But s/he feels quickly labelled, and can respond explosively to feedback. By identifying with expert skills, one does achieve a belief system independent from mere social conformity. But this identification is too narrow to be able to take on the complexity of in-service reality, The 'me' is left exposed and insecure. Because the belief structure does not encompass enough of practical reality, the 'me' is threatened by unexpected challenges and unforeseen problems.

5 **Achiever**: Crucial to this phase of development is the emphasis on real results and goal accomplishment. The achiever is pro-active, s/he takes initiative and follows through. The person is clearly focused on, and identifies with, a concrete organizational goal. If s/he's not achieving that goal s/he wants to know why, and will make changes to get things right. Achievers will seek out negative feedback, but they won't question their goals. Their reasoning is often very powerful; the results can be impressive, just as long as their assumptions are correct. But because achievers do not see their own way of doing things as just one of many possible frameworks, their logic — heuristics and assumptions — remains unexamined. Axioms are understood as 'given'; logic is instrumental. An achiever doesn't imagine that his/her own goal oriented behavior could be counter productive (for instance, one's own leadership style demotivates one's team, making a goal unreachable). Because the achiever can only make incremental changes to her/his

logic, if the achiever's categories to not fit the needs of the organization s/he is easily overwhelmed by external forces.

The achiever takes responsibility for actual goal accomplishment, instead of excusing non-performance by claiming *'No one asked me to check on that'*, or *'That's not my department's responsibilty'*, or *'It isn't in the curriculum.'* But the either/or reasoning (for instance, school performance is either 'good or bad') leads easily to win/lose dynamics. (*You can do it 'my' way, or the wrong 'old' way*), instead of to win/win solutions. This generates unproductive tensions and conflicts which lead to missed opportunities. The achiever is capable of successfully running a complex organization, involving continuous monitoring and the analysis of events, just as long as events do not invalidate his/her point of view. S/he is rationally aware, within the limits posed by the perceptual model used, of reality's demands; this makes him/her relatively effective and confident. Since the achiever is open to new information about his/her own functioning, s/he copes more effectively with the 'I/me' divide. But 'belief' is a blind spot; the achiever has lost contact with the intuitive dreams that inspire cooperation and therefore easily alienates him/herself from others (students, colleagues, clients) that s/he is supposedly serving.

6 **Strategist:** In this phase one is not bound to a particular framework such as the diplomat, technician or achiever are; one makes use of different frameworks when they contribute to the achievement of one's goals. S/he is unanchored in any particular taken-for-granted frame. S/he accepts the continual imminent necessity of developing a theory-in-use, i.e. of continually (re-) inventing a means of making sense of in-practice reality. The strategist realizes that one's interpretation of events depends on one's frame(s) of reference. No single frame is thought to be demonstrably superior; there are no objective criteria of selection, superior to all frames.

The strategist continually re-explores the authority and the legitimacy of the various structures, strategies and systems with which s/he works. As lecturer s/he deliberately fosters inquiry into her/his school's educational mission and into its realization (by examining whether the organizational structure, didactical practice and social outcomes are consistent with the mission). S/he rejects single outcome criterion of success (such as: exam results or the school's academic rating) and embraces multiple criteria of success. A balance is sought between short-term efficiency (meeting deadlines, getting decisions made, running the programme), middle-term effectiveness (a consistent, intellectually strong programme), and long-term legitimacy (shared goals and purpose). Lecturing is to be self-amending — i.e. the lecturers are able to think about and if need be change basic assumptions. This self-evaluating, self-regulating process goes much further than what normally is meant by feedback. The 'I/me,' 'self/other,' 'beliefs/reality' relationships are maximally creative and dynamic.

To summarize: The diplomatic lecturer will be a conformist who is highly motivated to get along with colleagues and who primarily needs to feel accepted. The technician will be content directed, strong in skill mastery and oriented towards academic expertise. The achiever will work systematically within set boundaries to create an effective programme. The strategist will contribute to the building-up of a self-transforming creative programme, with strong shared goals.

The research question: Can one distinguish (in the career history data I have collected) the phase(s) the lecturers are in? And if so, is this a powerful means to understanding Polytechnic careers?

To turn to the second analytic cadre, the chief strength of the situational approach is that it understands education in its interactive context. This approach tries to see how situations influence individuals, and how individuals influence situations.

To illustrate: If we examine Torbert's stages of development from this perspective, we see that he seems to be assuming a developmental pyramid (lots of diplomats, many technicians, few achievers and even fewer strategists) that looks suspiciously like a job hierarchy. This raises the question of the developmental scheme as a justification (in disguise) of meritocracy. Torbert's data: first-line supervisors are mostly technicians (68 per cent) though there's a strong minority of diplomats (24 per cent), junior and middle managers are mostly technicians or achievers (both $+/-40$ per cent), and senior managers are technicians (47 per cent), achievers (33 per cent) or strategists (14 per cent).[7] Thus, higher niveaus on the developmental ladder correlate with societal success. The situational issue: what is cause and what is effect? Are pathfinding skills — the ability to find and effectively pursue the right goals — a prerequisite to leadership, or a result of having exercised it? Is insight into the frameworks that can be used to perceive and act on reality a result of personal development or a result of societal position? The ramifications: what are the politics of Torbert's developmental theory? Should the influence of the small elite of strategists or perhaps even better of super strategists, who are called 'magicians', be greater since they have insight into reality which the rest of us do not possess? The seemingly innocent description of career development seems to have a frightening political Janus face.

I have presented elsewhere the results of the longitudinal research I did on the theme of the polytechnic instructor's awareness of practice.[8] This work was strongly rooted in the context of teaching, it was based on an experiential description of the instructor's situational understanding. The phases through which the instructor evolved are each characterized by a distinct world view, each following phase is more inclusive than the preceding one. Torbert's (1987) description of this phenomenon: 'In each transformation, what has been subject becomes object; the world view that the person was (controlled by) becomes a capacity that the person has (control of)'.[9] Two things differentiate my research from Torbert's. Firstly, I interrelate the developmental phases to the surrounding social reality. The phases are not merely forms of individual psychology, they are social codes which are held in place by others. A phase is a form of interaction, it persists because persons in one's (direct of indirect) surroundings want it to persist. If one wants to understand the power that a phase has over persons, it is necessary to see which forces are working for, and which against, its continuation. I see the movement from phase to phase as a process of social conflict where codes that one has (more or less) shared with others are broken. Most often the others resist and try to prevent change. Torbert sees the movement from phase to phase as a moment of spiritual turmoil — he emphasizes the unknown quality of the new paradigm for the person and the uncertainty involved in trying out a new way of thinking. I stress the continuing conflict between the immediate will to experience and the hold that established codes have on us. I assert that there is an epistemological schism between openness to circumstance and the adherence to closed systems. The issue: does meaning have to be created and recreated in direct interaction with events, or does reality's significance precede consciousness? For some consciousness has to make circumstance mean, others assume that meaning is pre-existent to consciousness. On the one side there is entenderment — the will to experientially learn, motivated by a caring attitude to life, a fascination for existence and an attempt to embrace human creativity. And on the other, there is angel-ism — the assumption that meaning precedes and is of a higher order than consciousness. In this case, the achievements of consciousness are necessarily very limited – consciousness produces itself mere sub-realism.

When you get right down to it, Torbert's is an individual developmental psychology and mine a situational conflict psychology.

The seven steps to development which I have described:

1   *An unstructured emotional phase* wherein the instructor faces the class for the first time. Herein we find the well-known fight for survival, the confusion between pedagogic goals and the need to keep order, the shock of being confronted with students, colleagues, adminstrators, stakeholders who could not give a damn about what one has taken years to learn. In this period the 'me' is put under new and often unfamiliar pressures. One's beliefs may not seem attuned to reality. There is a cruel polarization between experiential or intellectual values and one's surroundings. One's lifeworld appears to split along the lines: warmth for learning (which I've called entenderment) versus the survivalist rejection of speculative or critical thought (dubbed sub-realism). The relationship between action and statement seems to fall apart.

2   *A phase wherein attention to 'the other' predominates;* a referential group is constructed wherein one shares a belief structure. In my case this was with students, sometimes it is with colleagues or ex-classmates. Mere professional survival is transcended, lecturing starts to seem worthwhile. If outsiders to one's reference group, attack the group

norm the group's right to exist is challenged. This can lead to a more or less fierce struggle.

3   *A growing awareness of the role of self and of the other in the educational system and/or curriculum.* The lecturer masters his/her professional role, only to be threatened with a spectre of the role mastering him/her! The trap is that one will settle into a (successful) instructional role and become a second-rate actor, doomed to play the same role over and over again. Having mastered the appearance of schooling one can lose all contact with learning. Learning is much more demanding than schooling; it depends on one studying reality, a process which always threatens to fail.

4   *An explicit but simple concept of teaching, which is one-sidedly voluntaristic or deterministic* governs the instructor's thinking. The machine of teaching can take over, leaving response curiosity and awareness in ruins. However creativity, innovation and immediacy can become a new mannerism. There are two extremes: teaching as merely so many rational rules; teaching as pure innovation, exploration and renewal. Both attitudes are excessively extreme. One cannot sustain either position. The instructor who sees teaching merely as rule-governed behavior cannot react to unexpected discussions, personal responses, or unusual ideas. S/he will glide ever deeper into conflict: students feel themselves unheard and colleagues ignored. The individual self-image will be confronted with the message that one has failed. But the effort to sustain total creativity will be exhausting. Burn out is in the offing. A compromise between a purely situational/experiential approach, and the traditional transmission of knowledge, has to be found.

5   *A more complex concept of teaching, which is more inclusive but highly subjective* emerges. Meaning, it turns out, demands creativity, entenderment, experience, but also language continuity, and abiding commitment. On the individual psychological level solutions begin to emerge for the conflicts between openness and rigidity, experimentation and tradition; expression and discipline. The person discovers that in the one factor there is always the other. An appreciation for the paradoxical nature to experience, creativity, and knowledge emerges.

6   *A statement of practice based on one's own teaching experience* becomes possible. One begins to gain enough distance from one's own practice that it becomes describable. One is no longer immersed in the conflicts which have made one into the sort of teacher one is. The contours to one's own progress become visible. The developmental process is winding down. A comparison between one's own practice and one's educational goals is made. One asks: What are my social ethics? And one examines: What effect do I have on my students and colleagues?

7   *The retrospective examination of one's own development, coupled to questioning its value for others* begins. In order to transcend the impasse of the previous phases, one has had to abandon the logic of intellectual/social conflict. Instead of experiencing the polarization entenderment versus sub-realism from within, one becomes an observer of its effects and rationale. Ethnological questions are posed. What sort of society is it wherein these conflicts take place, in this manner? What sort of instructors do these conflicts produce?

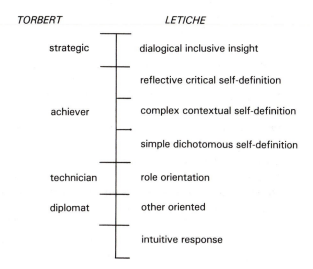

When we compare the two descriptions of development we see:

At no point do I show the instructor totally encapsuled in a phase. Already in the initial subjective awareness of teaching, there is the strategic awareness that the various ways of seeing the educational reality are constructs which different persons are using to manipulate reality. The instructor slowly earns his/her way to an overview, but meta-level insights occur on each level. In fact they form the aha insight which moves one from step to step.

The question 'What interest do others have that circumstances are seen in this way?' plays for me a crucial role; this question does not seem very important in Torbert's thought.

The second step described above resembles the diplomatic phase; the third step is a critique of the one-sided behavior of the technician; the fourth, fifth and sixth steps are grappling with effectiveness, i.e. achievement, and the seventh step centers on strategic insight.

For me the movement from step to step is more the product of a social dialectical struggle than the product of individual psychological progression. One doesn't master a previous phase as much as one fights one's way through an interactive conflict. The logic of the steps is progressive, the one issue propels one along to the next.

Torbert seems to believe that it is increasingly difficult to achieve each progressive stage beyond that of the technician. On the other hand, he states that adults who have not transcended the opportunistic or diplomatic phases will find it very difficult to develop further.

I believe that the first step is the most difficult to take. Once the developmental spiral begins it carries one along, but many are frightened to step into the spiral. The instututional sanctions and social barriers against investigating one's own practice are very real.

Torbert seems to assume that society values knowledge, I assume that it is afraid of it. Contemporary societies are afraid of feedback — i.e. of knowledge about their own functioning. One is not supposed to hold a mirror up to how one 'learns' in one's own society!

Torbert and I agree that learning is a paradoxical activity of continuity and discovery, where ways of understanding reality are applied, developed and exchanged.

The research question: Can one analyze, with the themes just described, the force(s) that lead to lecturer change? And if so, is this a powerful means to understanding polytechnic careers?

Methodology

In order to answer the research questions, whose career history was collected and how? The interviewees (in the order they were interviewed):

Mrs A   Lectures and is assistant chairperson in an advanced nursing course for surgical operation assistants. She had worked five years in initial training before she was appointed four years ago to her present job. She has studied nursing (BA) and education (MEd)

Mrs B   Lectured in sociology at a polytechnic for seven years; she is presently Assistant Head of Personnel and Organization at a publishing house. She has an MPhil in sociology. Before becoming a polytechnic lecturer she worked for the labor unions, and before that she had been teaching assistant at a university.

Mr C   Lectured in didactics for five years in the Department of Initial Training for Secondary School Teachers. He has an MPhil in French and a minor in pedagogics. He taught secondary school for ten years before joining the polytechnic. He has accepted a new appointment at another polytechnic in the Faculty of International Business.

Mr D   Lectured in theoretical and philosophical pedagogics, psychology and didactics at a polytechnic for fourteen years. He was a physical education teacher at a secondary school before that. He has an MPhil in psychology and physical education.

Mrs E   Lectured pedagogics in an in-service psychiatric nursing course, and has worked in special education for eight years. She divides her time between staff responsibility for patient care, and lecturing. She did her MPhil in special education. This is her first job.

The interviewees were chosen on the basis of the following criteria:

— observers had told me that they were superior lecturers;
— they all lecture (at least in part) in the social sciences i.e. in pedagogics, sociology, or psychology;
— they lecture at different institutions and do not know one another;
— they are approximately forty years of age; and
— they are all experienced lecturers in mid-career.

The research population thus is not made up of average Polytechnic lecturers, but of expert instructors. I chose to interview lecturers in mid-career with superior reputations because I was more interested in investigating potential professional development than in ascertaining a mean level of performance. The results of this study are not meant to be representative of polytechnics in general, but to indicate the upper boundaries to staff potential. I assume that insight into this potential is necessary to define goals for (potential) professional development.

How were they interviewed? I met at least twice with each interviewee. The first meeting gave me a chance to corroborate what I had already been told, namely that the person was an expert instructor and to observe the interviewee in his/her natural setting. Depth interviewing took place thereafter at a spot chosen by the interviewee.[10] Each lecturer was interviewed for three to four hours. Typically the interviewees began as follows:[11]

I was twenty-four and came almost directly from graduate school. I knew nothing about teaching and had to lecture as well as develop a new curriculum. I had no practical background and I had to tell the students how they should be practically effective. I had no idea what psychiatric nurses ought to be able to do. And there were no upper division students, it was a totally new programme.(Mrs E)
Do I see a development of myself as a lecturer? I don't know, let me describe my experience and we'll see.

My first experience of the polytechnic was the job interview. What I remember is that there were several students present, but that they played no role. One of them spoke to me later, and I then realized that I had no recollection at all of which students had been there.

> Afterwards I thought, 'This is part and parcel of the democratic ideal, letting students be members of the appointments committee'. But they hadn't said anything. In fact I hadn't actually seen them. I didn't even remember if they had been men or women.(Mrs B)

The interviews proceeded informally, with the interviewee telling his or her story with a minimum of interference. During the last half-hour I examined five questions with the interviewee:[12]

1   What are the characteristics of your common-sense world — of yourself as unreflecting member of a professional culture?
2   What has been the role of significant others in your career: has there been a 'we' relationship?
3   What rules, codes, standards have you encountered — did your social action merge with/conflict with the social reality about you?
4   What has your process of development been like?
5   What have you done, which you would not have done if you had not been in this specific work situation?

I taped and transcribed the interviews.

Empirical Findings

The two research questions:

> Can one, in the career history data, distinguish the [social psychological] phase(s) of development described by Torbert? And if so, is this a powerful means to understanding polytechnic careers?
> Can one analyze the force(s) that have led to lecturer change with the situational theory I have presented? And if so, is this a powerful means to understanding polytechnic careers?

Both research questions are composed of two sub-topics. The first sub-topic focuses on the ability to apply the categories already described to the data; this is discussed in sections A and B which follow. At issue: Do the categories illuminate the career histories, and if so how? The second topic has to do with the relative value of analyzing the data in the two manners proposed. This is discussed in the Conclusion.

Section A

The categorization of the development phase(s) of the interviewees on the basis of Torbert's taxonomy: Mrs A is an achiever who is developing towards becoming a strategist.[13]

> You have to confront some pupils with their efforts to avoid their

responsibilities. Some students are always better at inventing excuses than you are at unmasking them. You have to confront them with their behavior. At first I didn't dare do that — you think it's all your own fault when students don't do their work. I sometimes ignored student behavior that I would now confront. I was unsure of myself: 'Can I match her?' — 'Can I take her on successfully?' Now I feel that we each have our own responsibility: I mine, the students theirs. If the two differ too much, then that has to be corrected. We have to sit down and talk matters through. That doesn't mean that I'm by definition right.

In this passage the achiever's goal directedness speaks clearly in what is said. Mrs A is not an expert lecturer, uninvolved in the broader issue of course effectiveness (a technician). She has indicated that when she first began to lecture, she sometimes ignored behavior that was in contradiction with course goals. This because she was afraid of conflict (diplomat). She has gotten beyond that stage now. While she acknowledges the relativity of her own perceptions, she does tend to stay in her own framework without doubting its overall worth or effectiveness. She does not switch easily to a metal-level, and ask herself 'What is this all about?' or 'What do we achieve here, and why?'

I have ambitions to go into administration, but not yet. I see administration as the stimulating of others: you have to be enthusiastic and communicate your ideas. But you also have to watch out that decisions are implemented. I am getting better in these things.

Her concept of leadership is more the achiever's (stimulate effective goal realization) than the strategist's (facilitate a self-amending system). But she is obviously searching for something more.

When I talk with my husband about my work, I do so in order to reflect on my strategy. I'll decide that I must not speak first at the next staff meeting, or that I must keep my emotions under control, or that I must not be dominant. When, for instance, I wanted to change my relationship with a colleague who felt herself threatened, I had to strive not to be too dominant. But I also have had to make sure that I did not act defensively. I've learned to be tactical. If you react solely intuitively and spontaneously, you are often not effective.

Her definition of strategy recognizes the importance of dealing with different perspectives. The emphasis on effectiveness gives support to the assertion that she is in the achiever phase. In the quote the dynamic between I/me predominates. She is obviously conscious of both factors and reports that she regulates the tension between them in her contact with her husband [self/other]. She explores the relationship between her beliefs (be spontaneous and direct, one should get one's tasks done) and reality (people are threatened, you must be indirect, many cannot get their work done) on this level.

Mrs E describes the transformation from technician to achiever which took place in the first two years of her career.

In the beginning my life was all work. I got up with the work and I
went to bed with it. Thirteen hour days at the Institute was normal,
and then I'd prepare lectures at home. I also had a pile of books on
psychiatric nursing to read. And if there was time over, there were
policy proposals to be examined.

Now my agenda it's full — staff meetings, work with students, etc.
etc.; back in the beginning my agenda was empty — I was everywhere
at once. I did everything; nothing was planned. When I was observing
patients, I was thinking I ought to be preparing a lecture. When I was
lecturing I was thinking I ought to be taking care of some crisis or other.

The technician's effort to master events with expertise, resulted in effectiveness
being lost from sight.

I spent a lot of time preparing lectures. We tried textbook after
textbook; we were never satisfied. One curriculum concept was tried
out after the other. But we were so busy with our own roles as lecturers
that we focused entirely on what had to be learned. All our energy was
devoted to what we were going to tell the students. We've evolved since
then; the students have more room now to be creative. We've gained
enough self-confidence that we can leave room for student initiative. If
classroom discussion begins to develop in a way that I don't want to
pursue, I can redirect the class's attention easily enough.

While I still know all the names of the first group, that's not the
case with the current group. Also, the exam results of that first cohort
were extremely good. I think they gained from us being so very involved
with them.

This passage is paradoxical. The technician's drive to get everything right has
something impersonal and overbearing to it. The intense involvement of the
novice teacher evidently off-set the negative influence of inexperience. The
achiever's effectiveness may be more open and flexible, but it may also be
impersonal and lead to a routine-like performance characterized by
uninvolvement.

In the treatment of the patients there's a staff/line split. The staff
determines the policies and sells them as best it can to the line. The line's
attitude: everything's fine, keep things as they are. The staff is pro-
active, and interested in improvement. The line is consumptive. In
general you can gain influence over the line by affirming that they have
done good work. As staff, you have to take the initiative. The line can
be made enthusiastic for change if you give them the feeling that they
are respected.

This quote is paradoxical. Mrs E is tactical, but is she strategic? Can she do
anything about the line/staff conflict? She seems to accept it as *fait accompli*.
She tries to manoeuvre, despite it, as best she can to improve the quality of care.

Insofar as effectiveness is the central theme to her functioning, and she does not transcend the logic of the situation, she is an achiever.

> The Director wanted our clinic to be exceptional. We were supposed to offer superior care and to be a centre-of-excellence for in-service training. Actually the care is good and the teaching programme is above-average; you probably cannot find anything much better. But you can find other institutions at the same level. The director is bitter because we are not unique. But his idea of the best care was never clear. What is this superior clinic supposed to look like? What are the criteria? He doesn't even know!

She has realized that her boss is not a strategist, but does this mean that she cannot become one herself? Her conclusion: she wants to get into organizational consultancy.

Mr D is a strategist:

> When I was appointed lecturer, practice (sports) and theory (pedagogics) had, in the Physical Education curriculum, nothing to do with each other. As I saw it, my task was to build up the interaction between the two. The results have been constructive, in the sense that the tension between the sport and pedagogical sides of our programme has become evident. This tension has had the effect of getting the instructors to think about their work. There are instructors who if asked 'What are the goals to your course? What are your assumptions?' can only answer 'Stop the ball. Run ten laps'. But there are others who ask themselves: 'Am I consistent? What are my basic goals?' For my part, I've learned to be less arrogant; I've realized that everyone has to conceptualize their practice themselves. Each lecturer has to discover what his/her own affective and cognitive principles amount to. I've learned to concentrate more on ideas-in-practice and less on intellectual debate. What counts is not what is theoretically true or false, but what is actually practised.
>
> The first year students are 17 years old. They come here with a naive idea of physicalness . . . they take hedonistic pleasure in bodily movement. Commonly, their attitude is: sport's great, don't think. During practice teaching they discover that a gym teacher doesn't have problems of the order: 'Have your pupils mastered the technique of the forward roll?', but is confronted with psycho-social issues. Lots of kids don't see physical activity as pleasure. Our students have to develop their naive concept of physicalness (i.e of pleasure in movement) into a pedagogic concept capable of answering some pretty difficult questions: 'Why should kids be required to do certain physical activity? How do you legitimize that demand?' Many freshmen don't like what I do to them. I don't give them security — I only diminish it. I demand that they learn to confront the central issues of physical education. I've

chosen a meta-position for myself. I clarify for the students what the results will be of interacting with children on the basis of a variety of different conceptions. The first thing I teach is that people are not things — kids will react to you differently depending upon how you approach them. The task is to understand and influence these relationships.

The lecturer strives to show his students that different first principles lead to different forms of practice. In his supervision of practice teaching, he forces them to recognize that they are choosing their own first principles. In his seminars he demands that they defend their choices. This lecturer has also shown himself a strategist in how he has recast his own faculty position:

At first I went to bed at midnight and got up at 4 a.m. Luckily I don't need much sleep. I spent a lot of time talking to students about their problems. My priorities have changed — I now put less emphasis on students and more on my own development. I used to want to teach the latest news from myself, i.e. what I had just learned. At a certain point you realize you cannot develop unlimitedly with the students. While there's a new group of freshmen every year, your own learning is continual.

I now want to see, with the knowledge and didactic skills I possess, how I can develop further. How can I improve my teaching? Of course I'll keep up with the professional literature and react to new developments. But how can one make instruction more intensive? To do that I'll have to work in a new setting. I've worked long enough at the poly in a framework of four years. Now I want to know what I can achieve in three times three days. The same effect? Can a process of questioning and rethinking of one's work be produced so quickly? In corporate training every step is planned. At the polytechnic we use time inefficiently. We know that we have four years to fill. But in management development you have to plan your work to achieve a powerful, dynamic effect in the shortest possible time. Of course what I am saying is part of the spirit of the 1980s. I'm not separable from contemporary history.

I've been appointed to set up a training center. I'll still lecture two days a week but three days a week I'll work on the new training center. My task is to make contact with the business world; to tell managers what we can do for them and to inquire about their needs. I'm not directly out to sell any programmes. But I've already had a couple of phone calls inquiring about possible further contacts.

In this passage self-redefinition and organizational development go hand in hand. This polytechnic is the first in the country to set-up a commercial training center as a spin-off to its academic programmes. [14]

The interviewees tell us how they have developed during their careers as lecturers. The autobiographical material displays instructor awareness of change. I have not made a longitudinal study of instructor-pupil or instructor-colleague interactions, which reveals change visible to an observer. In the following section I assume that the data, though a product of introspective reflection, provides valid information with which the second research question can be answered. To narrow down that question: *What in the eyes of Mrs B was the nature of the situational field within which her career as a polytechnic lecturer took place? Will the application of the categories I have developed allow us to understand that career more adequately?*

My predecessor — who had an excellent reputation — left without leaving any syllabi, lecture notes, reading lists, course descriptions behind. I came from a job where each of us made our individual contribution, but where we also worked together. We had course materials, curriculum plans, programme suggestions, etc.

At the poly you were required to work entirely alone, but you were supposed to stay within an unwritten code! The repressive tolerance got more repressive, and less tolerant, if you ignored that code. The norms were hidden and weren't supposed to be examined. In fact, you had to guess what the rules were — if you guessed right you could stay, if you guessed wrong they'd throw you out. The formal espoused code and the real code were so terribly different. The formal code was democratic, co-operative, collegial; the actual situation was quite the opposite. The sanctions for not accepting the informal rules were very severe. You simply were thrown out. Your possibilities to step outside the rules and still survive depended on your ability to be unique. But if you were too unique, then you were a threat and you also had to go. Some typical rules: lecturers don't help one other, the quality of the programme is undiscussible, lip-service is to be paid to democracy but the staff makes all decisions, Marxism is a truth which is neither to be criticized nor (in any depth) taught. The crux to the dominant culture was to be found in the sanction against communicating. The care or attention that people need to work well just wasn't approved of. Feelings or personal expression were banned. The individual was forced into his/her shell.

The contact I had with colleagues was one-sided. You could invest energy, interest, or creativity in a colleague, but you'd get nothing back in return. If you helped someone — the effect would be gone the minute you weren't there! Colleagues only had ears for their own situation and problems. They had no room to listen to anyone else.

At first I acted on what I had been told about the polytechnic. The chairperson had said that I was supposed to develop my programme with the students. So I asked them 'What should we study this semester?' I got a sea of blank looks! They had no idea. I had a week, thus, to develop a course.

It was supposedly a leftist polytechnic — in fact the poly was living off fame gained during the student protests of the sixties. It was the victim of old fame — everyone was keeping up an image which didn't correspond to the current reality. Policy was determined by feelings of twenty years ago. We were supposedly unique, oppositional and anti-establishment. The leftist image required the staff to be different and original. This ideology put uniqueness above team work. A lot of energy was wasted on cultivating the appearances of specialness. The weaker brothers, who couldn't teach very well, fell victim to this system. Those who didn't have the personal and academic strength to be successful soloists risked destruction. There was a lecturer with whom it became impossible to communicate; she had a nervous breakdown. Another colleague so entirely lost his self-esteem that he committed suicide.

There was also a pariah. He was too unique for the rest! He broke all the codes; despised the leftist myth and went about unmasking it. I actually thought he was a fine chap, if a bit eccentric. But colleagues put me under pressure to reject him. A pregnancy got me off the hook — when the conflict really got out of hand I was home with sick leave. The uniqueness code had the disastrous effect on the weaker figures. Because they believed in the code, it was impossible for them to identify with each other. They were too isolated to realize that they were all in a similar position and should help one another.

In this description one can recognize two forces at work in a polarized social field. Mrs B describes one force in terms of feedback, collegiality, and openness, and the other in terms of a code of leftist uniqueness, institutionalized in hidden social norms. What is the effect of all this on Mrs B?

I decided to search for another job. The patterns I saw were so negative that I thought 'Someone else had better take over here'. When I think about all the new experiences and challenges I have encountered since I've left, I'm very glad I left. It's so hard to know how much you've been influenced; in so far as there has been an influence it will have become a part of me. Since I still find collegiality so important, I must not have been influenced on that point. I'm stubborn enough to be able to take the freedom offered and do what I want to do with students. The emphasis on individuality and creativity fitted my needs fine. But you had to be a soloist also when you didn't want to. I can work alone, but you need a dialogue if you're going to stay fresh and creative.

In the beginning there was the challenge of understanding the codes. But I got the feeling that I was being pumped empty and wasn't receiving anything of value in return. To think of it, I learned more in the two years of my job with the unions than I did in the seven and a half at the poly.

In Mrs B's description of her career as a polytechnic lecturer we can distinguish the following themes:

— an intuitive phase of shock caused by the recognition that the formal code and reality were divorced from one another. The result of the dichotomy is seen to be dehumanizing; one is confronted with other people who cannot really meet, hear or influence.

— another oriented reaction, focusing on who the students and colleagues are. If one invests energy in the other s/he becomes dependent; the other will not become more active thanks to one's relationship with him/her.

— a role oriented concern, where Mrs B fulfills all her responsibilities but is threatened by her very success. Predictability lulls her to sleep; passivity vitiates her energy; this work just does not produce worthwhile results.

— a simple self-definition is developed wherein the social field is split between strong and weak, unique and victim.

— a more complex self-definition emerges, centering on the paradoxes of academic liberty. Liberty is experienced as intellectually satisfying but in this case also as socially destructive. A paradoxical code demands creativity while denying the possibility of communication; for whom is one supposed to be creative — is it yet another autistic activity?

— a statement of practice is made, based on further analysis of the paradoxes. Academic work has to remain a challenge to be rewarding. A teaching position has to stretch one's capabilities if it isn't going to become deadening.

— the link is drawn between the polytechnic's fate and what has happened to leftists [in Holland] in the eighties. But ethnological questions, pertaining to the social or historical significance of the phenomena, are not posed.

The data do not support a precise phasing of all of the elements. Nonetheless, the general theoretical framework is reaffirmed. A developmental line, from level to level, through conflict is recognizable:

— When Mrs B saw that the poly was not what it pretended to be, she began to look closer at the others who lectured and studied there;

— when she discovered that these others remained passive, and would not join with her, she re-examined her role;

— when she realized that her success in the teaching role enclosed her in the code rather than allowing her further liberty, she looked to herself;

— once she defined herself as creative and collegial, she realized that the paradoxes of the polytechnic were not some sort of inevitable fate;

— when she stood back from herself and the polytechnic, she found that work can be challenging;
— once she chose for challenge, she left the polytechnic for another job.

The relationship of Mrs B to the last (contextual and dialogical) phase is complex; did she want to enter into it? She states that she prefers being a doer to being reflective.

> Others were involved in paradigms and theories of social science. My goal was to prepare students so they could react to practical situations and could derive pleasure from concrete activity. I don't now think that initial training can achieve those goals. If I ever teach again, it would be in an in-service course where you're close to the daily reality of professional work.

Mrs B's insight into her work is dialogical, i.e. she looks at the effects and rationale of her work from a series of perspectives and reflects on the interaction between them. But her behavior according to her own report was soloistic; she resigned and took another job. While her reflection was inclusive, i.e. encompassed the situational limits to initial training and the problems of leftists in the 1980s she fled both issues in her behavior. Mrs B's learning is paradoxical: she's concluded that polytechnic teaching is not worth her while because the social preconditions for challenge (permanent learning) are absent. Her conclusion: There is not much to value in a situation without dialogue. But the ethnological issues are not explored. What are the generalizable lessons to be learned from this experience? What has been revealed about oneself, the situation and society? To extrapolate from the data: the human quality of work depends on the demands colleagues and clients make of one. If these are superficial or alienating, involvement will degenerate into uninvolvement, interaction into bitterness and learning into sleep.

To repeat the research question: *What was the nature of the situational field within which Mr C's career as a polytechnic lecturer took place? Would the application of categories I have developed allow us to understand that career more adequately?*

> The merger of the initial training and the in-service programmes has created nothing but problems. The two had been totally separate. They're legally one team now, but there has never even been a meeting of the full staff! I haven't even met some of my so-called colleagues.
>
> You notice informally, for instance in the staff room, a tremendous animosity. The inset staff claim that initial training is a luxurious life where one has to lecture a lot less. The inset instructors have an attitude: It's about time that they get down to work. All the time spent in initial training on individual, student supervision is ignored. Only lecturing is work. The inset people will have to lecture in the initial training programme this autumn — their first reaction was: Let the initial training staff work harder.

In three years the government has shortened our programme, abolished the distinction between major and minor fields of study, required us to develop a further education programme, cancelled several of our degree programmes, introduced admissions limits reducing the number of students, ended the funding of cooperation with the secondary schools, and declared 40 per cent of our staff redundant. No one knows if their job is really permanent or not. And it's going to stay that way. Every change forces yet another re-organization which in turn creates still more conflict. The increased work load has to be borne by a demoralized staff. Since no one wants to be utterly depressed, everyone flees — you put all your energy into other things.

I feel myself deserted, left to fend for myself. The Deans only produce an endless series of redundancy lists, all of which contradicted one another. Of course, rumours become rife. Ultimately the Deans retreat into their offices and send around nasty notes telling us that we should learn to apply more effectively for new jobs. As if it was our fault.

The lecturers have no energy to protest. Our will has been broken. You accept everything after a while. Once you realize that re-training and/or searching for a new job is your fate, you adopt the attitude: Let the damn poly burn down for all I care.

The only result of the fight to save what had been built up, was anger. It is so dishonest — all the work and effort that had gone into making a good and effective programme — everything thrown away. Now I choose for security. I'm over forty; I cannot choose to earn half as much. You might think that I'd feel ashamed, now that I have been appointed to another job. You simply have to choose for yourself — my idealism has been dented. The idealistic young lecturer who saw the potential of initial training and had the will and ideas to try and do things, has been made redundant.

I'm glad I'm going. Between now and 1995 no one will know if their job is safe. You won't know if it's worth renewing the programmes. For students it is terrible. Staff members leave and there are no replacements. The building isn't even kept properly clean anymore.

When I was first appointed I was very happy. I had the feeling it was a big step forward — to be promoted from secondary school teacher to poly lecturer. The sense of being rewarded for work well done gave me lots of energy. And when I began I felt myself welcome and appreciated. Of course the idea I had that poly students would all be highly motivated was pure bunk. But I could get them to work. I may have been very idealistic, but if the government hadn't made everything topsy-turvy a lot of the goals would have been realized.

Work has become a very practical matter — I have to have a job.

Content has to come second. What's important is to have a safe salary. Once I've got that, then I can discover the creative possibilities that the job offers.

The sphere at my new job will be very different. You feel in the staff room that the instructors come, lecture and leave. After having been appointed a future colleague showed me about; two of the people he wanted me to meet were having such a furious fight in the corridor that we simply had to walk on. The first impression is one of tension; but also of growth and change. There are chances to specialize and develop oneself, but before I can make use of them I'll have to feel really safe.

My career objective was to become a poly lecturer. When that was taken away from me, I became very dependent. My feelings were: Can I please stay? Will I really have to go? Will I be able to stay after all? But when it gets through to you that the axe has really fallen, you ask yourself: When will I be dismissed? What sort of re-training is there? You feel yourself helpless. They are deciding for you. I felt very threatened — my ability to believe in myself was under attack. And there was the constant anger — the absurdity of it all. After five years of hard work everything we'd achieved destroyed, thrown away.

The risk of getting bored after five years at any one job may be enormous, but I didn't get the chance to discover it.

In Mr Cs reportage we can see the following aspects:

— an initial intuitive phase of enthusiasm, accompanied by a strong sense of achievement. The appointment at the polytechnic was experienced to be in recognition of his excellence as a teacher and to be an earned promotion.
— an Other oriented reaction, focusing on his polytechnic colleagues. This was a constructive experience. His interaction with students was less positive, but he evidently accepted that in his stride.
— a simple idealistic self-definition follows. As a polytechnic docent you can explore your creative potential.
— a more complex self-definition emerges as government policy infringes on his idealism. Nothing, it turns out, guarantees that innovation and experimentation can continue.
— a statement of practice grappling with institutional dependence ensues. Economic and social security is prerequisite to achieving educational goals. Individual self-interest has to be met, before shared collective goals can be realized.
— the lecturer has not yet begun to question the general significance of what he's experienced. The ethnological issues aren't discussed. For instance, why was major funding of new polytechnics undertaken and then cut back by half?

If we examine Mrs B's and Mr C's careers, as analyzed by my categories, do we gain in insight? In these two career histories the theme of conflict — between openness or creativity on the one hand, and social codes or rules on the other — predominates. Forces stronger than the individual make human dialogue, expressivity and creativity ineffective. In the one case, it is the code of the polytechnic which overrules collegiality and cooperation. In the other, government policy reigns as some sort of blind fate which destroys indiscriminately the work of the individuals. In both instances, the lecturer tries to flee the situation which s/he experiences as virtual terror. In fact, all five career histories document the flight from polytechnic lecturing.

My assertion that there is a crucial initial intuitive reaction to a work situation which takes place before the person develops a pattern of response, is supported by the research. The data repeatedly reveals that lecturers have a gut feeling about a new job which is very indicative for their future development [for Mrs B the faceless, voiceless students which haunted her; for Mr C the elatedness of belonging to the polytechnic team].

The crucial experience is of conflict. What is the broader situation which these career documents reflect and illuminate? It must be one of tremendous social violence. Mrs B and Mr C perceive the organizing principle to their social ethics to be in contradiction to the society's, they stress mutual cooperation and interactive decision-making. They state that the person needs to perceive him/herself as needed, before a learning experience can be effective. Their politics of education is based on a commitment to awareness and consciousness. They want to develop the contact between the student as individual and the knowledge to be learned. Their focus is on unity between the espoused and done, learned and applied.

Key Issues: is the demand for integration between knowledge and action justified? What are the causes of the failure? Is the migration out of teaching into business consultancy and training a good solution? Since there are no answers to these questions in the data, I have to conclude that the seventh ethnological facet to professional development has not been illustrated.

Conclusions

Is it a fluke of my data that the lecturers do not (wish to) remain at a polytechnic? On a meso-level they were all very successful teachers. Mrs B, Mr D and Mrs E are confronted on the micro-level with the problem that they no longer find their work challenging or creative. Mr. C wonders if this problem wasn't looming for him but the macro-crisis came first. For these individuals the meaning of learning is to be found in the relation between knowledge and action. When the integration of the two levels fails, they (of/or not of their own free will) move on.

The normative thrust to Torbert's conceptualization asserts that professionals should learn to be effective in action. The normative assumption to my work is that practitioners should learn to appreciate and interact with OTHERNESS (other persons, other ways of seeing things, other behavior). Both systems have descriptive value; you can use them to analyze career history data.

Torbert's developmental system leads to a concept of leadership; my interpretative grid to an affirmation of dialogue. He assumes that it is the mark of maturity to be able to be effective in an organization. I am less volunteristic: the logic of the situation often prevails, despite what individuals do. I assert that anxiety, insecurity, and despair are very real; lecturers will meet them all if they hold a mirror up to actual circumstance. Torbert's strategists seem unmoved (untouched by doubt, immune to tragedy) movers (leaders able to change things). The strategist has a very powerful action repertoire, but there is nothing in the theory to tell us how s/he is going to use it. Someone who has worked their way through the seven steps I've sketched, has seriously asked themselves what the potential significance of their experience is for others. This sounds like a much more modest achievement, but is it?

To summarize the findings: for the polytechnic lecturer to develop an increasingly more encompassing insight into his/her career, s/he must have sufficient personal, collegial, institutional and social commitment.

1 If the personal commitment to learning, openness and the meeting new challenges is lacking, there will be little or no development at all.
2 If collegial solidarity is lacking, the individual will choose to look elsewhere for a job.
3 If the institution destroys more than it constructs, it will make personal development ineffective.
4 If the individual does not investigate the link between individual and general experience, learning will remain particular.

The zone of potential development which emerges from the research centers the fourth theme. Because the polytechnics as institutions have failed to/or have been prevented from providing the organizational prerequisites for lecturer development onto this level, a flight from teaching has resulted. If career development is to occur, the process of reflective critical self-definition has to be strengthened and the movement into dialogical inclusive insight has to be facilitated.

Notes

1 To see how the sample was formed see the discussion of methodology. I stress that the lecturers had never met; that they work at a variety of institutions, and that the idea of a *negative discourse* was NOT amongst my initial hypotheses.
2 Hugo Letiche, *Learning and Hatred for Meaning*, (Amsterdam/Philadelphia: John Benjamins Publishing, 1984).
3 See D. Katz, 'The functional approach to the study of attitude change', in *Public Opinion Quarterly*, vol. 24, 1960, pp. 163–204, and D. Ball, 'Self and identity in the context of deviance: the case of the criminal abortion,' in R. Scott and J. Douglas (Eds) *Theoretical Perspectives on Deviance*, (New York, Basic Books,

1972), cited in J. Nias, 'Reference Groups in Primary Teaching', in *Teachers' Lives and Careers*, S. Ball and I. Goodson, (Eds) (Lewes, Falmer Press, 1985) pp. 105--19.

4 J. Nias, *ibid.*, p. 107.

5 William Torbert, *Managing the Corporate Dream*, (Homewood Ill., Dow-Jones Irwin, 1987).

6 While the developmental phases are derived from Torbert's work — the descriptions of these phases include paraphrased passages from his book, both the use of the three perspectives (I/me, I/Other, belief/reality) and the applications to education are my responsibility. Torbert concentrates on management and MBA student maturity.

7 William Torbert, 'Management Education for the Twenty-First Century', Selections, 1987, pp. 31–36.

8 Hugo Letiche, *Learning and Hatred for Meaning*, (Amsterdam/Philadelphia, John Benjamins Publishing, 1984).

9 W. Torbert, *Managing the Corporate Dream*, (Homewood Ill., Dow-Jones Irwin, 1987) p. 226.

10 At his/her work or at his/her home.

11 All quotes from interview data have been translated from Dutch to English. In the longer quotes I have omitted my questions.

12 The questions were adapted from Gareth Jones' article 'Life History Methodology', in Gareth Morgan (Ed), *Beyond Methodology*, (Beverly Hills: Sage, 1983) pp. 147–59.

13 While I want to present long enough quotes that they are more than mere illustrations, my space is limited. Thus a compromise; I will present data from Mrs A, Mrs E, and Mr C in section A, and from Mrs B and Mr C in section B.

14 I would have categorized Mrs B as a strategist; and Mr C as leaning towards strategist but with aspects of the achiever. I would have quoted Mrs B on respecting and valuing diverse points of view, and Mr C on what he thinks his lecturing has meant for students. I would have analyzed how Mrs B's tolerance benefited her colleagues — i.e. how she created a more humane situation. And I would have analyzed how Mr C understands perspectivism and its creative worth, but has had too passive a role to be a strategist.

References

NIAS, J. (1985) 'Reference Groups in Primary Teaching', in BALL, S. and GOODSON, I. (Eds) *Teachers' Lives and Careers*, Lewes, Falmer Press.

TORBERT, W. (1987) *Managing the Corporate Dream*, Homewood Ill., Dow-Jones Irwin.

Chapter 19

Social Aspects of Teacher Creativity

Peter Woods

Teaching is regarded as an uncreative activity by some, and there are fears that it may become even more routinized. Others by contrast, point to teachers' developing professionalism, and see their handling of complex teaching situations as an art.

Some primary school research revealed a considerable degree of creative teaching, judging it as activity that exhibited innovation, ownership, control and relevance. Illustrations are given of creative teaching around a structured base, teaching as discovery, breakthroughs and creative projects. The conditions necessary for this kind of teaching include time, resources, a supportive school ethos, and a matching pupil culture.

Teaching: Dead or Alive?

There is a view that teachers, almost by definition, are uncreative. This is not a judgment on them as persons. It is what teaching does to them. The classic analyst in this tradition, Waller (1932, p. 391) 'is puzzled to explain that peculiar blight which affects the teacher mind, which creeps over it gradually, and, possessing it bit by bit, devours its creative resources'. This 'deadening of the intellect' (*ibid.*) in teachers has been noted by others. Elbaz (1981, 1983), for example, points out that because of emphases in curriculum research and study, there has been 'little encouragement for teachers to view themselves as originators of knowledge.'

As well as these studies directed toward the intrinsic nature of teaching, others argue that political and economic developments are progressively de-skilling teachers and proletarianizing the profession (Lawn and Ozga, 1981; Apple, 1982; Apple and Teitelbaum, 1986). By this argument, if they were not before, they certainly are now becoming mere technicians in the service of the ideas of others. What invention and spontaneity there used to be is, some claim, being driven out. Thus Brighouse (1987, p. 11) gives the example of an innovative teacher forced to leave the profession, who told him: 'The profession will need "systems people" in future — all schemes of work, work cards and rigidly sticking to the syllabus'. For some, the Education Reform Act of 1988 raises the spectre of 'an inevitable return to such anti-educational practices as cramming, teaching to the test, rote learning and regurgitation of inert knowledge, didactic teaching styles and streaming' (Haviland 1988, p. 85).

While not denying the threat in these developments and the potentially constraining nature of the teacher's job, it is possible to construct another argument, one that points to their developing professionalism, growing self-awareness, increasing skills and control, and more opportunity for personal innovation. The considerable 'action research' movement has shown that many teachers investigate their own practice, submitting their teaching to critical scrutiny, and experiencing a sense of improving their craft (Nixon, 1981; Carr and Kemmis, 1986; Hustler *et al.*, 1986). The associated 'Continuing Professional Development' movement is also becoming something of an industry (Todd, 1984; 1987). Much of this is underpinned by the conception of teacher knowledge advanced by Schön (1983), Eisner (1987), Zeichner (1983) and others. Schön argues that a technical-rationality model has been influential in the past. According to this, the practitioner utilizes technical skills based on systematic and standardized knowledge that is then applied. The implications for training and evaluation are clear — competence is a matter of building up to preconceived norms, and it can be judged by the degree to which a teacher's behaviour measures up to them. By contrast, Schön's 'reflective practitioner' is altogether more innovatory and creative, discovering problems and issues, inventing and experimenting in the search for solutions, and continuously adapting. As Clark and Yinger (1987, p. 98) argue, many of the teacher's problems are 'uncertain practical problems which require unique and idiosyncratic approaches to solution because of their strong ties to specific contextual factors, the uncertainty and competition among goals and the grounds for decision, and the unpredictability of uniquely configured events.' Consequently, 'the skill required is that of intelligent and artful orchestration of knowledge and technique' (*ibid.*). This is similar to Connelly's (1972) conception of the teacher as 'user-developer', which recognizes the autonomous decision-making function of the teacher in adapting and developing materials to particular situations. It is not far removed, also, from the view of 'teaching as an art', associated with, for example, Eisner (1979; 1985). For Eisner (1985, p. 104), educational improvement comes not from the discovery of scientific methods that can be applied universally, but from 'enabling teachers and others engaged in education to improve their ability to see and think about what they do. Educational practice as it occurs in schools is an inordinately complicated affair filled with contingencies that are difficult to predict, let alone control. Connoisseurship in education, as in other areas, is that art of perception that makes the appreciation of that complexity possible.'

Creativity

The incidence and educational importance of teacher creativity was brought home to me in some recent primary school research. Before I give some examples, we need some idea of what is intended by the term. There seem to be four basic criteria: innovation, ownership, control and relevance. Innovation may, as Pribram (1964) argues, extend the boundaries of the conventional, involving first a thorough knowledge of the relevant field (see also Bruner, 1962). It can result from a new combination of known factors, or from the introduction of a new factor into a prevailing situation. Yet, as Clark and Yinger (1987) note, each teaching situation is unique, and thus teachers might be said to be always creating to resolve the problems thrown up by the complexity, uncertainty, instability, and value conflict of the classroom. Occasionally a breakthrough may be achieved. It may be planned in the sense that it is the product of deliberate experimentation, or it may be unusual, unexpected, serendipitous. Miracles do happen (Jackson, 1977). But they must be grasped, apprehended, and the opportunity seized. More often the level of novelty is less dramatic, and less perceptible, especially the more sophisticated the teacher is in his or her craft.

The innovation belongs to the teacher concerned. It may be the teacher's own idea, or it may be an adaptation, perhaps in new circumstances, of someone else's idea. Some novel aspect of the process is produced by the teacher concerned. The teacher is at the centre of activities here, as catalyst, a position overlooked by curriculum studies that focus purely on intended outcomes (Reid and Walker, 1975).

The teacher has a certain autonomy here, and control of the process. It is a situation where the more spontaneous 'I' can flourish in interaction with the socialized 'me', where the 'self' is fully reflexive (Mead, 1934). In routinized situations, the 'I' is suppressed, perhaps to emerge triumphantly elsewhere. Others are dictating the agenda. There is an affective element involved here. Nias (1988, pp. 203–4) illustrates the personal satisfaction of teachers who reported 'you're the one who is making it happen at first hand', or 'it's you who's instigating things in the classroom'. The end result of this, Nias reports, was that such teachers felt 'more intuitive, relaxed and spontaneous', more able to be 'adaptive and flexible'. There are two points here. One is that, in order to be creative, teachers need to be in control and not, for example, being dictated to by higher authority or by pupils. The other is that they also need this for their own realization of self as teachers. As Eisner (1979, p. 166) notes, 'it is easy to neglect the fact that teachers have needs that must be met through teaching' and he refers to 'the human need for pride in craftsmanship and being able to put something of oneself into work'.

If the 'I' is important, so is the 'other'. In 'taking the role of the other', teachers must perceive accurately the attitudes and meanings brought to the situation, the personal and social resources that underpin them, and the possibilities for future action. The 'other' is both a validator and motive-spring (Perinbanayagam, 1975). There are situations where a teacher's ideas do not bear fruit. A brilliant and original programme of work cultivated over a weekend might fall on stony ground on Monday morning, forcing a fall-back on to routines. The situation in its complexity cannot always be predicted. It depends in large part on pupils, and their collective and individual attitudes do differ (Riseborough, 1985; Sikes *et al.*, 1985). The others here must be receptive, though the creative act may make them receptive. The teacher, thus, must be culturally attuned to his or her pupils, and to other aspects of the situation, some of which may be beyond the teacher's immediate control — school policy, parental background, the weather....Creative acts bring change. They change pupils, teachers and situations. But the teacher's perceptions of the situation must be as accurate and complete as possible.

In some instances what a teacher regards as a creative act might lead to destruction. A creative act leads to results, not blockage. Something is transformed in consequence. It creates a product, in this case pupil learning. In Sprecher's (1959, p. 294) words, 'A truly creative product has the characteristic of being itself creative in the sense that it generates additional creative activity.' The teacher casts a new light and pupils 'have their eyes opened', or helps to unify a great deal of information and expressing it in a highly condensed form reveals essences which lead to new lines of thought (Jackson and Messick, 1965) or introduces a new activity and stimulates pupils' inspiration.

These criteria are advanced by the ability to take the role of the other, and to rehearse in advance of the event potential interactions. This process is accompanied by adaptability, flexibility, and a willingness and facility for improvization and experimentation. Considering the pupils, the time of day, the classroom context, previous and surrounding activities and so on, the teacher will interpose a new factor, or arrange a new conjunction several times over, envisaging the possible consequences. This is a 'playing with ideas', an exploiting of opportunities as they occur with an end in view which nevertheless might be altered in the working out of the ideas in practice. A range of scenarios needs to be rehearsed, numerous options envisaged. Whether they will work in practice remains to be seen. Mistakes may be made, and successes, when they come, may appear to happen almost by accident. A teacher told me, 'you don't know what's going to work, that's the point, so you must be prepared for failure, but when it does work it's marvellous.'

Mackinnon (1975, p. 73) notes that 'there can be little doubt that the "chance" occurrence of an event at the appropriate time during the creative process may be signally important in providing the cue or material necessary for the creative act.' This might seem to defy analysis. Some of these occurrences, teachers would claim, cannot be described in rational terms, preferring to attribute their actions to intuition — 'it just felt right to do it that way' (Jackson, 1977). However, though the intricacies of the situation are such that a measure of luck or an extraneous variable might act as a trigger, all else has been arranged and made highly conducive to such an outcome. The chance element would not work in any situation, for example one that encourages conformity, getting the one 'right' answer, and discourages guessing.

Since the unusual and unexpected might happen, creative acts are often accompanied by feelings of anticipation before and excitement aftwards. The thrill of discovery and of breakthrough is integral – it is part of the product for both pupil and teacher. A feature of the creative act, therefore, is a certain holism, one characteristic of which is the combination of cognitive, cultural, social and affective factors. Another characteristic is the combining in thought of public and private, formal and informal, school, and out-of-school. Teachers and pupils are not encased within their formal roles, nor their activities compartmentalized into discrete sections of time and subject, nor certain of their characteristics isolated from others (Elbaz, 1981). Holistic thinking is necessary for a number of reasons. It establishes the widest possible 'play-base', and also the most valid one. In order to know and negotiate with the other, knowledge is required of the other's construction of self, much of which has taken place outside the school's orbit, and which has a considerable history.

Some psychologists contrast holistic with algorithmic thinking, the one being creative or autistic, the other rational. Both are necessary. McKellar (1975), for example, sees the first as author of the creative act, with rational thinking being the editor. Thus a teacher might have a profusion of ideas, some of which work, some of which do not, with a fair degree of unexpectancy and accident. The application of those ideas, and certainly their evaluation, will require more systematized, step-by-step working-out and analysis.

Creative Teaching

I turn now to some examples of 'creative teaching', that I observed during some recent work in primary schools. They are intended to convey the flavour of the activity rather than represent an exhaustive list.

Creative Teaching Around a Structured Base

Sue was charged with the task of assisting two pupils adjudged to be in need of special teaching, a boy and a girl, both aged seven. She worked under the direction of an external supervisor, who provided a heavily structured programme for Sue's use. Sue wove a series of creative activities around this programme, converting it into a live, experimental, relevant scheme which teacher and pupils could engage with and regard as their own. They had 'Crown Readers', graded reading books which aim to build up vocabulary and idiom through repetition of words and association with pictures, while holding the child's interest through a simple but imaginative story with clearly defined characters with whose activities the child can identify. After reading each book, the child completes a workbook, designed to test and consolidate. Book 1 begins:

THE CASTLE
This is the castle
It is big
It is old
It is big and old

THE KING

I am the king
I live in the castle
The castle is big
It is big and old

There is also a 'big guard' and a 'little guard' and a baby, always appealing
to young children and useful for repetition

'Big and old' the baby said
'Big and old'

The Crown Readers are typical of reading schemes designed as a complete
exercise which a teacher could 'take pupils through', and from which they
would no doubt learn something. However, Sue was not happy to work within
this scheme, preferring to see it as a resource which required considerable
modification. She therefore adapted it to a new learning form by encouraging
Sarah and Robert to make and perform a play of their own, based on some of the
stories. They each had a crown and a cloak, and they 'loved it'. Sue asked Sarah
if she would like to make the props and she eagerly accepted, making the
crowns, pots of paint etc. Sarah insisted on wearing the crown and cloak
whenever she had to say anything. When another girl was drafted in to take
Robert's part when he was away, Sarah insisted she put on the crown and cloak.
She even wore them when sitting down and reading. The end product was a
playlet 'We will mend the castle', based on the Crown Readers' vocabulary up to
and including Book 4, which could be recorded as a radio play, or acted out.
Sarah and Robert did give a performance before an audience of their class. They
had chosen and written the words and made the props, with help of course. The
play now began:

Queen: Look at the castle
King Robert
Look at the doors, the windows, and the walls
King: The doors are broken, Queen Sarah
The walls and the windows are broken
Baby: Broken, broken, broken

Stephanie, another 'slow learner' had to be drafted in to play the baby, which
was regarded as a star role. Later, they were inspired to make up another play of
their own based on Robert's suggestion of 'The Three Bears'.

'Let us make some porridge
Yes, we will make some porridge
Let us go down to breakfast . . . !'

The framework is still that of the Crown Reader, but this time the words are
theirs. The play, it will be noted, contains another star role, that of Baby Bear,
and there were squabbles over who was to play this. Robert seemed to think he

had author's rights. Sarah just felt she would do it better. The matter was resolved by the toss of a coin which Sarah lost, but accepted.

This shows how the project provided other forms of learning, in this case to do with social behaviour and rules of conduct. Sue's part in all this was to mediate, arbitrate, enable. The play was theirs, but she prompted and made suggestions: 'What's the story, what would you do there, what would you say . . .' The project shows an interesting combination of associationist and constructivist principles, and of transmissional and pupil-centred teaching. The adaptation established ownership, control and relevance, conveyed excitement and novelty, and provided opportunities for play wherein the teacher participated as facilitator. It thus became part of the pupil's world.

This is particularly important, it might be argued, for pupils from working-class homes. Sue reported that middle-class parents were very supportive of traditional forms. They would reinforce the teacher's work by faithfully taking their children through the Crown Readers again. But Sarah, for example, had no such culture of support.

Teaching as Discovery

The need to attune to a pupil's culture is illustrated in another episode with Sarah, where Sue was trying to teach her how to count money. This proved difficult to begin with, for Sarah could not recognize coins. Then the teacher was provided with a clue, which she pursued like a true investigator. The clue was Sarah's recognition of a 50p coin — the only one she identified. How did she know that?

> 'Because we put them in the tele, of course.'
> 'How long does it last?'
> 'About eight minutes.'
> 'What happens when it runs out and you haven't any more 50ps?'
> 'My dad goes down the pub and asks the pub man.'
> 'All right. I'll be the pub man and you be your dad coming for some 50ps. There you are, there's a pound, how many 50ps do you want?'

Occasionally they switch roles, and Sarah is the 'pub-man'. And Sue rings other changes. What programmes does Sarah like to watch?

> 'Oh, it's run out. This time you've only got 10ps. How many are you going to give the pub-man for one 50p? etc. etc.

Sue says you have to experiment. 'You try all sorts of things. Some work, some don't. You have to have a stream of things to do, a great variety, with plenty of props. It's no use just presenting formal activities. You have to improvise.'

Breakthroughs

At times in teaching, a pupil's learning achieves a quantum leap; a particularly intransigent blockage is freed, or a transformation in attitude and motivation undergone. While many factors contribute toward these, not all of them understood, creative teaching can be one of the motive forces. At another school, Sue was assisting with some ethnic minority children who spoke English as a second language. One of them, Gita, was an elective mute. She spoke fluent Bengali at home and was said to be competent at English, but had not been perceived to utter a word at school to anyone during her eighteen months there. Gita did her work for Sue competently enough, showing herself to be very capable, but would not communicate, other than writing her name for Sue when asked. In small group work, Gita would not talk, other pupils telling Sue 'Gita can't talk!' She kept her head down at first, but as tensions eased and laughs came, she smiled. She also nodded at some questions, and shook her head for 'No.'

The following week, Sue took Gita into the library where other people were working silently. She showed her the 'What's Wrong' cards. Gita wouldn't look at them to begin with.

> Then I put one in her hand and watched. She looked up from under her eyebrows. I fingered the cards, pointing out the mistakes. Soon she did this herself and showed me what was wrong. We did not speak. Once she smiled broadly. After this I played a 'copy me' game. Gita copied me and soon was obviously enjoying the game. Touch my head, eyes, shoulder, floor. I got quicker and she copied. Then I touched my mouth, and opened it wide. Gita would not do this. I left the mouth and went back to other areas but I had lost her completely . . . In class I discovered that Gita does talk with Rufin in the playground. I asked her to ask Gita what we were doing in the library.
> (Teacher's notes)

The next week:

> With Gita, we played copycat game, then Gita did it and I copied her. When I asked her how old she was, she indicated she was 3 years old, and her baby brother 5 years old. At break, I went in the playground. Gita and Monwara came and held my hand firmly.

One week later:

> I took Gita in the library for five minutes. Played the copycat game. I started and once begun she was happy to follow. I got quicker. Then I asked Gita to lead. She did so very confidently and smiled and laughed. After play, Mrs Jones asked why the elephant children must look after their masks and Gita put her hand up to volunteer an answer. When asked, she couldn't say anything, but it was the first time she has done

this. During the acting of the play Mrs Carr came in to collect Gita to 'read' (the attempt was regularly made). At 3.30 pm she brought her back and said Gita had read five books aloud (in a whisper).

Great breakthrough! Jill over the moon, lifted Gita up high in the air. Yellow table allowed to go first because of a 'special reason.' Mrs Carr said she had assumed, as always, that Gita would read. Her lips began to move, then out came a whisper.

From then on, Gita behaved normally, seemingly enjoying school, relating well to her peers and teachers, and talking.

Not enough is known to provide a full analysis of what lead up to this breakthrough. But Sue's contribution almost certainly helped. What she achieved, it might be argued, by trial and error was a means of communicating with Gita, and by which Gita could communicate with her with confidence and enjoyment. What we see illustrated is a 'conversation of gestures' (Mead, 1934). From a position of former isolation, Gita reaches out and happily engages in meaning construction. This, we might argue, is an important step for Gita's construction of self. We could say that in Gita's case the 'me' — the self as object was underdeveloped at least in the school area. She found it difficult to 'take the role of other' (not uncommon among 5–6 year olds). The lack of interaction between the 'I' and the 'me' was reflected in her lack of communication with others. The case was complicated by Gita being an ESL child. The indications were that she behaved normally at home, but could not transfer that self to school. Once she had found a way of conveying her own meanings and confidently predicting the other's response, she achieved a certain equilibrium. Sue thus acted her part as 'significant other' (Kuhn, 1964). Possibly the real breakthrough occurred when Gita began to participate in this 'conversation' for language is only one form of gesture, and arguably a natural sequel to what occurred. Sue's insight was to locate communication with Gita on a broader range of gestures than simply language. This lead not only to the conveying of information, but to enjoyment and reward on Gita's part and a close relationship with the teacher concerned. Once the communicating and relationships had been established with one teacher, the development of that communication might be expected to follow with another teacher in whom she felt similar confidence.

Creative Projects

Here I refer to compilations of teaching activity on a broader front involving groups or classes of pupils, and possibly more than one teacher.

A creative piece of team teaching was the school exchange that I have discussed elsewhere as a good example of 'matching' along all aspects of a 'learning and teaching opportunities model', that is one where teacher intentions match practice, where task matches pupils' abilities, where context and relationships match social relevancies, where teacher and pupil motivation are taken into account, and so on (Woods, 1988 and 1989). One aspect of this is teacher initiation and involvement. Much of the idea, or if not that, its implementation, is theirs, and such is its novelty they, as well as the pupils, are not left untouched by it. They learn with the pupils; creativity builds on creativity.

A previous exchange with a different school had not worked so well, because, in the words of one of the teachers, it had been 'thrust on them'. This one, by contrast, had been their idea. It began thus:

> *Miss B.* I was at my dad's. Julie came round to see my dad, and we got talking about children and schools and what we all did in our schools. And we said wouldn't it be a good idea if we joined forces and your class wrote to my class and so on . . . . So we all said, well we'll go and ask our head. So I went and asked David (her head teacher). And David said 'oh that was fine' and then she did the same. And then we started planning what we wanted and she thought she'd like children to see the village because that is a completely different environment to what they are used to. And I said well it would be nice if our children could see the Hindu Temple because that would come in part of their sort of religious syllabus apart from anything else. To see other religions. And then we thought about well what else could we do if we exchanged and I sort of tentatively said well wouldn't it be nice if our children could use your apparatus, because we haven't got any . . . . And we were talking about it, and we decided that we had this week when we had a minibus so that week we would be able to get over to see them. Then we had a meeting with Mr Jones (Headteacher) at which we all discussed it all and sort of well I'd already told David what the programme was and persuaded everybody around to our idea of the programme, what we wanted. By sort of making it seem as if it was somebody else's idea . . .

The other teacher (Julie), interviewed later, confirmed this, and made this significant comment:

> It came from a spontaneous meeting between myself and Deirdre. There was a spark between two teachers and two different schools that had been missing from the previous thing. So we built it up outside school first in every aspect. And that was the difference in the preparation — that you got the teachers sparking each other off.

This notion of 'spark' is clearly important in this kind of creative endeavour and draws attention to the chemistry of the interrelationship and the circumstances in which it occurred. Clearly all this has to be got right. The final remark of Miss B's indicates how in the power relationships of a school, a creative strategy is sometimes required to implement creative teaching.

Creative Conditions

What conditions are necessary for teacher creativity? Hargreaves (1988) has drawn attention to a number of factors that constrain teachers to act in conservative and routinized ways, such as: the demands of controlling cohorts, rather than individuals; situational constraints, such as teacher–pupil ratios, standards in school buildings; public examinations, which some argue promote transmission teaching; subject specialism; status and career factors; and teacher isolation. To these might be added: reformist pressures that are exerted on teachers, demands for greater accountability, teacher appraisal, and a weakening of their control over the curriculum, examinations and school processes in general.

It might be inferred that their opposites — more individual, non-examination, inter-subject teaching etc. — might be indicated for a more innovative style. But this is not so simple. Examinations, for example, can sometimes be a considerable resource, and we have yet to see the full effects of the GCSE, which was designed in part to tackle some of these problems. These factors, therefore, are debatable. They are the means through which more basic requirements may or may not be met. These requirements I would suggest, at least as far as creativity is concerned, are fourfold, and they reflect the criteria mentioned earlier. First, for ideas to be produced and take root, inspiration and incubation is needed. The prime element here is time. This is not just hours and days, but subjective time involving ownership and control. This yields time to reflect on which is needed, on countless interactions of past experience, on the composition of the likely situation, and to play with various permutations and combinations, experimenting with interjecting various extraneous factors, and setting up hypothetical programmes which are then tried out in practice. They might not always work, so latitude is needed in which a few mistakes are accepted as part of the enterprise. This is not simply, or even necessarily, a matter of more free periods and fewer duties, though that would no doubt help. In creative activities, time is often created where formally none was suspected to exist — outside school hours, in-between lessons, a snatched moment in the course of a lesson. Even whilst one is teaching, in the maelstrom of activity something might occur that creates the germ of an idea at the back of the mind, to be held there until further reflection could be brought to bear. More important here than actual time, perhaps, is the amount that is the teacher's own time, and the freedom he or she has to exercise the mind in spontaneous and innovative ways.

Secondly, resources are needed. The more money that is put into teaching, the better the buildings and equipment, the greater the range of opportunities. Again, however, this is not simply a matter of money. Indeed on occasions hardship can promote creativity. Primary school teachers avail themselves of all manner of materials, from toilet roll cardboard cylinders to milk bottle tops and cornflake packets. 'This snakes and ladders board will help my children to count;' 'with a few adaptations this method of making Chistmas trees on "Blue

Peter" can be employed by my pupils — all they need is some coloured paper;' 'I'll take these old photos in of my forefathers, and ask the children to bring in theirs as a basis for discussion about life earlier this century;' 'you need a stream of things to do.' The teacher who made this comment seemed to be in a state of continual awareness about what she could appropriate to aid her teaching. 'Don't throw that away, I can use that.' Having said this, such initiative can be blunted if inadequate official resource is put into the school, if, for example, the supply of basic materials is depleted, or if conditions affect pupils and teachers working normally. It can be considerably enhanced if an LEA, for example, is particularly supportive of teacher-centred activities. Aspinwall (1989), for example, describes how an LEA helped to give teachers a sense of empowerment through sponsoring them to revitalize their curricula.

Thirdly, a teacher requires a supportive school ethos, one wherein teacher creativity is valued and encouraged. Authoritarian regimes do not do so, and to these, creative teachers are a nuisance. Fontana (1986, p. 101) notes that 'creativity involves an independent and original approach to life and sometimes the creative person has to show a touch of ruthlessness in giving his (*sic*) creative work precedence over the social demands made upon him by others.' The hierarchy will be no less ruthless, with the result that creativity becomes displaced into strategical thinking. Creative teaching favours a participatory-democratic environment, a 'bottom-up' management structure to match the 'bottom-up' model of teacher knowledge discussed earlier (Sikes *et al.*, 1985; Hunter and Heighway, 1980). Such models have the teacher's self at their centre. It is allowed to flourish within them. In this sense, this is teacher-centred teaching. The principles of ownership and control discussed earlier are intrinsic to it.

There is more to school ethos than management structure. Teacher culture is clearly important — relationships with one's peers and the 'way of doing things' that most schools seem to develop. Ideally it is one that both contributes to, and takes from individuals in balanced interaction which allows for the growth of both. Thus individuals are neither fully determined by school cultures, nor are they permitted to run wild. A good example of such an enhancing environment is provided by Gates (1989) who describes how the staff of his comprehensive school engaged in long-term, systematic 'mutual support and observation'. For them, teacher isolationism was not a problem. The teacher self gained another perspective on performance which aided self-evaluation. By contrast, in heavily constrained circumstances like 'Black School' (Webb, 1962), 'Lumley' (Hargreaves, D., 1967) and 'Lowfield' (Woods, 1979), creative teaching is difficult. One's ingenuities are diverted towards coping and survival.

Pupil culture is also important and herein lies the fourth factor. For, as noted earlier, teacher creativity must bring a response. Certainly a teacher's skill in negotiation may affect pupil motivation. But there are factors beyond the teacher's control also exerting influence. Social class, 'race', gender, age, neighbourhood factors, employment prospects, and a pupil culture that may have grown up in response to these and many more, including situational variables such as school organization, and which may be fairly impervious to change — all these help guide the nature of the pupil response. If creative teaching is aimed at generating creative learning, then it has to be noted that this does not occur in a social vacuum — that creativity, or at least our perceptions of it, is not a single, absolute quality. In some contexts creative pupils can be a problem for teachers. They make unexpected responses, do strange things, create diversions, ask embarrassing questions (Cropley, 1967). A pupil's creativity may not match a teacher's. It might draw on different social class or ethnic, perhaps, referents and not be recognized for what it is. It might be displaced, like teachers' on occasions, into strategical thinking (for example, Willis, 1977). It may lie dormant, conditioned by years of socialization, and untapped by teachers' overtures, as perhaps in the case of girls' approach to science (Kelly, 1985). Thus teacher creativity requires a response, but that response needs to be correctly identified.

A Concluding Comment

The literature abounds with examples of the sheer tedium and ineffectiveness of unrelieved, systematic transmission teaching, of routinized teachers regimented 'like horses, all running on the same track at the same speed' (Elbaz, 1981, p. 64). We know, too, that there are so many different, emergent, changing and conflicting factors in teaching that they require either that kind of treatment, or a divergent cast of mind. As one teacher records, 'we fly by the seat of our pants most of the time' (Abbot *et al.*, 1989).

As noted at the beginning, there seem to be conflicting trends in motion at the moment, some of which appear increasingly to direct, others to free the teacher. After periods of 'black box' teaching (before the 1970s, when the teacher did not appear to exist as a factor), 'bashing' the teacher in the 1970s, and 'directing' the teacher in the later 1980s, perhaps we are due for a period of 'freeing' the teacher in the 1990s, when they might be allowed and encouraged to use their own considerable inspiration. This might seem to be flying in the face of some current prognoses. However, there is plenty of evidence of teacher ingenuity. It is so much part of minute-to-minute activity, so integral to a stream of events, and in an ironical way a taken-for-granted element in the teacher's day-to-day job, that it is in danger of being overlooked. A resurrection of interest in creativity, but this time directed more toward the teacher, and situating such studies within their appropriate social referents might give a boost to a new trend which seeks to display the educational promise of individual innovation and experiment in balance with a thorough grounding in basic knowledge and more traditional techniques.

References

ABBOTT, B. *et al.* (1980) 'Towards anti-racist awareness: confessions of some teacher converts', in WOODS, P. (Ed.) *Working for Teacher Development*, Cambridge, Peter Francis.

APPLE, M. (1982) *Education and Power*, London, Routledge and Kegan Paul.

APPLE, M. and TEITELBAUM, K. (1986) 'Are teachers losing control of their skills and curriculum?' *Journal of Curriculum Studies*, 18, 2, pp. 177–84.

ASPINWALL, K. (1989) ' "A bit of the sun": teacher development through an LEA curriculum initiative', in WOODS, P. (Ed.) *Working for Teacher Development*, Cambridge, Peter Francis.

BRIGHOUSE, T. (1987) 'Goodbye to the head and the history man', *Guardian*, 21 July, p. 11.

BRUNER, J. S. (1962) 'The creative surprise', in GRUBER, H. E., TERRELL, G. and WORTHEIMER, M. (Eds) *Contemporary Approaches to Creative Thinking*, Atherton Press, New York.

CARR, W. and KEMMIS, S. (1986) *Becoming Critical*, Lewes, Falmer Press.

CLARK, C. M. and YINGER, R. J. (1987) 'Teacher Planning', in CALDERHEAD, J. (Ed.) *Exploring Teachers' Thinking*, London, Cassell.

CONNELLY, M. F. (1972) 'The functions of curriculum development', *Interchange*, Vol. 3, Nos. 2–3, pp. 161–77.

CROPLEY, A. J. (1967) *Creativity*, London, Longmans.

EISNER, E. W. (1979) *The Educational Imagination*, London, Collier MacMillan.

EISNER, E. W. (1985) *The Art of Educational Evaluation: a personal view*, Lewes, Falmer Press.

ELBAZ, F. (1981) 'The teacher's "practical knowledge": report of a case study', *Curriculum Inquiry*, Vol. 11, No. 1, pp. 43–71.

ELBAZ, F. (1983) *Teacher Thinking: a study of practical knowledge*, London, Croom Helm.

FONTANA, D. (1986) *Teaching and Personality*, London, Blackwell.

GATES, P. (1989) 'Developing consciousness and pedagogical knowledge through mutual observation', in WOODS, P. (Ed.) *Working for Teacher Development*, Cambridge, Peter Francis.

HARGREAVES, A. (1988) 'Teaching Quality: a sociological analysis', *Journal of Curriculum Studies*, Vol. 20, No. 3, pp. 211–31.

HARGREAVES, D. H. (1967) *Social Relations in a Secondary School*, London, Routledge and Kegan Paul.

HAVILAND, J. (Ed.) (1988) *Take Care Mr Baker!*, London, Fourth Estate.

HUNTER, C. and HEIGHWAY, P. (1980) 'Morale, Motivation and Management in Middle Schools', in BUSH, T., GLATTER, R., GOODEY, J. and RICHES, C. (Eds) *Approaches to School Management*, Milton Keynes, Open University Press.

HUSTLER, D. *et al.* (1986) *Action Research in Classrooms and Schools*, London, Allen and Unwin.

JACKSON, P. W. (1977) 'The Way Teachers Think', in GLIDEWELL, J. C. (Ed.) *The Social Context of Learning and Development*, New York, Gardner Press.

JACKSON, P. W. and MESSICK, S. (1965) 'The person, the product and the response: conceptual problems in the assessment of creativity', *Journal of Personality*, Vol. 33, pp. 309–29.

KELLY, A. (1985) 'The construction of masculine science', *British Journal of Sociology of Education*, 6, 2, 133–54.

KUHN, M. H. (1964) 'The reference group reconsidered', *Sociological Quarterly*, Vol. 5, pp. 6–21.

LAWN, M. and OZGA, J. (1981) 'The educational worker: a reassessment of teachers', in BARTON, L. E. and WALKER, S. (Eds) *Schools, Teachers and Teaching*, Lewes, Falmer Press.

McKELLAR, P. (1957) *Imagination and Thinking*, London, Cohen and West.

MACKINNON, D. W. (1975) 'IPAR's contribution to the conceptualization and study of creativity', in TAYLOR, I. A. and GETZELS, J. W. (Eds) *Perspectives in Creativity*, Chicago, Aldine.

MEAD, G. H. (1934) *Mind, Self and Society*, Chicago, University of Chicago Press.

NIAS, J. (1988) 'What it means to "feel like a teacher": the subjective reality of primary school teaching' in OZGA, J. (Ed.) *Schoolwork: approaches to the labour process of teaching*, Milton Keynes, Open University Press.

NIXON, J. (1981) *A Teacher's Guide to Action Research*, London, Grant McIntyre.

PERINBANAYAGAM, R. (1975) 'The significance of others in the thought of Alfred Schutz, G. H. Mead and C. H. Cooley', *The Sociological Quarterly*, XVI Autumn, pp. 500–21.

PRIBRAM, K. H. (1964) 'Neurological notes on the art of education', in HILGARD, D. R. (Ed.) *NSSE Yearbook*, LXII, Chicago, University of Chicago Press.

REID, W. A. and WALKER, D. (Eds) *Case Studies in Curriculum Change*, London, Routledge and Kegan Paul.

RISEBOROUGH, G. F. (1985) 'Pupils, teachers' careers and schooling: an empirical study', in BALL, S. J. and GOODSON, I. F. *Teachers' Lives and Careers*, Lewes, Falmer Press.

SCHÖN, D. A. (1983) *The Reflective Practitioner: How Professionals Think in Action*, London, Temple Smith.

SIKES, P., MEASOR, L. and WOODS, P. (1985) *Teacher Careers: Crises and Continuities*, Lewes, Falmer Press.

SPRECHER, T. B. (1959) 'Committee report on criteria of creativity', in TAYLOR, C. W. (Ed.) *The Third University of Utah Research Conference on the Identification of Creative Scientific Talent*, Salt Lake City, University of Utah Press.

TODD, F. (1984) 'Learning and work: directions for continuing professional and vocational education', *International Journal of Lifelong Education*, 3, pp. 89–104.

TODD, F. (Ed.) (1987) *Planning Continuing Professional Development*, London, Croom Helm.

WALLER, W. (1932) *The Sociology of Teaching*, New York, Wiley.

WEBB, J. (1962) 'The sociology of a school', *British Journal of Sociology*, Vol. 13, pp. 204–72.

WILLIS, P. (1979) *Learning to Labour*, Farnborough, Saxon House.

WOODS, P. (1979) *The Divided School*, London, Routledge and Kegan Paul.

WOODS, P. (1988) 'Learning through friendship: teaching and learning opportunities in primary school', in BURGESS, H. (Ed.) *Teaching in the Primary School: Careers, Management and Curricula*, London, Croom Helm.

WOODS, P. (1989) 'Opportunities to learn and teach: an interdisciplinary model', *International Journal of Educational Research*.

ZEICHNER, K. (1983) 'Alternative paradigms of teacher education', *Journal of Teacher Education*, Vol. 31, pp. 3–9.

Notes on Contributors

Miriam Ben-Peretz is Dean of the School of Education at the University of Haifa, Israel, where she has been a faculty member since 1969. She was previously a biology teacher, then director of a biology curriculum project. Her main research areas are; the role of teachers in curriculum development and implementation, issues in teacher thinking and education and cross-curricular research on teaching. She has published numerous articles in scholarly journals and books and has been visiting Professor at the Ontario Institute for Studies in Education, Stanford University, Michigan State University, the Johannes Gutenberg University in Mainz, the University of Calgary, and Monash University.

Alan F. Brown is Professor of educational administration at the Ontario Institute for Studies in Education, University of Toronto, Canada. He is a former president of Canadian Association of Professors of Education, and the founding president of Canadian Educational Researchers' Association. He likes to do constructivist studies of organizational behaviour, especially of the cognitive, reflective and interpersonal acts of teachers and their administrators, each with their own wills, thoughts and hopes.

Margaret Buchmann is Senior Researcher at the Institute for Research on Teaching and Professor in the Department of Teacher Education at Michigan State University. With a background in philosophy and sociology, she has conducted conceptual and empirical work on the contributions of formal knowledge and experience in teaching and learning to teach. Her current research interests include the foundations of teacher education, curriculum, and conceptions of teacher thinking, knowledge, and judgment. Her work on knowledge utilization and research communication, teaching knowledge and the teaching role, practical arguments and deliberation has appeared in numerous books and journals inside and outside the United States.

Ingrid Carlgren is an Assistant Professor at the Department of Education, University of Uppsala, Sweden. She has worked as a school psychologist, and her research interests include classroom conflicts (and how teachers cope with them) and conceptions of teachers' knowledge and practice within the teacher education field.

Christopher Day is Reader in Education and Head of the in-service unit, School of Education, University of Nottingham, England. He has worked as a classroom teacher, initial teacher trainer and local education authority adviser. His research interests centre upon school-based curriculum and professional development, and in-service teacher education, in particular ways in which action research and external consultants assist teachers' development of personal practical knowledge. Recent publications include *Reconceptualizing School-Based Curriculum Development* (with Marsh, C., Hannay, L. and Leiberman, A.), Falmer Press, 1990, and 'In-Service as Consultancy; the evaluation of a management programme for primary school curriculum leaders', in Aubrey, C. (Ed) (1990) *Consultancy in the UK — its Role and Contribution to Educational Change*, Falmer Press.

Pam Denicolo is assistant head of the Department of Educational Studies, University of Surrey, England, and **Maureen Pope** is Professor of Community Studies and Education at Reading University. Both have degrees in psychology and continue to teach psychology of education and research methods on a number of undergraduate and postgraduate courses, and are active in the field of human counsel and staff development.

They have worked together on several research projects concerned with teacher thinking, professional development and study learning. A particular research interest of Maureen's is teachers' theories of teaching and she has published widely on Personal Construct Psychology. Explanations — how they are given and why — has been a focus for much of Pam's research. A joint current interest is in developing methods of helping teachers reflect on and develop their professional roles at any point in their careers and in relation to external pressures on the profession.

Freema Elbaz teaches in the School of Education at the University of Haifa, Israel, is interested in the development of reflective and critical approaches to teaching, in curriculum development, evaluation and criticism (and teacher involvement in these in particular). She is especially concerned with the use of cross-cultural perspectives in furthering understanding of the various 'cultural maps' within which and through which education works. Publications include *Teacher thinking: a study of practical knowledge* (Croom Helm and Nicolls, 1983) and 'Critical reflection on Teaching: Insights from Freire' in *Journal of Education for Teaching*, 1988.

Sigrun Gudmundsdottir is Associate Professor of Education at the Pedagogisk Institutt of the University of Trondheim, Norway. Previously she lectured in the Department of Education at the University of Iceland. She earned a Ph.D. in 1988 at Stanford University School of Education (California). In her doctoral thesis 'Knowledge use among experienced teachers: Four case studies of high school teaching', she explored the knowledge base of experienced veteran teachers who were considered excellent by their peers and students alike. Sigrun Gudmundsdottir's research interests include the knowledge base of teaching (its growth among novice teachers and development among veterans), qualitative research methodology and the use of stories as a tool to organize the curriculum. These interests have grown out of her teaching experience in Linlithgow, Scotland, and Reykjavik, Iceland, where she taught at an innovative primary school that was implementing the British tradition in open education.

Udo Hanke is an Assistant Professor in the Department of Sport Science at the University of Heidelberg. His research interests include the development of methods for the investigation of teacher and student cognition, and the development of cognitive training instruments for teachers and coaches. He is currently conducting a research project to analyze the knowledge structures of teachers and coaches.

Lynne Hannay and **Wayne Seller** are both field centre faculty members of the Ontario Institute for Studies in Education. Lynne is Head of the Midwestern Centre while Wayne is Head of the Northwestern Centre. As Field Centre faculty, both have been actively involved in conducting field-based research related to their development projects in the areas of curriculum development, peer coaching and the general process of change.

Along with Colin Marsh, Chris Day and Gail McCutcheon, Lynne has recently co-authored a book on re-conceptualizing school-based curriculum development. She has also published in the areas of inquiry learning, planned change, professional development and action research.

Wayne Seller has co-authored 'Curriculum Perspectives and Practice' with John Miller and has also published in the areas of peer coaching, planned change, professional development and the role of the OISE field centres.

Gunter L. Huber went through the first and second phase of German teacher training and studied psychology and pedagogics at the University of Munich. A main area of interest is the application of psychology to pre- and in-service training of teachers. He does research on effects of implicit theories on teachers' classroom behaviour, and he participated in the development of materials for teacher training based on this approach. As methodological tools for his studies he wrote some programs for computer-assisted analysis of qualitative data.

Michael Kompf and **Donald Dworet** teach in the graduate and pre-service departments of the College of Education at Brock University, St. Catherines', Ontario, Canada. Michael is currently co-ordinator of a pilot programme of graduate studies for Community College personnel. His research interests are eclectic and include studies examining teachers' ideal-type constucts, the use of experts as school volunteers, general use of school volunteers, teachers' lies as coded communications, career-span personal and professional development of teachers, attitudes and reflections of retired teachers and programme development in adult education.

Prior to working at Brock, Donald Dworet was a special education teacher in Toronto and New York City. He has been extensively involved in teaching special education at the pre-service, in-service and graduate levels. His current research interests focus on those processes teachers must learn in order to provide effective instruction in both regular and special education classes, and special education — specifically concerning education of the behaviourally disordered student. He is the recipient of the R. W. B. Jackson award presented by the Ontario Educational Research Council and is currently a Regional Co-ordinator of the Council for Children with Behavioural Disorders.

Lya Kremer-Hayon is Associate Professor at the University of Haifa, Israel. Prior to this she was an elementary school teacher, initial training teacher and has worked for the Ministry of Education. She is currently Head of the Centre of Educational Administration and Evaluation. She has published widely on Attitude-Behaviour Links in Teaching and Teacher Professional Development. She has published two books, one on Developing Writing Skills, and the other on Teachers' Professional Deliberations in the Teaching Process.

Hugo Letiche lectures in qualitative research methods and management development at the Rotterdam School of Management, Erasmus University, Rotterdam; and is course chairman of the M.Ed. in Management and Policy at the Nutsseminarium, Amsterdam. His chief areas of research include adult learning processes, institutional analysis, career development in higher education and mis-communication in international interaction/business. His publications include *Zelf-Evaluatie* (Assen, van Gorcum, 1988), *From Europe to the Teaching Team* (Delft, Eburon, 1986) and *Learning and Hatred for Meaning* (Amsterdam/Philadelphia, J. Benjamins Publishing, 1984).

Joost Lowyck was Chair of ISATT from 1985–1988. He is Professor, Head of Educatec (Research Centre on Educational Technology) and coordinator of the University Department of Course Development (UDC) at the University of Leuven, Belgium. In his research endeavours, the cognitive psychology, linguistics and teacher thinking studies are linked to instructional design. Thus the research experience in the field of teaching and teacher thinking is used as the framework for entering the domain of educational technology.

Don Massey and **Charles Chamberlin** are Associate Professors at the University of Alberta, Edmonton, Canada. Charles has worked as a primary school teacher and has undertaken several teacher education projects with preservice and inservice teachers over the past twenty years.

One strand of his research has examined the evolution of teacher perspective. His current research is attempting to illuminate the relationships between university and school roles in the socialization of beginning teachers, particularly the balance between reflection-in-action and master-apprentice learning.

Don has worked as a teacher and teacher consultant in the public schools resulting in an interest in teacher preparation programs. His research on children's thinking includes an interest in two aspects of perspective: (1) how it is created and managed for children in classrooms through textual materials; and (2) how it is influenced in teachers through teacher education programs. Publications include *Communities Around the World*, Ginn, 1984, *Canada: Its Land and People*, Reidmore, 1985, and *Our World*, D.C. Heath, 1989.

Lars Naeslund is a research coordinator and evaluator of educational programmes at the Swedish National Board of Education. He has recently completed a four year research project on the working conditions of teachers.

John Olson is Professor of Education at Queen's University, Canada, where he teaches courses in science methods and curriculum change. He is interested in the culture of teachers, and in teacher thinking as it illuminates the meaning of classroom events. His recent book *Schoolworlds/Microworlds* (Pergamon Press, 1988) collects together studies undertaken over the last five years using mostly rep grid method of the impact of computers on school life.

Jurgen H. W. Roth also studied pedagogics and psychology after finishing teacher training. In his teaching activities at the University of Munich as well as in his research, children's view of reality and teachers' implicit theories play a main role. Based on his experiences in training and practice as a psychoanalyst he studies educational settings under psychoanalytic perspectives, and he does counselling with groups and individuals. At the moment he is developing a supervision model for teachers.

Peter Woods is Professor of Education at the Open University, and Director of the Centre for Sociology and Social Research. After graduating in history at University College, London, he taught for a number of years in primary and secondary schools in Norfolk, London, and Yorkshire. He studied education and sociology at the Universities of Sheffield, Leeds and Bradford, before joining the Open University in 1971. He has contributed to several courses there, including 'Contemporary Issues in Education' and 'Exploring Educational Issues'. His books include *The Divided School, Sociology of the School, Inside Schools* and *Teacher Skills and Strategies*, and he has written many articles for the academic and educational press.

Subject Index

Author Index